The Psychology of Sex Differences

ELEANOR EMMONS MACCOBY &
CAROL NAGY JACKLIN

Volume I: Text

STANFORD UNIVERSITY PRESS

STANFORD, CALIFORNIA

Stanford University Press
Stanford, California
© 1974 by the Board of Trustees of the
Leland Stanford Junior University
Printed in the United States of America
Cloth ISBN 0-8047-0859-2
Paper ISBN 0-8047-0974-2 (Volume I),
0-8047-0975-0 (Volume II)
Original edition 1974
Paperback edition, in two volumes, 1978
Last figure below indicates year of this printing:
87   86   85   84   83   82   81   80   79   78

Dedicated to equity, affection,
and greater understanding
   Among women
   Among men
   Between men and women

Preface to the Paperback Edition

Except that it is divided into two volumes—one of text, the other of bibliography—this paperback edition does not differ from the original hardcover edition published in 1974. The Annotated Bibliography (pp. 395–627 of the original work) occupies Volume II; everything else, including the Index, is in Volume I. The Preface to the hardcover (1974) edition explains how this book relates to the earlier volume *The Development of Sex Differences* (Maccoby, 1966), and there are notes on text pages 8–9 and 377 and back-matter page xix of Volume I, and on page 395 of Volume II, that give further information on the relationship.

A number of users of the hardcover edition have said that they found the Annotated Bibliography to be a useful foundation and supplement for the text. In including the bibliography in the first edition, it was our hope that readers would use it to check our conclusions, to make their own summaries of topics not fully treated in the book, and to combine the studies reviewed there with newer work, not yet available at the time we went to press, to amplify or modify our treatment. We have reason to believe that a number of readers have, indeed, made use of the Annotated Bibliography in these ways. Other readers, however, have different purposes, and many have little need for the sort of detail about the research cited in the text that the Annotated Bibliography provides. It is for these readers that the text material has been made available in a separate volume, at a more modest price. For others, the two paperback volumes duplicate the original 1974 hardcover edition, and the hardcover edition itself remains in print.

Preface

In this book we have assembled a large body of evidence concerning how the sexes differ, and how they do not differ, in many aspects of psychological functioning. We do not deal with sexual behavior per se, but rather are concerned with intellectual performance and social behaviors that are not specifically sexual but have been thought to be differentiated by sex. Our objective is to sift the evidence to determine which of the many beliefs about sex differences have a solid basis in fact and which do not. In addition, we discuss the major theories of how psychological sex differentiation comes about. Throughout we are interested in *development*—in the way sex differentiation appears (or, occasionally, disappears) in the course of the life cycle. The book is a sequel to the earlier volume *The Development of Sex Differences* (Maccoby, ed., 1966), but whereas that book was composed of contributed chapters by different authors, this one attempts a more uniform treatment and a more comprehensive coverage of the various behavioral topics taken up. Like the earlier book, it includes summary tables of data and an annotated bibliography; it does not reprint entries included in the 1966 volume, but lists primarily research published since that date.

The preparation of this book has involved the devoted labors of many people. The effort to make the bibliography as complete and accurate as possible required untold hours of searching the literature, writing abstracts, checking references, and writing to authors for clarification or amplification of published materials. Mary Clare Jacobson and Chris Cozzens worked assiduously on these tasks. Mary Anderson rendered invaluable service in the early stages of the library search. Sharon Nash did a complete editing of the annotated bibliography, rewriting many entries for clarity and uniformity of style, with considerable checking back to original documents. Our most especial thanks go to Greg Buckle, who became the bibliography's gatekeeper for accuracy, and with a fierce integrity worked to keep the rest of us from overinterpreting the data or ignoring the nuances of findings. Much of this bibliographical work was underwritten by Ford Foundation grant 72-429, and we are most grateful for this support.

The preparation of a manuscript of this kind, with its many tables and references, imposes especially heavy demands upon a secretarial staff. We can only say that without the extraordinarily careful and sustained work of Ruth Prehn, Jo Denham, and Susanne Taylor, the manuscript would never have come into being.

A number of people read portions of the manuscript at various stages of preparation and gave us their critical comments. Especially helpful was the commentary by William Kessen, who served as the publisher's primary reader and gave us our first feedback on the book as a whole. On the basis of his suggestions we revised the chapter organization and rewrote several sections extensively. We believe that his critique resulted in a manuscript that was considerably more coherent than the first draft, and we are grateful to him.

We are painfully aware that despite all the efforts of ourselves and our co-workers, our coverage of the existing body of research and interpretive writing on sex differences is not complete. The ever-present problem of publication lag has meant that work completed during the past year could not be included in our summaries. We can only apologize to those whose contributions have been missed, and hope that the main themes that have emerged from our study do rest on a body of evidence sufficient to allow them to stand the test of time and replication.

Contents

Tables

The Psychology of Sex Differences

Volume I: Text

CHAPTER ONE

Introduction

Questions about the psychological nature of man and woman are currently under intense debate. Do the sexes differ in their emotional reactions to people and events? Do they differ in the vigor with which they attack the life problems confronting them? Do they have equal potential for acquiring the knowledge and skills necessary for a variety of occupations? If psychological differences do exist, on the average, are the differences great enough to impose any limits on, or indicate any especially promising directions for, the kinds of lives that individuals of the two sexes may reasonably be expected to lead? And, perhaps most important, where the differences do exist, how did they come about? Are they inevitable, or are they the product of arbitrary social stereotypes that could be changed if society itself changes?

In this book we address all these questions, but we have proceeded on the assumption that before we can attempt to understand the "why" and "how" of psychological sex differentiation, we must have as accurate and detailed a knowledge as possible concerning the nature of existing differences and the changes these differences undergo at successive ages. In Chapters 2–7 we attempt to establish precisely what the differences are that need to be explained. We then turn to the three major psychological theories that purport to explain them. These theories (in highly encapsulated form) are that psychological sex differentiation occurs:

1. Through imitation: children choose same-sex models (particularly the same-sex parent) and use these models more than opposite-sex models for patterning their own behavior. This selective modeling need not be deliberate on the child's part, of course.

2. Through praise or discouragement: parents (and others) reward and praise boys for what they conceive to be "boylike" behavior and actively discourage boys when they engage in activities that seem feminine; similarly, girls receive positive reinforcement for "feminine" behavior, negative reinforcement for "masculine" behavior.

3. Through self-socialization: the child first develops a concept of what

it is to be male or female, and then, once he has a clear understanding of his own sex identity, he attempts to fit his own behavior to his concept of what behavior is sex-appropriate.

Of course, the third process calls upon the other two. A child's conception of what is appropriate behavior for a male or female will depend both upon what he sees males and females doing and upon the approval or disapproval that these actions elicit differentially from others. Both of these kinds of events constitute information the child can draw upon in building his concept of sex-appropriate behavior, but in theory 3 neither modeling nor reinforcement is thought to operate in any automatic way to produce sex-typed behavior.

In Chapter 8, then, we assemble the evidence concerning whether, at what ages, and under what circumstances, children imitate same-sex models (theory 1), and ask whether selective imitation precedes or follows the development of behavioral sex-differentiation and a sex-typed self-concept. In Chapter 9, we examine the available information on how the two sexes are socialized, to see what kinds of differential rewards and punishments are known to occur (theory 2) and to determine how well the socialization pattern fits the developing behavioral differences and similarities charted in Chapters 2–7. In Chapter 10 we discuss theory 3, and also consider in what way all three processes, acting jointly, might function in such a way as to account for the phenomena documented in the earlier chapters.

In the explanatory chapters, _psychological_ processes are stressed, but this is not to deny the impact of biology. An individual's sex is obviously both a biological and a social fact. If biological sex turns out to be linked with psychological functioning, the study of this linkage should help to deepen our understanding of a more basic matter: the way in which biological "predispositions" interact with the impact of social experience to shape the psychological makeup of the person. Few psychologists now believe that all newborn human individuals are alike in their potential reactions to the experiences they will have. A few brave students of human development have attempted to identify temperamental "types" or individual styles of thought and action that appear to be pervasive and stable, that affect the individual's response to experience, and that may have a biological basis. But so far, the biological base cannot be inferred with confidence. Of course, it is very difficult to know whether a psychological sex difference has a biological origin; but since sex itself _is_ a biological variable, there is hope that something can be discovered concerning the role that sex hormones and other genetically sex-linked aspects of the body's functioning play in influencing an individual's reactions to his environment. It will be just as important to know what functions are _not_ affected as to identify those that are.

The writers are neither geneticists nor biologists, and are therefore not equipped to undertake an in-depth account of these factors. But wherever we are familiar with genetic or biochemical information bearing upon sex differentiation in a particular sphere of behavior, we have made reference to that information. For example, the influence of sex hormones on aggression and dominance is discussed in Chapter 7; and the question whether there is any sex linkage in the genetic control of intellectual abilities is discussed in Chapters 3 and 4.

Sexual behavior per se may of course be the sphere of behavior most affected by the biology of sex. The reader should be forewarned, however, that this book does not deal with sexual behavior in the usual sense of that term. Sexual behavior is a topic widely written about, and we leave it to the sexologists. Our concern is with other aspects of psychological sex differentiation, although of course we will be interested in whether this differentiation in any degree reflects the roles the two sexes play in sexual encounters.

THE NATURE OF THE EVIDENCE

A number of the physical differences between the sexes are obvious and universal. The psychological differences are not. The folklore that has grown up about them is often vague and inconsistent. We believe there is a great deal of myth in the popular views about sex differences. There is also some substance. In Chapters 2–7, we hope to be able to identify the generalizations that may be relied upon with some confidence. Our primary method will be a detailed examination of the findings of research in which the social behavior, intellectual abilities, or motivations of the two sexes have been systematically studied.

There are some distinct limitations on what can be learned from the published body of research. In the next few pages we shall discuss briefly some of the methodological problems we have encountered in attempting to summarize and interpret the available data. Readers who do not have a technical interest in such issues are invited to turn to p. 8.

A first problem has to do with the incompleteness of the information upon which we must rely. Some information is lost owing to the selection that occurs in the publication process itself. We invite the reader to imagine a situation in which all psychological researchers routinely divide their subjects into two groups at random, and perform their data analyses separately for the two halves of the sample. Whenever a difference in findings emerges between the two groups (and this would of course sometimes happen by chance even when no difference exists that would replicate with further samples), our imaginary researcher tests the difference for significance, and any significant differences are included in the published report of the study. If we are not told that the original subdivision has been made at random, we might misspend a great deal of time attempting to explain the differences.

In a sense, this book is dedicated to testing the null hypothesis that sex differences are of this same order: that assigning cases to groups by sex is no more meaningful, for purposes of understanding the behavior of the subjects, than assigning them at random.

Let us hasten to add that we do not believe the null hypothesis for all aspects of psychological sex differences. The problem is to sift the differences that are "real" from those that are not. Let us also emphasize that we do not believe that a sex difference, to be real, must be replicable on all populations. As an example, consider the greater vulnerability of the male fetus and infant to damage by pathological prenatal or perinatal conditions. Any behavioral anomalies resulting from such damage would be more frequent in boys. However, improvements in prenatal medical care, and in the care of mothers and infants at the time of delivery, should reduce the sex difference, or conceivably eliminate it. The underlying fact, that males are more vulnerable, would continue to be true, but would only manifest itself under certain conditions. Similarly, behavioral sex differences that are the outcome of differential socialization practices could be expected to exist only in some cultures, but where they occur they are nonetheless real.

We emphasize the null hypothesis because of the way most data on sex differences find their way into the psychological literature. Researchers frequently match their experimental and control groups by sex, to guard in advance against the possibility that sex may turn out to be related to the behavior under investigation. Having so designed the study, they are then in a position to analyze by sex—and frequently do so only to confirm that this variable can be ruled out for further analysis. If the analysis yields insignificant results, the researcher usually breathes a sigh of relief and sees fit not to report his negative findings in print. If sex differences do emerge, they are often regarded as a nuisance, and the researcher may settle upon a strategy of reporting them only if he must do so in reporting significant interactions in which sex is one of the factors. There are some exceptions: when there is controversy concerning what sex differences may be expected, then the researcher may report his mean differences as of some interest in their own right. More often, the problem lies in the failure to report findings of *no* difference.

There are instances in which there has been direct pressure to keep findings out of the published literature when they do not agree with the accepted view of some process or relationship. In one instance we know of, an established figure had built a considerable theory about sex differences around the findings from a test he had employed. When a young researcher later failed to find a sex difference on the test and wrote to the senior person about her findings, she was told there must be something wrong with either her method or her sampling—that her results were "just wrong"; she then omitted reference to her contrary findings in the published report of the study.

Of course, not all negative findings are equally worthy of attention. In some cases, measures are unreliable, and any sex differences that might exist go undetected. However, when measures do demonstrate some power (in the sense of being reliable and sensitive to experimental treatment or of showing other group differences) but still do not distinguish between the sexes, there is more reason to include them in a tally as genuinely negative findings. We are aware, of course, that no amount of negative evidence "proves" that no sex difference exists. In the pages that follow we have sometimes used the phrase "There is no sex difference with respect to ..."; this is simply a way of saying, "No sex difference has been shown." It is always possible that the wrong techniques of measurement have been used, or that the problem has been wrongly defined, and that sex-difference effects will emerge in future work with different methods.

Although negative findings probably constitute the most frequent omissions from the literature, there are some instances in which positive findings are omitted as well. We have been told of instances in which editors have insisted on the omission of significant sex-difference findings from papers on verbal memory, for example. We sympathize with the editors' problem of conserving journal space, and recognize that the deleted findings may not be central to the primary message of a study, but such rulings do hamper our efforts to discover whether the rate of significant sex differences for a given behavior is different from chance. On the whole, we believe that the omission of negative findings is considerably more frequent than the omission of positive findings, though we cannot be sure.

The reader will no doubt find that the best evidence for the sexes' not differing in some respect is to be found at the two extremities of the hypothetical distribution of differences—that is, when there are as many studies showing relatively high scores for boys as there are showing high scores for girls. A more interesting case occurs when the distribution is lopsided —when beyond the many studies showing no difference there are many others demonstrating a difference that is always (or almost always) in one direction. We take this kind of result to mean that there is something "real" about the difference but that there are triggering factors in the eliciting conditions for the behavior; we attempt in these cases to deduce what the factors are that must be present for the sex difference to appear.

It is regrettable that so few research studies have been deliberately directed toward the discovery of these factors. It continues to be true that most of the findings reported are accidental, or at least incidental to other scientific concerns. We expect that as the reader joins us in an effort to "explain" the differences that do turn out to be consistent, he will come to feel, as we do, that the time has come for research focusing directly upon manipulation of the conditions that ought to elicit differential behavior from the two sexes.

However that may be, we shall return now to the importance of the null hypothesis—to point with some alarm to the tendency for isolated positive findings to sweep through the literature, while findings of no difference, or even later findings showing opposite results, are ignored. Studies with nonreplicable positive findings are reprinted in books of readings, cited in textbooks, and used to buttress theories about the nature of the development of sex typing. It is easy to understand how this happens, for it is an extraordinarily time-consuming task to comb through the masses of published data for all the instances—positive and negative—that bear upon an issue. It is our hope that the present volume will serve as a resource and will save researchers at least part of this burdensome but necessary task.

In our review of the literature, we have encountered some peculiarities of *interpretation* of data, distortions that occur frequently enough to deserve comment here. Writers sometimes refer to studies that included subjects of only one sex as if they had demonstrated a sex difference. This occurs when a within-sex correlation suggests a hypothesis about between-sex differences. As an example: R. Q. Bell, reporting on an all-male sample, said that activity level was high in newborn boys who had suffered some degree of birth complications, compared with those who had not. He speculated that, since boys more often suffer birth complications, this might explain a higher neonatal activity level among boys. This was later reported by others as an instance in which boys had been found to have a higher activity level than girls, although Bell had not in fact studied girls.

In other instances, though the correlation for one sex is significantly different from zero, the correlation for the other is not. These facts are then interpreted as if there were a significant difference *between the correlations*. There are instances in which the correlations for the two sexes are only a few points apart, but one reaches the .05 level of statistical significance and the other does not. For example, a study might find that the correlation between the amount of mother-child interaction in infancy and the child's later IQ was .40 for boys, .30 for girls. Let us suppose that for the sample size used in this hypothetical study, only the correlation for boys is statistically significant. In the published report of the study, the authors might choose to include in their tables only those correlations that reached significance. The information available to the reader, then, would be that there was a significant correlation for boys but not for girls. He might be tempted to assume that the girls' correlation must have been zero, and might proceed to spin out a theory about how different causal factors affect intellectual development in the two sexes. But with our hypothetical sample size, a correlation of .40 is not significantly different from one of .30. We have found a number of instances in which correlational data have been misinterpreted in this way. In analysis of variance terms, to support conclusions about differential effects it is necessary to show that the *interaction* is significant, not just that there is a significant main effect within one sex but not the other.

Different patterns of findings *within* each sex have sometimes been mistaken for sex differences. A case in point is the comparison of verbal and physical aggression. Sears et al. (1965)[R] found that among a sample of preschool girls verbal aggression was more frequent than physical aggression. Among boys the reverse was true. Although there was no ambiguity about the presentation of the original findings, they were later interpreted as showing that girls were higher than boys in verbal aggression. In fact, boys showed *more of both kinds of aggression* than girls showed.

We can only caution the reader against these pitfalls, and hope that the text will help to correct such misinterpretations where we have detected them.

A basic problem with the research on sex differences is that it is almost always impossible for observers to be blind to the sex of the subjects. Stereotypes about what kind of behavior is to be expected from the two sexes run very deep, and even when sex differences are incidental to the main focus of a study, the observers must almost inevitably be biased to some extent. There are a number of instances in which a commonly believed sex difference is confirmed when ratings by parents, teachers, or other observers are used, but is not confirmed when simple frequency counts of relatively unambiguous categories of behavior are tallied in the course of direct observation.

Rater bias does not always take the form of "seeing" stereotypic behavior with greater frequency than it actually occurs. As Meyer and Sobieszek have shown (1972), there are instances in which a rater is more likely to notice a bit of behavior if it runs *counter* to his stereotype. In this case, it stands out more against the rater's adaptation level. It is our judgment that behavior observation, though not free from bias, is less influenced by the observer's expectations than rating scales are, and we have therefore placed somewhat more reliance on observational data in our text discussions. And although it would be desirable to do more research under conditions where the observer does not know the subject's sex, this can usually be managed only under highly contrived, artificial conditions; under normal conditions, the very fact that the subject's sex is known to others around him is part of the network of phenomena surrounding the sex-typed social behavior that is under study, and to change this would be to distort the behavior. Perhaps all that can be done is to make greater efforts to evaluate the degree of observer bias, so that it can be allowed for in the interpretation of findings.

ORGANIZATION AND TREATMENT OF THE MATERIAL

The present book is a sequel to the volume *The Development of Sex Differences* (Maccoby 1966b[R]). Like that book, this one focuses upon the development of sex differences through childhood and adolescence, although more work with adults is included in the present volume. The text of the earlier book consisted of six contributed chapters covering selected issues and reflecting the diverse viewpoints of different authors. The present book attempts to be more comprehensive in its topical coverage and, having uniform authorship throughout, reflects a more consistent point of view. It includes a revised and updated version of the earlier chapter on sex differences in intellectual functioning (Chapter 3), but with that one exception the chapters in the present volume are not meant to supersede those in the old one. The earlier chapters are, in our opinion, still highly relevant discussions of some of the theoretical issues in this field, and we expect teachers and researchers will find that joint use of the two books presents a fuller picture than the present book alone can offer.

The 1966 book included an annotated bibliography and a set of summary tables on selected topics. Volume II of the present work is an annotated bibliography of studies published since the 1966 book (or not included in that book) but does not reprint the entries annotated earlier. The summary tables in the present book are now integrated in context in the topical chapters (those in the 1966 volume were collected in a single grouping). The organization of topics in the topical summaries is somewhat different from that in the earlier summaries; and studies annotated for the previous book are included in the present summary tables where they are relevant to new topics. Studies have been included in the new Annotated Bibliography only if they included subjects of both sexes; within-sex experiments and within-sex correlational analyses are cited in the text when they appear to shed light on some of the between-sex comparisons, but are listed only in the References Cited section (pp. 377–91 of this volume).

The system that we have used for references in the body of the text is as follows: when a work is cited, the author's name is given, along with the year in which the study was published. The reader will find most of these references (all of those not furnished with a superscript R) listed alphabetically in the Annotated Bibliography (Volume II). Works cited that bear the superscript letter R after the year will be found in the References Cited section. This section has been reserved for studies cited in the text but not included in the Annotated Bibliography; *some* of these studies (those indicated, in the References Cited section, by an asterisk) appear in Roberta M. Oetzel's Annotated Bibliography in the 1966 volume (pp. 223–321), where they are annotated much in the manner of the present Annotated

Bibliography. (All text-table references bearing the superscript R are given in the Annotated Bibliography in the 1966 volume, as well as in the References Cited section in the present volume.)

In making up the summary tables, we have listed a study as showing a sex difference if the statistical test yielded a probability value of .05 or less. The difference is listed as a "trend" if the p value is between .10 and .05. Otherwise it is listed as "no difference." Readers who wish to make their own sign tests might have preferred to have the direction of difference indicated even when it did not reach the .10 level, but such directional information would not have been interpretable without standard deviations; furthermore, many publications, while reporting p values, do not give either means or standard deviations, and our tables would have become more complex and less complete. We recognize, of course, that readers will not be satisfied merely to count studies as if they were all of equal value, and we have accordingly reported sample sizes in the summary tables, so that the reader can have some basis for assigning weights to different studies. In addition, in reporting the work on tested intellectual abilities, we have made separate tabulations of the large-sample studies showing not only the direction of the sex differences but the magnitude of the differences in z-score units. But large samples, too, must be interpreted with care; although such studies have a firmer data base, they are also capable of showing a sex difference to be significant even though it is very small, relative to a distribution.

Some difficult decisions had to be made concerning how to describe, in an economical way, the samples that had been used in the studies listed in text tables. The large bulk of the psychological work covered here has been done with white, middle-class American children and adults, studied in nursery schools, public schools, and colleges (this of course reflects no choosing on our part, but rather the population usually selected for research studies). In order to save space, we decided not to include a sample description (other than age) when it was a "standard" sample in the above sense. We did believe, however, that the reader would want to be informed when the sample deviated from this pattern—when the subjects came from, say, a different country, an ethnic American subculture, a parochial school, or a homogeneously low-income group of families. A number of the studies included in our summary tables are taken from the growing body of data on Head Start and Follow-Through children—children from low-income families who are usually, though not always, from black, Spanish-American, or American Indian backgrounds. We have designated these varying sample characteristics in the summary tables without wishing to be in any way invidious, but in the belief that there is something to be learned by determining whether a sex difference is, or is not, found across a variety of cultural settings.

There are some instances in which the literature contains several reports from a given body of data. This is especially likely to be true in large-scale longitudinal studies. Sometimes different reports have provided data for overlapping samples, with the data for a subgroup of subjects being later incorporated into a different report on a larger sample. It is not always clear when this has been done; in the instances where we are aware of it, we have included only one report for a given sample of children on a given measure at a given age, and have tried to choose the most comprehensive report when more than one source was available.

In this book, like the previous one, we have listed studies in the summary tables in order corresponding to the age of the subjects. We have done this in an effort to trace developmental patterns. In a few instances, sex differences are shown to be a transitional phenomenon—at an early point, the sexes are similar, after which they briefly diverge and then resemble one another closely once again. This can happen when one sex develops faster with respect to a particular behavioral domain; it can also happen when the two sexes take different developmental paths to reach the same mature level of proficiency. Such patterns are particularly important for students of development, even though developmental "paths" are difficult to trace in view of the changes in the nature of measures that can be appropriately used at widely differing ages.

We have not prepared summary tables (or corresponding text) on all the topics that have been included in the studies in the Annotated Bibliography. In the discussion of cognitive styles, for example, we have focused upon the dimensions where sex differences had been shown or alleged, and concerning which a body of research aimed at explaining such differences was available; we have not prepared summary tables on category breadth, focusing vs. scanning strategies, tolerance for ambiguity, or a number of other topics that may be of interest to some readers. (Data relevant to these topics may be found in the Annotated Bibliography, however, and it is our hope that readers with special interests will thereby be assisted in producing summaries in addition to those we have undertaken in the text proper.)

We have attempted to be thorough in our review of the literature. We began by reviewing all issues from January 1966 to spring 1973 in a selected set of journals in which findings of psychological sex differences are most frequently reported. We then followed leads from the reference lists of papers in these journals, and used the *Psychological Abstracts* and relevant books and review chapters as guides to still other bodies of data.

In an attempt to improve our coverage, we wrote to a number of authors whose published reports indicated that sex had been a variable in a study design but for which no analysis of sex differences was reported. In response we received many helpful letters and supplementary tables of data, and we have incorporated this additional information into our summaries in numerous instances. We have also run statistical tests in instances where authors did not report them, but for which sufficient information was given to do so; these results too have been included in our report. Even so we are aware that gaps remain. Furthermore, we have tried to acknowledge our indebtedness to the writings of others whenever we are aware of it, but it is to be expected that some of the conclusions that emerge from our review will have been anticipated, without our knowledge, in the wisdom of earlier writers, and we trust we shall be forgiven if we fail to acknowledge this specifically in every case.

Writing a book about sex differences almost forces an author into being a "trait" psychologist. The very process of arranging researches under topical headings tempts the reader—and the writer—into believing that all the items listed are indices of the trait that is named in the table title. In our discussion, we shall attempt to resist this temptation. We are aware that behavior is situation-specific. Indeed, one of our objectives is to identify the situations in which a given sex difference in behavior may be expected to occur, and the situations in which it may not. The "trait" labels that have been used in our summary-table titles have been dictated, to a large extent, by the topics that have been selected for research on sex differences—by the kind of trait psychology, in other words, that is implicit in the work that psychologists do. The summaries provide some insights into whether clusters of behavior that psychologists have included under the same label do in fact cohere, in the sense of yielding consistent findings.

We are constrained by the data in another way: there are certain restricted aspects of behavior that have been extensively studied; at the same time, many broad areas have received little research attention. The recent history of psychology and its focus of interests are reflected in our summary tables. An initial classic study, using an ingenious technique or posing an interesting issue, will be followed up by a large number of studies, some parametric, some introducing experimental refinements to shed light on interpretations of earlier findings. Thus there are masses of studies on the effects of modeled behavior on acquisition and performance; on attachment as revealed in Ainsworth's Strange Situation; and on social influence in an Asch-like situation; etc. The reader may feel that it represents overkill to summarize 21 studies on the Prisoner's Dilemma, for example, and that the usual performance of the two sexes could have been documented sufficiently with a subset of the evidence. But we have decided to present all the evidence available to us, chiefly because there was no reasonable basis for selecting some studies and excluding others (and to select would have been to run the risk of bias), but also because there are some areas (and the Prisoner's Dilemma is a good case in point) in which an early study reported a sex difference that was not replicated in many subsequent attempts. As noted above, it is our impression that there is a substantial primacy effect in beliefs about scientific truths—that it takes a great deal of evidence to refute an original erroneous impression. We have therefore reported the literature as it exists, with all its peculiarities of distribution. But the very process of scanning the topics that have been heavily researched, and noting the gaps, should assist the reader in identifying areas where further work is needed.

In dealing with the traditional topic "sex typing" or "masculinity and femininity," we encountered an organizational problem. The term "sex typing" sometimes refers to the process whereby social pressures are brought to bear upon the individual to make him or her conform to the social definitions of appropriate behavior for his or her sex. This aspect of sex typing has been dealt with in the chapter on differential socialization of boys and girls. But there is another meaning of the term "sex typing." Tests of "masculinity" and "femininity" are made up of items on which the two sexes are known to differ. In this sense, Chapters 2–7 are all focused on sex typing, since each asks how the sexes differ. Once this is known, it is easy to define the individual as "masculine" or "feminine" according to whether he or she shares the characteristics usually displayed by males or females. This meaning of the term "sex typing" renders it entirely redundant with the topic "sex differences."

However, the term "sex typing" can have narrower meanings. In one usage, a "masculine" man or a "feminine" woman is simply one who is sexually attractive to members of the opposite sex. Another meaning has to do with an individual's adopting interests and behavior related to the roles that his sex would normally play in the society in which the individual is growing up. Our treatment of this topic is to be found primarily in Chapter 8. From still another point of view, sex typing deals with the individual's adoption of a sex identity. In childhood, a boy usually comes to understand that he is and always will be a boy, comes to feel that he *wants* to be a boy, and is motivated to behave according to his conception of what boylike behavior is. In rare cases, of course, an individual resists adopting the appropriate sex identity, and the result may be transsexuality. The present volume deals only very tangentially with abnormalities of sex-identity development. This is a complex and specialized matter that is beyond the scope of our work. The reader is referred to the recent volume *Man and Woman, Boy and Girl*, by Money and Ehrhardt (1972)[R], for an extensive treatment of this issue. Our own discussion of the normal course of development of sex identity will be found chiefly in Chapters 8 and 9.

We cannot close this introduction without saying a word about the authors' own biases. We are both feminists (of different vintages, and one perhaps more militant than the other!), and although we have tried to be objective about the value-laden topics discussed in this book, we know that we cannot have succeeded entirely. We doubt, in fact, that complete objectivity is possible for anyone engaged in such an enterprise, whether male or female. If our own interpretations bear the marks of feminist bias, this will be detected soon enough by hawk-eyed readers with points of view different from ours. We expect to be challenged. We can promise the reader only that we have attempted to set forth the reasoning behind our positions as clearly as possible, so that future argument will not be diverted into irrelevancies.

PART ONE

Intellect and Achievement

The intellectual functioning of human beings has been studied from several widely divergent points of view. A large body of work deals with the processes whereby the individual comes to have the intellectual skills he does possess—how he learns, and in what way he stores the products of previous learnings in memory in such a way that previous experience can be made use of in solving new tasks. A second approach to intellect involves the assessment of "abilities," and the identification of patterns or clusters among these abilities. It might be expected that there would be a clear relationship between learning and abilities. That is, the person who learns easily should accumulate a fund of knowledge and skills that would emerge in the form of a high score on an abilities test, and if a person's learning experiences have been focused primarily in a particular subject-matter area, then his abilities should be stronger in this area than in others. In fact, however, there has been a discontinuity between studies of learning and studies of ability patterns. Studies of learning have dealt primarily with the learning process itself, and only tangentially with individual differences in how learning takes place or what is most easily learned. Studies of abilities have been focally concerned with individual differences, but only marginally with perceptual, mediational, or mnemonic processes that may underlie these differences. Indeed, assessment of an individual's abilities leaves open the question whether his achievements are a result of past learning, inherent capacity, motivation and interests, or some interweaving of these factors.

In Chapter 2, we compare males and females with respect to the basic psychological processes that are involved in intellectual functioning: perception, learning, and memory. In Chapter 3 we turn to tested abilities, and consider whether the sexes differ with respect to the profile, or pattern, of abilities that they normally display. Intellectual achievement, however, clearly depends not only upon the strategies a person can employ in perceiving, learning, and memory and upon the pattern of abilities he has devel-

oped to date, but also upon his motivation for achieving in the intellectual sphere. In Chapter 4 we take up the question of whether the two sexes have different degrees of interest in achievement for its own sake, and whether they normally try to achieve in different spheres, or work for different kinds of goals.

CHAPTER TWO

Perception, Learning, and Memory

PERCEPTION

It is alleged that the sexes differ in their perceptions. For example, Garai and Scheinfeld say: "One might postulate a 'visual stimulus hunger' of the boys and an 'auditory stimulus hunger' of the girls. From the foregoing studies we may conclude that boys tend to be showing an inherently greater interest in objects and visual patterns, while girls are congenitally more interested in people and facial features" (1968, p. 193)[R].

The statement implies two things: that boys perceive more through *looking*, girls through *listening*; and that girls are more interested in social stimuli of all kinds, whereas boys are more interested in "things." It would seem that the two tendencies should sometimes reinforce each other, sometimes cancel each other. For example, faces are perceived visually, but they are also social, so that boys and girls might be equally interested in them for different reasons. If the two tendencies do exist, they ought to show themselves more clearly in cases where they coincide, such as human voices or a variety of nonhuman visual patterns.

If the two sexes did begin life with different perceptual biases, this might have far-reaching effects upon their development, and would help to explain certain differences in aptitudes or interests that can be detected at a later point. Garai and Scheinfeld suggest (*ibid.*) that "a difference in sense modality between the sexes, ... if corroborated ... would provide an explanation for the apparent tendency of girls to develop superior verbal skills, as well as for that of boys to excel in spatial perception."

Some of the research that Garai and Scheinfeld use as a basis for their position has been done with very young infants. It may seem far-fetched to suggest that the perceptual tendencies an infant shows during the first few days of life would have any bearing upon the way he behaves several years later. But in fact, such relationships have been shown. For example, R. Bell and his colleagues (1971) have found that a newborn infant's sensitivity to touch predicts certain aspects of his play behavior when he is observed at the age of 2½. Similarly, J. Kagan (1971) reports that infants who spend only a short time looking at visual displays when they are four months old tend to be "flighty" in their play patterns two years later; that is, they shift the focus of their activity rapidly from one place, or one toy, to another. The links between infant perception and childhood behavior that have been uncovered by Bell and Kagan were found in both sexes. They suggest that if the two sexes did have different patterns of perception in infancy, this fact might indeed be important in explaining sex differences at later ages.

Is there any physiological reason why infant boys and girls should perceive differently? Conel (1941, 1947)[R] has shown that the visual system is neurologically somewhat more mature (i.e. more myelinated) in early infancy than the auditory system. If girls mature at a more rapid rate than boys, there may be a period of time during which both sexes have fairly mature visual systems, but the girls have progressed farther than the boys in the development of those portions of the neural system that are relevant to hearing. During such a period, the girls ought to be more responsive to sounds.

The hypothesis is intriguing, but in fact it is not known that the relevant portions of the nervous system do develop at different rates in the two sexes. It *is* known that girls are skeletally somewhat more mature at birth, as measured by the hardening of the wrist bones. However, their advantage in this respect is short-lived; boys are somewhat ahead in skeletal development by the end of the first year and continue to be so to about the age of 8 (Flory 1936[R]). In any case, the initially greater skeletal development of girls may not mean much for perception—the maturation of different physiological systems proceeds at different rates, and skeletal maturation does not seem to be a good index to the maturation of other parts of the body. Behavioral measures of maturation, such as the age of first sitting up, the age of beginning to crawl and walk, and the age of achieving each of the developmental stages in the use of the hand and the fingers for prehension, do not show a sex difference (Bayley 1936[R]; Table 3.1 of this book). If there were a general sex difference in the rate of maturation of the nervous system, the infant developmental scales would show it. Of course, direct measures of the nervous system itself would be the most conclusive sort of evidence. Conel (1939, 1941, 1947, 1951, 1955, 1959, 1963)[R] has produced the definitive work on the myelination of different parts of the nervous system at successive ages, but he has not had enough cases at each age to permit meaningful analysis by sex. Thus it is simply not known whether there is any sex difference in the rate of maturation of the specific parts of the brain that control vision, audition, and the other sensory systems.

Assuming for the moment that the auditory system does develop somewhat faster in girls, it might be expected that their advantage in auditory perception would be brief, and that boys would show as much responsiveness to sounds as soon as their neural growth had caught up. Another possibility (suggested by Sherman 1971[R]) is that a modality preference is established early and maintained subsequently, so that boys come to rely on vision during the time when audition is not fully functional, and continue to rely upon it even after the time when they would be physiologically able to make greater use of audition.

All this is speculation, however, for it does not rest on a solid foundation of neurological knowledge. Before we attempt to explain perceptual sex differences in these terms, it would obviously be wise to determine as precisely as possible what phenomena need to be explained. In the sections that follow, sex differences (and similarities) in chemical, tactile, auditory, and visual perception are discussed and charted. When information about each of these sense modalities is in hand, it will then be possible to address more clearly the question of modality *preferences*, which calls for comparisons among modalities as well as between sexes. Finally, we shall examine responsiveness to social as compared with nonsocial stimuli in the modalities for which information is available.

Taste and Smell—The Chemical Senses

There is good reason to expect sex differences in the chemical senses. Changes in estrogen levels during the normal fluctuations of these hormones in women are associated with changes in the acuity of the sense of smell. With increased estrogens after puberty (Le Magnen 1952, reported in Money and Ehrhardt 1972[R]) and during the menstrual cycle (Schneider and Wolf 1955[R]), women become considerably more sensitive to odors. Furthermore, olfactory sensitivity in animals has been linked to sexual behavior, which of course in its turn is functionally related to levels of sex hormones. These facts would strongly suggest that there ought to be sex differences in smell sensitivity, at least during certain portions of the life cycle or certain portions of women's monthly cycles. However, there are almost no relevant data. Two studies of responsiveness to several odors among newborns found no sex difference (Lipsitt and Jacklin 1971, Self et al. 1972). Although these infants were not assayed for sex hormones, recent work has found sex differences in both androgens and estrogens in the newborn, with the male infants, surprisingly, having higher levels of *both* kinds of hormones.[*] It is not known how androgens affect smell sensitivity, or how their effects might interact with varying levels of estrogens; thus it is not clear whether the neonatal hormone patterns might be expected to produce any sex differences in smell sensitivity or not. It would

[*] C. H. Doering, Department of Psychiatry, Stanford University, personal communication, 1973.

be especially interesting to know about smell thresholds at later points in the life cycle, when the hormonal patterns of the two sexes are more strongly differentiated, but this information is not available to date.

With respect to taste sensitivity, there is a report (Nisbett and Gurwitz 1970) showing that newborn girls increase their sucking rate for sweet solutions while newborn boys do not. Of course this simple fact does not reveal whether male infants cannot discriminate between sweet and neutral solutions, or whether they discriminate but do not especially like the sweet taste. With adult subjects who can report their taste thresholds, women prove to be more sensitive to bitter tastes (Kaplan and Fischer 1964[R]). In rats, estrogen injections increased saccharin preference (Zucker 1969[R]). Thus the evidence, though sparse, indicates that females are more sensitive to at least some tastes.

The Sense of Touch

Infant girls are thought to be more sensitive to touch, and this is seen as an important precondition for later sex differences: "They [females] also have a greater reactivity to physical stimuli, as evidenced by their lower tactile and pain thresholds, their greater irritability during physical examinations, and their higher skin conductance. The idea that this early sensitivity is a necessary precondition for empathy and imagination is supported by studies of older girls and women" (Bardwick 1971[R], p. 102).

Tactile sensitivity in infants has been measured in a number of ways. Bell and his colleagues (R. Bell et al. 1971) have used an "aesthesiometer," which is a series of nylon filaments graded in diameter. Starting with the thinnest filament, each filament is applied with gently increasing pressure to the heel of a sleeping infant until the filament bends. If the infant has not given a reflex withdrawal of the foot, the next-thicker filament is applied, and so on until the filament is reached that will reliably elicit a foot-withdrawal response. Other measures used to measure tactile sensitivity include a jet of air applied to the infant's abdomen (with air pressure being increased gradually to the point where a general body movement occurs), brushing the infant lightly on the mouth, and touching him with a cold disk.

An important initial question is whether these procedures measure anything that is a stable characteristic of an individual child. Bell reports that aesthesiometer measures showed reasonably good test-retest reliability when two measures were taken hours apart during the first four days of life. Bernstein and Jacklin (1973), using the same method of measurement, tested infants at age 3½ months and again one week later, and found that there was considerable intrapersonal stability over this time period, although the 3½-month measures did not correlate with tactile sensitivity measures that had been taken by Stanton with the same infants on their

TABLE 2.1
Tactile Sensitivity

Study	Age and N	Difference	Comment
R. Bell et al. 1971	Newborns (75)	Girls	Tactile sensitivity (aesthesiometer; breast-fed infants)
		None	Tactile sensitivity (bottle-fed infants)
R. Bell & Costello 1964	Newborns (21)	Girls	More movement after removal of a covering blanket
	Newborns (17)	Girls	Lower threshold, stimulation of abdomen by air jet
		None	Air jet to cheek
Birns 1965	Newborns (30)	None	Motor response to cold disk
Lipsitt & Levy [R] 1959	Newborns (36)	Girls	Lower threshold to electroactual threshold (1 or 2 studies)
Stanton [R] 1972	Newborns (40)	None	Tactile sensitivity (aesthesiometer)
	Newborns (24)	None	Tactile sensitivity (second- and later-borns)
Turkewitz et al. 1967	Newborns (51)	None	Head turning to touch of brush on mouth
G. Weller & Bell 1965	Newborns (40)	Girls	Higher skin conductance (more sensitive)
Yang & Douthitt 1974	Newborns (43)	None	Air jet to abdomen
Bernstein & Jacklin 1973	3½ mos (38)	None	Tactile sensitivity (aesthesiometer)

second day of life. The measures do appear to be sufficiently reliable for a short time period that they should be capable of revealing sex differences if they exist. As Table 2.1 shows, there are eight studies of tactile sensitivity with neonates. Three of these have found a sex difference, with the girls having lower touch thresholds (being more sensitive) in each of the three cases. But five studies show the two sexes to be much alike, and the Bernstein and Jacklin study with infants of 3½ months also failed to find a sex difference.

The discrepancies among studies are so far unexplained. They do not appear to be a function of the measures used, since studies using the same method have sometimes found a sex difference, sometimes not. They do not seem to be a function of infant state; however, state has not always been measured or held constant. They also do not appear to be a function of whether the sample included firstborns. Rosenblith* has suggested that birth weight may account for some of the sex differences when they are found. A "chubbiness ratio" (a ratio of weight to length) has sometimes been used as an index of body conformation in newborns, and surprisingly, lean babies are relatively insensitive (R. Bell and Costello 1964). However,

* J. F. Rosenblith, Brown University, personal communication, 1973.

it is difficult to see how chubbiness could account for the fact that girls are more sensitive to touch in some samples of babies but not in others. It may be true that in some samples girls are chubbier, and hence more sensitive, whereas in other populations, with different diets and different maternal care, the sex difference in chubbiness does not appear. At the moment, however, there seems to be no good reason why the relation between chubbiness and sex should vary from one group to another.

The evidence is weak, but if we assume for the moment that newborn girls are indeed more sensitive, we may then ask: What would the implications of this fact be? If being sensitive to touch were equivalent with finding touch pleasant, an implication might be that girls would be easier to soothe by holding, swaddling, or stroking.

The possibility that girl infants are easier to soothe than boys was suggested by Moss (1967). In attempting to explain a negative relationship at age 3 months between infant crying and maternal handling that was found for boys only, he speculated: "Mothers of the more irritable boys may have learned that they could not be successful in quieting boys, whereas the girls were more uniformly responsive to (quieted by) maternal handling."

The matter of what will quiet an infant has received little systematic study. Sternglanz (1972)[R] waited for newborns to cry, and then wrapped them in a blanket with either a synthetic fur surface or a soft, smooth cotton-fabric surface touching their bodies (with temperature, infant orientation, and movement held constant). The fur was a more effective quieter, but the sexes did not differ in "quietability" with either type of surface. A similar procedure was used by Bernstein and Jacklin (1973), working with infants aged 3½ months. The crying infant was wrapped loosely in a synthetic fur blanket and brought to the shoulder, and an observer noted how quickly (or whether) the infant stopped crying. Although there was great variation among infants in how easily they could be soothed, these variations were not related to sex. Thus it has not been demonstrated that infant girls' greater tactile sensitivity (if indeed *this* is a reliable phenomenon) makes them more susceptible to tactile soothing. From a commonsense standpoint, being highly sensitive to touch could mean that touch is either more irritating or more soothing than for insensitive persons. It is not intuitively obvious which way the effect should go.

As mentioned above, R. Bell et al. (1971) have explored whether neonatal tactile-sensitive measures would predict behavior later in childhood. They found that high tactile threshold (low sensitivity) in infancy was related in both sexes to vigorous attack on barriers and sustained goal orientations at age 2½. Conversely, low threshold (high sensitivity) was related in both sexes to lethargic and briefly sustained goal behavior. Thus behavior at birth predicts much the same things in both sexes at preschool age; but the study does not reveal whether tactile threshold is itself a stable characteristic of individuals over several years' time.

We are unable to find any research in which measures of tactile sensitivity have been used as a basis for predicting behavioral characteristics in adolescence or adulthood. We are therefore unable to support Bardwick's contention that tactile sensitivity is a "necessary precondition for empathy and imagination," although of course later research may demonstrate that this is so.

Much of the work on tactile thresholds in older children and adults was done many years ago when there was less interest in sex differences. We have been able to locate only one study on sex differences in tactile sensitivity beyond infancy. Ghent (1961) found that girls aged 6, 7, and 9 were more sensitive on their nondominant than their dominant thumbs; no such difference emerged for boys. No direct comparison between sexes was made.

It is important to distinguish between sensitivity and tolerance, particularly where pain is concerned. It is possible for a person to be highly sensitive to painful stimuli (in the sense of being able to detect the first beginnings of pain at a low intensity of the stimulus) while at the same time being able to tolerate fairly high levels of painful stimulation. In a large-scale study (using over 40,000 adult subjects) Woodrow et al. (1972)[R] tested tolerance for pressure on the Achilles tendon. The mean tolerance for men was 28.7 pounds per square inch, for women 15.9 pounds. Thus men showed considerably greater tolerance for pain. Pain threshold was not measured in this study, however, and evidence is sparse concerning sex differences in either pain or touch thresholds among adults. Citing a review by Notermans and Tophoff (1967)[R], Woodrow et al. note that previous work on pain thresholds has found either no sex difference or greater sensitivity in women. No studies have found greater sensitivity in men. There has been considerable work on perceiving through touch (haptic perception), and a number of these studies permit sex comparisons. In some cases the subject is required to feel an object behind a screen and either recognize it or learn to distinguish it from other touched objects. In other instances he must match a touched object, or a length measured with the hands, to an object or length presented visually. Studies of tactile perception are summarized in Table 2.2. Out of 11 studies, 9 find no sex difference. The two that do report a difference both show girls as having finer discrimination using the sense of touch.

If a sex difference exists in touch sensitivity and in the ability to make fine discriminations by the use of this sense, our survey has revealed only hints of it. The reader, of course, can set his own criteria for the level of proof he is willing to accept, but a conservative reading of the evidence is that no such difference has been demonstrated.

TABLE 2.2
Tactile Perception

Study	Age and N	Difference	Comment
DeLeon et al. 1970	3-4 (48)	None	Correct response in haptic or haptic-visual shape discrimination
Podell 1966	3-11 (112)	None	Perceived orientation of figures traced on forehead
Abravanel 1968	3-14 (200)	Girls	Greater accuracy at 4 yrs and 12-14 yrs in moving unseen machines along rod to equal a seen distance, and at 7, 8, and 9 yrs matching visual length of tactile stimulus applied to forearm
Butter & Zung 1970	5-8 (144)	None	Recognition errors in visual stimuli varying in size, shape, and orientation after Ss saw, felt, or saw and felt stimuli
A. Siegel & Vance 1970	5, 6, 8 (64)	None	Haptic oddity discrimination in size, form, and texture
Gliner 1967	5, 8 (160)	Girls	Tendency to get more smooth-textured discrimination correct ($p < .1$)
Gliner et al. 1969	5, 8 (160)	None	Transfer trials (after redundant stimuli) in which stimulus shape or texture was the basis for haptic discrimination
Jackson 1973	6, 8, 10 (120)	None	Shape recognition tactual (tactual-visual)
Schiff & Dytell 1971	7-19 (293)	None	Number of letters identified after tactual presentation (hearing and deaf Ss)
Natsoulas 1966	18-21 (96)	None	Correct identification of drawings of letters or angles traced on heads
P. Wilson & Russell 1966	18-21 (60)	None	Estimation of how high Ss lifted weights when blindfolded

Audition

What is meant by saying that a person is "responsive" to sounds? The implication may be that he hears well—that he can make finer discriminations between similar sounds than many other people can. Or it may be that he is sufficiently interested in sounds so that he will attend to them more focally than to other available stimuli, and perhaps therefore remember them better. Especially in infancy, it is difficult to distinguish between these implications. An infant is presented with a sound, and he is observed, to see whether (and how soon) he responds. In some research, his heartbeat is monitored, and a sudden deceleration of the heartbeat is taken to indicate that he is attending to the sound. Similarly, a sudden cessation or acceleration of arm movements, or a turning of the head and eyes toward the source of sound, is used as an indicator of his having heard the stimulus and being interested in it. When children are old enough to talk and to follow an experimenter's instructions, it is possible to ask them whether two sounds are the same or different, and to find out what they remember from a set of simultaneously present stimuli.

TABLE 2.3
Audition

Study	Age and N	Difference	Comment
Birns 1965	Newborns (30)	None	Intensity of motor response to loud and soft tones
Brackbill et al. 1966	Newborns (24)	None	Crying, motor, or cardiac response to music, voice, heartbeat, metronome, or silence
F. Horowitz 1973	Newborns (44)	None	Response decrement bell and rattle and orientation to animate auditory stimuli
Porges et al. 1973	Newborns (24)	None	Cardiac response to tone
Simner 1971	Newborns (94)	Girls	Longer cry to tape of newborn crying (trend, $p < .1$)
	Newborns (155)	None	Duration of cry to tape of newborn crying (3 experiments)
Bernstein & Jacklin 1973	3½ mos (38)	Girls	Alerting to social and nonsocial sounds (sing test), 1 of 2 samples t test
Brotsky & Kagan 1971	4, 8, 13 mos (70)	None	Cardiac deceleration to male voice
J. Kagan 1969	4, 8, 13 mos (150)	None	Vocalizations or cardiac deceleration to male voices
S. Cohen 1973	5, 8 mos (96)	None	Fixation of mother or stranger when each speaks with congruous or incongruous taped voice
J. Kagan & Lewis 1965	6 mos (32)	Boys	Greater cardiac deceleration to tone
		Girls	Greater cardiac deceleration to music and more vocalizations to each of 5 stimuli (sign test); when all 5 pooled, n.s.
		None	Arm movements to tone, music, and voice
	13 mos (30)	None	Cardiac deceleration to tone, music, and voices
J. Kagan 1971	8, 13 mos (180)	None	Vocalization, orientation to speaker, activity level, cardiac deceleration to male voice tapes
Templin[R] 1957	3-8 (480)	None	Sound discrimination, ages 3-7
		Girls	Sound discrimination, age 8
Kimura 1967	5	Girls	Right ear effect on dichotic listening task
	6-8 (142)	None	Right ear effect (low-middle SES)
J. Hall & Ware 1968	5-7 (86)	None	Identifying spoken words
Knox & Kimura 1970	5-8 (80)	Boys	Correct identification of nonverbal and animal sounds
Gardner 1973	6, 8, 11, 14, 18, 19 (100)	None	Previously heard matching musical passages
Bryden 1972	11 (40)	None	Auditory oddity discrimination
Corah & Boffa 1970	18-21 (40)	Women	Rated sound as producing more discomfort
		None	Galvanic skin response
Slobin 1968	18-21 (46)	None	Matching English antonym pairs with Thai and Kanarese antonym pairs

Table 2.3 summarizes studies on audition in which the sexes have been compared. A variety of response measures and auditory stimuli have been used. Despite the alleged "hunger" of girls for auditory stimuli, the evidence for a sex difference in responsiveness to auditory stimulation is not impressive.

Newborns of the two sexes are very similar in the speed and duration of responses to a variety of auditory cues. Among older infants, the results seem to depend somewhat upon what measures are used to assess the infant's response. J. Kagan and Lewis (1965), for example, working with a group of 6-month-old infants, found no sex difference in arm movements to a variety of sounds; when cardiac deceleration was used, boys were more responsive to some sounds, girls to others; when vocalizations were taken as a measure, girls were more responsive. However, at age 8 months there were no sex differences with any of the measures used (J. Kagan 1971). In the Bernstein and Jacklin study, sounds were presented at random intervals over speakers placed on each side of the infant's head. Observers noted whether the infant alerted to the sound. In the first of two testing sessions, girls showed more alerting when the responses were summed across stimuli. But in the second session, there was no sex difference. In another study with somewhat older infants, the two sexes were similar in the degree to which they looked toward the mother or a stranger when either one began to speak (S. Cohen 1973).

There is a suggestion in these results that there may be a greater responsiveness to sounds among girls using some measures, but the difference, if it exists, appears to occur in a very narrow age span. The bulk of the evidence over the period from birth to 13 months shows that the sexes are highly similar in their attentiveness to auditory stimulation.

Among children old enough to talk about what they hear, the findings also indicate sex similarity. Some measures test essentially how "sharp" the person's sense of hearing is (e.g. Templin 1975 [R], Bryden 1972), and here the sexes do not differ. Other studies might be more aptly described as measuring what the individual has paid attention to (e.g. identifying previously heard sounds). Here too, there is not any consistent sex difference.

There is reason to believe that the processing of speech sounds in adults is localized to some degree in the left hemisphere of the brain. Kimura (1967) has used a dichotic listening procedure (presentation of different sounds to the two different ears) to determine whether the degree of lateralization is different for boys and girls. Kimura has presented evidence that girls lateralize for speech sounds at a somewhat earlier age than boys; however, this fact of course does not imply that either sex hears more acutely or is more interested in sounds.

In a series of studies on selective listening (Maccoby 1969[R]), two different messages were presented simultaneously by two voices. The subject was asked either to select one voice or to report what both voices had said. In these studies, the data were scanned initially for sex differences. None were apparent, and sex was therefore not included in the analysis and reports. On the basis of this informal evidence, it would appear that neither sex is more skillful at selecting from among a variety of auditory stimuli, or at processing several such stimuli at one time. In sum, the case for a greater "hunger" for auditory stimulation among girls has not been proved.

Vision

Vision is the sense modality in which the most extensive research has been done. In recent years there has been a proliferation of studies with infants. Usually records are made of infants' eye movements in response to a variety of visual displays. It is a common procedure to show a stimulus (or pair of stimuli) briefly, then another stimulus, and so on through a series of trials, sometimes including the same stimuli several times in the series. A number of scores can be used to assess the degree of an infant's interest in a particular stimulus: one is the length of time he looks at it upon first presentation; another is the decrement in looking-time over a series of presentations (habituation). Habituation, of course, may be taken as a measure of speed of learning, or of memory (or retention), as well as of degree of interest in the stimulus. Furthermore, the various measures of an infant's interest sometimes yield different answers to the question of which children are showing the most interest in which kinds of stimuli. It frequently happens that the child who looks longest at a stimulus when it is first presented turns away from it more quickly on later presentation (habituates faster) than the child who gives it only a brief glance on first presentation. We have charted the results of habituation measures (Table 2.4) separately from other measures of response to visual stimuli, in order to permit analysis of whether sex differences appear on one kind of measure but not on others. As Table 2.4 shows, there are no sex differences in habituation to visual stimuli during the first few days of life. Thereafter, the results are inconsistent. Boys are found to habituate more rapidly than girls in three studies, but the difference is in the opposite direction for one study, and no difference is found in three others. Taken jointly, the results tend slightly in the direction of boys habituating more quickly than girls, but whether this signifies a lower level of interest in visual cues or a greater ability to process them quickly can only be determined by examining the findings of studies that use other measures.

In the tables that follow, the studies have been divided by age. The newborn period is unambiguously free of demonstrated sex differences (see Table 2.5) in response to visual stimuli, whether visual response is measured by fixation time, cardiac response, sucking, or EEG.

TABLE 2.4
Habituation to Visual Stimuli

Study	Age and N	Difference	Comment
Friedman 1972	Newborns (40)	None	Habituation of fixation to checkerboard
Friedman et al. 1970	Newborns (40)	Boys	Decrement in fixation to low-redundant stimuli (2x2 checkerboard)
		Girls	Decrement in fixation to high-redundant stimuli (12x12 checkerboard)
Friedman et al. 1973	Newborns (26)	None	Habituation of fixation to checkerboard
Haith 1966	Newborns (41)	None	Habituation of nonnurturative sucking to light panel
Horowitz 1973	Newborns (44)	None	Response decrement to light, orientation to inanimate and animate stimuli
Greenberg 1971	2, 2½, 3 mos (36)	Boys	More rapid habituation (longitudinal)
R. Caron & Caron 1969	3 mos (96)	Girls	Faster habituation rate (geometric designs and checkerboard patterns)
McCall et al.[R] 1973	3-4 mos (120)	None	Habituation to discrepant stimuli
Cohen et al. 1971	4 mos (64)	Boys	Habituation of fixation to geometric patterns
Pancratz & Cohen 1970	4-5 mos (32)	Boys	Habituation of fixation to geometric shapes
J. Kagan & Lewis 1965	6 mos (32)	None	Habituation of fixation to blinking lights
	13 mos (30)	Boys	More rapid habituation to blinking lights
Shipman 1971	3-4 yrs (1,194)	None	Habituation or recovery to redundant and varied pictures (low SES)

During the year following birth, the results are more variable. For most samples and most stimuli, sex differences are not found. When a difference is found, it favors one sex nearly as often as the other (Table 2.6), with a slight balance in favor of boys.

From the first birthday to adulthood, the very large majority of studies report no sex difference in visual perception (see Table 2.7).

There is an exception to the general picture of sex similarity in response to visual displays. Table 2.8 shows charted studies on afterimages and illusions. No sex trends may be seen in susceptibility to illusions in childhood, but in adulthood there are some intriguing findings. Brownfield (1965) reports that men have longer afterimages. In two studies out of three, men are found to be more susceptible to the autokinetic effect in studies of apparent motion (McKitrick 1965, shorter latency). There still is not a large enough body of evidence to establish these differences firmly, but if the phenomena prove to be replicable, they may be related to proficiency in spatial visualization, which tends to be an area of male strength from adolescence onward (see Chapter 3).

Preference for Auditory vs. Visual Stimulation

If a review of the evidence on responsiveness to auditory and visual stimulation had shown that the sexes differed in their responses to either kind of stimulus, it would then have been of some interest to explore whether the sex differentiation involves different sensory thresholds (dif-

TABLE 2.5
Vision in Newborns

Study	Age and N	Difference	Comment
Friedman 1972	Newborns (40)	None	Fixation to novel checkerboard
Friedman et al. 1970	Newborns (40)	None	Fixation to checkerboard
Friedman et al. 1973	Newborns (26)	None	Fixation to checkerboard
Friedman & Carpenter 1971	Newborns (96)	None	Fixation to checkerboard
Haith 1966	Newborns (41)	None	Nonnurturant sucking to light panel
Jones-Molfese 1972	Newborns (40)	None	Fixation to black squares against a white background
Korner 1970	Newborns (32)	None	Frequency and duration of visual pursuit to swinging object
Lodge et al. 1969	Newborns (20)	None	ERG and EEG responses to orange or white light
Miranda 1970	Newborns (54)	None	Fixation to stimuli: faces and geometric designs

TABLE 2.6
Vision in First Year of Life

Study	Age and N	Difference	Comment
Giacoman 1971	1 mo (32)	Girls / Boys	Greater visual pursuit, first observation period / Greater pursuit, second observation period
Fitzgerald 1968	1-2 mos (30)	None	Diameter of pupil and pupillary activity to photos of own mother or unfamiliar female face, checkerboard or triangles
Greenberg & O'Donnell 1972	1-2 mos (72)	Girls / None	Fixated longer on checkerboard / Fixation to dots or stripes
J. Weizmann et al. 1971	1-2 mos (32)	Boys	Fixation to stabile (1 of 2 groups)

(continued)

TABLE 2.6 *(cont.)*

Study	Age and N	Difference	Comment
Greenberg 1971	2, 2½, 3 mos (36)	Girls None	Longer fixation, 2x2 checkerboard (2 mos only) (longitudinal) Complex checkerboard (longitudinal)
Greenberg & Weizmann 1971	2-3 mos (24)	Girls	Longer fixations to more complex checkerboard patterns (24x24; 8x8 over the 2x2)
McKenzie[R] 1972	2-5 mos (40)	None	Fixation time on cubes at 4 distances, with real size or retinal size constant by group
	2½, 3, 4 mos (40)	None	Fixation times on 2- and 3-dimensional objects of different sizes
Watson 1966	2, 3, 4, 6 mos (48)	None	Sensitivity to orientation of 3 faces (mother's, E's, cloth mask), measured by smiling; sensitivity to orientation of schematic face, measured by fixation time
	2, 4 mos (32)	None	Fixation time on cube varying in real size, retinal size, and distance
D. Collins et al. 1972	2, 4 mos (48)	None	Limb movement and sucking to flashing light
	2, 4, 6 mos (24)	Boys Girls None	Fixation time on *small* illuminated checkerboard ($p < .05$) and total fixation time, summed across stimuli Fixation time on *large* illuminated checkerboard ($p < .05$) Fixation times for horizontal or vertical patterns
Moss & Robson 1968	3 mos (54)	Boys	Longer fixation to geometric shapes and faces
L. Cohen 1972	3-4 mos (36)	None	Latency to fixate and length of fixation to varying checkerboards
McCall et al.[R] 1973	3-4 mos (120)	None	Fixation to discrepant stimuli
Fagan 1972	3-4 mos (52)	None	Fixation to novel, or unfamiliar, relative to familiar photos of faces
	4-6 mos (34)	None	Fixation to novel relative to familiar photos of faces
	4-6 mos (36)	None	Fixation to line drawings of faces; and to novel relative to familiar line drawings of faces
	5-6 mos (72)	None	Fixation to photos of faces; and to novel relative to familiar photos of faces
	5-6 mos (56)	None	Fixation to masks; and to novel relative to familiar masks
	5-6 mos (24)	None	Preference for photos of faces over plain gray forms, measured by fixation time
	5-6 mos (16)	None	Fixation to novel relative to familiar masks
Fagan 1971	3-8 mos (24)	None	Fixation times to novel black and white patterns relative to familiar ones
K. Nelson 1971	3-9 mos (80)	None	Visual tracking and reversals of model train

(continued)

TABLE 2.6 *(cont.)*

Study	Age and N	Difference	Comment
Lewis 1969	3, 6, 9, 13 mos (120)	Boys None Girls	Longer fixation on male faces at 3, 6, 9 mos Fixation time at 13 mos Vocalized more to each visual stimulus at each age; smiled differentially to stimuli, whereas boys did not
Bernstein & Jacklin 1973	3½ mos (38)	None	Fixation and smiles to faces and scrambled faces
L. Cohen et al. 1971	4 mos (64)	Girls	Higher fixation to geometric patterns
J. Kagan et al. 1966	4 mos (34)	Boys	Longer first and total fixations to face masks
McCall & Kagan 1967	4 mos (36)	None	Fixation time, vocalization time, smiling frequency, and cardiac deceleration to geometric shapes
McCall & Kagan 1970	4 mos (72)	None	Fixation time to geometric shapes
Pancratz & Cohen 1970	4-5 mos (32)	None	Fixation to colored geometric stimuli (novel and familiar)
Brotsky & Kagan 1971	4, 8, 13 mos (79)	None	Cardiac deceleration to outlines of faces, 3D doll models (longitudinal)
J. Kagan 1969	4, 8, 13 mos (150)	None	Vocalization to clay masks of faces (scrambled, normal, and missing features; longitudinal)
J. Kagan 1971	4, 8, 13 mos (180)	None	Vocalization, fixation smiles, activity level, and cardiac deceleration to 2- and 3-dimensional faces and human forms (longitudinal)
Meyers & Cantor 1966	5 mos (24)	Boys	Cardiac deceleration to pictures of ball, clown, bear, and doll
Wilcox & Clayton 1968	5 mos (10)	None	Fixation to color movies of a woman's face
S. Cohen 1973	5, 8 mos (96)	None	Fixations to mother or stranger
J. Kagan & Lewis 1965	6 mos (32)	Boys Girls None	More vocalizations to light patterns Fixation to pictures of faces and designs, 3 of 5 episodes (no difference, all episodes combined) Arm movements, vocalizations and cardiac deceleration to faces and designs; fixation time, arm movements, and cardiac deceleration to light patterns
	13 mos (30)	None Girls	Fixation to light patterns (trials 1-9) Fixation to light patterns (trials 9-12)
Lewis et al. 1966	6 mos (64)	None	Fixation and cardiac responses to light matrix
Meyers & Cantor 1967	6 mos (44)	Boys None	Greater cardiac change to new stimuli Fixation time
Rubenstein 1967	6 mos (44)	None	Looking at and manipulating stimuli
Parry 1972	10-12 mos (48)	None	Fixation time to wooden dishes with 1 or 4 black dots

ferent acuity of the sense organs or their attendant cerebral projection areas), or whether it is true that the sexes simply differed in their interest in the two kinds of stimulus inputs. However, no differences were documented in either modality. Of course, comparing the audition experiments with the vision experiments taken as a whole is an insensitive method for testing the hypothesis. It involves comparing not only different stimuli but different subjects and different response measures.

It would be preferable to compare responses to visual and auditory stimulation within the same group of subjects. Although of course sights and sounds are measured in different units and cannot be directly compared, it is at least possible to use the same response measure, and to look for an interaction of sex with stimulus modality. That is, if boys are more attentive than girls to visual displays in a given experiment, and girls are more attentive than boys to sounds—the same measure of attentiveness being used in each case—this would constitute support for the hypothesis that the sexes differ in modality preference.

J. Kagan (1971) has used this approach, presenting infants with a variety of sounds and visual stimuli, and using cardiac deceleration and vocalization as measures of the infant's attention to each kind of stimulus. With these measures, he did not find sex differences in attention to either kind of stimulus, and therefore of course no interaction of sex with modality.

Watson (1969) used a similar design, but used the infant's rate of conditioning to either auditory or visual reinforcement as an index of modality preference. In the initial study, 10-week-old girls showed conditioned fixation with auditory reinforcement (or auditory plus visual), but not with visual reinforcement alone. Boys, in contrast, conditioned with visual reinforcement. This experiment has been one of the pieces of evidence most often cited in support of the view that the sexes have different modality preferences. In two follow-up studies, however (Ramey and Watson 1972ᴿ, Dorman et al. 1971), these effects were not replicated. Dorman et al. found better conditioning of visual fixation with visual reinforcement for both sexes. Ramey and Watson found no conditioning in either sex with auditory reinforcement. Conditioning was successful (at least for boys) with visual reinforcement, but a between-sex analysis was not made. Other studies addressing the audiovisual difference have been made with older subjects. Bryden (1972) presented patterns, two at a time, to 11-year-old subjects, and asked them to judge whether the two were the same or different. On some trials, one of the patterns was visual-sequential (a series of flashing lights) and the other auditory (a series of tones); on other trials two visual patterns were compared—a visual-sequential pattern, and a visual-spatial pattern made up of dots. There were no sex differences in performance on visual-auditory matches, or on visual-spatial vs. visual-sequential patterns,

TABLE 2.7
Vision, Second Year to Adulthood

Study	Age and N	Difference	Comment
Roberts & Black 1972	1 (40)	None	Visual regard of series of 16 toys
J. Kagan 1971	2 (180)	None	Fixation, smiles, verbalizing, cardiac deceleration to colored slides of people and object
Lewis et al. 1971a	2 (60)	None	Fixation, cardiac response, arm movement, smiling, pointing, and vocalizing to human forms varying in incongruity
DeLeon et al. 1970	3-4 (48)	None	Latency of errors in shape discrimination
Heider 1971	3-4 (71)	None	Choice of basic or nonbasic colors
Kraynak & Raskin 1971	3-4 (64)	None	Matching animal or geometric stimuli
C. Dodd & Lewis 1969	3½ (52)	None	Fixation, smiling, pointing, and surprise at pictures of family and designs
Clapp & Eichorn 1965	4-5 (24)	None	Response to tachistoscopic presentation of geometric figures, drawings
Wolff 1972	4-7 (97)	Girls	Matching to standard (reach criterion faster; trend, $p < .1$)
Gaines 1972	5-6 (47)	Boys Girls	Fewer errors at midchroma Fewer errors, color perception at high and low chroma
Hecox & Hagan 1971	5-7 (52)	None	Proportion estimations by moving lever in matching task
Butter & Zung 1970	5-8 (144)	None	Matching shapes from cutouts
Gliner et al. 1969	5, 8 (160)	None	Same/different shape judgments or transfer trials in discrimination task in which stimulus shape or texture was used
Jackson 1973	6, 8, 10 (120)	None	Shape recognition visual (or visual-tactile)
Kaess 1971a	6, 8, 10 (54)	None	Shape identification of rectangular forms in different orientation
Bosco 1972	6, 8, 11 (180)	None	Processing speed of tachistoscopically presented geometric figures (high and low SES)
Wohlwill 1965	6, 9, 13, 16 (96)	None	Relative distance perception
P. Katz et al. 1971	6, 11 (300)	None	Similarity judgments of visual nonsense items
Keenan 1972	7, 9, 11 (48)	None	Tachistoscopic presentation, English letters, Hebrew letters, or binary patterns
Kaess 1971b	7, 9, 11, 18 (80)	None	Comparing rectangles to standard forms
Gummerman & Gray 1972	7, 9, 11 18-21 (48)	None	Verbal report of letter position in tachistoscopic presentation

(continued)

TABLE 2.7 *(cont.)*

Study	Age and N	Difference	Comment
L. Miller 1971	7, 11, 20 (72)	None	Visual-target letter-selection task
Baltes & Wender 1971	9, 11, 13, 15 (120)	None	Preference of random dots and random-shape patterns (German)
Saltzstein et al. 1972	12 (63)	Boys	Fewer errors judging lengths of paper strips (group testing)
Weber 1965	16-25 (72)	Men	Better identification of steady-interval flashing light from set with varying intervals
Iverson & Schwab 1967	18-21 (80)	None	Fusion judgments of faces shown stereoscopically
Koen 1966	18-21 (72)	None	Time to match photos of same individual
W. Lambert & Levy 1972	18-21 (40)	None	Rate of using fully available visual stimuli

TABLE 2.8

Visual Afterimages and Illusions: Observational Studies

Study	Age and N	Difference	Comment
A. Hill & Burke 1971	4-20 (97)	None	Judging relative sizes of triangles under framed (illusion) and no-frame conditions (normal, retardates)
Hartmann et al. 1972	6, 7, 8, 9 (50)	None	Mueller-Lyer Illusion
Gough & Delcourt 1969	8-16 (1,065)	None	Geometric illusion (Swiss and American)
Spitz et al. 1970	9, 15, 35 (112)	None	Poggendorff and Oppel-Kundt (filled space) illusions
Brownfield 1965	18-20 (30)	Men	Longer duration of afterimages
Bogo et al. 1970	18-21 (97)	None	Autokinetic effect
McKitrick 1965	18-21 (200)	Men	Shorter latency to perceive autokinesis

indicating that stimuli in the two modalities were as easy to deal with for one sex as the other.

An experiment by Mendelsohn and Griswold (1967) can also be interpreted as reflecting modality salience. Subjects memorized a list of 25 words presented visually, while listening to 25 different words being played on a tape recorder. The subjects then attempted to solve 30 anagrams, 10 of which had appeared on the visual list, 10 on the auditory. There were no sex differences in anagram solutions of words from either the visual or auditory list, indicating that in a situation of conflicting information from two sensory channels, the sexes did not differ in frequency of noticing and remembering the items that came in auditory, as compared with visual, form.

The simple fact appears to be that the two sexes are very similar in their interest in, and utilization of, information that comes to them via hearing and vision. Indeed, unless a child has a hearing defect or impaired vision, it is difficult to see why any consistent modality preference should develop. Of course, for some purposes, visual cues may be more useful than auditory ones, or vice versa. In learning a language, for example, it is more useful to hear other speakers of the language than to watch their lips moving. Reliance upon auditory vs. visual information should vary from one situation to another, then, but there seems to be little reason to expect that some persons should be more attuned to one sensory channel than the other in many situations. Rosner (1973)[R], however, has recently identified individual differences among first- and second-grade children in the competent use of information contained in visual vs. auditory stimulus patterns, and has found that the "visual" children do better in arithmetic, the "auditory" children in reading. He does not report whether there are sex differences in the perceptual orientations he has identified. Judging from our Tables 2.3–2.8, it is doubtful whether they will be found. Furthermore, as will be seen in Chapter 3, sex differences in reading and arithmetic achievement are minimal during the early school years. It remains an intriguing possibility, however, that modality preferences during the early school years might feed into the development of different subject-matter skills at a later time. At present it has not been demonstrated that either sex is more "visual" or more "auditory" than the other.

Orientation to Social vs. Nonsocial Stimuli

Much of the research on perception in infancy has involved presenting infants with various representations of the human face. It has been argued that, from an ethological standpoint, the human face should be a particularly salient stimulus for the human infant. Face stimuli that have been used include line drawings, three-dimensional clay masks (in color or black-and-white), photographs of real faces, or in some instances the actual human face itself, either held immobile or shown smiling and talking. Distorted representations of the face have also been used, with features missing or scrambled. In some studies, faces have been compared with nonsocial stimuli such as a checkerboard, geometric forms, random shapes, or familiar objects.

As we have seen, sex differences are not found among newborns in their attention to any of the many visual stimuli, both social and nonsocial, that have been presented to them. There is more variation in the findings of studies with infants following the neonatal period through the remainder

TABLE 2.9

Response to Social or Nonsocial Visual Stimuli in First Year

Study	Age and N	Difference	Comment
Greenberg & O'Donnell 1972	1-2 mos (72)	Girls	Nonsocial: fixation
Weizmann et al. 1971	1-2 mos (32)	Boys	Nonsocial: fixation
Greenberg 1971	2 mos (36)	Girls	Nonsocial: fixation
Greenberg & Weizmann 1971	2-3 mos (24)	Girls	Nonsocial: fixation
McKenzie[R] 1972	2, 4, 6 mos (24)	Boys Girls	Nonsocial: fixation to small checkerboard Nonsocial: fixation to large checkerboard
Moss & Robson 1968	3 mos (54)	Boys	Social and nonsocial: fixation
Lewis 1969	3, 6, 9 mos (120)	Boys Girls	Social: fixation Social: vocalization
L. Cohen et al. 1971	4 mos (64)	Girls	Nonsocial: fixation
J. Kagan et al. 1966	4 mos (34)	Boys	Social: fixation
J. Kagan & Lewis 1965	6 mos (32)	Boys	Nonsocial: vocalization
	13 mos (30)	Girls	Nonsocial: fixation

of the first year. Can some of this variation be accounted for by whether the stimuli are social? Using Table 2.6 as a starting point, we have first selected the studies where a significant sex difference was found on at least one measure, and then charted them according to whether the stimuli were social or nonsocial. Table 2.9 displays the result of this procedure.

As noted earlier, the majority of studies done in this age range found no sex differences. When significant differences were found, they sometimes favored one sex, sometimes the other. The direction of the difference does not appear to be accounted for by whether or not social stimuli were used. When nonsocial stimuli are used, boys and girls are about equally likely to come out with a higher average attention score. With social stimuli, boys somewhat more often have higher scores, but a sign test does not reach significance and the conservative conclusion is that the sexes do not differ in their interest in visual social stimuli. No social preference is revealed for either sex in responses to visual stimuli at later ages (see Table 2.7), or for social versus nonsocial sounds (see Table 2.3).

There are instances in which boys and girls show a different pattern of preferences among visual stimuli, without a significant between-sex difference. A frequently cited finding by Lewis et al. (1966) is a case in point: girls (aged 6 months) looked significantly longer at faces than they did at nonhuman patterns, whereas boys distributed their attention fairly evenly across all the stimuli presented to them. However, it was not reported that girls looked at faces significantly longer than boys, though the experiment is sometimes cited as though girls had indeed shown a greater interest in social stimuli.

When social and nonsocial stimuli are compared, they obviously differ from one another with respect to many characteristics other than their social quality. Complexity (specifically, amount of contour) has been found to be an important determiner of the amount of attention an infant gives to a stimulus: if an infant looks longer at a face than, say, a line drawing of a triangle, this may simply occur because the face is more complex. The same problem exists in comparing the human voice with tones or other nonhuman sounds (J. Kagan and Lewis 1965).

Bernstein and Jacklin (1973) compared the attentiveness of 3½-month-old infants to social and nonsocial stimuli that had been equated for other stimulus parameters. The visual social stimuli were normal faces; the nonsocial stimuli were mosaics assembled from fairly small segments of the normal faces and equated with them for contour, intensity, chroma, and filled area. The auditory social stimuli were taped words ("hello" and "baby") spoken by either a female or male voice, and the nonsocial sounds were non-speech-sounding noises, equated with the words for fundamental frequency, intensity, complexity, and contour of the sound wave. Visual interest was measured in terms of fixation time, interest in auditory cues in terms of whether the infant alerted at the presentation of the sound. Both boys and girls preferred social to nonsocial pictures and sounds, but there was no difference between them in the degree of preference.

Thus, with careful control of some of the stimulus dimensions that usually are allowed to vary, the same conclusion must be reached as before: there is no evidence that girls are more interested in social, boys in nonsocial stimulation.

Summary: Perception

There is reason to believe that females may be both more sensitive and more variable in their response to taste and smell cues, but the research base is very thin and generalizations are really not warranted at this time. The work on touch sensitivity also presents an inconclusive picture: most studies find no sex differences among newborns, but those that do show girls to be more sensitive. It is not known whether any initial differences in touch sensitivity continue after the first few days or weeks of life. Even if they do not, the early differences may be important, in the sense that at least for one sample of children they have been found to be predictive of other behavioral characteristics at a later time. These continuities need further exploration.

Boys and girls have been found to be remarkably similar in responsiveness to visual and auditory cues. The view that one sex is oriented more toward auditory stimuli and the other toward visual cannot be supported by existing evidence. The same is true when social and nonsocial stimuli are compared: neither sex consistently shows more interest in social stimuli (i.e. faces and voices) than the other.

If there are sex differences in vision and audition, the research methods used so far have not revealed them. It is possible that the approach to these matters has been too reductionist; perhaps differences, if they exist, involve the sequential and organizational properties of perception, so that experimental presentation of stimuli one at a time, isolated from their context, may have been a self-defeating strategy. However, the more important truth may be that the sexes really are very much alike in the amount and kind of information they are capable of extracting from the milieu of stimulation in which they must function.

Perceptual Motor Abilities

Summaries of early work on sex differences (e.g. Anastasi 1958[R]) conclude that boys show greater speed and coordination of gross bodily movements, whereas girls excel in manual dexterity. More recent work has not tested for individual differences in gross bodily movement, so nothing new is to be added to the earlier conclusion except to note that physical strength may be involved in the sex difference.

Manual dexterity has been studied in recent years, using a variety of different tasks. It appears that the rubric "manual dexterity" is too broad to encompass the results. Table 2.10 lists the recent studies. When speed measures are used, girls tend to score higher (Laosa and Brophy 1972, Droege 1967, Very 1967, Backman 1972, Strutl et al. 1973). Backman reports the performance of the two sexes at high school age on a speeded test of visual-motor coordination and finds girls' performance to be approximately 5 percent better than that of boys. In the Droege study, high school girls score about 8 percent higher than high school boys, on the average, on finger dexterity, and 9 to 10 percent higher on tests of motor coordination. It is worth noting, however, that whereas girls have somewhat better *finger* dexterity, there is no sex difference in *manual* dexterity —a finding that underlines the importance of the distinction between large-muscle and small-muscle movements, or fine vs. relatively gross movements.

Are there sex differences, possibly due to a difference in willingness to tolerate repetitive tasks, involved in the findings on perceptual motor tests? Cantor approached this issue by varying the interest of tasks for 6-year-olds. One group saw colored slides of high interest, another saw one geometric figure repeatedly (on successive trials), and reaction times were measured. No sex differences were found in reaction times (as measured

TABLE 2.10
Perceptual Motor Abilities

Study	Age and N	Difference	Comments
Anyan & Quillian 1971	1-8 (605)	None	Figure copying
Beiswenger 1971	2-4 (48)	None	Motor responses to visual and auditory stimuli
Eckert 1970	3-4 (22)	None	9 visual-motor tasks
Birch 1971	3-6 (35)	None	In coordination of vocal and manual responses – latencies and accuracy measures
Hamilton 1973	3, 4, 7 10 (72)	None	Ability to form imitative facial expressions
Strayer & Ames 1972	4-5 (40)	None	Form board, errors or response latencies
Laosa & Brophy 1972	5-7 (93)	Girls	Perceptual speed subtest of Primary Mental Ability test
Davol et al. 1965.	5-8 (64)	None	Rotary pursuit board
Cantor 1968	6 (60)	None	Reaction time to visual stimuli
A. Siegel & McBurney 1970	6-13 (96)	None	Matching handgrip to line and length or verbal numbers
Smothergill 1973	6, 7, 9, 10, 18-21 (60)	None	Visual or proprioceptive localization of spatial targets
Strutl et al. 1973	6, 9, 12 (54)	Girls	Speed of card sorting
Kubose 1972	7 (60)	None	Response and movement time in lever-pull task
Arnold 1970	7-8 (96)	None	Simultaneous verbal and motor tasks
McManis 1965	10-13 (96)	None	Accuracy in pursuit rotor (normals, retardates)
Droege 1967	14-17 (20,541)	Girls	Clerical and form perception, motor coordination, finger dexterity
		None	Manual dexterity
Backman 1972	17 (2,925)	Girls	Perceptual speed and accuracy (Project Talent Test Battery)
Koen 1966	18-21 (72)	None	Ability to form imitative facial expressions
Very 1967	18-21 (355)	Women	Perceptual speed and accuracy: visual motor velocity, number comparisons

by start speeds and "travel" speeds). However, nonbored girls reacted more quickly than bored girls, whereas the reverse was true for boys. These findings do not help to clarify previously found sex differences in perceptual motor performance, but they do indicate that task interest should be taken into account when examining sex differences.

LEARNING AND MEMORY

Students of the learning process have concerned themselves primarily with general laws that apply to all learners. In considering the possibility that there may be sex differences in learning, we are entering the ill-charted realm of individual differences in learning abilities and learning styles. What can be meant by the question of whether people differ in the way they learn? A first meaning has to do with a generalized capacity to learn. Are there some people who learn more readily than others, regardless of the nature of the material to be learned or the nature of the incentive offered for learning? If a high level of such a generalized learning capacity were a stable characteristic of some persons, it would clearly enter into our measures of general intelligence, and as such it is treated in Chapter 3. However, there are other ways in which the learning performance of individuals might differ. For example, people probably differ considerably in their motivations for learning. Perhaps some people learn primarily to please others, whereas others may be more intrinsically motivated, attempting to meet some standard of excellence that they impose on themselves. It has been alleged that girls are especially likely to work in order to win the approval of others, and hence it is possible they might learn best under social reinforcement, whereas boys might learn better with some other sort of incentive. (See Chapter 4 for a more detailed discussion of this issue.)

People may also differ in the preestablished biases they bring to a learning situation. Stevenson notes (1970, p. 919)[R]: "Even young children enter the experimental situation with strong response biases and stimulus preferences which, if in accord with correct response, lead to rapid learning and otherwise interfere with performance."

When experimenters speak of response biases, they usually mean something very specific, such as a tendency to choose the right-hand member of a horizontal grouping. Such a bias could presumably stem from handedness, from previous experience with directionality, or both. Seligman (1970)[R] has recently summarized evidence for a more intriguing kind of bias—a "preparedness" on the part of the organism for associating only certain kinds of cues with certain kinds of responses. It has been found, for example (Garcia and Koelling 1966[R]), that rats can associate flashing lights or noises with shock, and can use them as avoidance cues. But they cannot use taste cues in this way. They can associate tastes with becoming ill several hours later, and will learn to avoid tastes that have had a delayed association with illness, but they cannot form such an association between illness and lights or noises. Seligman stressed species differences in preparedness to make certain associations. It is conceivable that there might be sex-linked, within-species differences as well in preparedness for certain specific learnings. If this were so, the two sexes would differ not in any overall learning ability but in their readiness to learn associations that are especially relevant to their sex. It will be reasonable to examine the learning literature with this possibility in mind.

Flavell (1970)[x] has noted that children of different ages differ in the strategies they employ in learning and remembering a list or set of objects. A subject may improve his memory by verbal rehearsal of the names of the things to be remembered or by grouping (e.g. noting that several items are all fruits). Other subjects have discovered the value of tying unrelated sets of items together in a "story" invented for the occasion. Flavell shows that even when a child knows how to use a strategy of this kind, he may not make use of it spontaneously; however, once he does use it, his performance is improved. The superior performance of older subjects on recall tasks is at least in part a function of their having acquired a varied repertoire of strategies, good judgment about which strategy to use, and whatever motivation or skill it takes to put to use the strategies that they "know." As far as individual differences are concerned, it would clearly be possible for some persons to progress more rapidly than others through the developmental sequence of strategy acquisition and use; furthermore, different persons could come to rely upon different strategies. And finally, persons could differ in the associative richness (based on breadth of experience) that they brought to bear in weaving relevant stories in aid of recall. The sexes might differ with respect to any of these processes that support the retrieval of learned and "stored" material.

A distinction has sometimes been made between different "kinds" of learning. That is, it is thought that a person can learn either by simple rote association, based on repetition (as in the traditional methods of learning the multiplication tables), or with "understanding"—that is, with greater involvement of higher cognitive processes. White (1965)[x] has elaborated this distinction, arguing that young children learn primarily by association, whereas older children learn more "cognitively," and that the second phase calls for the inhibition of the first. He cites a number of developmental changes in learning as evidence, including the facts that younger children are more susceptible to simple conditioning, more susceptible to position and order effects in a series of learning trials, and less likely to combine separately learned elements by the use of inference. Stevenson also notes a developmental change in the nature of the learning process: "Young children seem to be more dependent upon the characteristics of the external situation than are older children. Older subjects are more likely to respond in terms of their own hypotheses and expectations" (1970, p. 919)[R].

It has been alleged that the sexes differ in the developmental level of the learning processes they employ. Feldstone (1969), using White's distinction, has suggested that girls may be using a developmentally more "primitive" method of learning than boys, at least when the response to be acquired is an inhibitory one. Broverman and his colleagues (1968)[R] have argued that females are superior to males in "simple overlearned repetitive behavior," whereas males excel in "complex behaviors requiring problem-solving, delay, or reversal of usual habits."

The Broverman hypothesis will be taken up later, in the section on intellectual abilities (Chapter 3) and in Chapter 7, where his theory of the possible biological foundations for different intellectual processes is discussed. At present, the theory will be referred to only as it bears specifically upon learning.

In the following pages, we chart studies that have compared the sexes on a variety of different learning tasks. The tables are arranged roughly in order from the simpler, more associative learning processes to those that are more obviously complex. Let us say at the outset, however, that we do not find the distinction between simple and complex learning processes a convincing one. As Rescorla (1967, 1969)[R] has pointed out, even in "simple" conditioning with animals, the subjects appear to be engaged in a complex computation of the probabilities of certain contingencies rather than a simple cumulative building of associative connections between stimuli and responses. A similar case has been made for discrimination learning. It seems difficult to keep organisms, particularly human ones, from engaging in "higher mental processes" even on simple tasks, and we suspect this generalization applies even to females. But let us see what the relevant research reveals.

Conditioning

Broverman et al. included conditioning in their list of "female" abilities. The belief that women condition more easily than men probably stems from early work on eyelid conditioning (see Spence and Spence 1966[R] for a review of this work). We shall return to this work shortly. But let us review the rather sparse evidence on sex differences in conditioning during childhood.

We have referred earlier to the work of Watson and his colleagues. They attempted to condition visual fixation in 10-week-old infants. In Watson's original report, although boys and girls did not differ in ease of conditioning, they did differ in the nature of the reinforcement that seemed most effective. However, these findings were not replicated in two subsequent studies. A number of other researchers have used conditioning procedures with infants; among those who have analyzed their findings according to the sex of the subjects, sex differences have not been found. For example, in a series of studies with a variety of reinforcements with newborns, 3-month-old infants, and 5-month-old infants, Papousek (1967) has not found sex differences in the acquisition of a conditioned head-turning response. At 3 months, Banikiotes et al. (1972), Rheingold et al. (1967), Haugan and McIntire (1972), and R. Caron et al. (1971) also found no sex differences.

The same situation prevails in studies with older children. Cantor and Whitely (1969) conditioned high- or low-force target-striking in 4- to 5-year-olds. Moffatt (1972) conditioned an avoidance response in children of 6 years; Walls and DiVesta (1970) also used children of 6 years and conditioned a verbal response. None of these experiments showed sex difference. The exception is an experiment by Werden and Ross (1972), who reported that boys aged 4–6 acquired a conditioned eyelid response more readily than girls of the same age.

A number of studies have conditioned verbal responses in children and adults. The results are straightforward and consistent with the findings of studies using other responses: there are no sex differences (Birnie and Whitely 1973, Slaby 1973, J. Grusec 1966, Sarason and Ganzer 1962, Insko and Cialdini 1969, Greenbaum 1966, Koenig 1966, Weiss et al. 1971, Doctor 1969, and Yelen 1969).

The one exception to the generally negative picture is in classical eyelid conditioning in adults. Here women do condition more readily. In their review of this literature, Spence and Spence note that more highly anxious subjects (as measured by the Manifest Anxiety Scale) usually show more rapid eyelid conditioning, using a standard conditioning procedure. However, when a "masked" conditioning procedure is used (where the conditioning is a byproduct of procedures ostensibly designed to measure something else), anxiety no longer affects the readiness to acquire the conditioned response. Under "masked" conditions, the sex difference also disappears. The implication is plain that women's somewhat higher level of manifest anxiety (see Chapter 5) may be responsible for the sex difference in eyelid conditioning under the normal procedure, although a direct causal link has not been established. In conditioning studies in which levels of anxiety have been experimentally varied (Stone and Hokanson 1969, Buss and Buss 1966[R]), no sex differences were found. In any case, it seems clear that "conditionability" per se is not the factor differentiating the sexes.

Conditioning has been thought of as a rather automatic process, in which stimuli become connected with responses with a minimum of involvement of the subject's higher mental processes. As noted above, conditioning is probably more complex than this; at the least, it may call for the subject's deliberately holding his higher mental processes in abeyance. Whatever abilities are called for at various ages, the two sexes seem to possess them in approximately equal degrees.

Paired-Associates Learning

A widely used method for studying learning is the paired-associates method. The subject is usually given pairs of words, or pairs of words and symbols, and asked to associate them so that when the first member of the pair is given, he can produce the second. Matching of names to faces is a real-life example of paired-associates learning. It is an area of learning in which there is some reason to expect a sex difference, since the material to be learned is usually at least partly verbal. Furthermore, it is simple associative learning (if any learning can properly be described as such), and according to the Broverman hypothesis should fall into the category of "female" skills. Table 2.11 summarizes the studies of paired-associates learning that have compared the performance of male and female subjects. The studies are remarkably consistent in finding no sex difference.

It is clear that "simple associative learning," whether in the form of conditioning or paired-associates learning, is not a function characterizing one sex more than the other. We now turn to learning that involves some degree of delay or inhibition of a competing response, where a sex difference has also been alleged. The ability to extract a stimulus from a salient context, or to restructure the elements of a problem during problem solving, will be taken up in Chapter 3, as will the ability to postpone gratification (wait for a delayed reward). In the present section we take up discrimination learning, oddity learning, studies of delayed and partial reinforcement, and the restriction of responses to the low-amplitude range.

Discrimination Learning

The subject's task in a discrimination-learning experiment seems quite simple. He is asked to choose the correct stimulus from an array, or to say whether two stimuli are the same or different. However, Stevenson (1970, p. 868)[a] points out some hidden complexities: "It is assumed that he [the subject] is capable of attending to the relevant stimuli, of inhibiting attention to irrelevant cues, of discriminating the differences among the stimuli, of remembering the stimulus chosen, of being appropriately influenced by the consequences of his response, of being motivated to persist in trying to be correct, and of not elaborating the problem so that it becomes more difficult than it actually is."

Inhibition is involved in discrimination learning: the subject must either inhibit attention to irrelevant cues, avoid responding to these cues once noticed, or both. Suppose a subject is asked to press a button whenever a stimulus with a characteristic appears on a screen before him, but is asked

TABLE 2.11
Paired-Associates Learning

Study	Age and *N*	Difference	Comment
H. Reese 1972	2-6 (48)	None	Paired associates in slide presentation
H. Reese 1970	3-5 (71)	None	Original learning or relearning of paired associates
Hoving et al. 1972	5-11 (72)	None	Learning, relearning, or errors in paired associates
Gahagan & Gahagan 1968	6-7 (54)	None	Verbal paired associates
Hoving & Choi 1972	6-8 (40)	None	Learning or relearning paired association
Fraunfelker 1971	6, 8 (80)	None	Trigram and color paired associates
Shultz et al. 1973	6, 10 (160)	None	Stimuli with or without specific labels (low, middle SES)
P. Katz et al. 1971	6, 11 (240)	None	Learning verbal labels of stimuli
H. Stevenson et al. 1968a	8-12 (475)	None	Paired associates with abstract words as response stimuli
H. Stevenson & Odom 1965	9, 11 (318)	None	Trigram and word paired associates
S. Shapiro 1966	10, 11, 13, 14 (80)	None	Aurally presented paired associates
Carroll & Penney 1966	11 (56)	None	Competition of words in paired associates task
McCullers 1967	11 (144)	None	Paired associates with varying interference
H. Stevenson et al. 1968a	12-14 (256)	Girls	Paired associates with abstract forms as response stimuli (high IQ subsample only; no difference, middle and low IQ subsamples)
		None	Paired associates with abstract words as response stimuli
H. Stevenson et al. 1970	14 (96)	None	Paired associates under different testing conditions (educable retardates)
Pallak et al. 1967	18-21 (39)	None	Retention of paired associates

not to press for similar patterns that are different with respect to some critical attribute. During the early stages of learning, the subject will press indiscriminately. Then, quite often, he will solve the problem abruptly, shifting from a chance level of responding to 100 percent correct. He must now inhibit the tendency to respond to attributes of the stimuli that do not distinguish the correct from the incorrect instances.

Discrimination learning studies are summarized in Table 2.12. Studies using oddity problems are shown in Table 2.13. Oddity problems are a

TABLE 2.12
Discrimination Learning

Study	Age and N	Difference	Comment
Reppucci 1971	2 (48)	None	2-choice discrimination learning
J. Turnure 1971	3-4 (40)	None	Discrimination learning under distraction and no-distraction conditions
Campione 1971	3-5 (64)	None	Discrimination transfer under high or low redundancy conditions
Friedrichs et al. 1971	3-5 (50)	None	8 discrimination-learning tasks
Campione & Beaton 1972	3-6 (100)	None	Successive or simultaneous discrimination-learning task (2 experiments)
L. Brown 1969	4-5 (64)	None	2-choice discrimination task with different reward levels
Berman et al. 1970	4, 6 (16)	None	Win-stay, lose-shift principle in discrimination task
Mitler & Harris 1969	5-9 (77)	None	Errors to criterion in discrimination task
Elkind et al. 1967	5-11 (120)	None	2-choice discrimination task
Scholnick 1971	5, 7 (96)	None	Discrimination learning with differing verbalization training
Rieber 1969	5, 7, 9 (120)	None	2-choice discrimination of 3-dimensional objects
W. Siegel & Van Cara 1971	5, 7, 9 (108)	None	3-part successive discrimination tasks to different reinforcement conditions
Harter et al. 1971a	6-7 (210)	None	2-choice size-discrimination task (normal, retardates)
Harter & Zigler 1972	6-7 (80)	None	2-choice discrimination task with different rates of stimulus presentation (normal, retardates)
Odom & Mumbauer 1971	6-19 (277)	None	Errors to criterion on discrimination task
Pishkin 1972	6, 7, 9	Girls	Made fewer errors with right or right-wrong cues in discrimination
	8 (144)	Girls	Fewer errors on concept identification task
Achenbach & Zigler 1968	7-9 (40)	None	Large-small discrimination
Spence 1966	7-9 (96)	None	Verbal discrimination task with varied feedback
Scholnick & Osler 1969	8 (192)	None	Discrimination learning with or without pretraining (low, middle SES)
Cairns 1967	9 (40)	None	Acquisition or extinction of Wisconsin Card-Sorting Test
McCullers & Martin 1971	9 (72)	None	Discrimination task with varied feedback

(continued)

TABLE 2.12 *(cont.)*

Study	Age and N	Difference	Comment
Ratcliff & Tindall 1970	9 (72)	Boys	2-choice discrimination with loud tone for incorrect responses
		None	2-choice discrimination, 2 other feedback conditions
F. Horowitz & Armentrout 1965	9-11 (48)	Boys	Trend ($p < .1$) improved over trials of simultaneous or successive discrimination tasks
Achenbach 1969	10-11 (514)	None	Discrimination-learning tasks with cues provided
Pishkin et al. 1967	10-18 (270)	Girls	Wisconsin Card-Sorting Task in several conditions
H. Stevenson et al. 1968a	12-14 (256)	Girls	Discrimination-learning tasks (with IQ subsample)
H. Stevenson et al. 1970	14 (96)	None	Shape-discrimination task (educable retardates)
Laughlin & McGlynn 1967	18-21 (192)	Women	Shorter time to solution in a visual discrimination problem

variant of discrimination learning in which the subject must choose the odd stimulus from a set of three or more—the stimulus that is unlike the others with respect to one or more attributes. As may be seen from the tables, no pattern of sex differences has been shown.

In some studies of discrimination learning, the subject's task is made more complex by changing the rules in midstream. Stimuli that were once correct are now called incorrect. These rule changes provide a direct test of the Broverman hypothesis that females have especial difficulty in tasks calling for the inhibition of an already learned habit in favor of a new habit. In some instances, the new rules are a direct reversal of the old ones—if all

TABLE 2.13
Oddity Problems

Study	Age and N	Difference	Comment
Friedrichs et al. 1971	3-5 (50)	None	Oddity discrimination
Saravo et al. 1970	3-7 (144)	Girls	Faster on learned oddity-pretraining task
Levin & Maurer 1969	4-6 (82)	None	Oddity or matching problems
Gaines 1969	4-7 (30)	None	Error rate of oddity problem
S. Hill 1965	4, 6, 9, 12 (114)	None	Oddity problem with 2 kinds of training
J. Turnure 1970	5-7 (90)	None	Oddity problem with and without distractions

TABLE 2.14
Reversal and Nonreversal Shifts

Study	Age and N	Difference	Comment
Campione & Beaton 1972	3-6 (176)	None	Intra- and extradimensional shifts
Beilin & Kagan 1969	4 (78)	None	Reversal shifts
Kendler et al. 1972	4-5 (80)	None	Pre- or post-reversal shift discrimination
Schell 1971	4-5 (72)	None	Reversal shifts
Dickerson et al. 1970	5 (96)	None	Reversal or extradimensional shifts
Heal 1966	5 (24)	None	Reversal shift performance with and without overtraining
Crowne et al. 1968	10-11 (63)	None	Intra- and extradimensional shifts

large stimuli were formerly correct, all small stimuli are now correct. In other instances, the new rules call for attending to an entirely different attribute of the stimulus. Table 2.14 summarizes the findings on reversal and nonreversal shifts. There is no indication of sex difference in performance on these tasks. Of course, many additional studies have been done with shift problems in which experimental and control groups have been equated for sex but in which the final report does not include an analysis of sex differences. This omission, we suspect, usually reflects the fact that there were no differences to report. In fact, one experimenter has written to us: "We routinely counterbalance for sex in our experiments, and at least initially look for differences associated with sex. In every instance we have failed to find such differences."

Delay of Reinforcement, Partial Reinforcement

Increasing the time interval between a response and its reinforcement increases the probability that other responses will interfere with learning the correct response. Such interfering responses must be inhibited during the delay period. Similarly, reinforcing only a portion of the correct responses probably makes it more likely that other responses will occur and compete with the correct response. Studies of delayed reinforcement are summarized in Table 2.15, studies of partial reinforcement in Table 2.16. In neither case are sex differences evident.

Incidental Learning

While a subject is learning the material that he has been instructed to concentrate on, he may or may not also be noticing and remembering other

TABLE 2.15
Delay of Reinforcement

Study	Age and N	Difference	Comment
Loughlin & Daehler 1973	2-4 (51)	None	Delayed reaction with and without filled delay
Ferraro et al. 1971	4, 5, 6, 8, 10 (40)	None	Panel-pressing matching task with varying delays
S. Goldstein & Siegel 1971	8 (48)	None	Empty or filled delay in discrimination task
S. Goldstein & Siegel 1972	8-9 (84)	None	Immediate reinforcement or empty or filled delay

things that occur at the same time. Some experiments are deliberately set up so that "incidental" stimuli will be available that are either redundant or entirely irrelevant to the stimuli that are clearly task-relevant. In other instances, the subject does not have a specific task, but there are nevertheless some events that may be considered more incidental than others. For example, in a standard fictional film, some events are part of the plot and of the development of the motivations of the central characters as they relate to the plot; other events, such as the striking of a clock in the distance or the color of the clothes worn by one of the characters, have little to do with the story, and remembering these events may be classed as incidental learning.

Incidental learning may or may not reflect absence of inhibition on the part of the learner. As Hagen (1967)[8] has shown, when one increases the

TABLE 2.16
Partial Reinforcement

Study	Age and N	Difference	Comment
Hamilton 1970	3-4 (28)	None	In extinction after direct or vicarious reinforcement in marble task
Hamilton 1972	4 (24)	None	Discrimination learning in partial and continuous reinforcement
Ryan & Voorhoeve 1966	5 (120)	None	Partial or continuous reinforcement in lever-pulling task
Stabler & Johnson 1970	5 (64)	Girls	Longer to extinguish in partial reinforcement
Bresnahan & Blum 1971	6 (60)	None	Partial or continuous reinforcement in concept-acquisition problem
Warren & Cairns 1972	7 (100)	None	Partial or continuous reinforcement in discrimination learning
Nakamura 1966	9 (32)	Boys	Longer to extinguish in low-reward condition in dissonance reduction

TABLE 2.17
Incidental Learning

Study	Age and N	Difference	Comment
Wheeler & Dusek 1973	5, 8, 10 (144)	None	Incidental learning in memory task
A. Siegel & Stevenson 1966	7-14 (96)	None	Incidental learning in discrimination tasks
Hale et al. 1968	8-12 (444)	Girls	Incidental learning in film observation
	18-21 (275)	None	
H. Stevenson et al. 1968a	8-12 (475)	Girls	Incidental learning in film observation
	12-14 (256)	Girls	Incidental learning in film observation
Hawkins 1973	8, 10, 12, 14 (306)	None	Incidental learning in film-watching task
A. Siegel 1968	8, 14 (96)	None	Incidental learning in discrimination task
Dusek & Hill 1970	9-10 (72)	Girls	More response patterns in 3-choice probability task
Hagen & Hyntsman 1971	9, 11 (21)	None	Incidental learning of pictures (retardates)
Druker & Hagen 1969	9, 11, 13 (240)	None	Incidental learning scored by matching (black working class)
H. Stevenson et al. 1970	14 (96)	Girls	Recalling details from films (in individually tested subsample only; educable retardates)

difficulty of the task to the point where the subject cannot process all the available information, a negative correlation is found between the amount of irrelevant detail a subject remembers and the amount learned on the central task. In other words, it is necessary to inhibit attention to irrelevant information in order to cope with the information-processing demands of a difficult task. Under most conditions, however, the correlations between task-relevant and incidental learning are zero or positive. That is, it is possible to attend to (and remember) both task-relevant and task-irrelevant materials, and the most skillful subject can often do both well. Under such conditions, inhibition is not required, and incidental learning may simply be taken as a measure of ability to encode and remember a wide range of stimulus inputs simultaneously.

Table 2.17 summarizes the studies of incidental learning. Two studies show an advantage for girls, both being film studies in which there was no loss of plot-relevant content as a result of remembering incidental material. We therefore take these studies to reflect breadth of memory. However, the major conclusion from the table is that the sexes do not differ in their ability to process incidental information, or to inhibit attention to it when necessary.

Learned Low-Amplitude Responding

Feldstone (1969) has used an ingenious method for charting the acquisition of a learned inhibition. The experimental subjects are reinforced for low-amplitude responding (turning a crank slowly, squeezing a dynamometer weakly), and over a series of trials the experimental group comes to respond with lower amplitude than a control group. In most instances, Feldstone finds no sex differences in the speed of acquistion of this inhibitory behavior, although when sex differences do appear, they show acquisition to be faster in girls. Feldstone, however, is especially interested in testing the White model that there are two kinds of learning processes: a simple, fast-acting associative process, and a more complex cognitive learning process, the latter being developmentally more mature. Feldstone examines his acquistion curves for evidence that these two processes occur successively. For example, if for a given group of subjects the experimental and control groups diverge at a fairly early point in a series of trials, then converge, then diverge again, he would interpret the first divergence as an instance of simple associative learning which was then briefly interfered with by the second "cognitive" learning process, which "took over" at the second divergence. In one group (the older girls) there was only one divergence. The question is whether this divergence means that the girls learned to inhibit on the basis of simple associative learning and failed to switch to a more cognitive process, or whether they turned to the more advanced process immediately without using the less mature learning style at all. Feldstone sought to determine which interpretation was correct by interviewing his subjects to find out whether they were able to verbalize the reinforcement contingencies, and whether their verbal reports corresponded with their behavior. If the correspondence was high, he thought this would indicate the mature, type 2 learning processes. The older girls showed a high degree of understanding of the contingencies, and a high degree of correspondence between their verbalizations and their behavior, but Feldstone nevertheless concluded that their performance probably represented the immature, type 1 kind of learning, and that their cognitive behavior was probably not regulating their motor behavior. We find this conclusion mysterious.

Obviously there are great difficulties in interpreting the trial-by-trial differences between an experimental and a control group. Feldstone suggests no statistical test for identifying the number of convergences and divergences. The work is provocative, but in our view it has not succeeded in demonstrating the operation of two learning processes, much less a sex

TABLE 2.18
Probability Learning

Study	Age and N	Difference	Comment
Wittig & Weir 1971	4-5 (80)	Boys	More response patterns in 4 alternative probability tasks
		None	2 alternative probability tasks
Gruen et al. 1970	6, 9 (121)	None	3-choice probability task (lower and middle SES)
Deffenbacher & Hamm 1972	7-8 (96)	None	Probability learning in 2-digit-number tasks
	13-15 (96)	None	
	19-20 (96)	None	
Endo 1968	8 (96)	None	2-choice probability task
Lewis 1965	8 (150)	None	2-choice probability task
H. Stevenson et al. 1968a	8-12 (475)	None	3-choice probability task
	12-14 (256)	None	3-choice probability task
Weinberg & Rabinowitz 1970	12-19 (48)	Boys Girls	More maximizing strategy More matching strategy
Rosenhan & Messick 1966	18-21 (116)	None	2-choice probability of smiling or angry faces
F. Todd & Hammond 1965	18-21 (72)	None	Multiple-cue probability task

difference with respect to these processes. The main conclusion from his work would appear to be that the sexes are much alike in acquiring an inhibitory response, with girls possibly having a slight advantage.

Probability Learning

Some learning studies are set up so that there is no response the subject can make that is correct 100 percent of the time. If he has before him a set of three buttons to press, for example, the buttons might be programmed so that one will yield reinforcement 50 percent of the time and the other two 25 percent of the time. The subject's task is to determine how to maximize his own reward. In working on such a task, most subjects do not behave as though there were any simple increase in the strength of the tendency to push each button depending on the number of reinforcements it has delivered. Rather, they attempt to discover what the sequential pattern of reinforcement is, and adopt a problem-solving strategy to guess the "system." In this sense, it is a task that calls upon higher cognitive processes rather than simple associative learning. As may be seen in Table

2.18, the large majority of studies that have analyzed their findings by sex of subject have found no sex differences.

We have reviewed the research on a number of different traditional learning problems. Some are thought of as fairly simple associative forms of learning; others involve the delay or inhibition of an initial response tendency. There is no evidence of sex difference in either kind of task. From the learning literature alone, then, we found no basis for Broverman's contention that there is a linkage between sex and proficiency on one type of task as compared with the other.

Learning Through Imitation

We turn now to the question of whether girls are more "social," and whether this has any bearing upon their learning or memory. We have already seen, in the section on perception, that both sexes are interested in social stimuli and that neither sex has a consistently higher level of interest, although there was a tendency for boys to show somewhat more interest during the first year of life. Chapter 4, achievement motivation, takes up the question of whether girls are more motivated to work for social approval, and summarizes the evidence on the responsiveness of the two sexes to social reinforcement. Chapter 5 considers whether girls are more social in the sense of spending more time interacting with others, or in the sense of being more "empathic"—more sensitive to the needs and emotional states of others. In the present chapter we consider the literature on learning through modeling. In so doing, we have made a rather arbitrary distinction. There are some experiments in which imitation might be said to be incidental. That is, the subject is exposed to a model and is then observed at a later time to see whether he imitates the model, although he has not been instructed to imitate. This is the procedure in many studies of the effects of films, where a group of children are shown an aggressive film, for example, and then observed on a playground to determine the level of aggression as compared to a baseline. In other experiments, the model explicitly shows the subject how something is to be done—solves a puzzle, pronounces a word, etc.—and the model's actions are a good (or perhaps the only) source of the information the subject needs to solve the problem set for him. It is this second kind of modeling study that is charted here. Studies of spontaneous imitation are reviewed in Chapter 7, under "conformity." Table 2.19, then, includes the research on what might be called "instructed" or "learning-set" imitation. It is reasonable to suppose that if either sex were more "social"—more oriented toward people than impersonal objects or abstract ideas—members of that sex would find it especially easy to learn through modeling.

There has been an enormous amount of work on observational learning. The large majority of studies summarized in Table 2.19 find no sex differ-

TABLE 2.19
Learning Through Modeling

Study	Age and N	Difference	Comment
J. Grusec & Mischel 1966	3-4 (28)	None	Reproduction of models; neutral and aversive behavior
Bandura & Menlove 1968	3-5 (48)	None	Change in dog avoidance after model interacted with dog
Friedrichs et al. 1971	3-5 (50)	None	Puzzle-completion task modeled
McDavid 1959	3-5 (32)	Boys	Imitated model's choice of door in search for candy, without knowledge of model's success
Mehrabian 1970	3-5 (127)	None	Imitation of sentences
Liebert & Swenson 1971a	4 (48)	Girls	Higher recall of items model chose
Masters & Driscoll 1971	4 (48)	Boys	Toy arrangement
	4 (40)	None	Toy arrangement
Osser et al. 1969	4-5 (32)	None	Imitation of sentences read by model
Liebert & Fernandez 1970	4-6 (48)	None	Matching model's responses to stimulus items
Hetherington[R] 1965	4-11 (216)	Girls	Imitation of parents' aesthetic preferences
B. Coates & Hartup 1969	4, 5, 7, 8 (72)	None	Number of accurate reproductions of filmed model's behavior
Kuhn 1972	4, 6, 8 (87)	None	Object-sorting task after watching an adult model
Bruning 1965	5 (144)	None	Lever-movement response
Rickard et al. 1970	5 (40)	None	Imitation of animal names after hearing varying number of animal names
Staub 1971c	5 (75)	Boys	Helping child in distress after role-playing practice coupled with positive comments from E (trend, $p < .1$)
		Girls	Helping child in distress following role-playing practice
Elliott & Vasta 1970	5-7 (48)	None	Sharing behavior after exposure to altruistic model
Yando & Zigler 1971	5-6, 9-10 (192)	None	Imitation of model's designs (normals, retardates)
Presbie & Coiteux 1971	6 (64)	None	Imitation of sharing (vs. stingy) behavior
Thelen et al. 1972	6-8 (60)	None	Imitation of filmed model's button-pressing responses

(continued)

TABLE 2.19 *(cont.)*

Study	Age and *N*	Difference	Comment
Liebert et al. 1969a	7 (48)	None	Imitation of self-reward patterns in bowling game
Rosenthal et al. 1972	7 (80)	Boys	More imitation of model's clustering of stimulus objects
Zimmerman 1972	7 (36)	Boys	Asked more questions in retraining after modeling
Akamatsu & Thelen 1971	7-8 (48)	None	Button pressing after model was rewarded or not rewarded
W. Mischel & Liebert 1967	7-8 (56)	None	Imitation of self-reward patterns
Bandura & Kupers 1964	7-9 (160)	None	Imitation of model's self-reinforcing behavior in bowling game
M. Harris & Hassemer 1972	7-9 (48)	None	Sentence modeling (two-thirds bilingual)
Hildebrandt et al. 1973	7-9 (96)	None	Self-reward in bowling game after exposure to lenient or stringent models
J. Grusec 1971	7-11 (88)	None	Donating behavior after exposure to altruistic model
Cheyne 1971	8 (30)	None	Word choices after observing model receive varying reinforcements
Rosenthal & White 1972	8 (112)	None	Word association arrays
Rosenhan et al. 1968	8-9 (72)	None	Imitation of self-reward
Stouwie et al. 1970	8-9 (156)	None	Self-reward after watching adult model's self-reward
Debus 1970	8-10 (100)	None	Latency and error scores after viewing reflective and/or impulsive models
Bandura & Whalen 1966	8-11 (160)	None	Modeled self-reinforcement
Lamal 1971	8, 10, 12 (72)	None	Performance on "20 questions" type of problems after observing model
Hanlon 1971	9 (52)	None	Imitation of taped British accent
W. Mischel & Liebert 1966	9 (54)	None	Self-reward in bowling game
Zimmerman & Bell 1972	9-12 (84)	None	Modeled rule learning
Thelen 1970	10-12 (38)	None	Self-blame statements after exposure
Bandura & Jeffery 1973	18-21 (88)	None	Complex motor configuration after observing filmed model
Gerst 1971	18-21 (72)	None	Complex motor responses after exposure to a filmed model

(continued)

TABLE 2.19 *(cont.)*

Study	Age and N	Difference	Comment
E. Jones et al. 1968	18-21 (140)	None	Recall of model's problem solving
Larsen et al. 1972	18-21 (79)	Men	Shocked victim more (intensity, duration) after exposure to model who ended up shocking the victim at maximum level
		None	Total voltage administered
Yelen 1969	18-21 (96)	Women	Imitation of peer-partner's rating of nonsense syllables on semantic scale

ences. Among the studies that do, males are approximately as likely as females to obtain higher scores. We have not charted studies according to the sex of the model. A number of reports in the literature indicate that a child's imitation of a model may depend on whether the model is of the same sex. As we shall see later in reviewing the work on spontaneous imitation, some kinds of behavior are thought to be more appropriate for a model of a given sex; for example, children of both sexes are more likely to copy aggression if it is displayed by a male rather than a female model. But we have not been able to detect any overall tendency for subjects to learn more successfully from a same-sex or opposite-sex model, and this conclusion applies to both spontaneous imitation and explicit learning-set imitation.

Memory

The distinction between learning and memory is an arbitrary one. What is remembered must have been learned. What has been learned can usually only be determined through asking persons to recall or recognize the learned material. However, traditional "memory" research has differed somewhat from the work on "learning" in its methods and phrasing of questions to be answered. We have taken the easy way out of the difficult decisions over whether individual studies should be classified under learning or memory, and simply listed under memory the studies the authors labeled in this way.

We do not regard memory as a "capacity" but as a set of processes. Individuals (and groups) differ in their skill in using these processes. Furthermore, there can be differences among individuals or groups in *what* is remembered. That is, in a subject-matter area where an individual already has a good deal of information and where his interest is high, he has a substantial body of related material with which to associate new, incoming information; furthermore, he is motivated to employ whatever strategies he knows how to use, such as active rehearsal of the new material, in order to ensure that it will be available for later retrieval. If there are sex dif-

TABLE 2.20
Verbal Memory

Study	Age and N	Difference	Comment
J. Hall & Halperin 1972	2½ (23)	None	Recognition of previously heard word list
Sitkei & Meyers 1969	3-4 (100)	Girls	Sentences presented aurally (for black, middle SES subsample only)
J. Hall & Ware 1968	5-7 (86)	None	Recognition of previously heard words
Weener 1971	5-8 (90)	None	Recall of 5-word strings with 4-month follow-up
Cramer 1972	6, 7, 10, 11, (96)	None	Recall of list of 12 words (3 instruction conditions)
Cole et al. 1971	6, 8, 13 (120)	None	Number of object names recalled
	6, 9, 11, 14 (82)	None	Number of words recalled
Shepard & Ascher 1973	6, 11, 18-21 (96)	Girls	Higher total number of words recalled
Amster & Wiegand 1972	7, 11 (64)	Girls	Higher overall recall for words used in sorting tasks
H. Stevenson et al. 1968a	8-12 (475)	None	Answering questions about orally presented story
	12-14 (256)	Girls	Answering questions about orally presented story (high- and low-IQ subsamples; no difference, middle-IQ subsample)
Felzen & Anisfeld 1970	8, 11 (80)	Girls	Shorter latency in recognizing unfamiliar words in recall task
		None	Errors
Finley & Frenkel 1972	9, 12 (48)	Girls	Tachistoscopic presentation, girls recalling more words
Kossuth et al. 1971	11 (80)	Girls	Better recall and more word clustering
H. Stevenson et al. 1970	14 (96)	None	Answering questions about story heard (educable retardates)
Sarason & Harmatz 1965	15 (144)	None	Sexual learning task
Tulving & Pearlstone 1966	15-17 (929)	Girls	Immediate recall and cued recall of category name tests
Backman 1972	17 (2,925)	Girls	Verbal memory: Project Talent Test battery
DeFazio 1973	18-21 (44)	None	Repeating strings of words
Milburn et al. 1970	18-21 (134)	Women	Words recalled
Laurence & Trotter 1971	23, 75 (72)	None	Words recalled per trial

TABLE 2.21
Memory for Objects and Digits

Study	Age and N	Difference	Comment
Fagan 1972	3-6 mos (266)	None	Fixation times to novel relative to familiar stimuli (6 experiments)
Fagan 1971	3-8 mos (24)	None	Fixation times to novel relative to familiar stimuli and to less familiar relative to more familiar stimuli
C. Allen 1931	1 (100)	None	Toy hidden under 1 of 3 boxes — delayed response task
Sitkei & Meyers 1969	3-4 (100)	Boys	Object memory (for lower SES white subsample only)
		Girls	Recall of sequences of letters (for middle SES black subsample only)
		None	Visual Sequence Memory; ITPA Vocal Sequencing
Friedrichs et al. 1971	3-5 (50)	None	Serial recall of line drawings of common objects
L. Horowitz et al. 1969	3-5 (108)	None	Pictures of objects (3 experiments)
Hagen et al. 1973	4-7 (48)	None	Serial recall of pictures of animals
Rothbart 1971	5 (56)	None	Recall of toys seen in playroom
McCarver & Ellis 1972	5-6 (60)	None	Digit span, short-term, memory of location of drawings of objects
Mathews & Fozard 1970	5-8, 11-12 (128)	None	Recency judgments on picture pairs
Flavell et al. 1966	5, 7, 10 (60)	None	Serial recall of pictures of familiar objects
McCarver 1972	5, 7, 10, 18-21 (160)	None	Serial position, probe-type, short-term memory
Steele & Horowitz 1973	6 (72)	None	Recall of line drawing
Moynahan 1973	6, 8, 10 (144)	None	Recall of line drawings of common objects (categorized, noncategorized)
B. Ross & Youniss 1969	6, 10 (64)	None	Recognition of pictures under 2 delay periods
G. Harris & Burke 1972	7, 9, 11 (90)	None	Recall of grouped or ungrouped digits
Keenan 1972	7, 9, 11 (38)	None	Recall of sequences of English letters, Hebrew letters, binary patterns (tachistoscopic presentation)
Sabo & Hagen 1972	8, 10, 12 (240)	None	Short-term memory of location of pictures

(continued)

TABLE 2.21 *(cont.)*

Study	Age and N	Difference	Comment
Spitz et al. 1972	8, 17 (60)	None	Digit recall
	9, 13, 20 (90)	None	Digit recall
	14-17 (44)	None	Digit recall
	Adults (22)	None	Digit recall
Hagen & Huntsman 1971	9, 11 (21)	None	Short-term memory of location of pictures (retardates)
Druker & Hagen 1969	9, 11, 13 (240)	Boys None	Better recall of location of drawings / Matching previously seen line drawings of animals and household objects
Anders et al. 1972	19-21 (10)	None	Latencies of response to short digit lists
Blum et al. 1972	64, 84 (54)	None	Wechsler-Bellevue: Digits Forward, Digits Backward (longitudinal); annual rate of decline over the 20-year period

ferences in interests, areas of knowledge, and abilities, then, we would expect these to be reflected in memory. The specific areas of strength of the two sexes are discussed in later chapters (see especially Chapter 3). In the present section we anticipate the distinctions made there, and summarize the studies that deal with memory for verbal content in Table 2.20, those using objects or digits in Table 2.21, and those calling for memory of a combination of verbal and nonverbal materials in Table 2.22.

Girls show somewhat better memory for verbal content. More than half the studies have found no sex differences, but when differences are found, girls have higher scores in every case. The superiority of girls in verbal memory is especially clear after about the age of 7. By contrast, sex differences are seldom found for objects or digits. The one study with children older than preschool age showing a sex difference finds boys better at recalling designs, a task that probably relates to the area of visual-spatial skills in which boys of this age frequently excel. The studies that used tasks calling for memory of both verbal and nonverbal materials present a mixed picture, but on the whole do not show superiority of either sex. In a study of recall of a model's performance, J. Grusec (1972) found that boys remembered more performed than verbalized material, whereas girls recalled both equally well.

To summarize, verbal content in a memory task may give some advantage to girls, but it clearly cannot be said that either sex has a superior memory capacity, or a superior set of skills in the storage and retrieval of information, when a variety of content is considered. Nor does existing evidence point to a difference in choice of mnemonic strategies.

TABLE 2.22
Memory for Words and Objects

Study	Age and N	Difference	Comment
Sitkei & Meyers 1969	3-4 (100)	Boys	Picture memory (for lower SES black subsample only)
		None	Paired pictures
Ward & Legant 1971	3-4 (20)	None	Pictures with and without verbal labels
	4 (29)	None	Pictures and color stimuli, with and without verbal labels
Appel et al. 1972	4 (20)	None	Memory task for pictures and names
	7 (40)	Girls	Remembered more names of pictures
	11 (40)	None	Pictures and names
Rothbart 1971	5 (56)	None	Recall of names of zoo animals in picture
McCarver & Ellis 1972	5-6 (60)	None	Recall of location of previously labeled and non-labeled drawings
Wheeler & Dusek 1973	5, 8, 10 (144)	Boys	Matching previously seen line drawings (8-year-old sample only)
		Girls	Better recall of location of previously labeled and nonlabeled line drawings
G. Davies 1972	8-9 (100)	None	Names or pictures of objects
Koen 1966	18-21 (72)	Men	Recalled pictures seen if no labeling was allowed
		Women	Recalled picture seen if verbal labels or acting out was used

Social Memory

In an early study, Witryol and Kaess (1957)[R] reported that women college students were better able than men to remember the names associated with photographs of faces, and better able to remember the names of people they had met briefly. Primarily on the basis of this study, it has been thought that females have superior "social memory." Garai and Scheinfeld say (1968, p. 206)[R]: "The greater facility in the recall of names and faces by girls may be the result of their greater interest in people, while the better retention of information by boys appears to be related to their greater interest in objects, which is manifest in infancy."

In the earlier portion of this chapter, we were not able to find evidence that infant boys are more interested in objects, or infant girls in people. But of course this would not preclude the development of differences in social interests at a later time that could be reflected in social memory.

To our knowledge, there has been no attempt to replicate the Witryol and Kaess study directly. An indirect replication (Messick and Damarin

TABLE 2.23
Social Memory

Study	Age and N	Difference	Comment
Leifer et al. 1971	4, 7, 10 (60)	None	Memory of characters in fairy tale
G. Leventhal & Anderson 1970	5 (144)	None	Recall of own and fictitious partner's performance scores in game
Zussman & Reimer 1973	9, 10 (64)	None	Memory of what characters said in puppet show
Isen 1970	18-21 (30)	None	Recall and recognition of confederate's behavior
A. Lott et al. 1970b	18-21 (52)	None	Association of nonsense syllables with names of liked, disliked, and neutrally regarded acquaintances

1964[B]) found no sex differences. We have charted in Table 2.23 the studies that test for recall of material appearing to have some social content, and no sex difference emerges. However, the evidence is scanty, and the research has not been focused on the social-nonsocial distinction. It would be useful to have more information on the recall of names and faces in naturalistic situations. Meanwhile, the existing evidence on social memory is consistent with what has been found with respect to perception of social cues and learning through modeling: the two sexes seem to be equally oriented toward social stimuli, and equally able to recall them, at least through the college years. We have no doubt that certain adult occupations call for special skill in identifying people and recalling their names. The receptionist, bank clerk, head waiter, insurance salesman, nurse, doctor, and teacher all find it advantageous to know the names of the people with whom they deal. Most people in these occupations develop the relevant memory skills with practice. If women, more often than men, have jobs requiring these skills, it is to be expected that a sex difference in "social memory" might emerge during the post-college years. If so, it would appear that the social skills of adult women are not rooted in any childhood patterns that have emerged so far. But this issue will be reexamined in the chapters that follow.

To summarize: beginning in early infancy, the two sexes show a remarkable degree of similarity in the basic intellectual processes of perception, learning, and memory. Although the possibility remains open that females are more sensitive in the modalities of touch and smell, we found no evidence to support the contention that boys are more oriented toward vision, girls toward hearing. Hence we do not see differences in sensitivity to these two kinds of stimulation as being the foundation of any sex differences in language acquisition, or in the processing of visual-spatial materials.

The allegation that girls learn best by rote processes, boys by some more advanced form of reasoning, is clearly not supported by the evidence. If learning tasks are classified in terms of whether they call primarily upon the formation of simple associations or upon higher-level processes (such as the inhibition of previously acquired responses), there is no trend whatever in the direction of girls excelling on some classes of learning tasks and boys on others. Nor have we been able to find evidence for the widely held belief that girls are more skillful at perceiving, learning, and remembering materials that have a "social" content. However, most studies of perception, learning, and memory do not vary systematically the nature of the content to be learned. The present chapter has shown clearly that there is no difference in *how* the two sexes learn. Whether there is a difference in *what* they find easier to learn is a different question. Whether either sex is in any sense readier to respond to certain kinds of inputs from the environment is a question that will continue to be examined in Chapters 3–7, where the acquistion of specific classes of behavior by the two sexes is reviewed.

CHAPTER THREE

Intellectual Abilities and Cognitive Styles

To anyone accustomed to thinking in terms of the theories and concepts of developmental psychology, the factor-analytic studies of "abilities" have an alien ring. They address themselves to few developmental issues. An exception is the question of whether separable "abilities" become more differentiated or more integrated as intellectual development proceeds through childhood and adolescence. But this question is only tangentially linked to theories concerning the changes in information-processing strategies which are a primary concern of current developmental psychology. The ability factors that emerge from factor-analytic studies do not always make sense in terms of these processes and their developmental changes. For example, the distinction between "verbal" and "quantitative" skills poses problems. Numbers are frequently expressed in words. In what sense, then, are mathematical skills also not verbal? If the distinction has to do with the manipulation of symbols, words as well as numerals and conventional mathematical notations are symbols. There does not seem to be a clear distinction between solving a verbal syllogism and solving a mathematical problem that is couched in "if-then" terms. It would appear that complex manipulation of symbols can occur with the use of either mathematical symbols or verbal symbols. Individual differences in intellectual abilities in adolescence and adulthood should have to do with processes that are not specific to either sphere, but that ought to be better understood by reference to processes such as those described by Piaget in his analysis of "formal operations." If one thinks in these terms, it does not come as a surprise that verbal and mathematical skills are usually quite strongly correlated, or that quantitative ability has sometimes not emerged as a distinct factor in factor-analytic work (Flanagan 1961). It *does* come as a surprise if two groups of people differ in one direction on "verbal" ability and in the opposite direction on mathematical ability.

Similarly, the distinction between "spatial" abilities and other abilities is puzzling. It is widely alleged (e.g. Bruner et al. 1966[R], pp. 21ff) that young children tend to use "ikonic" (pictorial) representations in organizing, storing, and retrieving the products of their experience. With development such representations are presumably superseded, to a considerable degree, by nonpictorial symbols, including both quantitative and nonquantitative words. As the person develops, he presumably begins to solve even spatial problems (such as the representation of three-dimensional space in a two-dimensional perspective drawing) in nonpictorial ways, with increasing use of verbal symbols. A developmental psychologist might be tempted to suppose, then, that "spatial visualizing" might emerge as a factor in intellectual abilities in early and middle childhood, but that it would merge with other factors with approaching maturity; or if it continued as a distinct factor, it would represent a lower level of intellectual maturity. Such an assumption would not be warranted by the findings of the factor-analytic studies. Spatial ability does not become less distinct as a factor with increasing age, but probably more so. Little is known concerning the role that spatial-visual imagery plays in mature, complex thought, but it now seems possible that ikonic representation does not give way to other "more advanced" forms of thought, but rather can be retained and utilized as part of the most advanced levels of information processing.

Developmental psychology has focused on a single ladder of intellectual development, describing individuals in terms of the height they have reached on this ladder. Factor-analytic studies suggest that there are diverging paths of development—that there may be different "types" of advanced thought.

In comparing the intellectual development of groups of individuals (e.g. social classes, firstborns vs. later-borns, ethnic groups, males vs. females), one can ask two questions: (1) Do they differ in their rate of progress, and in the level ultimately reached, on a unidimensional developmental ladder? (2) Does one group have a higher representation than the other among certain "types"? (Are there distinct ability profiles?) The two questions can be combined, if one thinks in terms of distinct developmental progressions for different abilities, into the question: Do the groups differ in the height they reach (or their rate of progress) on the separate ability ladders? Our analysis will be primarily focused on the last question. We will not have a free choice of the content of these different ladders. We will be constrained by the nature of the tests that have been given and the clusters of abilities that have emerged from them in the course of the psychometric work that has been done.

It has been customary in the testing field to distinguish between tests of achievement and tests of ability. Achievement tests are normally focused on a range of subject matter on which training has been given. Tests of ability have been designed primarily to predict individuals' future success on particular kinds of tasks. Achievement tests are likely to emphasize *knowledge*, then, whereas ability tests include items intended to reveal how quickly a person can learn something new. In practice, the distinction becomes blurred. The products of past learning form the basis for new learning. The same processes that enabled the person to amass knowledge in past learning situations can be utilized to acquire new information. "Achievement" quite often takes the form of having learned *how to learn*, rather than merely storing learned information. Thus, although we recognize that the distinction has been a useful one for certain purposes, it is not particularly useful for our present purposes, and we will analyze the two kinds of data jointly.

This chapter, more than others in this book, takes the form of a sequel to a chapter called "Sex Differences in Intellectual Functioning," which appeared in the 1966 *Development of Sex Differences*. The tables included in this chapter summarize the research that has been done since the previous summaries were prepared (plus a few items omitted from those summaries), and although the previous summaries have not been repeated here, they will be referred to where relevant to the discussion.

GENERAL INTELLECTUAL ABILITIES

It is still a reliable generalization that the sexes do not differ consistently in tests of total (or composite) abilities through most of the age range studied. As Table 3.1 shows, girls do appear to have a slight advantage on tests given under the age of 7: out of 18 such studies, 8 found girls to have higher scores, whereas only 1 (with kibbutz children under the age of 2) found higher scores for boys. There is some question, of course, whether tests given during the first year of life may be considered tests of "intellectual" ability in any meaningful sense. By necessity they must rely upon perceptual performance and motor skills, and they do not predict later intellectual achievements, so it is difficult to interpret any group differences that occur at this age. Tests from age 2 to 7 do come closer to measuring abilities that will be involved in later intelligence, and when there is a sex difference in this age range, it favors girls. It is tempting to view this early superiority of girls, when it is found, as reflecting a differential rate of maturation in the two sexes, but there are two reasons to be cautious about such an interpretation. First, Bayley (1956)[R] has shown that the rate of intellectual development is not positively related to indexes of physical growth (indeed, that the correlations tend to be negative), so that if intellectual development is a function of physical maturation, it would have to be maturation of a different system than that reflected in height or bone development. A second issue is that of cultural differences. The higher scores of girls tend to be found in studies of "disadvantaged" children. The one instance of higher scores in boys comes from a special subculture: Israeli kibbutzim. Unless rates of maturation are affected differently in the two sexes by cultural conditions, the cultural effects would

TABLE 3.1
General Intellectual Abilities

Study	Age and *N*	Difference	Comment
Leiderman et al. 1973	0-2, 3-5 mos (64)	None	Bayley Scales of Mental and Motor Development (premature, full-term)
Kohen-Raz 1968	1, 3, 4, 8, 10, 12, 15, 18, 24, 27 mos (207)	None	Bayley Scales (Israeli sample)
	6 mos (32)	Boys	Bayley Mental Scale (Israeli infants reared in kibbutzim and institutions
		None	Bayley Motor Scale
	6 mos (18)	None	Bayley Scales (Israeli infants reared in private homes)
R. Wilson & Harpring 1972	3, 6, 9, 12 18, 24 mos (261 pairs of twins)	Girls	Bayley Motor Scale (at 9 mos only); Bayley Mental Scale (at 18 mos only)
T. Moore 1967	6, 18 mos (76)	None	Griffiths's Scale of Development (longitudinal)
	3, 5, 8 (76)	None	Stanford-Binet (longitudinal)
Goffeney et al. 1971	8 mos (626)	Girls None	Bayley Scales – fine motor Bayley Scales – mental, gross motor
	7 yrs (626)	None	WISC, Bender-Gestalt
Ireton et al. 1970	8 mos (536)	None	Bayley Scale
Willerman et al. 1970	8 mos (3,037)	Girls None	Bayley Motor Scale Bayley Scale
	4 yrs (3,037)	Girls	Stanford-Binet (longitudinal)
Beckwith 1971	8, 10 mos (24)	None	Cattell, Gesell
D. Stayton et al. 1971	9-12 mos (25)	None	Griffiths's Scale of Development
Clarke-Stewart 1973	10-12, 17-18 mos (36)	None	Bayley Scales (longitudinal)
Lewis et al. 1968	3 (57)	Girls	Stanford-Binet
Dickie 1968	3-4 (50)	None	Stanford-Binet (black sample)
Shipman 1971	3-4 (1,474)	Girls	Caldwell Preschool Inventory (black and white disadvantaged sample)
Zigler 1968	3-4 (52)	None	Stanford-Binet
McDavid 1959	3-5 (26)	None	Stanford-Binet Form L

(continued)

TABLE 3.1 *(cont.)*

Study	Age and N	Difference	Comment
Klaus & Gray 1968	3, 4, 5, 6, 7 (88)	None	Stanford-Binet, WISC (low SES black; longitudinal)
	6 (80)	None	Metropolitan and Gates Reading Readiness tests
	6, 7 (80)	None	Metropolitan Achievement Test (longitudinal)
	7 (30)	None	Stanford Achievement Test
Quay 1972	4 (50)	None	Stanford-Binet (black disadvantaged sample)
Radin 1973	4 (52)	None	Stanford-Binet
Massari et al. 1969	5 (33)	None	Stanford-Binet
Winitz 1959	5 (150)	Girls	WISC Performance Scale IQs
F. Brown 1944	5-6 (432)	None	Stanford-Binet Form L (multiracial sample)
Kaufman 1971	5-6 (103)	None	Large-Thorndike Intelligence Tests
SRI 1972	5, 7 (7,301)	Girls	Wide Range Achievement Test
Dykstra & Tinney 1969	6 (3,283)	Girls	Pintner-Cunningham Primary test of intelligence
G. Prescott 1955	6 (800)	Girls	Metropolitan Readiness Test Score
Goldschmid 1967	6-7 (81)	None	Pintner-Cunningham or Otis
V. C. Crandall & Lacey 1972	6-12 (50)	None	Stanford-Binet
Sundberg & Ballinger 1968	6-13 (807)	None	Goodenough Draw-a-Man Test (Nepalese sample)
Havighurst & Hilkevitch 1944	6-15 (670)	None	Arthur Point Performance Scale (Indian sample)
Schubert & Cropley 1972	6-15 (211)	None	WISC (Canadian, Indian, and white subsamples)
V. C. Crandall 1969	7-12 (41)	None	Stanford-Binet
Parsley et al. 1963	7-13 (5,020)	None	5 tests in 4 achievement areas
Eska & Black 1971	8 (100)	None	Otis-Lennon Mental Ability Test
Solkoff 1972	8-11 (224)	Boys	WISC — Coding WISC — Picture Completion and Object Assembly

(continued)

TABLE 3.1 *(cont.)*

Study	Age and *N*	Difference	Comment
Faterson & Witkin 1970	8-13 (53)	Girls	Articulation of Body Concepts (longitudinal)
	10, 14, 17 (60)	Girls	ABC at 14 yrs only (longitudinal)
Curry & Dickson 1971	8, 11 (16)	None	Stanford-Binet
Dreyer et al. 1971	9-16 (22)	None	Sophistication of body concept on Draw-a-Person Test (longitudinal)
Lekarczyk & Hill 1969	10-11 (114)	Girls	Kuhlmann Anderson, Forms E and F; Stanford Achievement Test
Achenbach 1970	10-13 (1,085)	Girls	Higher IQ, all ages
S. Stayton 1970a	16 (112)	None	Stanford-Binet (retardate sample) Science Research Associates Test of Educational Ability (normal sample)
Bayley 1957	16, 18, 21 (33)	None	Gains in intelligence (longitudinal)
Wyer 1967	18 (2,000)	None	ACT
Rosenberg & Sutton-Smith 1966	18-20 (600)	Women	Total score—ACE
Baltes et al. 1971	21-70 (280)	None	General Intelligence factor score (Primary Mental Abilities Test, Test of Behavioral Rigidity)
E. Lane 1973	27-46 (22)	None	Average IQ increase from second to eighth grades
Kangas & Bradway 1971	39-44 (48)	Men	Larger gains in IQ over a 38-year period

seem to weaken the maturational interpretation and point to environmental reasons for whatever sex difference is found.

A major issue in determining whether a given study finds a sex difference, of course, is the nature of the items included on the test. Some tests, such as the Stanford Binet, have been standardized in such a way as to minimize sex differences; other tests, such as the Thurstone Primary Mental Abilities Test, have not. Since boys are better at some kinds of tasks and girls at others (see below), the sexes can be made to differ in either direction, or to be the same, depending on the mix of items included in a test. The majority of studies of general ability with subjects over the age of 6 seem to have used well-balanced tests: they find no sex differences. The studies showing higher scores for girls seem to have used tests that rely heavily on verbal skills. If the scores obtained by boys and girls in a particular study are determined by the weighting given to certain specific abilities, then any sex difference that emerges is of little general interest. We shall turn shortly to an analysis of sex differences in specific abilities. But first we shall discuss an issue with respect to general intelligence: the question of its heritability, and whether heritability is equivalent in the two sexes.

Do the Sexes Differ in Heritability?

Bayley and Schaefer[R], in their 1964 monograph on development of mental abilities in relation to certain aspects of the behavior of the mothers in their longitudinal studies, say: "The impact of the environment (maternal behavior) on infant boys is persistent: both their behavior and their intellectual functioning tend to become fixed by the third year and to persist at least through 18 years. The girls' intellectual functioning, on the other hand, appears to be more genetically determined."

The suggestion is, then, that the path of development is somehow more fixed by biology for girls than it is for boys. The argument is partly based on the evidence concerning genetic factors from Skodak and Skeels' study of adopted children. In their reanalysis of these data, Bayley and Schaefer show that the IQs of girls are significantly correlated with the IQs of their natural mothers (from whom they have been separated since birth), whereas the IQs of boys are not significantly related to those of their natural mothers. The Bayley and Schaefer hypothesis is also an inference, based on evidence that the male of the species is more affected by environmental variations than the female. Bayley and Schaefer's data showed higher correlation between maternal behavior and the social and intellectual characteristics of boys than girls.

Before we continue with analysis of the evidence relevant to the Bayley-Schaefer hypothesis, it should be noted that although it was originally stated in the context of the inheritance of intelligence, the hypothesis applies to the heritability of other characteristics as well. Because most of the evidence we draw upon comes from studies of mental abilities, we include the discussion of heritability in the present chapter, and broaden the discussion to cover nonintellectual aspects of behavior whenever they bear upon the general issue of sex differences in heritability.

We discuss later (in the section on variability, p. 119) the matter of greater male vulnerability. We take it as demonstrated that there are certain kinds of powerful environmental insults—perhaps especially those that occur prenatally or paranatally—that affect the male more than the female. What relation does this fact have to the role of genetic control over the growing individual? Is it a reasonable inference that if one sex is more affected by certain aspects of the environment, the other must be more susceptible to genetic influence? Let us consider the case of twins. If one twin is subjected to a powerful environmental hazard while the other is not, then the twins should become more unlike than they would otherwise be. The degree of unlikeness produced by the environmental effects would be at least as great for fraternal as for identical twins. Thus the greater genetic similarity between identical twins would be gradually outweighed by the cumulative impact of environmental events for any group of twins that are highly vulnerable to such events. Heritability coefficients, as these are normally computed, would go down. Thus the argument seems persuasive that if boys are more vulnerable, they ought to show less heritability, at least when heritability is measured through twin resemblances.

We shall first examine the direct evidence that can be found concerning heritability in the two sexes, and then shall return to the issue of the relationship between heritability and environmental effects. The scarcity of data is a handicap. There are many studies of heritability, of course, and most of them include subjects of both sexes, but either the data are not analyzed by sex, or sex differences in heritability are reported only if they are positive, not if they fail to appear.

First we take studies of heritability in animals; here the amount of heritability is usually determined by relating similarities among individuals to their degree of genetic similarity. This can be carefully controlled by the use of back-crosses and other selective breeding programs. The heritability of activity level has been studied separately by sex in fruit flies and mice (Connolly 1966[R], DeFries et al. 1966[R]); Thompson (1953)[R] studied the heritability of food drive, emotionality, and exploration in mice. Dominance, aggression, and sexual behavior have been studied in chickens (Craig and Baruth 1965[R], Guhl et al. 1960[R], Wood-Gush 1960[R]). In none of these studies was heritability greater for one sex than the other. An interesting exception is a study of alcohol consumption in rats. Eriksson (1968)[R] found that females had a higher heritability for alcohol consumption than males, and linked this to a sex difference in alcohol elimination. However, the general conclusion is that when both sexes are studied in a variety of animal behaviors, there is no sex difference in heritability.

In humans, the constraints on experimentation mean that the available evidence will be less direct than that for animals. There are two main kinds of evidence: parent-child correlations and twin studies.

Parent-child correlations of mental abilities. Parent-child resemblances in IQ have been the major focus of study, with very little research being available on parent-child similarities in attributes other than intelligence. And even in the IQ studies, the data are often incomplete. Sometimes IQ scores from the parental generation are available only for mothers, not fathers. More of a problem is the fact that the parental data are sometimes *estimates*, based on education, occupation, or some other indirect index. Sometimes the measures of the parent or the child represent an incomplete coverage of the domain of mental abilities—for example, only verbal tests may have been given. This turns out to be important, for there is now some reason to believe that certain components of mental abilities may be more heritable than others. Most studies of parent-child resemblances deal with total IQ scores, and there might be more useful information if subscores were available as well. Total IQ scores may mask some parent-child resemblances that exist for some components but not others.

A final problem in the studies of parent-child resemblance has to do with the ages at which the measures are taken. Usually there is a child's score, obtained when the child is young, and this is correlated with the parent's score, obtained from an adult. Since IQ tests measure different things at different developmental stages, parent-child resemblances may be attenuated by the age differences. If a genetic substratum is accounting for some of the variance in the two distributions, this fact might be more apparent if both parent and child were measured at the same age. Obviously, it is only very extended longitudinal studies that will yield data of this kind.

The earliest report from a longitudinal study is by Conrad and Jones in 1940[R], in which estimated IQs of mother and father were correlated with measured IQs of children. In this report, boys' and girls' scores showed similar degrees of relationships with their parents' IQs, although the girls' correlations were somewhat higher. Honzik (1963)[R] and Bayley and Schaefer (1964)[R] later reported data from the Berkeley longitudinal samples. Bayley and Schaefer, using estimated IQs for the mother (estimated on the basis of a mother interview) report correlations ranging from .48 to .55 between the IQs of girls and their mothers; for boys, the comparable relationships are .34 to .48. No test was reported for the significance of the difference between these correlations. With the sample sizes involved (15 boys and 16 girls), it would not appear to be significant. Here is an instance, then, in which girls tend to show slightly more heritability than boys, but not significantly so. Honzik, working with larger numbers of families from the Berkeley Guidance Study, used estimated IQs for the parents, and she reports a tendency for boys' correlations with parental IQs to be higher than girls'; however, the significance of this difference was not tested.

The Fels longitudinal study also provides us with some interesting data on parent-child resemblance. Kagan and Moss (1959)[R] report relationships between child IQs and the IQs of their parents measured during the parents' adulthood. The parent-child resemblances were of the same magnitude for boys and girls. More recently, McCall et al. (1973)[R] have reported on families in which the parents were themselves subjects in the Fels longitudinal study as children; now that their children are also being tested, it is possible to study parent-child resemblances between IQ scores taken at the same age. The changing patterns of correlation depending upon the age of measurement are of interest in themselves; for our present purposes, however, the main point is that there are no sex differences in the degree of correlation between parents and children, regardless of whether the measures of parent IQ are taken in childhood or adulthood. One sex difference has been reported by both McCall and Honzik: for both sexes, children's scores show little resemblance to parental scores when the children are very young; as they grow older, the correlation increases. Girls reach the point of maximum correlation with parental scores at an earlier age than boys do, a fact that Honzik attributes to the more rapid maturation of girls. In any case, the bulk of the evidence indicates that the ultimate level of resemblance in IQ does not differ for the two sexes.

As mentioned above, the Bayley and Schaefer reanalysis of an earlier study of adopted children revealed a higher relationship for girls than boys between the child's IQ and that of its natural mother. There is now reason to believe that this sex difference will not replicate on other samples of children. Although the data are not yet published, the scores of a group of adopted children on the Ravens Progressive Matrices test have been related to the educational level attained by the children's natural mothers.[*] The correlations are virtually identical for the two sexes.

Later in this chapter, the studies comparing parents and children with respect to their spatial abilities are reviewed. It will be shown that children's spatial abilities are moderately related to those of the cross-sex parent. For our present purposes, the main point of interest is that the degree of correlation with the cross-sex parent does not appear to differ by sex, so that even if the attribute is sex-linked, this does not mean it is more genetically controlled in one sex than the other.

It would be very useful indeed to have parent-child correlation data, separately by sex, for psychological measures other than IQ. Our conclusions from the existing data can only be tentative, but the existing studies of parent-child resemblance would seem to indicate no sex difference in heritability.

Twin studies. Two questions are usually addressed by twin studies. One is whether male identical twins are more similar to each other than female identical twins. The other rests on a comparison between identical and fraternal twins of a given sex. Let us consider first the work with identical twins only. Lyon (1961)[ᴿ] has suggested that female monozygotic twins have somewhat more room to differ from one another than do male monozygotic twins, because females have two X chromosomes and only one of these will become apparent in the phenotypes—which one being a matter of chance. More recent work on this subject indicates that which X is activated is random within each cell, so that an individual female has a mosaic pattern of X activation throughout her body. Female identical twins, then, can be somewhat more unlike than male identicals with respect to any characteristic carried on the X chromosome but not so unlike as fraternals. To the extent that the X chromosome is implicated in a wide range of

* Personal communication from S. Scarr-Salapatek, University of Minnesota, 1973.

physical and psychological attributes, then, female identical twins should show less congruence than male identical twins. Vandenberg (1962)ᵃ has found that this seems to be true on a range of physiological measures, and also on the verbal subtest of the Primary Mental Abilities test. Similarly, Humphreys* finds somewhat less congruence in monozygotic girl twins from the Project Talent sample on spatial tests, although it is not clear whether the difference between male twin congruence and female twin congruence is statistically significant.

The second approach with twins is to compare the correlations between identical twins with the correlations between fraternal twins. If there is no genetic contribution to a particular ability, one would expect the two kinds of twins to be equally correlated. Heritability can be computed by first finding the correlation between identical twins, then finding the correlation between fraternal twins, and expressing these two numbers as a ratio. Humphreys has done this for a variety of IQ subtests, and finds that for girls, correlations between identical twins and those between fraternal twins are somewhat more similar than for boys. Thus, girls show somewhat less heritability by this measure. The difference between the sexes is greatest for spatial abilities. That is, this ability seems to be a more genetically controlled attribute in boys than it is in girls. Again, the statistical significance of the sex differences has not been reported.

In summary, on the narrow range of attributes that have been studied, we find that the sexes show similar degrees of genetic control on the basis of parent-child resemblance, but that boys may show somewhat more genetic control if data from twin studies are used.

Heredity and Environment

There is a dilemma: we noted initially the greater vulnerability of male infants and children, and the fact that Bayley and Schaefer reported a greater relationship between maternal behavior and the child's intellectual development for boys than for girls. If it were generally true that males were more susceptible to environmental influence than females, there appears every reason to expect that heritability ought to be greater for girls. Instead, heritability is either very similar for the two sexes or on some measures higher for boys. How is it possible for one sex to show both more heritability and more susceptibility to environmental influence?

Perhaps the dilemma is not real. That is, it may be based upon false assumptions or incomplete information. Having examined what is known about heritability, let us return to the issue of whether one sex is really more susceptible to environmental influence than the other. It would be a formidable task to review all the socialization studies to see whether the correlations between parent behaviors and child characteristics are gen-

* L. G. Humphreys, personal communication, University of Illinois, 1972.

erally higher for boys than for girls. We have, however, reviewed a selected set of studies (Bayley and Schaefer 1964[R]; the Fels longitudinal study, reported in Kagan and Moss 1962[R]; Honzik 1967[R]; Bing 1963[R]; Hetherington 1967[R]; R. Sears et al. 1965[R]) with this question in mind.

Taken as a whole, these studies do not indicate that either sex is generally more susceptible to home influence. There is the further question of whether the other major sources of environmental influence—school, peer group, climate, ecological factors such as crowding, or an unlimited list of other possibilities—affect the two sexes to different degrees. For the present, it may be taken as a reasonably strong hypothesis that they do not; at least, we know of no evidence that they do.

There is still, however, the substantial evidence for the greater vulnerability of the male infant, referred to earlier. How can it be that this vulnerability exists and is not reflected in lowered heritability figures for males? Two possible resolutions to the problem come to mind. The first is that some of the prenatal and paranatal defects that are found more commonly in boys are genetic. This is not a new suggestion. Potentially injurious genetic attributes tend to be recessive. (Indeed, if they were not, they would not survive in the gene pool unless they simultaneously controlled characteristics needed for survival along with their injurious side effects.) Whenever such attributes are sex-linked (that is, carried on the X chromosome), the female has the protection of a second X chromosome, and the chances of a dangerous recessive trait being present in both her X chromosomes are small. When the male gets the recessive trait with his single X chromosome, there is no available suppressor for it, and it does whatever developmental damage it is capable of doing. If the problem is genetic in this sense, then of course it will affect both members of an identical twin pair, more so than in the case of fraternal twins.

The case of prenatal or paranatal problems that are *not* genetic is different, but it would appear to have the same outcome. That is, suppose a mother contracts rubella at the third or fourth month of pregnancy. It will presumably affect both her unborn twins. And it ought to affect identical twins in more precisely the same way than fraternals, since the nature of the effects seems to depend in a very detailed way upon the point a fetus has reached in its development when the disease strikes. Incidentally, it may be that girls' somewhat faster rate of prenatal development reduces their period of maximum vulnerability and helps to account for the lower rate of intrauterine damage among female fetuses. But to return to the matter of effects of such hazards as rubella upon twins: fraternal twins may develop at somewhat different rates, whereas identicals do not (except for those attributes that are affected by crowding in the placenta). Hence, the effects of the disease would be more similar for identicals than fraternals. Hence, also, the measures of heritability that involve comparing identical with fraternal twins would continue to reveal high heritability figures, even in the face of an environmental factor with a severe impact. Thus, the fact that males are more vulnerable to certain sorts of damage is not incompatible with the fact that they show somewhat greater heritability in twin studies. We need not accept the proposition that if one sex is more vulnerable, then the other must by definition show more heritability.

Our survey has led us to agree with the often-cited generalization that boys are more vulnerable than girls to certain physiological stressors. However, we think it is fallacious to infer that because male bodies are more vulnerable, males must therefore also be more capable of learning from experience—more susceptible to environmental feedback of all sorts. It is a great leap from the evidence of more frequent male stillbirths to an expectation that boys ought to be more affected than girls by their parents' socialization practices. A brief review of the relevant studies has led to the conclusion that, although the sex difference in physical vulnerability does exist, a sex difference in the effects of learning and teaching environments probably does not. As to the question of genetic control of behavior, the twin studies point to somewhat greater effects of heredity for boys than girls, but studies of parent-child resemblance do not bear this out. On the whole, to the extent that biology is destiny, it would appear that it is about equally so for the two sexes.

SPECIFIC ABILITIES

Verbal Abilities

Female superiority on verbal tasks has been one of the more solidly established generalizations in the field of sex differences. Recent research continues to support the generalization to a degree. It is true that whenever a sex difference is found, it is usually girls and women who obtain higher scores, but the two sexes perform very similarly on a number of verbal tasks in a number of sample populations. In particular, it may be that some of our earlier views concerning the course of development of sex differences in verbal skills should be reconsidered.

It has been thought that sex differences begin very early—from the time of the utterance of the first word or even earlier, in babbling, and diminish as the boys "catch up." A source of this generalization is the 1954[R] McCarthy summary of studies of language development. The differences reported in that study tended to be small, and many, as McCarthy noted, were not significant even on large samples. However, when there was a difference it almost always favored girls, and the many studies taken together added up to a significant trend.

The same was true generally in the studies done between the McCarthy study and our 1966 review, although the study with the largest sample (Templin 1957[R]) found no sex differences between the ages of 3 and 6. Conclusions concerning the first few years of life, however, are still

TABLE 3.2
Spontaneous Vocal and Verbal Behavior

Study	Age and *N*	Difference	Comment
S. J. Jones & Moss 1971	2 wks, 3 mos (28)	None	Vocalizations in each of 5 states: active and passive awake, drowsy, active and passive asleep
Lewis & Freedle 1972	3 mos (40)	Girls None	Respond vocally to mother behavior Vocalization frequency (home observation)
Rheingold et al. 1967	3 mos (21)	None	Vocalization to E
J. Kagan 1969	4, 8, 13 mos (150)	None	Mean vocalization time to clay faces and verbal stimuli
L. Yarrow et al. 1971	5 mos (41)	None	Frequency of positive vocalization (home observation)
Lewis 1969	6 mos (64)	Girls	Vocalization to mother during free play
Rheingold & Eckerman 1969	9-10 mos (24)	None	Spontaneous verbal behavior
B. Dodd 1972	9-12 mos (15)	None	Spontaneous utterances: number, range, length
Clarke-Stewart 1973	9-18 mos (36)	None	Vocalizations to mother, total number of vocalizations (home observation; longitudinal)
Rheingold & Samuels 1969	10 mos (20)	None	Frequency of spontaneous vocalizations (mother present)
H. Ross et al. 1972	11-12 mos (8m, 4f)	None	Number of vocalizations during experimental session
Roberts & Black 1972	18-22 mos (40)	None	Mother's reports of language production
P. Smith & Connolly 1972	2-4 (40)	Girls	Talked more frequently to other children; made more play noises
R. Bell et al. 1971	2½ (74)	Girls	Teachers rated as higher in speech development
Halverson & Waldrop 1970	2½ (42)	Girls	Talking to mother
Mueller 1972	3-5 (48)	Boys	Verbalizations in free play with same-sex peer
Hartig & Kanfer 1973	3-7 (261)	None	Verbalization of instructions to self in resistance-to-temptation task
Kohlberg et al. 1968	4-5 (34)	None	Egocentric speech recorded while S performed various tasks (Americans, Norwegians)
Szal 1972	4-5 (60)	Boys None	Spontaneous verbalizations (competitive) in cooperative-competitive games Spontaneous verbalizations (cooperative, uncooperative)
Wolff & Wolff 1972	4-5 (55)	None	Verbal output, verbal skill (teacher rating)
B. Coates & Hartup 1969	4-5, 7-8 (72)	Girls	Appropriate verbalizations during movie

(continued)

TABLE 3.2 *(cont.)*

Study	Age and N	Difference	Comment
Kohlberg et al. 1968	4-10 (112)	None	Percentage of egocentric speech while constructing sticker designs with adult
Shrader & Leventhal 1968	6-17 (599)	None	Parents' reports of speech problems
Greenglass 1971b	9-10, 13-14 (132)	Girls	Requests for information or evaluation from mother (Canadian sample, ages 9-10 only)
		None	Requests for information or evaluation from mother (Italian sample)
Sarason & Winkel 1966	18-21 (48)	None	Incomplete sentences, sentence corrections, or serial repetition of words
		Women	Emitted fewer "ah's"

based upon very early work. There has been almost no work with children under 2½ or 3 of a normative sort, involving large and unspecialized samples of children, since the 1930's and 1940's. Work in the field of language development has been very intensive during the past 15 years, and understanding of this development has been greatly enhanced, but the work has tended to be focused upon very small and rather highly selected groups of children; it does not reveal whether there has been a change in the relative standing of the two sexes at these early ages with respect to articulation, length of utterance, or early vocabulary. Recent, relatively small-scale studies seem to indicate that the presumed advantage of girls in the first two years of life is tenuous. Lewis and Freedle (1972) did find such an advantage at age 3 months, in terms of the frequency with which the infant responds vocally, rather than in some other way, to stimulation by the mother. T. Moore (1967) found that girls had higher "speech quotients" at age 18 months, though not earlier or later. Clarke-Stewart (1973) found girls to be ahead in both comprehension and vocabulary at 17 months. However, 8 other studies made with infants and children up to the age of approximately 2 find no difference (see Tables 3.2 and 3.3).

In Table 3.2 we have charted studies of spontaneous vocalizing and speaking, most of which involve fairly small samples. After the age of 2, when speech is beginning to be acquired, no trends are apparent in the amount of spontaneous talking that the two sexes do in the course of their daily activities. Table 3.3 summarizes a very large number of studies conducted in testing situations using a variety of standardized stimulus materials. Here, beginning at age 2½, several large-sample studies appear. McCarthy and Kirk (1963) tested children ranging from 2½ to 9 to obtain norms for the Illinois Test of Psycholinguistic Abilities. They found no consistently significant sex differences in overall linguistic ability. The only consistent trend across age levels was that boys were better at "visual de-

TABLE 3.3
Tested Verbal Abilities

Study	Age and N	Difference	Comment
T. Moore 1967	6, 18 mos (76)	Girls	Speech quotients higher at 18 mos (longi-tudinal)
		None	Amount of vocalization at 6 mos; vocal communicativeness at 18 mos
	3, 5, 8 yrs (76)	None	Vocabulary, verbal behavior (longitudinal)
Clarke-Stewart 1973	17 mos (36)	Girls	Language competence
Lewis et al. 1971a	2 (60)	None	Vocalization to human forms
Reppucci 1971	2 (48)	None	Vocabulary naming and recognition
Rhine et al. 1967	2-5 (50)	None	Picture vocabulary
McCarthy & Kirk 1963	2½-9, at 6-mos intervals (700)	Boys	Visual Decoding (at 4½, 8½, 9 yrs only) Motor encoding (at 5½, 9 yrs only)
		Girls	Battery of Illinois Test of Psycholinguistic Abilities (at 7½ yrs only) Auditory Decoding (at 3½, 7 yrs only) Visual-Motor Association (at 3½, 8 yrs only) Auditory-Vocal Sequencing (at 7½ yrs only) Visual-Motor Sequencing (at 7 yrs only) Auditory-Vocal Association (at 5, 6 yrs only)
		None	Vocal Encoding, auditory-vocal automatic
Herriot 1969	3 (24)	None	Understanding tenses
Dickie 1968	3-4 (50)	None	Expressive Vocabulary Inventory, Peabody Picture Vocabulary Test (PPVT), Vocal Encoding and Auditory-Vocal Association subtests of the Illinois Test of Psycholin-guistic Abilities (black sample)
Sitkei & Meyers 1969	3-4 (100)	Girls	Action-Agent Divergent (lower and middle SES black subsample only); ITPA Vocal Encoding (lower SES black subsample only)
		None	PPVT, Action-Agent Convergent, Picture Description, Orpet Utility, Monroe Lan-guage Classification (lower and middle SES black and white samples)
Shipman 1971	3-4 (1,000-1,400)	None	ETS: Matched Pictures Language Comprehen-sion Task I, Story Sequence I, PPVT, Mimicry of Meaningful Words
		Girls	Mimicry of Nonsense Words
T. Williams & Fleming 1969	3-4 (36)	None	PPVT and verbal and visual associative tasks
H. Brown 1971	3-5 (96)	None	Choice of pictures after hearing descriptive sentences
Friedrichs et al. 1971	3-5 (50)	None	Carrying out simple and complex verbal instructions

(continued)

TABLE 3.3 *(cont.)*

Study	Age and N	Difference	Comment
Mehrabian 1970	3-5 (127)	None	Picture vocabulary, comprehension, and judgment of grammaticalness of sentences
Shipman[R] 1972	3-5 (820)	Girls	ETS: Matched Pictures Language Comprehension Task II, Story Sequence II
Parisi 1971	3-6 (144)	None	Syntactic comprehension
Klaus & Gray 1968	3, 4, 5, 6, 7 (88)	None	PPVT (low SES black sample; longitudinal)
	5 (88)	Boys	Greater number of words used in descriptions of pictures
	5, 6, 7 (88)	None	ITPA, total scores (longitudinal)
	6 (88)	None	Metropolitan and Gates Reading Readiness Tests
Matheny 1973	3-8 (44)	Girls	Templin-Darley Articulation Test
Jeruchimowicz et al. 1971	4 (79)	None	PPVT, Expressive Language task (black sample)
Radin 1973	4 (52)	None	PPVT (lower SES)
Shure et al. 1971	4 (62)	None	PPVT (black sample)
W. C. Ward 1969	4 (55)	None	Fluency (Uses, Patterns, and Instances tests)
Ali & Costello 1971	4-5 (108)	None	Standard and modified PPVT (disadvantaged black sample)
A. Harrison & Nadelman 1972	4-5 (50)	None	PPVT
Osser et al. 1969	4-5 (32)	None	Verbal imitation and comprehension
Suppes & Feldman 1971	4-6 (64)	None	Response to verbal commands testing comprehension of logical connectives
James & Miller 1973	4-7 (32)	None	Identification, explanation, and conversion of meaningful and anomalous sentences
Masters 1969b	4-9 (72)	None	Word-association and word-definition tests
Brimer 1969	5 (867)	None	Orally administered English Picture Vocabulary Test 1
	5-8 (3,240)	Boys	Higher on orally administered vocabulary tests at each age level except 5 yrs
	6-8 (2,373)	Boys	EPVT 1
	7-11 (5,084)	Boys	EPVT 2
Winitz 1959	5 (150)	Girls	Mean length verbal response, fluency (1 of 4 measures)
		None	Vocabulary, articulation, WISC verbal scale

(continued)

TABLE 3.3 *(cont.)*

Study	Age and N	Difference	Comment
McCarver & Ellis 1972	5-6 (60)	None	PPVT
Milgram et al. 1971	5-7 (99)	None	Verbal reproduction of story heard (half of sample disadvantaged)
Saltz & Soller 1972	5-6, 8-9, 11-12 (72)	None	Matching pictures to concept words
SRI 1972	5, 7 (7,111)	Girls	Language ability
	5, 7 (13,155)	Girls	Reading knowledge
Cowan et al. 1967	5, 7, 9, 11 (96)	None	Mean length of response to picture
Routh & Tweney 1972	5, 10 (60)	None	Verbal free association
F. Darley & Winitz 1961	6 (150)	None	WISC Verbal Scale IQ
Sharan (Singer) & Weller 1971	6 (357)	Girls	More descriptive categorization and grouping in verbal responses to object-sorting task
O. Davis 1967	6-7 (238)	None	Reading achievement test
Dykstra & Tinney 1969	6-7 (3,283)	Boys	Orally administered vocabulary test (at age 6 only); spelling test (at age 7 only)
		Girls	5 measures of reading readiness; several subtests of 2 verbal achievement tests
Gahagan & Gahagan 1968	6-7 (54)	None	Number of verbs produced in a stimulus response language task
Lesser et al. 1965	6-7 (320)	None	Total verbal ability (some sex differences in ethnic subgroup)
France 1973	6-9 (252)	Boys	PPVT administered by taped voices of students (multiracial sample)
Graves & Koziol 1971	6-9 (67)	None	Plural noun formations
Braun & Klassen 1971	6, 9, 11 (216)	Girls	Higher frequency of noun, relative clause, and object transformations (German-, French-, and English-speaking samples)
		None	29 other linguistic indexes (e. g. number of subordinate clauses, redundancies, etc.)
Bandura & Harris 1966	7 (100)	None	Frequency of passive or mean number of prepositional phrases
J. Kagan et al. 1964	7-8 (135)	Boys	Higher verbal fluency scores
Penk 1971	7-11 (100)	Girls	Fewer mediational faults in word association task
Gates 1961	7-13 (13,114)	Girls	Speed of reading, level-of-comprehension, reading vocabulary

(continued)

TABLE 3.3 *(cont.)*

Study	Age and *N*	Difference	Comment
Parsley et al. 1963	7-13 (5,020)	None	Reading vocabulary, reading comprehension
M. Harris & Hassemer 1972	7, 9 (96)	None	Length and complexity of sentences in composed stories
Lipton & Overton 1971	7, 9, 11, 13 (80)	None	Anagrams task
Zern 1971	7, 9, 12 (69)	None	In time or error scores on questions requiring several mental steps of negation
Eska & Black 1971	8 (100)	None	Response latency and mean length of stories in picture description task
Eisenberg et al. 1968	8-10 (64)	Girls	Better understood on tapes by teachers
Corah 1965	8-11 (60)	Boys	Vocabulary IQ
Hoemann 1972	8-11 (80)	None	Communication of information of a task or game rules
H. Stevenson et al. 1968a	8-12 (475)	Girls	Anagrams task
	12-14 (256)	Girls	Anagrams task (low IQ sample)
		None	Anagrams task (middle, high IQ samples)
H. Stevenson et al. 1968b	8-14 (529)	Girls	More words generated from a single word
Palmer & Masling 1969	8, 9, 15, 16 (48)	None	Vocabulary for skin color (black and white subsamples)
B. Cohen & Klein 1968	8, 10, 12 (240)	None	Verbal communication skill
Hopkins & Bibelheimer 1971	8, 10, 12, 13 (354)	None	Language IQ: California Test of Mental Maturity (longitudinal)
Cotler & Palmer 1971	9-11 (120)	Girls	Fewer errors in reading
Nakamura & Finck 1973	9-12 (204)	Boys	Fewer errors on easy similes
		Girls	Fewer errors on hard similes
Moran & Swartz 1970	9-17 (280)	None	Free association test scored for types of responses (3 longitudinal samples)
Penney 1965	9-11 (108)	None	PPVT
Preston 1962	9, 11 (2,391)	Boys	Reading comprehension and reading speed at age 11 (German sample)
		Girls	Reading comprehension and reading speed (American sample); reading speed at age 9 (German sample)
		None	Reading comprehension at age 9 (German sample)
H. Stevenson & Odom 1965	9, 11 (318)	None	Anagrams task

(continued)

TABLE 3.3 *(cont.)*

Study	Age and N	Difference	Comment
Shepard 1970	9, 11, 13 (137)	Girls	More syntagmatic responses in a word association task (at 9, 11 yrs only); more complex word definitions
		None	Number of simple functional word definitions
T. Baldwin et al. 1971	10 (96)	None	Verbal communication of pictures to another child (black and white)
Herder 1971	10 (143)	None	Descriptions of abstract and face stimuli (black and white)
Achenbach 1969	11 (164)	None Girls	WISC–information WISC–vocabulary
Cicirelli 1967	11 (609)	None Girls	Reading achievement Higher in language achievement
Kellaghan & MacNamara 1972	11 (500)	None	Drumcondra verbal test (Irish)
Weinberg & Rabinowitz 1970	12-19 (48)	None	Vocabulary scores of WISC
Svensson 1971	13 (8,905) 13 (7,694)	Girls None Girls None	Verbal achievement Verbal intelligence (Swedish) Verbal achievement Verbal intelligence (Swedish)
H. Stevenson et al. 1970	14 (96)	Girls	Anagrams task, 1 of 2 testing conditions (educable retarded)
Flanagan et al. Project Talent 1961	14, 17 (4,545)	Boys Girls	Vocabulary Disguised words, English language; reading comprehension
Walberg 1969	16-17 (1,050) 16-17 (450)	Girls Girls	Verbal factors in IQ, scientific processes, and understanding science (physics students) Henmon-Nelson Intelligence Test, Form B
Backman 1972	17 (2,925)	Girls	English language (Project Talent Test battery)
Monday et al. 1966-67	18 (238,145)	Women	ACT English scores
Rosenberg & Sutton-Smith 1966	18-20 (600)	None	Linguistic scale ACE
Bieri et al. 1958	18-21 (76)	None	SAT verbal
DeFazio 1973	18-21 (44)	None	Verbal fluency, advanced vocabulary test
Feather 1968	18-21 (60)	None	Anagrams task
Feather 1969b	18-21 (167)	None	Anagrams test
Koen 1966	18-21 (72)	None	Verbal communication of information about photography
Laughlin et al. 1969	18-21 (528)	None	Synonyms and Antonyms

(continued)

TABLE 3.3 *(cont.)*

Study	Age and *N*	Difference	Comment
Marks 1968	18-21 (760)	None	SAT verbal, Advanced Vocabulary Test
Mendelsohn & Griswold 1966	18-21 (223)	None	Vocabulary Test of the Institute of Educational Research
Mendelsohn & Griswold 1967	18-21 (181)	None	Anagrams task
Sarason & Minard 1962	18-21 (96)	None	Vocabulary subtest of WAIS
Very 1967	18-21 (355)	Women	Moore-Castore Vocabulary, Moore-Castore Paragraph Reading, English Placement Vocabulary
Rosenberg & Sutton-Smith 1964	19 (377)	Women	Linguistic scale ACE
Rosenberg & Sutton-Smith 1969	19 (1,013)	Women	Linguistic scale ACE
Sutton-Smith et al. 1968	19 (1,055)	None	ACE verbal
Bayley & Oden 1955	29, 41 (1,102)	Men	Overall score on Concept Mastery Test (at 41 yrs only), Analogies subtest score (longitudinal study of gifted sample and spouses)
		None	Synonyms and antonyms subtest score
	29 (168)	None	Overall score on Concept Mastery Test (gifted sample)
	41 (227)	None	Overall score on Concept Mastery Test (gifted sample)
Blum et al. 1972	64, 84 (54)	Women	Wechsler-Bellevue: similarities; Stanford-Binet: vocabulary (at 84 yrs only; longitudinal)
		None	Annual rate of decline over 20-year period

coding"—pointing at named objects when the stimulus was visual. Girls tended to be somewhat better at *productive* naming. A set of 13 other recent studies involving children of preschool age have found no sex differences on a variety of verbal tasks. A major exception is the work done by the Educational Testing Service (Shipman 1971) with children from impoverished families. Here, girls are clearly ahead on a number of language measures, though not on all measures used. Another large-scale study of disadvantaged preschoolers (Stanford Research Institute 1972) also finds girls ahead on language measures.

As we move into the next age range, the early school years, there are again few differences. Brimer (1969), who gave receptive vocabulary tests to very large samples in England, found, in fact, higher average scores for boys at each age from 6 through 11. Most studies in America, however, including the ITPA norming sample mentioned above, detect no consistent sex differences, and these include tasks involving productive "fluency" as well as tests of understanding. The primary exception is found in the work of the Stanford Research Institute, with very large samples of disadvantaged children in Follow-Through programs from kindergarten through the second grade. Here the girls clearly test higher in a variety of language skills, including reading, vocabulary, and the understanding of relational terms. Johnson (1973–74)[n] suggests there are sex-specific cross-cultural differences in the reading of English. Males have fewer reading problems in England. This may explain the difference in direction of sex difference of Brimer's work.

It is at about age 10 or 11 that girls begin to come into their own in verbal performance. From this age through the high school and college years we find them outscoring boys at a variety of verbal skills. Sex differences are not found in every study; the findings seem to depend in part on whether tests of general knowledge are called verbal tests—boys tend to do at least as well as girls on such tests and, in the Project Talent sample, substantially better. But in tests of verbal power, girls above age 11 frequently do better, and in some studies the difference is fairly large in absolute terms.

Table 3.4 shows the studies with the largest samples, and gives the magnitude of the sex differences found, as well as their direction. Since units of measurement are not comparable from one study to another, the magnitude of the mean sex difference has been expressed in standard deviation units. The female advantage on verbal tests ranges from about .1 to nearly .5 SD, with the usual difference being about .25 SD. One longitudinal study (Droege 1967) that followed a large group of high school students from the ninth to the twelfth grade found that the superiority of girls on verbal tasks increased through this period. This study is especially interesting, since its longitudinal design permitted a control for differential dropout. We think it important to be clear that the measures reported cover much more than spelling, punctuation, and talkativeness. Included as well are considerably higher-level skills, such as comprehension of complex written text, quick understanding of complex logical relations expressed in verbal terms, and in some instances verbal creativity of the sort measured by Guilford's tests of divergent thinking.

We suggest that there are distinct phases in the development of verbal skills in the two sexes through the growth cycle. One occurs very early—before the age of 3. We emphasize that the studies documenting sex differences at this age are very old. More recent studies tend not to show superiority for girls in spontaneous vocalization or in picture vocabulary after the understanding of speech has begun. Whether a sex difference would still be found with large samples on age of beginning to speak, age of first combining words into sentences, or mean length of utterance, we do not know. If girls do have an early advantage with respect to these aspects of language development, it is short-lived. At about 3 the boys catch up, and in most population groups the two sexes perform very similarly until adolescence. When there are differences, they favor girls; these exceptions tend to occur in populations of underprivileged children, where girls maintain an advantage to a later age. It is possible that boys' greater vulnerability to hazards of all sorts, including those prevailing prenatally, means that the poorer the prenatal and postnatal nutrition and medical care prevailing in a population, the greater the sex difference in early performance will be and the higher the age to which the difference will persist, owing to the presence of larger numbers of low-scoring boys who have suffered some sort of systemic damage in the population most at risk. We shall return shortly to the matter of variability and its possible causes; but now let us simply note that for large unselected populations the situation seems to be one of very little sex difference in verbal skills from about 3 to 11, with a new phase of differentiation occurring at adolescence.

Quantitative Ability

The earliest measures of some aspect of quantitative ability begin at about age 3 with measures of number conservation, soon followed by enumeration. As Table 3.5 shows, there appear to be no sex differences in performance on these tasks during the preschool years, or in mastery of numerical operations and concepts during the early school years, except in disadvantaged populations. Here again the data from the large studies conducted with Head Start and Follow-Through children show the girls to be ahead. The majority of studies on more representative samples show no sex differences up to adolescence, but when differences are found in the age range 9–13, they tend to favor boys. After this age, boys move ahead, and the sex differences become somewhat more consistent from one study to another, though there is great variation in the degree of male advantage reported. Table 3.6 shows the magnitude of the sex differences (in standard score units) in the studies with large samples. It may be seen that Flanagan et al. (1961, Project Talent) find that boys' math scores are .66 SD better than girls' at the twelfth grade, whereas Droege (1967), also using thousands of cases, finds no significant sex difference in high school, and a large Swedish study finds a difference of less than .2 SD. It is not possible at this point to estimate how large the sex difference in quantitative performance is likely to be in any given population.

It is frequently suggested that boys' superiority in math during the high school years simply reflects their greater interest in this area (perhaps based on greater expectations that they will need to use math for their later careers). It is true that boys tend to take more math courses when they have a choice. Is their better performance in math tests due to the fact that their interests have led them to take more courses, rather than due to any difference in aptitude? Project Talent analyzed math scores in the senior

TABLE 3.4

Sex Differences in Verbal Ability: Magnitude and Variability

Study	Age	Sample size		Mean scores		Size of mean difference*	Sex scoring higher	Standard deviation		More variable sex
		Boys	Girls	Boys	Girls			Boys	Girls	
Shipman ETS (1971):										
Peabody PVT (receptive)	3-4	1,198		25.9	26.8	-.07	F	13.10	12.58	M
SRI (1972):										
Reading	5	4,838	4,831	32.57	36.15	-.23	F	14.99	15.37	F
	7	1,768	1,718	55.01	62.09	-.26	F	26.17	26.39	F
Language	5	1,842	1,762	12.09	12.53	-.13	F	3.36	3.26	M
	7	1,774	1,723	18.36	19.69	-.18	F	7.16	7.28	F
Gates (1961): †										
Reading speed	7	938	888	7.37	8.43	-.19	F	5.11	5.73	F
Vocabulary	7	938	888	9.41	11.26	-.26	F	7.18	6.99	M
Comprehension	7	938	888	7.05	8.66	-.26	F	6.06	5.97	M
Reading speed	10	1,027	933	19.63	20.94	-.15	F	8.69	8.25	M
Vocabulary	10	1,027	933	26.36	28.16	-.18	F	10.63	9.04	M
Comprehension	10	1,027	933	22.60	23.64	-.12	F	9.20	7.43	M
Reading speed	13	846	811	20.07	21.49	-.18	F	7.84	7.62	M
Vocabulary	13	846	811	37.15	39.60	-.21	F	11.90	10.72	M
Comprehension	13	846	811	30.49	31.33	-.10	F	8.21	7.22	M
Brimer (1969) (England)	8	584	605	17.60	15.98	.22	M	7.48	6.65	M
	9	639	546	22.36	19.34	.37	M	7.96	8.00	F
	10	616	537	26.80	23.60	.40	M	7.84	8.05	F
	11	537	515	29.20	26.88	.30	M	6.91	8.29	F

(continued)

TABLE 3.4 *(cont.)*

Study	Age	Sample size		Mean scores		Size of mean difference*	Sex scoring higher	Standard deviation		More variable sex
		Boys	Girls	Boys	Girls			Boys	Girls	
Svensson (1971) (Sweden):										
School I – 1961	13	2,950	2,878	87.54	89.61	-.12	F	16.79	16.36	M
School II – 1961	13	1,499	1,578	88.69	90.18	-.09	F	16.78	15.99	M
School I – 1966	13	731	769	114.58	123.32	-.30	F	29.22	27.97	M
School II – 1966	13	3,097	3,047	54.61	58.36	-.23	F	15.77	15.50	M
Droege (1967); GATB (verbal subscore)	14	3,398	3,680	93.20	95.55	-.19	F	11.97	12.16	F
	15	3,348	3,491	96.60	100.03	-.26	F	12.83	13.47	F
	16	3,229	3,395	98.70	102.93	-.29	F	13.57	14.11	F
	17	3,028	3,139	100.19	103.38	-.21	F	14.22	14.80	F

*The difference between the means has been divided by the weighted mean of the standard deviations of the two sex distributions; that is, the difference is expressed as a standard score.

†We are reporting three of the seven ages studied.

TABLE 3.5
Quantitative Ability

Study	Age and N	Difference	Comment
Potter & Levy 1968	41 mos (29)	None	Enumeration (point once and only once at each member of a set)
	47 mos (29)	Girls	Enumeration
Shipman 1971	3-4 (1,395)	Girls	Enumeration, low SES sample
Farnham-Diggory 1970	4-9 (282)	None	Mathematical synthesis tasks
SRI 1972	5, 7 (6,607)	Girls	Quantitative scores (New York Alpha)
Ginsburg & Rapoport 1967	6, 11 (76)	None	Estimating proportions
Parsley et al. 1963	7-13 (5,020)	None	Arithmetic Fundamentals and Reasoning Tests
B. Ross 1966	7, 9, 11, 13, 15 (80)	None	3 tests of probability estimating
D. Pedersen et al. 1968	8 (24)	None	WISC arithmetic subtest
Hopkins & Bibelheimer 1971	8, 10, 12, 13 (354)	None	Nonlanguage IQ: California Test of Mental Maturity (longitudinal)
L. Siegel 1968	9, 11 (192)	None	Digit-processing tasks
T. Hilton & Berglund 1971	10, 12, 14, 16 (1,320)	Boys	STEP math test, at 12, 14, 16 yrs only; SCAT quantitative test, at 16 yrs only (longitudinal sample of college-bound students)
	10, 12, 14, 16 (539)	Boys	STEP math test, at 16 yrs only; SCAT quantitative test, at 16 yrs only
		Girls	SCAT quantitative, at 10 yrs only (longitudinal sample of vocational students)
Cicirelli 1967	11 (609)	None	California Arithmetic Test
Keating & Stanley 1972	12-13 (396)	Boys	SAT math, Math Level I Achievement Test (gifted sample)
Svensson 1971	13 (8,905)	Boys	Math achievement, math reasoning (Swedish)
	13 (6,144)	Boys	Math achievement, math reasoning (Swedish elementary school sample)
Droege 1967	14, 17 (7,078)	Boys	General Aptitude Test Battery (GATB): Numerical Aptitude (longitudinal)
	15, 17 (6,839)	Boys	GATB: Numerical Aptitude (at 15 yrs only, longitudinal)
	16, 17 (6,624)	None	GATB: Numerical Aptitude (longitudinal)
	17 (6,167)	Boys	GATB: Numerical Aptitude

(continued)

TABLE 3.5 *(cont.)*

Study	Age and N	Difference	Comment
Flanagan et al. 1961	14, 17 (4,545)	Boys	Mathematics ability
Walberg 1969	16-17 (1,050)	Boys	Physics achievement (physics students)
Backman 1972	17 (2,925)	Boys	Mathematics (Project Talent battery)
Monday et al. 1966-67	18 (238,145)	Men	Math subscore of ACT
Rosenberg & Sutton-Smith 1964	19 (377)	None	Quantitative score, ACE
Rosenberg & Sutton-Smith 1969	19 (1,013)	Men	Quantitative score, ACE
Sutton-Smith et al. 1968	19 (1,055)	None	Quantitative score, ACE
Rosenberg & Sutton-Smith 1966	18-20 (600)	Men	Quantitative score, ACE
Bieri et al. 1958	18-21 (76)	Men	SAT Quantitative
Jacobson et al. 1970	18-21 (276)	None	Digit symbol test of WAIS
Sarason & Minard 1962	18-21 (96)	None	Digit symbol subtest of WAIS
Very 1967	18-21 (355)	Men	Arithmetic Reasoning, Division, Mathematical Aptitude, General Reasoning, Moore-Castore Arithmetic, Moore-Castore Algebra
		None	Addition, Subtraction, Arithmetic Computation, Number Arrangement, Ship Destination

year of high school, after equating the two sexes on the number of math courses taken. The boys still emerged with substantially higher average scores, a finding that suggests it is not merely the amount of training the two sexes have received that is responsible for the difference in their performance at this age.

During adolescence, boys' superiority in math tends to be accompanied by better mastery of scientific subject matter and greater interest in science. The two disciplines are of course closely linked in that science relies heavily upon math in formulating its problems and finding their solutions. One may ask whether male superiority in science is a derivative of greater math abilities or whether both are a function of a third factor. In this connection, some findings of the Harvard Project Physics (Walberg 1969) are interesting. Physics achievement tests were given to a large sample of high school students. On the portions of the test calling for visual-spatial skills, the male physics students did better; on verbal test items, female physics

TABLE 3.6

Large-Sample Studies of Quantitative Ability: Magnitude of Sex Differences and Within-Sex Variability

Study	Age	Sample size		Mean scores		Size of mean difference*	Sex scoring higher	Standard deviation		More variable sex
		Boys	Girls	Boys	Girls			Boys	Girls	
SRI (1972)	5	1,799	1,724	25.46	27.40	-.12	F	7.93	7.35	M
	7	1,596	1,488	38.44	40.58	-.16	F	13.28	12.16	M
Svensson (1971) (Sweden):										
School I – 1961	13	2,950	2,878	41.53	39.85	.17	M	9.72	9.07	M
School II – 1961	13	1,499	1,578	41.72	40.02	.17	M	9.73	9.34	M
School I – 1966	13	731	769	35.14	34.09	.08	M	13.02	12.71	M
School II – 1966	13	3,097	3,047	37.26	35.02	.16	M	13.67	12.80	M
Droege (1967); GATB (numerical subscore)	14	3,398	3,680	97.70	100.19	.18	F	13.57	13.81	F
	15	3,348	3,491	99.37	101.74	.16	F	14.15	14.32	F
	16	3,229	3,395	102.76	103.08	.02	F	15.26	15.15	M
	17	3,028	3,139	106.54	105.70	.05	M	14.36	14.60	F
Project Talent; Flanagan et al. (1961)	14	1,152	990	7.14	5.81	.36	M	3.92	3.33	M
	17	1,153	1,250	11.58	7.86	.64	M	6.25	5.34	M
ACT 1966 norm manual (math subscore); Monday et al. (1966-67)	18	133,882	104,263	21.10	18.0	.47	M	6.3	6.2	M

*The difference between the means has been divided by the weighted mean of the standard deviations of the two sex distributions; that is, the difference is expressed as a standard score.

students obtained higher scores. It would appear that verbal and spatial factors account for some of the variance in science achievement.

Factor analysis of mathematical aptitude tests suggests that a similar situation exists in mathematics. Mathematical ability is not a unitary factor (see Smith 1964[R] and Werdelin 1958[R] for reviews). Moreover, a space factor emerges as an element in mathematical skills for boys but not for girls (Werdelin 1961[R], Mellone 1944[R]). Evidently there are different ways to attack mathematical problems, and individuals differ in the cognitive skills they characteristically bring to bear on such problems. In a letter, Steven Vandenberg* tells us: "Rumor has it that Karl Pearson did everything by algebra and Fisher thought geometrically, and that that was the reason why they were not on speaking terms even though they had offices in the same place." It is evident that more needs to be understood about such differences in "mathematical styles" before we can hope to understand sex differences in mathematical ability.

Spatial Ability and Disembedding

Spatial ability, even more than verbal or quantitative ability, is difficult to define. Should it include, for example, skill in auditory localization? Accurate maintenance of size-distance constancy? Tactual recognition of objects as they change orientation in space? Spatial ability first emerged as a distinct factor in the early work of Thurstone. His Primary Mental Abilities test had a Spatial subtest, including the Flags test. In this test, each item has a standard American flag, and a set of four from which the subject must choose those that are the same figure rotated in the plane of the page; false choices are mirror-reversals. A later version of the PMA includes items in which the subject is given a set of segments of figures and is asked to identify which segments would fit together to form the standard, if rotated in two-dimensional space. Other spatial tests have involved such stimuli as (1) drawings of systems of gears, with the subject being asked to determine what motion in one part of the system would be produced by a given motion in another part of the system, and (2) a two-dimensional representation of a three-dimensional pile of blocks, with the subject's task being to estimate accurately the number of surfaces visible from a different perspective than his own. The Block Design subtest of the WISC has been used as a measure of spatial ability, as have mazes and form boards.

In our earlier review (Maccoby 1966a[R]), following Witkin's interpretation, we listed the Embedded Figures Test and the Rod and Frame Test under "Field Dependence"—a cognitive style variable that was thought to reflect analytic ability. Both these tests require the subject to separate

---

* Steven Vandenberg, University of Colorado, 1974.

TABLE 3.7
Spatial (Visual, Nonanalytic) Ability

Study	Age and N	Difference	Comment
Shipman 1971	3-4 (1,460)	Girls	Reproduction of geometric forms
	3-4 (1,411)	None	Identifying matching geometric shapes
	3-4 (1,129)	None	Seguin Form Board
Kraynak & Raskin 1971	3-4 (64)	None	Matching 2- and 3-dimensional geometric stimuli
Kubzansky et al. 1971	3-6 (64)	None	Size constancy with 2- and 3-dimensional stimuli
Fishbein et al. 1972	3-9 (120)	None	Matching photos to room from different orientations
Strayer & Ames 1972	4-5 (40)	None	Latencies or number of errors on form board, copying geometric shapes
G. Burton 1973	4-7 (111)	None	Linear patterning tasks
Caldwell & Hall 1970	4-5, 7-8 (144)	None	Match forms to standard under different orientations
Brainerd & Huevel 1974	5-6 (120)	None	Choosing 2-dimensional drawings to represent 3-dimensional objects
Cronin 1967	5-6 (216)	None	Discrimination of triangles and mirror image reversals of them
Hecox & Hagan 1971	5-7 (52)	None	Proportion estimations matching a standard
Farnham-Diggory 1970	5-9 (332)	Girls	Maplike synthesis (1 of 2 experiments)
Conners et al. 1967	5, 6, 9, 12 (80)	None	Identification of geometric figures by touch
Coryell 1973	5, 7, 9 (90)	None	Matching pictures to room objects in different orientations
Kershner 1971	6 (160)	None	Reproducing spatial relations of cars and houses
A. Long & Looft 1972	6-12 (144)	None	Distinguishing right from left, east from west, top from bottom
Smothergill 1973	6-7, 9-10, 18-21 (60)	None	Localization of spatial target
Kaess 1971a	6, 8, 10 (54)	None	Shape identification under different orientation
Wohlwill 1965	6, 9, 13, 16 (96)	None	Perception of relative distance in third dimension
Ruble & Nakamura 1972	7-10 (56)	None	Assembling puzzles

(continued)

TABLE 3.7 *(cont.)*

Study	Age and N	Difference	Comment
Kaess 1971b	7, 9, 11, 18 (80)	None	Form constancy with rotated shapes
Keogh 1971	8-9 (135)	Boys None	Reproduced patterns by walking more accurately Copying geometric patterns
Nash 1973	11 (105)	None	Differential Aptitudes Test (DAT): Space Relations
	14 (102)	Boys	DAT
Stafford 1961	13-17 & adults (232)	Boys & men	Identical Blocks Test
Droege 1967	14-17 (26,708)	Boys	Spatial aptitude (General Aptitude Test Battery)
Flanagan et al. 1961	14, 17 (4,545)	Boys	2- and 3-dimensional visual spatialization (Project Talent Test Battery)
Backman 1972	17 (2,925)	Boys	Visual Reasoning (Project Talent Test Battery)
Brissett & Nowicki 1973	18-21 (80)	None	Angle-matching task
Kidd & Cherymisin 1965	18-21 (100)	Men	Reversal rate test
Very 1967	18-21 (355)	Men	Cards, cubes, spatial orientation, spatial relationships
A. Davies 1965	20-59 (540)	Men	Maze performance
	60-79 (540)	None	Maze performance

an element from its background, ignoring the latter, and in this sense it is analytic. However, the EFT loads heavily on a spatial factor when it is included in a battery with other visual-spatial tests (e.g. Goodenough and Karp 1961[R]). Sherman (1967)[R] has argued that it is the spatial component of these tests, rather than their analytic component, that is responsible for sex differences in performance on them. Another issue is whether sex differences in spatial ability are confined to the visual modality. With these questions in mind, we discuss separately the few studies that deal with nonvisual spatial skills, and have divided the visual-spatial tasks into two groups: those that appear to call for analytic processes as well, and those that do not.

In our earlier review (Maccoby 1966) we noted that visual-spatial ability, as measured by the spatial subtests of the Differential Aptitudes Test and the Primary Mental Abilities Test, and by mazes, form boards, and block-counting, showed an advantage for boys beginning at about age 6–8.

We have located few recent studies in which these tests have been used. These and studies using a variety of measures that would appear to have a spatial component are charted in Table 3.7. On the whole, they show no sex differences until adolescence, though Keogh (1971), using a sample of moderate size, does report higher scores for boys at age 8–9. Two studies (Droege 1967, Flanagan et al. 1961) have given space-factor tests to large samples of high school students. They both find that boys' superiority on this factor increases through high school, and that the boys' scores exceed the girls' by at least .40 standard score units, on the average, by the end of this time.

Table 3.8 shows studies using versions of the Embedded Figures Test, the Rod and Frame Test, the Body Adjustment Test, and Block Design.

The original Gottschaldt and Witkin Embedded Figures tests have been modified for use with younger subjects, and children's forms (CEFT, PEFT) have been given to children of preschool age by several researchers (Reppucci 1971, Shipman 1971, Sitkei and Meyers 1969, and S. Coates 1972, 1973). In only one of these (Coates) was a sex difference found, and this was in favor of girls. An unpublished study with French kindergarten children* found higher scores for boys on an EFT adapted for this age level. On balance, however, the EFT studies do not show a sex difference for ages 3–5, and the same is true for the early school years. Beginning at about age 8 and continuing into adulthood, studies become inconsistent. A substantial number of studies find no sex difference, but when differences are found, they show higher scores for boys and men into adulthood, with a suggestion that the differences may disappear in old age (D. Schwartz and Karp 1967). Some of the inconsistencies in Table 3.8 may possibly be accounted for by the inclusion of studies with populations from nonindustrial cultures. This issue will be discussed below. Meanwhile, it should simply be noted that not all the inconsistencies can be accounted for by variations in any obvious sample characteristics.

Tables 3.7 and 3.8 have shown that visual-spatial tasks that involve disembedding, and those that do not, have a similar developmental course. The male advantage emerges in early adolescence and is maintained in adulthood for both kinds of tasks. Thus there is no indication, if one considers simply the timetable for change, that the disembedding process contributes anything to the sex difference, beyond what would be produced by the visual-spatial component of the embedded figures tasks or the Rod and Frame test. However, comparison of the two tables does not provide a definitive answer to whether there is such a contribution. What is needed is tasks that are not visual-spatial but that do involve disembedding (or "decontextualization," as it is sometimes called). Witkin and his colleagues

---

* E. Vurpillot, Laboratoire de Psychologie Expérimentale et Comparée de Paris–Sorbonne, personal communication, 1972.

TABLE 3.8
Spatial (Visual-Analytic) Ability

Study	Age and N	Difference	Comment
Reppucci 1971	2 (48)	None	Preschool Embedded Figures Test (PEFT)
Shipman 1971	3-4 (1,288)	None	PEFT
Sitkei & Meyers 1969	3-4 (100)	None	Design discrimination
S. Coates 1972	3-5 (247)	Girls	PEFT
S. Coates 1973	4-5 (53)	Girls	PEFT; trend, $p < .1$
Mumbauer & Miller 1970	4-5 (64)	None	Children's Embedded Figures Test (CEFT)
Bigelow 1971	5-10 (160)	None	CEFT
D. Goodenough & Eagle 1963	5, 8 (96)	None	PEFT
Curry & Dickson 1971	5, 8, 11 (24)	None	Visual Closure Subtest of ITPA
Hartmann et al. 1972	6-9 (50)	None	Mueller-Lyer Illusion
V. C. Crandall & Lacey 1972	6-12 (50)	None	EFT
V. J. Crandall & Sinkeldam 1964	6-12 (50)	None	Embedded Figures Test (EFT), time measures
Schubert & Cropley 1972	6-15 (211)	None	Block Design subtest of WISC
J. Kagan et al. 1964	7 (180)	None	Hidden Figures Test (HFT)
Keogh & Ryan 1971	7 (44)	Boys	Rod and Frame Test (RFT); pattern walking test
		None	CEFT; pattern drawing test
Ruble & Nakamura 1972	7-10 (56)	None	Gerard rod-and-frame test
Wapner 1968	7-16 (192)	Boys	Apparent Vertical and Apparent Body Axis Position
Stouwie et al. 1970	8-9 (156)	None	EFT, time measures
Corah 1965	8-11 (60)	None	CEFT
	Adults (120)	Men	Solutions faster

(continued)

TABLE 3.8 *(cont.)*

Study	Age and N	Difference	Comment
Witkin et al. 1967	8, 13 (47)	Boys	RFT (longitudinal)
	8, 10-13, 15, 17-21 (515)	Boys None	RFT, EFT Body Adjustment Test (BAT)
	10, 14, 17 (51)	None	RFT (longitudinal)
Bergan et al. 1971	9 (48)	Boys	Block Design, WISC
Immergluck & Mearini 1969	9 11, 13 (120)	Girls None	EFT EFT
MacArthur 1967	9-15 (167)	None	EFT (Eskimo sample)
Saarni 1973	10-15 (64)	Boys	RFT
Berry 1966	10–adult (122)	None	Kohs Blocks, Morrisby Shapes, EFT (Eskimo sample)
Nash 1973	11 (105)	None	Group Embedded Figures Test (GEFT)
	14 (102)	Boys	GEFT
Okonji 1969	12 (33)	Boys	CEFT (rural Nigerian sample)
	21-27 (25)	Men None	RFT (Univ. of Nigeria sample) EFT
	Adults (65)	Men None	CEFT (rural Nigerian sample) RFT
Weinberg & Rabinowitz 1970	12-19 (48)	None	Block Design, WISC
Fiebert 1967	12, 15, 18 (90)	Boys	RFT, CEFT (deaf sample)
J. Silverman et al. 1973	14-17 (16)	None	RFT (patients with behavior disorders)
	13-20 (15)	Boys	RFT (siblings of above sample)
	18-22 (30)	Men	RFT
F. Gross 1959	17-25 (110)	Men	RFT
Stuart et al. 1965	17-25 (64)	None	EFT
Green 1955	17-40 (60)	Men	RFT (2 of 3 series) Tilting Room Test (2 of 4 series)
		None	EFT
D. Schwartz & Karp 1967	17, 30-39 58-82 (120)	Men None	RFT, EFT, BAT RFT, EFT, BAT

(continued)

TABLE 3.8 *(cont.)*

Study	Age and *N*	Difference	Comment
Bieri 1960	18-21 (60)	None	EFT
Bieri et al. 1958	18-21 (110)	Men	EFT
Bogo et al. 1970	18-21 (97)	Men	RFT (portable)
A. Goldstein & Chance 1965	18-21 (26)	Men None	EFT, faster discovery times, first 10 items Discovery times, last 10 items
Kato 1965	18-21 (60)	Men	RFT
Morf et al. 1971	18-21 (82)	None Men	RFT, trials 1-8 RFT, trials 9-16
Morf & Howitt 1970	18-21 (44)	None	RFT
Oltman 1968	18-21 (163)	None	RFT (standard and portable)
Sarason & Minard 1962	18-21 (96)	Men	Block Design subtest of WISC
Vaught 1965	18-21 (180)	Men	RFT
Willoughby 1967	18-21 (76)	None	HFT (Hidden Figures Test)
Gerace & Caldwell 1971	25 (40)	Men	Ames distorted room (portable model)
Blum et al. 1972	64, 84 (54)	None	Block Design (Wechsler-Bellevue)

(1968) have devised a battery of such tests for blind subjects, and used them with 20 congenitally blind and 20 sighted subjects aged 12–18. They found:

Tactual block design test	No sex difference
Tactual embedded figures test	No sex difference
Auditory embedded figures	No sex difference
Tactile matchstick problem	Girls superior

Witkin notes that the last result is the opposite of the sex differences usually obtained on the visual form of this task.

In this one small-sample study, then, it would appear that girls' difficulty with disembedding may be specific to visual-spatial tasks. Or, to put a somewhat different interpretation on the matter, it may be that, as Sherman has suggested, their poorer performance on visual "field independence" tasks may simply be a reflection of their lesser visual-spatial ability and have nothing to do with "decontextualization." It is risky to pin this conclusion to a single study, however, and we must look further for work in which nonvisual disembedding has been studied.

One may interpret the studies of selective listening as measures of auditory disembedding. In these studies, a subject is asked to listen to one voice and ignore another. If he is unable to separate the desired message from its auditory context, he will make intrusive errors. That is, he will interpolate words spoken by the undesired voice into his report of the content spoken by the target voice. In a series of studies of selective listening with children ranging in age from 5 to 15 (Maccoby 1969[R]), no sex differences have been found. Thus the male advantage in visual decontextualization does not appear to generalize to the auditory modality.

It is difficult to distinguish disembedding from other forms of "analytic" responding. The matchstick problems referred to above are a good case in point. These tasks were used by Guilford (1957)[R]. In these problems the subject is given a figure made out of matchsticks in the form of a lattice; he is asked to remove (or change the position of) a specified number of matches, to form a specified new figure. The test is similar to the Embedded Figures Test in that the subject must free himself from the binding organizational properties of the initial configuration and discover new organizational properties inherent in portions of the figure. Performance on the visual form of this task is substantially correlated with the EFT (Guilford 1957[R]; Witkin et al. 1962[R]). In Guilford's work, this test is also correlated with others, such as the Dunker insight problems, which call for the subject's breaking a preestablished set. Guilford identifies a factor contributing to performance on a variety of such tests as the "adaptive flexibility" factor.

The nonvisual measures of disembedding frequently involve restructuring, or set-breaking, and therefore relate to the larger issue of analytic abilities, as well as to the narrower issue of perceptual "field independence." Set-breaking, in its turn, is related to the ability to inhibit an initial dominant response while exploring alternative solutions. We therefore turn now to studies of these kinds of "analytic abilities," and will return to the issue of visual-spatial vs. other measures in the course of discussing these studies.

Analytic Abilities

The factor-analytic literature on the dimensions of perceptual and intellectual abilities is voluminous, and we cannot hope to do justice to it here. For our present purposes, the important point is that a number of workers have identified some aspect of set-breaking, or restructuring, as an important dimension of problem-solving ability; furthermore, it has frequently been reported that males perform better than females on tests calling for this ability. For example, as we noted in Chapter 2, Broverman et al. (1968)[R] distinguish "simple, overlearned, repetitive" behaviors (at which females are alleged to be superior) from tasks that involve inhibition of initial response tendencies, mediation of higher mental processes, and production of novel solutions (at which males are alleged to be superior). We have already seen (Chapter 2) that no superiority of males is found in learning tasks that involve inhibition of already learned responses. However, it is conceivable that differences that do not emerge in learning tasks might be found in measures of "abilities." Parlee (1972)[R] has presented some cogent evidence in opposition to the Broverman classification of sex-linked abilities, and our own review in this chapter and Chapter 2 certainly supports the Parlee position. However, the point of interest here is whether males are in fact better at tasks that call for the inhibition of previously learned (or initially probable) response tendencies.

The Stroop color-word test would appear to provide a measure of at least one aspect of this ability. In this test, the subject is given a set of color names, printed in the wrong-color ink. The subject must "read" the page by giving, for each word, the color of the ink, suppressing his strongly established tendencies to read the printed word. In one version of the test, the subject's performance on this task is contrasted with his performance when he needs only to name small color blocks that are the same size as printed words but that do not give conflicting color names. Podell and Phillips (1959)[R], in factor-analyzing the Stroop test along with Witkin's field-independence measures, found that performance on the Stroop was factorially quite independent of the visual-spatial field-independence tests. In the original report by Stroop concerning this test (1935)[R], data are presented separately by sex for three successive samples of college students. It is shown that the sexes are very similar on this task, with no sex difference in the effects of introducing conflicting stimuli for which the response must be inhibited. Thus the Stroop test provides an instance of a set-breaking task (one requiring inhibition of a dominant response) in which no sex difference is found.

Another approach to the measurement of inhibition of initial response tendencies is found in the studies of reflectivity-impulsivity, initiated by Kagan, and usually employing the Matching Familiar Figures test (MFF). The subject must select a match for a standard figure from a set very much like it, but where some of the figures differ in small details from the standard. An "impulsive" child makes errors because he decides too soon that there are no differences, without systematically checking each picture, in all its details, against the standard. J. Kagan et al. (1964), in an early report using this measure, did not find sex differences on either response latency or errors. The work done since that time supports this conclusion (see

TABLE 3.9
Impulsivity, Lack of Inhibition

Study	Age and N	Difference	Comment
W. Mischel & Underwood 1973	2-5 (80)	Boys	Wait shorter time for less preferred reward
Baumrind & Black 1967	3-4 (103)	None	Observer ratings: impulsiveness, impetuousness
Shipman 1971	3-4 (1,399)	None	Matching Familiar Figures (MFF) test (low SES, largely black sample)
	3-4 (1,458)	None	Delay of gratification (low SES, largely black sample)
Friedrichs et al. 1971	3-5 (50)	None	Motor inhibition task
Klaus & Gray 1968	3-7 (80)	None	Delay of gratification (low SES black; longitudinal)
	5 (80)	None	MFF
A. Harrison & Nadelman 1972	4-5 (50)	Boys	MFF, shorter response times, higher error rate; faster responses on 2 motor inhibition tests
Massari et al. 1969	5 (33)	None	Motor inhibition tests
W. C. Ward 1968b	5 (87)	Boys	More errors on impulsivity measure (estimating relative numbers of dots)
		None	Latency to most difficult items on dot test; 4 other impulsivity measures
Meichenbaum & Goodman 1969	5-6 (30)	Girls	MFF, shorter latency
Loo & Wenar 1971	5-6 (40)	Boys	Teacher ratings: impulsivity, low "inhibiting control"
		None	Motor inhibition tests
Sharan (Singer) & Weller 1971	6 (357)	Boys	Faster performance, motor inhibition test (draw a line slowly; Israeli sample)
Yando & Kagan 1968	6 (160)	None	MFF
Wallach & Martin 1970	6, 7, 11 (283)	None	Motoric expansiveness: amount of page used in line drawing (low, middle SES)
	9	Girls	More expansive (middle SES sample only)
J. Kagan et al. 1964	7 (69)	Boys	Shorter latency, Design Recall Test (DRT)
		None	Speed of performance, Draw-a-Line-Slowly Test; DRT, errors
	8 (66)	Boys	DRT, shorter latency
		Girls	DRT, more errors (1 of 2 measures); faster performance, Draw-a-Line-Slowly Test
	8-9 (113)	None	MFF, latency and errors
J. Grusec 1968	8 (40)	None	Delay of gratification

(continued)

TABLE 3.9 *(cont.)*

Study	Age and N	Difference	Comment
S. Goldstein & Siegel 1972	8-9 (84)	None	Effect of delayed or immediate reward
Ault et al. 1972	8-10 (29)	None	MFF, latency and errors
Debus 1970	8-10 (320)	None	MFF, latency and errors
Kopfstein 1973	9 (60)	None	MFF, latency and errors
Bandura & Mischel 1965	9-10 (120)	None	Delay of gratification immediately and 1 month later
W. Mischel & Grusec 1967	9-10 (96)	None	Delay of gratification
Achenbach 1969	10 (40)	None	MFF, latency and errors
Strickland 1972	11-13 (300)	None	Delay of gratification (black and white samples)
Staub 1972	12 (144)	Boys	Choice; immediate gratification
Zytkoskee et al. 1971	14-17 (132)	None	Delay of gratification (biracial sample)
Brissett & Nowicki 1973	18-21 (80)	None	Persistence in no-solution task
Marks 1967	18-21 (722)	None	Degree of stimulus ambiguity S will attempt to interpret (time to reach decision)
Marks 1968	18-21 (760)	None	Self-report: quick, intuitive behavior; lack of forethought

Table 3.9). Some studies report boys as more impulsive; some find girls more impulsive. The majority, working with children ranging in age from 3½ to 11, find no difference. Thus, on this measure, the sexes are much alike in their ability to inhibit an early, impulsive response and engage in whatever "higher mediating processes" are required (in this case, a systematic search) to find the correct answer.

Mischel has developed another approach to the question of whether a person can inhibit a dominant response. In this work, the person is offered a choice between taking a small immediate reward and waiting for a larger reward at a later time. It has been shown that impulsive children—that is, those who choose the immediate rewards—score lower on the average on tests of intellectual ability (Metzner and Mischel 1962[R]). As may be seen in Table 3.9, there is some evidence that boys are more impulsive on this measure during the preschool years, but the sexes do not differ consistently at later ages.

We do not find support, then, for the Broverman contention that girls are less able than boys to inhibit an initial response tendency while engaging in systematic problem solving. Nevertheless, there may be some sex differences in specific elements of the problem-solving processes that do not rely on any generalized ability in response inhibition. We discuss first some studies on "restructuring." There has been little recent work on insight in problem solving, and we must go back to the period before 1966 for evidence on this issue. Luchins (1942)[R] devised a set of problems that presumably tested a subject's ability to break away from a maladaptive set. The problems involved the measurement of liquids with jars of different capacities. One problem might be, for example, "How can you bring from the river exactly six quarts of water, when you have only a four-quart and a nine-quart pail to measure with?" An initial set of such problems calls for a fairly indirect, cumbersome solution. The next problems can be solved by the same indirect method, but there is also a simpler, more direct method. And, finally, a problem is given in which only the more direct method leads to the solution. Luchins reported that male subjects were more successful on these problems than female subjects. Guetzkow (1951)[R] used the same procedure, and distinguished *susceptibility to set* from the *ability to break set.* He found that the two sexes were alike in the degree to which they carried over into the second set of problems the cumbersome approach that had been successful in the first set. But male subjects were more able to break away from this set and use a different approach when the first approach no longer succeeded. Guetzkow also used the Dunker two-string problem and found male superiority in restructuring for this problem as well. It is worth noting that Guetzkow found success in restructuring on his two tasks to be correlated with performance on embedded figures tests but not related to measures of verbal fluency.

Sweeney (1953)[R] used a wider variety of problems (with college-age subjects), some calling for restructuring and some not. He found:

Verbal "trick" problems (requiring breaking set)	No sex difference
Tool problems (verbal, adapted from Dunker)	Men superior
Verbal posers (including verbal form of a Luchins-jar problem)	Men superior
Figural problems (including matchsticks) calling for breaking set	Men superior (trend in one study; significant in second study)
"Extension problems" (no set-breaking required)	No sex difference

Three of Sweeney's set-breaking tests were verbal; one of them did not yield a sex difference, two did. In attempting to solve the "verbal posers," some subjects reported that they employed visual imagery, and the question is whether visual-spatial ability contributes to the solution of these problems even though they are stated in verbal terms. However, an independent measure of spatial visualization did not correlate more strongly with the tests requiring restructuring than it did with those involving no restructuring, and the correlations were generally low, so that Sweeney concluded that restructuring and spatial visualization were independent elements in the solution of these problems.

Nakamura (1958)[R] used the Sweeney tests and several other tests, and found that his male subjects (again, of college age) did better on both the tests requiring restructuring and those not requiring restructuring, with no greater superiority on the one than the other. His study, then, is negative evidence for the hypothesis that restructuring per se primarily distinguishes the problem-solving ability of the two sexes. He did find that, although the women in his sample were more conforming than the men (on an Asch-type study of social influence), their conformity did not account for the differences in problem solving; when conformity was held constant statistically, the sex difference remained.

Cunningham (1965)[R] used the Luchins jars, and also a verbal restructuring test ("alphabet mazes") involving the formation and then breaking of a set for a given problem-solving strategy. Cunningham's subjects were younger (ages 7–12). The boys in his study did better than the girls on breaking set in the Luchins-jar problem, but not on alphabet mazes.

A well-known task calling for breaking set in a verbal context is the game of Anagrams. The subject must spell as many words as he can from a set of letters; once he has spelled one word, he must break up the configuration formed by that word in order to rearrange the letters into a new word. Podell and Phillips (1959)[R], working only with male subjects, included such a task in the battery they factor-analyzed and found that the loadings for the anagrams task were either close to zero (one sample) or negative (another sample) on the visual-spatial factor defined by mazes, block design, and an Embedded Figures Test. Similarly, Guilford found that a test calling for discovery of camouflaged words was not related to his "adaptive flexibility" factor. The implication of these findings is that there is no reason to expect the sex difference on visual-spatial disembedding tasks to be replicated with verbal tasks. There are a number of studies in which the sexes have been compared with respect to their skill at anagrams (see Table 3.10). Although not all studies find a sex difference, those that do report superiority for girls. It would appear that set-breaking is not a process that generalizes across tasks, and girls appear to find it relatively easy to restructure when the thing to be restructured is a word.

The term "analytic style" has been used with still another meaning. In a widely used procedure (Sigel's sorting task), the subject is shown three objects, or pictures of three objects, and asked to say which two "go together." He may group on any basis he chooses. There are three common types of groupings: *relational* (putting together objects that have a functional relationship to one another, such as an apple and a paring knife); *inferential* (putting together objects that belong to the same more inclu-

TABLE 3.10
Anagrams

Study	Age and N	Difference	Comment
Lipton & Overton 1971	7, 9, 11, 13 (80)	None	Anagrams task
H. Stevenson et al. 1968a	8-12 (475)	Girls	Anagrams task
	12-14 (256)	Girls None	Anagrams task (low IQ sample) Anagrams task (middle, high IQ samples)
H. Stevenson et al. 1968b	8-14 (529)	Girls	Anagrams task
H. Stevenson & Odom 1965	9, 11 (318)	None	Anagrams task
H. Stevenson et al. 1970	14 (96)	Girls	Anagrams task, 1 of 2 testing conditions (educable retardates)
Feather 1968	18-21 (60)	None	Anagrams task
Feather 1969b	18-21 (167)	None	Anagrams task
Mendelsohn & Griswold 1967	18-21 (181)	None	Anagrams task

sive class, such as apple and banana because they are both fruit); and
descriptive-analytic. The last type of grouping is based upon similarity
with respect to some selected detail; for example, a chair and a dog might
be grouped together because they both have four legs. This grouping has
been termed "analytic" because it involves responding to a part of an object
rather than to the whole, and ignoring attributes of the objects not relevant
to the basis for grouping. In a set of five studies with children ranging from
age 3 to age 16, no sex differences in the use of analytic-descriptive groupings have been found (A. Davis 1971, Kuhn 1972, Shipman 1971, K. White
1971, and Sharan and Weller 1971). In only one study (Stanes 1973), with
first-graders, was a sex difference found, with boys giving more analytic
responses.

To recapitulate: it is well known that males tend to score higher than
females on tests of "field independence" (embedded figures; Rod and
Frame test). It has been alleged that field independence forms part of a
larger cluster of abilities, sometimes called analytic abilities. A field-independent individual is alleged to be skilled in a large range of tasks that
require ignoring a task-irrelevant context or focusing upon only selected
elements of a stimulus display. Field independence has also been thought
to imply an ability to restructure a problem-solving situation—to inhibit
a well-established response in the interests of breaking away from an un-
productive set and taking a fresh approach to a problem. In our review we
have found the following:

1. Boys and men do perform better than girls and women on tests of field independence in many studies, but by no means all; the sex difference does not emerge consistently until approximately the beginning of adolescence. The development of sex differences in field independence parallels that in nonanalytic spatial abilities.

2. The sex difference in field independence is quite narrowly confined to visual-spatial tasks. In other tasks that call for ignoring an irrelevant context or for focusing upon an element rather than a whole gestalt, sex differences are not found. Specifically, the sexes are essentially alike on tests of selective listening (when potentially interfering messages must be ignored) and in tactual tasks requiring disembedding.

3. There is no reliable tendency for either sex to be generally more able to inhibit a dominant response while exploring potentially more successful solutions (Stroop 1935[R], measure of the reflective-impulsive dimension).

4. The use of an "analytic style" in grouping (grouping on the basis of isolated features of objects) is not more common in one sex than the other.

5. The results on set-breaking, or restructuring, are equivocal. On some verbal tasks calling for restructuring (e.g. anagrams) females do very well, and it is tempting to conclude that males are superior only on set-breaking tasks that are visual-spatial. Such a conclusion would be oversimplified, however. Judging from early studies, men appear to have an advantage on most of the Dunker and Luchins-jar kinds of problems, whether the problems are stated verbally or not. There are enough instances, however, in which the sexes do not differ on tasks that seem to call for restructuring that we cannot feel confident that set-breaking per se is the factor distinguishing the performance of the sexes. There is an elusive element in the sex differences on restructuring that we do not feel has been adequately identified.

Concept Mastery and Reasoning

Studies of concept formation overlap with studies of verbal and quantitative ability. Piagetian studies of conservation of number, mass, volume, etc., for example, are sometimes used as measures of readiness for math training in the early school years. And a number of concept-formation tasks are verbal in the sense that they require the child to know the meaning of relational terms such as "more," "longest," etc. The concept-formation tasks that focus specifically on the subject's speed of learning a concept, or the conditions governing the rate of learning, have been summarized in the learning section of Chapter 2. Table 3.11 shows studies that assess subjects' level of performance on Piagetian tasks, including conservation, transitivity, seriation, class inclusion, and other grouping problems.

As Table 3.11 shows, the research on Piagetian tasks is remarkably consistent in finding similar performance in the two sexes. The majority of studies have been done on conservation tasks, most of which are appro-

TABLE 3.11
Conceptual Level

Study	Age and N	Difference	Comment
K. Nelson 1971	3-9 mos (180)	None	Object constancy (visual tracking task)
D. Miller et al. 1970	6, 8, 10, 12, 14, 18 mos (84)	None	Object constancy (visual tracking task)
LeCompte & Gratch 1972	9, 12, 18 mos (36)	None	Object transformation tasks
Clarke-Stewart 1973	12-14 mos (36)	None	Uzgiris-Hunt Series: object permanence, schema development, object relations
Denney 1972b	2-4 (108)	None	Groupings of cardboard figures
Denney 1972a	2, 4, 6, 8, 12, 16 (96)	None	Groupings of colored blocks
A. Caron 1966	3-4 (192)	Girls	Far transposition
Shipman 1971	3-4 (1,274)	None	Numerical correspondence
Friedrichs et al. 1971	3-5 (50)	None	Object sorting
L. Siegel 1971	3-5 (77)	None	Equivalence, conservation, ordination, seriation
Lloyd 1971	3-8 (80)	Boys	Conservation of number with bricks (Yoruba sample)
		None	Conservation of number with candies
L. Siegel 1972	3-9 (415)	None	Seriation
Rothenberg 1969	4-5 (210)	None	Conservation of number
Brainerd 1972	4-6 (155)	None	Conservation of number
King 1971	4-6 (47)	None	Conservation of length
Pratoomraj & Johnson 1966	4-7 (128)	None	Conservation of substance
Kuhn 1972	4, 6, 8 (87)	None	Object classification
Curcio et al. 1972	5-6 (67)	None	Conservation tasks
Kaufman 1971	5-6 (103)	Girls	Battery of 13 Piagetian tasks
Moynahan & Glick 1972	5-6 (96)	Boys	Conservation of length, number, weight, and continuous quantity
Peters 1970	5-6 (131)	None	Conservation of number, difference, and area object-sorting task

(continued)

TABLE 3.11 *(cont.)*

Study	Age and N	Difference	Comment
Rothenberg & Orost 1969	5-6 (20)	None	Conservation of number
Roll 1970	5-7 (87)	None	Conservation of number (Colombian sample)
Roodin & Gruen 1970	5-7 (72)	None	Transitivity judgments
Wei et al. 1971	5, 7 (80)	None	4 Piagetian classification tasks
Gruen & Vore 1972	5, 6, 8, 10 (40)	None	Conservation of number, continuous quantity, and weight
P. Miller 1973	5, 8 (100)	None	Conservation of liquid
Youniss & Murray 1970	5, 8 (64)	None	Transitivity judgments of stick lengths
Snow & Rabinovitch 1969	5-13 (97)	None	Conjunctive and disjunctive card sorting
Figurelli & Keller 1972	6 (48)	None	Conservation (black sample)
Murray 1972	6 (108)	None	Conservation tasks
Goldschmid 1968	6-7 (81)	Boys	10 conservation tasks
Northman & Gruen 1970	6-7 8-9 (60)	None Boys	Equivalence and identity conservation Equivalence and identity conservation
Hooper 1969	6-8 (108)	Boys	Identity and equivalence conservation
Wasik & Wasik 1971	6-9 (117)	None	8 conservation tasks (white and black low SES)
Gelman & Weinberg 1972	6, 7, 8, 11 (80)	None	Liquid conservation and compensation
Furth et al. 1970	6, 8-12 7 (300)	None Girls	Match conjunctive and disjunctive symbols to pictures Match conjunctive and disjunctive symbols to pictures
Brainerd 1973	7-8 (120)	Girls None	Conservation (Canadian sample) Transitivity and class inclusion (Canadian and American samples); conservation (American sample)
	5, 6, 7 (180)	None	Transitivity, conservation, class inclusion (Canadian sample)
Cathcart 1971	7-8 (120)	None	Modes of rationalization for conservation
Brainerd 1971	8, 11, 14 (72)	None	Conservation of density and volume
Elkind et al. 1970	9, 14 (120)	None	Multiple classification

(continued)

TABLE 3.11 *(cont.)*

Study	Age and N	Difference	Comment
Saarni 1973	10-15 (64)	None	Specific gravity, chemical combination
Tisher 1971	12-14 (232)	None	"Formal" vs. "concrete" operational level: solution of scientific problems
Sullivan et al. 1970	12, 14, 17 (120)	None	Hunt and Halverson's Conceptual Level Questionnaire
A. Graves 1972	33 (120)	Men None	Conservation of volume Conservation of mass and weight (black and white minimally educated)

priate for preadolescent subjects. The majority of studies of more complex operations, made with preadolescent and adolescent subjects, have also found no sex differences.

The tests of "formal operations," made with these older subjects, bear a close resemblance to tests of reasoning growing out of psychological systems other than Piaget's. Many reasoning tests, like Piaget's assessments of formal operations, involve asking the subject to formulate and test hypotheses, using evidence to confirm or contradict them. Thus both inductive and deductive reasoning are involved. Studies of reasoning, using a variety of measures, are reported in Table 3.12. Included are studies using tasks that call for serial information processing.

Up to adolescence, studies are consistent in showing an absence of sex differences. In adolescence, the bulk of the evidence continues to show no differences, with certain exceptions. For example, Leskow and Smock (1970) gave three groups of subjects (ages 12, 15, and 18) sets of four numbers and asked them to make up as many license plates with these numbers as they could, using any system they chose. The systems used were analyzed; some of the subjects approached the problem in an unsystematic way that led to the repetition of particular combinations of numbers. Others operated by holding constant a systematic series of numbers. For example, a subject might use one of the numbers in first position, and vary the others; then put another in first position; then hold constant the first two numbers jointly, etc. There were no sex differences in the employment of such strategies. One strategy involved treating the numbers as subsets in mathematical groupings, and there was a trend ($p < .10$) for boys to do this more often. We have been unable to locate studies made since 1966 in which standardized reasoning tests have been given to subjects of high school age or older. The evidence from earlier work is that the sexes do not differ on such measures as the reasoning subtest of the

TABLE 3.12
Reasoning

Study	Age and N	Difference	Comment
Sitkei & Meyers 1969	3-4 (100)	Girls	Pre-Raven Matrices (white low SES sample only)
Goldberg 1966	3-5 (32)	None	Probability judgments
C. Davies 1965	3-9 (112)	Girls None	Probability judgments (age 7 only) Probability judgments (at other ages)
A. Siegel & Kresh 1971	4-8 (80)	None	Matrix completion (black and white)
Daehler 1972	4-7 (192)	None	Inference: 2-trial concept identification task
	8 (42)	None	Inference: 2-trial concept identification task
Scholnick 1971	5-7 (96)	None	Inferences about cue relevance from positive, negative, and mixed information
Lehman 1972	5, 7, 9 (60)	None	Use of relevant vs. irrelevant information in task performance
Jacobs & Vandeventer 1971	6 (61)	None	Double-classification matrices
Beilin 1966	6-7 (236)	None	Use of infralogical strategies in quasi-conservation task
Lesser et al. 1965	6-7 (320)	None	Reasoning subtest of Hunter College aptitude scales for gifted children
Greenberger et al. 1971	6-8 (113)	None	Problem-solving flexibility
McKinney 1973	7 (60)	None	Strategy in problem solving
Shantz 1967a	7, 9, 11 (72)	None	Raven's Progressive Matrices Test; multiple relations test
Eimas 1970	7, 9, 11, 13 (192)	None	Quality of questions asked in matrix solution
B. Ross 1966	7, 9, 11, 13, 15 (140)	Boys None	Predictions in concept probability task: "uneven odds" choice situations "Sure thing" and "even odds" choice situations (deaf and hearing samples)
Calhoun 1972	8-9 (12,350)	Boys	Raven's Progressive Matrices (abbreviated form)
Lamal 1971	8, 10, 12 (72)	None	Use of modeled hypothesis-scanning or constraint-seeking in problem solving
Laughlin et al. 1969	8, 10, 12 (216)	None	20 questions: number and quality of questions
Dusek & Hill 1970	9-10 (72)	Boys Girls	Correct responses, 3-choice probability learning task Variety of response patterns and use of win-stay and lose-shift strategies

(continued)

TABLE 3.12 *(cont.)*

Study	Age and N	Difference	Comment
Roberge & Paulus 1971	9, 11, 13, 15 (263)	None	Paulus Conditional Reasoning Test (if-then problems); Paulus-Roberge Class Reasoning Test
Zern 1971	7, 9-12 (69)	None	Latency and error scores on verbal problems involving multiple negation and decoding numbers to "odd" and "even"
Nuessle 1972	10 (40)	None	Concept identification task: use of consistent hypotheses, efficient use of feedback
		Boys	Shorter time taken to complete problems
H. Stevenson et al. 1968a	12-14 (256)	Boys	Concept of probability tasks (high IQ Ss)
		None	Concept of probability tasks (average and retarded Ss)
	8-12 (475)	None	Concept of probability tasks
Pecan & Schvaneveldt 1970	12-15, 35-45 (40)	Boys & Men	Probability learning
Weinberg & Rabinowitz 1970	12-19 (48)	Boys	Probability task: used maximizing strategy to a greater extent
Leskow & Smock 1970	12, 15, 18 (96)	None	Permutation problems: number of new permutations; use of "holding constant" strategy, trend $(p < .1)$; transformation with subgroups
Ziv 1972	13 (240)	None	Raven Matrix
Frederiksen & Evans 1974	18 (395)	Women	Number of acceptable hypotheses, Formulating Hypotheses Test
		None	Average judged quality and average scale value of hypotheses
Very 1967	18-21 (355)	Women	Logical Reasoning
		None	Deductive Reasoning, Letter Concepts, Inductive Reasoning, Picture Concepts, Letter Reasoning

Primary Mental Abilities test. The two studies with this age group listed in Table 3.12 show an advantage for females, but taking these studies in combination with earlier work, the overall picture remains one of little or no sex difference.

Creativity

In the most common meaning of the word, a "creative" person is one who produces something unique. An inventor who produces a new machine or a scientist who develops and proves a new theory is creative, just as the writer, musician, or graphic artist is when he produces a new work in his own expressive medium. Persons of great talent are, of course, rare, but there are lesser degrees of talent that may be seen in people with widely varying life styles. Creative people have been asked to introspect and describe the nature of the thought processes that go on during periods of artistic or scientific productivity. Wallach and Kogan (1965, p. 289)[R] conclude, after analyzing many such introspections, that the creative process involves "first, the production of associative content that is abundant and that is unique; second, the presence in the associator of a playful, permissive task attitude."

A number of researchers have attempted to measure the fluency and uniqueness of associative content. Guilford has done so in his work on divergent thinking. One of the best known of Guilford's measures is the "Uses" test, in which the subject is asked to list as many uses as possible for a familiar object (such as a brick). Torrance builds tests around the same view of the nature of creativity. He uses, for example, an "Asks" test, in which the subject is given a picture and is asked to write out all the questions he would need to have answered in order to understand the events in the picture. In another Torrance task, the subject is again presented with a picture, but this time is asked to guess at all the possible reasons why the pictured events might be occurring.

It is a far cry from the composer busy at his piano to the subject writing down answers to such test items; yet it is true that creative artists do score better on at least some such tests than matched groups of people who do not give evidence of creativity in their daily lives. (See Wallach 1970[R] for a review of evidence on the validation of creativity tests.)

It is well known that men are much more heavily represented than women in the ranks of outstanding creative artists, writers, and scientists. The question is whether this results from a greater male ability, on the average, to engage in creative thinking, or whether there is something about women's life situations that reduces the likelihood of their achieving creatively even though a creative style of thought is found among them as often as among men.

We have already encountered some work comparing the sexes on some aspects of creative thought. The Piagetian logical reasoning tasks used for testing at the level of formal operations (Table 3.11) and certain other measures of reasoning listed in Table 3.12 call for a form of problem solving in which the person must generate hypotheses to explain a phenomenon, and then either produce or use evidence to assess the truth value of the hypotheses. An important part of the process is, of course, the ability to think of a variety of alternative possibilities, which may then be tested. This aspect of intellectual performance was also discussed in the section on restructuring. No consistent sex differences emerged on the Piagetian tasks or on the other tests of reasoning; the evidence was equivocal on restructuring. We turn now to studies focused more directly on the "production of associative content that is abundant and unique."

TABLE 3.13
Divergent Thinking – Verbal Creativity

Study	Age and N	Difference	Comment
R. Bell et al. 1971	2½ (74)	None	Verbal originality (teacher rating)
R. Gross & Marsh 1970	3-6, 10, 15 (170)	None	Productivity and richness of thinking in construction of designs from geometric forms (black and white samples)
W. C. Ward 1969	4 (55)	None	Total number (fluency) and uniqueness of ideas (Uses, Patterns, and Instances tests)
Lichtenwalner & Maxwell 1969	4-6 (68)	None	Number of different verbal responses to styrofoam objects (Starkweather test)
W. C. Ward 1968a	4-6 (87)	None	Fluency and originality of ideas (Uses, Patterns, and Instances tests)
Cropley & Feuring 1971	6 (69)	None	Torrance Product Improvement Test: flexibility and originality; effects of creativity training
Torrance 1965	6-11 (555)	Boys	Product Improvement Task: originality, at 8 (1 of 2 conditions), 9 (1 of 2 conditions), and 11 yrs (1 of 2 conditions) only
		Boys	Fluency, at 8 yrs only
		Girls	Fluency, flexibility, at 10 yrs only
Ogletree 1971	8-11 (1,165)	Girls	Verbal battery of the Torrance Tests of Creative Thinking (English, German, Scottish samples)
Torrance & Aliotti 1969	10 (118)	Girls	Verbal originality, elaboration, and flexibility scores of Torrance Test (forms A and B)
Klausmeier & Wiersma 1964	10-12 (320)	Girls	Object Uses, flexibility; Plot Titles, fluency; Plot Questions; Expressional Fluency; Object Improvement
		None	Object Uses, fluency; Word Uses, flexibility; Plot Titles, cleverness; Sentence Improvement, metaphor, onomatopoeia
Cicirelli 1967	11 (609)	Girls	Verbal elaboration score of Minnesota Tests of Creative Thinking
		None	Combined verbal fluency-flexibility-originality score
Torrance 1965	11 (50)	Girls	Ask and Guess test: asking questions, causal hypotheses
		None	Consequential hypotheses
	12-13	Boys	Consequences Test, flexibility
	(75)	None	Consequences Test, fluency; Ask-and-Guess Test, Unusual Uses Test, Product Improvement Task (gifted sample)
Dewing 1970	12 (394)	None	Minnesota Tests of Creative Thinking: alternate uses of tin cans, alternate uses of bricks (number and uniqueness of verbal responses)
		None	Imaginative composition on "The Lion Who Couldn't Roar"
Raina 1969	13-15 (180)	Boys	Torrance Test total verbal score (India)

(continued)

TABLE 3.13 *(cont.)*

Study	Age and *N*	Difference	Comment
Frederiksen & Evans 1974	18 (395)	Men	Number of remote consequences (Guilford's Consequences test)
		Women	Number of obvious consequences
Abney 1970	18-21 (50)	Women	Remote Associations Test (RAT) (honors group)
	18-21 (118)	None	RAT (high, average GPAs)
Bieri et al. 1958	18-21 (111)	None	Bricks Test
Gall & Mendelsohn 1967	18-21 (120)	None	Baseline number of solutions, RAT
		Women	Number of solutions following opportunity to free-associate about missed items (no difference in 2 other conditions)
Keillor 1971	18-21 (22)	Women	RAT
Mendelsohn & Griswold 1966	18-21 (223)	None	RAT
Ohnmacht & McMorris 1971	18-21 (74)	Women	RAT

In most work on creativity, two measures are used: the *number* of different ideas produced and the *uniqueness* of the ideas produced. In Guilford's "Uses" test, for example, the response that a brick may be used "to build houses with" would be included as one item in a child's score for the number of uses offered but would not receive weight for uniqueness, since most other children would also mention this item. However, the response "You could write on the sidewalk with it" would contribute to both a number and a uniqueness score.

It should be noted that these tests tend to be verbal by their very nature; some writers (e.g. Bhavnani and Hutt 1972[R]) have equated them with measures of verbal fluency. We feel that a distinction should be made between sheer fluency of verbal output (which may be measured by mean length of utterance, length of papers turned in at school, amount of talking that occurs in social situations, etc.) and the number of different hypotheses or approaches generated in a test of creative thinking. We have summarized the measures of sheer fluency under verbal abilities, and have included in Table 3.13 the measures that might more properly be called measures of "ideational variety" or "hypothesis availability." Nevertheless, it is important to distinguish those measures of creativity that are entirely verbal from those that are not, and we have charted them separately.

As Table 3.13 shows, on verbal tests of creative ability no sex differences are found in the preschool and earliest school years, but from about the age of 7 girls show an advantage in a majority of studies. On nonverbal measures (Table 3.14), no clear trend toward superiority of either sex can be discerned. In general, then, it may be said that tests of creativity reflect the already documented difference between the sexes in verbal skills; clearly, girls and women are at least as able as boys and men to generate a variety of hypotheses and produce unusual ideas. Thus the underrepresentation of women in the ranks of the outstanding creative figures of earlier and present times would not appear to arise from any general deficiency in "the production of associative content that is abundant and unique."

Moral Judgments

We have included moral judgments with intellectual abilities because we believe, with Kohlberg (1964)[R], that these judgments are linked to the person's level of cognitive development while not being identical with it. Moral judgments are distinguished from moral behavior (as measured, for example, in tests of resistance to temptation). Studies with behavioral measures are included in Chapter 6. As Table 3.15 shows, the development of the two sexes with respect to the Kohlberg stages of moral reasoning appears to be quite similar. The finding of Saltzstein et al. (1972) is worth noting, in view of the fact that Turiel has also found* that girls tend to be overrepresented at stage 3—the level of "good boy" or "good girl" morality. The level just below stage 3 involves an orientation toward punishment; the level just above is "law and order" morality. It appears likely that both these levels have a greater element of aggression, and a greater orientation toward power, than stage 3. If so, a greater concentration of girls in stage 3, and of boys in the neighboring classes, would be understandable. However, three studies (Selman 1971a, Keasey 1972, and Weisbroth 1970) find no sex differences in levels of moral judgment, so perhaps an attempt at explanation is superfluous.

So far, we have been giving a descriptive account of the incidence and magnitude of sex differences on a variety of intellectual tasks. Before turning to a discussion of the "why" of these differences, there is one more descriptive issue to be taken up. This is the question of whether one sex is more variable than the other (whether the distributions of scores are different), even in the cases where mean values are the same.

VARIABILITY

The problem of differential variability was raised initially in Terman's work when he identified more boys as gifted (Terman et al. 1925[R]). The excess of boys having IQs over 140 was found on a test where there were no sex differences in the means of large samples; hence it appeared that

* E. Turiel, Harvard University, personal communication, 1973.

TABLE 3.14
Nonverbal Measures of Creativity

Study	Age and N	Difference	Comment
Baumrind & Black 1967	3-4 (103)	None	Observer ratings: imaginativeness, originality of work
Emmerich 1971	4-5 (415)	Boys	Fantasy activity during free play
		Girls	Classroom observations, early fall and late fall: artistic activity during free play (black and white low SES)
	4-5 (596)	Boys	Fantasy activity during free play
		Girls	Classroom observations, early fall and spring: artistic activity during free play (black and white low SES)
Torrance 1965	6-11 (320)	Boys	Picture Construction Test: originality, at 8 yrs (1 of 2 conditions) only; elaboration, at 10 yrs (1 of 2 conditions) only
		Girls	Picture Construction Test: originality, at 6 yrs only; elaboration, at 8, 9 (1 of 2 conditions) 10 (1 of 2 conditions), and 11 yrs (1 of 2 conditions) only
		Boys	Incomplete Figures Test: closure, at 8 yrs (1 of 2 conditions) only
		Girls	Incomplete Figures Test: originality, at 8 yrs only; elaboration, at 10 (1 of 2 conditions) and 11 yrs only; closure, at 11 yrs (1 of 2 conditions) only
	11 (50)	Boys	Parallel Lines Test: originality
		Girls	Elaboration
		None	Flexibility and fluency
	12-13 (75)	Boys	Torrance Tests, figural scores (gifted sample)
Ogletree 1971	8-11 (972)	Girls	Figural battery of the Torrance Tests of Creative Thinking (English, German samples)
	8-11 (193)	None	Figural battery, Torrance Tests (Scottish sample)
Torrance & Aliotti 1969	10 (118)	Boys	Figural flexibility (1 of 2 forms) and originality scores (Torrance Tests)
		Girls	Figural elaboration scores
		None	Figural fluency scores
Cicirelli 1967	11 (609)	None	Torrance Tests, figural scores
Dewing 1970	12 (394)	None	Minnesota Tests of Creative Thinking: Circles, Squares (number and uniqueness of responses)
		None	Teacher and peer ratings
Raina 1969	13-15 (180)	Boys	Torrance Tests, figural scores (India)
Mendelsohn & Griswold 1966	18-21 (223)	Women	Barron-Welsh Art Scale of creative potential

TABLE 3.15
Moral Judgment

Study	Age and N	Difference	Comment
Rhine et al. 1967	2-5 (50)	None	Identifying pictured actions as "good" or "bad"
Irwin & Moore 1971	3-5 (65)	None	"Justice" score, choosing just vs. unjust story endings
Wasserman 1971	4 (180)	Boys	Choice of humanitarian values, trend ($p < .1$) (multiracial lower SES sample)
		Girls	Choice of humanitarian values (multiracial, middle SES sample)
Jensen & Hughston 1971	4-5 (72)	None	Moral judgments
Hebble 1971	6-11 (944)	None	Judgments of "badness" of storied characters, stories varying in intent of actors and severity of physical consequences
Gutkin 1972	6, 8, 10 (72)	None	Moral judgments based on intent of actors in stories
Chandler et al. 1973	7 (80)	None	Judgments: videotaped and verbally presented moral dilemmas, varied as to intent and consequences
Jensen & Rytting 1972	7 (25)	None	Causal explanation: accidents related or unrelated to misdeeds
Lepper 1973	7 (129)	None	Attitudes toward moral offenses
Selman 1971a	8-10 (60)	None	Kohlberg's moral judgment stages
Luria & Rebelsky 1969	10-13 (80)	None	Projective: how deviant child felt before confession and the consequences of his confession
Dlugokinski & Firestone 1973	10, 13 (164)	Girls	Baldwin's test of moral understanding
Aronfreed 1961	11 (122)	Boys	More "internal" responses (projective story completion device)
Keasey 1972	11 (155)	None	Kohlberg's moral judgment stages
Turiel 1973	11, 14 17 (210)	Girls Boys None	Higher moral maturity Higher moral maturity Moral knowledge test
Saltzstein et al. 1972	12 (63)	Girls Boys	Representation at Kohlberg stage 3 Representation at both lowest and highest stages
LeFurgy & Woloshin 1969	12-13 (53)	Girls	More realistic moral judgments
McMichael & Grinder 1966	12-13 (98)	None	Responses of remorse, confession, and restitution to transgression stories (Japanese-American, Hawaiian, Caucasian Ss)
	12-13 (23)	Girls	Confession and restitution (Japanese-American rural sample)

(continued)

TABLE 3.15 *(cont.)*

Study	Age and N	Difference	Comment
Sullivan et al. 1970	12, 14, 17 (120)	None	Kohlberg's moral judgment stages
Porteus & Johnson 1965	14 (235)	Girls	Guilt in response to deviation stories; cognitive level of moral judgments
Coombs 1967	18-21 (369)	Men	Considered property crimes more serious than women did
		Women	Considered abortion a more serious crime than men did
Gorsuch & Smith 1972	18-21 (1,030)	Women	More severe in ratings on Crissman's moral behavior scale
Hass & Linder 1972	18-21 (150)	None	Judgment of guilt in bigamy trial
Rettig 1966	18-21 (160)	None	Predictions of moral behavior from stories
Shaw & Skolnick 1971	18-21 (116)	None	Attribution of responsibility to fictitious male
Walster 1966	18-21 (88)	Women	Judged fictitious male more responsible for seriously injuring a person than demolishing own car
Weisbroth 1970	21-39 (78)	None	Kohlberg's moral judgment stages

boys must be more variable, including more of both unusually high scorers and unusually low scorers. As Miles and Terman noted in the 1954 edition of the Carmichael *Manual,* the method of selection of cases for the Terman study made interpretation of the sex ratios difficult. The initial identification of high-scoring children was made by asking teachers to nominate children they considered to be especially bright; some additional children volunteered for the testing. We know that girls tend to underestimate their own intellectual abilities more than boys do, and so there is danger of sex bias in testing self-selected groups. Both Miles (1954)[R] and Terman and Tyler (1954)[R] reviewed a number of studies to find out whether there was a concentration of either sex among the very high scorers on tests of mental abilities. They concluded that there appeared to be no consistent tendency toward a higher incidence of gifted boys, and that the sex ratios in the gifted range depended on the content of the test.

What about variability in specific abilities? Considering the mean sex differences reported earlier on verbal, spatial, and mathematical tests, it should come as no surprise that there would be a higher incidence of very high-scoring boys on tests emphasizing content in which boys, as a group, do better. Presumably, if one looked for the exceptionally high scorers on verbal tests, one would find more girls. Of course, such results do not necessarily mean that one sex is more variable than the other—the two distributions could have equal standard deviations, with the distribution of one sex simply being displaced upward, yielding more cases above any arbitrary cutting-off point.

We shall first examine what information is available since the work of Miles, and Terman and Tyler, to see whether the new evidence points to a sex difference in variability. If it does, we will then consider the shape of the distributions, to determine whether any difference in variability is determined by one sex having more exceptionally low scores, or exceptionally high scores, or both.

In Tables 3.4 and 3.6, we showed data from studies with large samples, for which information is available on variability as well as mean scores. Beginning with verbal ability, it may be seen that studies of younger children do not show one sex to be consistently more variable than the other. At ages 3–4 (Shipman 1971) girls are more variable on two tests, boys on a third. In the Stanford Research Institute work (ages 5–7) girls tend to be more variable, and this is also the case in the work by Brimer (1969), in England, with children aged 8–11. Gates (1961) finds a fairly consistent picture of greater male variability over the age range 7–13, and this is also true in the work of Svensson in Sweden (1971, with 13-year-olds) and that of ACT norms based on tests with subjects of college age. Droege's work (1967), however, with subjects aged 14–17, consistently finds greater variability among girls, and Project Talent (Flanagan et al. 1961) presents a mixed picture depending on the age of measurement during the high school period. The differences found in variability are not large in an absolute sense. Taken together, the studies do not provide firm support for the hypothesis that males are more variable, although the trend is in this direction for subjects of 12 years or older.

There are fewer studies of quantitative ability that report measures of variability; here there is a fairly consistent trend in the direction of greater male variability, the exception being the work of Droege. In some cases, the difference in variability is substantial, male variability being up to 15 percent and 16 percent greater (Svensson, and Flanagan et al. 1961). We have not tabled the data for spatial ability, since there are only two studies (Droege, and Flanagan et al.) for which variability data are available. Both of these studies had subjects of high school age; both found greater variability among boys, and the difference in standard deviations was of the order of 7 to 8 percent.

In summary, we do find some evidence for greater male variability in numerical and spatial abilities but not consistently in verbal ability. The question is, when differences in variability are found, what does this imply in terms of the incidence of exceptionally high or low scores among the two sexes? Considering first the lower end of the ability scale, studies consistently indicate that more boys than girls suffer from learning deficits.

The greater vulnerability of the male child to anomalies of prenatal development, birth injury, and childhood disease is well known. For documentation, the reader is referred to review papers by Singer et al. (1968)[R], Bentzen (1963)[R], Bledsoe (1961), Garai and Scheinfeld (1968)[R], and Lapouse and Monk (1964). These reviews document a greater incidence among boys of a variety of developmental problems, ranging in severity from enuresis to mental retardation and autism. The incidence rates for the two sexes are substantially different. For example, stuttering is three to four times as common among boys, and reading disabilities are from three to ten times more common for boys, depending on how the disability is defined and what population is studied. The greater vulnerability of boys to this variety of problems, of course, affects the incidence of very low scores on tests of mental abilities. In school systems, children with exceptionally low scores tend to be siphoned off into classes for the educationally handicapped, and these classes may or may not be included in psychometric work. When they are included, or when the cut-off score for taking a child out of the normal classroom is very low, it may be expected that there will be more boys than girls with extremely low scores in a sampling of schoolchildren.

As noted in Table 3.4, Gates found greater variability in reading scores among boys from grades 2 through 7. After examining the distributions of these scores, he reports (1961, p. 432): "The distribution of scores on tests of reading ability shows that a relatively large proportion of boys obtained the lowest scores, without a corresponding increase in the number obtaining top scores." Gates notes that boys outnumbered girls among the lowest scorers by about 2 to 1 in the lower grades, with the ratio decreasing thereafter.

The situation is quite different with respect to mathematical ability. Work by Stanley et al. (1972)[R] on mathematically and scientifically precocious youth is relevant here. In one report (Keating 1972[R]), data are reported for 396 seventh- and eighth-graders who entered a science and math competition. Some of the children were nominated by their teachers as being especially talented, and some volunteered—the competition was well publicized. The subjects took the mathematics portion of the Scholastic Aptitude Test and the Mathematics Achievement Test Level I. The standard deviations of the boys' scores were higher than the girls', and considerably more boys scored at the top of the range. As noted elsewhere (Chapter 4), girls tend to have less confidence in their academic ability than boys, so that some girls with good mathematical skills might not have chosen to enter the competition. However, it seems unlikely that the girls who did enter would have less ability than the ones who did not. If the girls who entered include a reasonable representation of the best female math students, then this study, along with the previously reported work on retardation, indicates that the greater male variability in math scores reflects greater representation of males at both the high and low ends of the distribution. To our knowledge, no search for persons with outstanding spatial talents has been made, so we can only surmise that the situation would be similar in this domain as well.

In the verbal domain, the higher average scores of girls are not consistently accompanied by higher standard deviations; in fact, in some instances (e.g. Gates), the boys' scores are more variable and have a higher instance of low scores. In cases where girls earn higher mean scores but the standard deviations are similar for the two sexes, it would appear that the girls' distribution is simply displaced upward without changing its conformation; that is, there are more very high scorers and fewer very low scorers among the girls.

BIOLOGICAL AND ENVIRONMENTAL INFLUENCES

So far in this chapter, we have summarized the differences and similarities between human males and females in their intellectual functioning, as far as these are known. We have said little so far about the "why" of what has been discovered. There have been efforts to explain the sex differences in specific ability domains by reference to both genetic and experiential factors. We turn first to a review of the genetic argument and evidence, and then consider to what extent specific abilities appear to be a product of direct training or cultural factors. As we noted earlier, spatial ability enters into a variety of kinds of intellectual performance, including mathematics. When we discuss "explanations" of the sex difference in spatial ability, then, the explanations may be taken to apply to other kinds of performance, to the degree that spatial thinking is involved in them.

Genetic Factors in Specific Abilities

Until recently, most research on genetic factors in intellectual performance has been concerned with measures of general intelligence. When it comes to the inheritance of specific abilities, especially those that may be sex-linked, the genetics become more complex, and relatively little research is directly relevant. Vandenberg (1968)[R], in summarizing data from twin studies, reports that both spatial and verbal ability have high levels of heritability, with spatial ability seeming to be less influenced by educational and cultural factors than verbal ability. The fact that spatial ability appears to be both highly heritable and different in mean level for the two sexes has suggested a genetic sex linkage. Four studies (Stafford 1961, Corah 1965, Hartlage 1970[R], and Bock and Kolakowski 1973[R]) have now shown a pattern of cross-sex correlations between parents and children in spatial abilities. That is, boys' scores are correlated with their mothers' scores but not their fathers', and girls' scores are correlated with their fathers' scores and to a lesser degree with their mothers'. Stafford's hypothesis is that at least one important genetic determiner for spatial ability is sex-linked, being carried on the X chromosome and being recessive. Girls, with two X chromosomes, would have a relatively low chance of receiving two recessives, which would have to be the case for the trait to be manifest. Among boys, whenever the recessive trait was present, it would be manifest, since there would be no dominant X-linked character to suppress it. Since boys always receive their only X from their mothers, they would inherit the recessive trait through the mother, whether she expressed it phenotypically or not. Girls could only manifest the trait if they inherited a recessive from mother and father, but their phenotypical similarity would be greater to their fathers, since whenever he possessed the trait, it would be manifest, whereas the mother might carry it without its being expressed. It is possible to work out fairly precise predictions concerning what the correlations should be between children and their cross-sex or same-sex parents, and the correlations obtained in the four studies conform quite closely to these predictions. Bock and Kolakowski carry the argument one step further, using curve-fitting to test the hypothesis that spatial ability has two major components, only one of which is genetically sex-linked, and again, the predictions are quite accurate.

It appears likely, then, that there is at least some degree of sex-linked genetic control over spatial ability. Verbal ability also shows a significant degree of heritability (though not so high as for spatial ability).* However, there is no evidence of sex linkage in the inherited component of verbal abilities.

To say that there is a genetic component in spatial ability does *not* imply that this ability is something, like male genitals, that men have and women do not. With respect to a spatial gene that is sex-linked and recessive, some women will of course have two space-recessives, and their genetic potential for spatial ability will be the same as that of men who have a single recessive space gene on the X chromosome. The *proportion* of persons so endowed will be different for the two sexes—Bock and Kolakowski estimate that the ratio may be approximately 2 to 1, with 50 percent of men and 25 percent of women showing the trait phenotypically. But it should be noted that spatial ability, like all other human abilities, is genetically multidetermined. As noted above, Bock and Kolakowski hypothesize two specific determiners (only one of which is sex-linked), and there may very well be more. Furthermore, there are probably determiners of spatial performance that are not specific to this domain. Spatial ability is usually positively correlated with other kinds of cognitive per-

---

* L. G. Humphreys, University of Illinois, personal communication, 1972.

formance in which the sexes do not differ, or in which females are superior. Insofar as these other kinds of abilities have genetic components, they are not sex-linked, and any contribution they make to performance on spatial tasks will be impartial as to sex. All this is to say that a person may have a good genetic potential for the acquisition of spatial skills without having the X-linked space gene, and further, that both sexes do manifest the X-linked space gene, though in different proportions.

There is more than one way to attack almost any intellectual task. It is likely that problems such as the Luchins-jar problem may be tackled in one way by people with high spatial potential and in another way by people with a different pattern of abilities. Even more important, however, is the role of experience and training. To say that an ability has a genetic component is not to say that it is impervious to training. Obviously, a genetic potential has little meaning in the absence of the experiences and practice to actualize the potential. We shall return to this issue later.

Assuming that there is a genetically sex-linked component in spatial ability, in what way does it organize the body's functioning so as to produce the behavioral differences? One possibility is that the sex hormones are involved in the control system, but this is not the only way in which sex-linked traits are manifest. The development of secondary sex characteristics at puberty is determined both by prenatal programming (that occurs under the influence of testosterone) and by increasing levels of sex-appropriate hormones at puberty. On the other hand, certain sex-linked traits (e.g. color blindness) are not responsive to changes in the levels of sex hormones during the life cycle. What evidence do we have that the sex linkage of spatial ability operates through the hormonal system?

Hormones and spatial ability. Broverman et al. (1968)[ᴿ] have offered a theory concerning the relationship of sex hormones to intellectual performance. As noted earlier, they use a twofold classification of tasks: set A involves "simple, overlearned, repetitive" behaviors at which females are alleged to be superior; set B involves inhibition of initial response tendencies, and more complex information processing that calls for the reorganization of stimulus elements. As shown earlier in this chapter, this does not appear to be a useful classification for encapsulating sex differences. There is no consistent sex difference in tasks calling for inhibition of previously learned responses; boys excel at spatial tasks that do not call for the reorganization of stimulus elements (restructuring) as well as for those that do, and spatial tasks as a whole do not appear to call for any higher order of information processing than the verbal tasks at which girls characteristically excel. The differences in mathematical abilities do not fall easily into this classification—that is, higher mathematics is not simply a matter of the reorganization of stimulus elements. Furthermore, in the analysis of findings on sex differences in learning (see Chapter 2), no evidence emerged supporting the Broverman classification of functions; in fact, the evidence was inconsistent with this formulation.

However, we may consider the Broverman theory of hormonal effects apart from the validity of the classification of tasks. Briefly, the argument rests on the sympathetic and parasympathetic nervous systems and the balance in their functions: adrenergic (sympathetic) activating processes are alleged to support and stimulate the intellectual functions involved in set A types of tasks, whereas cholinergic inhibitory neural processes facilitate performance on set B types of tasks. As Parlee points out (1972)[R], both the sympathetic and parasympathetic nervous systems use acetylcholine as a transmitter substance; hence effects of varying amounts of sex hormones on the amounts of this substance available for neural transmission do not bear upon the issue of sympathetic-parasympathetic balance. There is a further problem in equating the sympathetic-parasympathetic balance with the balance between set A and set B tasks; as Parlee points out, the evidence summarized by the Broverman group of work prior to their own work does not establish any such connection. However, for present purposes the point is that the Broverman group did develop a hypothesis that they then tested with new data. The hypothesis (in simplified form) is that large amounts of either estrogens or androgens will tip the neural balance toward activating, rather than inhibiting, functions (toward set A tasks and away from set B tasks); however, estrogens are more powerful, so the balance is tipped further in females than in males.

In one experiment, Klaiber et al. (1971)[R] tested a group of normal adult male subjects on a simple "overlearned" task (serial subtraction). They then gave injections of testosterone to the experimental group, and of saline solution to the control group. Both groups declined in their performance on the task in the post-test, but the control group declined significantly more. The decline in the experimental group is troublesome for the hypothesis, but the authors suggest that the injection of testosterone prevented as great a decline as would normally have occurred as a result of the normal diurnal variation in testosterone levels: "The results suggest that infused testosterone positively affects performance of a repetitive mental task." It is unfortunate that this study used no tasks involving inhibition or restructuring, which presumably would be interfered with by testosterone. In another study by this group of investigators, however (Klaiber et al. 1967[R]), both kinds of tasks were used. The study is correlational rather than experimental. Male college students did some simple repetitive tasks (speed of reading repeated color names, speed of naming repeated pictured objects), and also were given two tests calling for restructuring: the WAIS Block Design subtest and the Embedded Figures Test. Measures were also taken of urinary 17-ketosteroids, and ratings were made of pubic hair growth, height, weight, and chest and biceps circumference. Both 17-KS scores and masculine physical characteristics (large chest and biceps, plentiful pubic hair) were found to be positively correlated with performance on the simple repetitive tasks and negatively correlated with the restructuring tasks. The correlations were not large in an absolute sense, but many were significant and they were consistent in direction.

The work cited so far has been done entirely with male subjects and with male hormones or their derivations. A finding that male hormones "feminize" performance among men hardly helps to explain sex differences, unless it can be shown that female hormones do so even more strongly. An interesting study by Petersen (1973) with subjects from the Fels longtitudinal sample does include female subjects, but still does not fill the gap. Measures were made of the degree of body "androgenization" in both boys and girls at three age levels: 13, 16, and 17 or 18. Scores were also available on spatial ability (measured by the PMA space test and the Block Design subtest of the Wechsler) and on "fluency" (measured by the Digit Symbol subtest of the Wechsler and the Word Fluency subtest of the Primary Mental Abilities test). The results for fluency are ambiguous, partly because it did not prove to be a coherent dimension. For spatial ability, however, the results show that at age 17 or 18 boys with a more masculine body type tended to have lower spatial scores. At age 13 this correlation was not present, and only marginally so at age 16. Among girls, the more androgenized body types (narrow hips, wide shoulders, solid muscles, small breasts) were associated with *higher* spatial scores, although the correlations were lower than for boys.

At first glance, the results with the female subjects seem anomalous: why should high body androgenization be associated with low spatial scores in boys (as the Broverman theory would imply) but with *high* spatial scores in girls? A possible explanation is that the endocrine picture among girls with masculine body types is one of low estrogen rather than (or in addition to) high androgen. From the Petersen data it is difficult to tell, and the puzzle probably will not be unraveled until direct measures of both male and female hormones have been made with subjects of both sexes and two types of tasks related to their performance: the tasks on which males normally excel and those showing female advantage.

To date, evidence does appear to be accumulating that, among males, highly "masculine" characteristics, either of physique or personality, are associated with *low* spatial scores. An additional item of evidence for this generalization was discussed in our 1966 review, in reference to a study of children who were relatively more skillful on spatial tasks than on verbal or quantitative tasks (Ferguson and Maccoby 1966). The boys with high spatial scores were rated by their peers as less "masculine" than boys with low scores; that is, 11-year-old peers rated high-score boys as unlikely to have those characteristics, such as fighting ability, that they thought most distinguished boys from girls.

Granted, for the moment, that spatial ability in boys is negatively related to various indexes of androgen level, where does this leave us in our attempt to explain sex differences in spatial ability? Clearly, if androgen were an important negative factor in this ability, it would be expected that boys, who have more androgen, would have lower spatial skills than girls. The Broverman case rests on the thesis that, although both male and female hormones are inimical to spatial ability, estrogens are more so than androgens. There is simply no evidence either to support or refute this latter claim. The negative effects of androgen are mysterious indeed when one considers the age curves for hormonal and intellectual development. Boys experience their greatest rise in spatial ability—and their greatest rate of divergence from girls' scores—from the beginning of adolescence until late adolescence, precisely when their androgen levels are rising most steeply. If androgens exercise a negative influence upon spatial ability, then there must be other powerful forces operating in an opposite direction to stimulate spatial development in adolescence and to more than neutralize the effects of the increasing androgens. It seems possible that the two sets of phenomena may actually be physiologically unrelated, even though both are sex-linked and occur at the same time.

We have one final note concerning hormonal effects on intellectual development: an early report of Ehrhardt and Money (1967)[R] found that fetally androgenized girls had unusually high IQs. The average IQ of the ten girls studied was 125, which the authors believed was higher than might be expected from socioeconomic predictors of their probable level, though no figures were presented on this point and there was no matched control group. Dalton, working with a group of English children whose mothers had received large amounts of progesterone (a female hormone) during pregnancy, found that both the male and female offspring of these mothers scored significantly higher than matched controls on general aptitude tests (Dalton 1968[R]). It seemed possible, then, that unusual amounts of either male or female hormone, present prenatally, might be a positive factor for intellectual development. However, a more recent study by Ehrhardt and Baker (1973)[R] found that fetally androgenized girls had higher-than-average IQs (see Chapter 5); but so did their normal sisters, who were the control group. Thus, the most likely explanation of the previous findings appears to be that there is a selective factor such that children who receive unusual dosages of hormones during prenatal life are more often found in families with a high likelihood of the children's having high IQs.

Brain lateralization. Another hypothesis concerns the way genetic factors may operate to affect intellectual functioning in the two sexes, one having to do with sex differences in cerebral dominance. It has been known for some time that the cerebral functions relevant to the perception and production of speech tend to be localized in the left hemisphere of the brain, those relevant to spatial perception and perception of nonverbal sounds in the right hemisphere. Kimura (1963)[R], using a dichotic listening technique, found that this localization had developed by the age of 4 among boys and girls of above-average IQ from professional homes, but that among less-advantaged children (Kimura 1967) left-hemisphere dominance had developed by age 5 among girls, and not till later among boys. Furthermore, it has been shown that boys with reading difficulties lag even further behind girls in the establishment of hemisphere dominance. The reader is referred to a summary of the work on sex differences in cerebral dominance by Buffery and Gray (1972)[R] for detailed documentation. The question of whether spatial abilities are more specifically localized in the right hemisphere for one sex than the other is not yet settled. Knox and Kimura (1970) and Kimura (1969) found greater localization among males for certain spatial tasks, with the sex difference being apparent as young as age 5. Buffery (1971)[R], however, found girls to be more fully lateralized on a spatial task, and more advanced in the development of handedness, beginning at ages 3–4. The Buffery and Gray thesis is that the earlier and stronger development of lateralization in females facilitates their verbal development, but that spatial skills call for a more bilateral cerebral representation and hence is facilitated in men, in whom laterality is not so strong or developed so early.

There is another, and somewhat contradictory, view about cerebral dominance. Sperry and his colleagues, working with patients in whom the functional connections between the two hemispheres of the brain have been severed, have argued that the localization of verbal functions in the left hemisphere and spatial functions in the right tends to be weaker in women. Levy-Agresti and Sperry (1968)[R] believe that strong cerebral dominance facilitates performance for spatial tasks, and they report that left-handed men (in whom cerebral lateralization is weak) are similar to women in obtaining low scores in spatial abilities. Thus Levy and Sperry believe that male superiority in spatial tasks stems from *greater* specialization of the two hemispheres among men than among women, whereas Buffery and Gray's position is that it results from a *lesser* degree of specialization. The issue is yet to be resolved. It may be, as Buffery and Gray suggest, that the findings on which the Levy-Sperry hypothesis is based apply to epilectic patients but not normals.

Some puzzling questions arise from the work on cerebral lateralization in the two sexes. One is that the "packages" of skills localized in each hemisphere do not correspond in detail to the known sex differences in abilities. Levy-Agresti (1968)[R], for example, has described the left hemisphere as being verbal, sequentially detailed, analytic, and computer-like.

Although girls are superior in a variety of verbal tasks, the rest of the description does not fit them better than boys. A theory that purports to account for female superiority on verbal tasks and inferiority on spatial tasks, in terms of stronger or earlier lateralization of the left hemisphere, would have to expect that the other functions controlled by this hemisphere would also be superior in girls.

A second problem has to do with timing, and whether the girl's early left-hemisphere dominance orients her toward the use of verbal means of problem solving. Sherman (1967)[R] suggests that girls develop verbally earlier than boys and that this operates to eliminate the need for the development of nonverbal (particularly spatial) thought. Do girls, as Sherman claims, have a head start in verbal development and do boys start out higher in spatial thinking? Do boys eventually catch up in verbal development and thereafter begin to equalize their ability to use alternative modes of thought? The developmental pattern, as we have seen, is quite different, with no sex differences found in verbal vs. spatial thought in the years boys are lagging behind girls in lateralization, whereas sex differences in modes of thought appear at an age when boys have caught up and become as lateralized as they ever will be. Perhaps Sherman is right that there is an early "bent twig" period during which a person establishes certain modes of problem solving, and continues, with the aid of sex-typed activities, to emphasize these modes after the original reason for doing so has disappeared.

We have reservations concerning this idea, because we believe that far-reaching, qualitative changes in intellectual processes occur with development; that large transformations in modes of thought do occur in middle childhood, after lateralization is virtually complete; and that the chances are slim that early habitual reliance on one kind of data will survive these transformations. However, the issue is an empirical one. To determine whether early language development in any way shuts off development of spatial ability, what appears to be needed is examination *within* *sex* of the relationship between the rate of early language development and later spatial skills. If boys who talk late have better spatial ability in later childhood than boys who talk early, this would be good evidence for the inhibiting effects of early left-hemisphere functioning on right-hemisphere functions. In the absence of this kind of data, the question remains open whether there is a critical period when the degree of lateralization is especially important for the future.

Effects of Training

All the abilities discussed in this chapter improve with age, from early childhood to adulthood. Our educational institutions are dedicated to the proposition that these changes are not entirely (or even primarily) a result of simple maturation—that verbal, mathematical, spatial, and conceptual skills can be taught, and indeed if they are not taught, they will probably not be learned to an adequate level of proficiency. This is not to say that success in teaching is independent of a child's already-developed readiness to learn a given task, or that success in training does not depend upon genetic factors (including those controlling maturation) and previous learning. However, if any group of children have not acquired certain intellectual skills that other children of their age possess, there is a reasonable presumption that at least part of the problem lies in deficiencies in the teaching they have received.

Witkin et al. have argued that training plays only a limited role in performance on the tests used to measure field dependence. It has been noted above that these talks have a large spatial component, and therefore the Witkin case is relevant to the "trainability" of spatial ability. The Witkin group trained subjects in estimating the upright in the Tilting-Rod-Tilting-Chair situation. The subjects improved, but their improvement did not generalize to performance on the standard Rod and Frame Test, or to the Embedded Figures Test. They also found that a group of dancers, who have extensive training in sensitivity to cues of body position, obtained higher-than-average scores on the Body Adjustment Test, but not on other measures of field dependence. They interpret this finding as follows (Witkin et al. 1962[R], p. 372):

These results suggest that no fundamental change in mode of field approach, in the sense of alteration of the subject's characteristic way of perceiving, occurred in consequence of training. Our observations of subjects during training tended to confirm this impression. We noted that subjects who improved their scores in the test on which they receive training accomplished this apparently by the acquisition of special techniques or "tricks" useful in correcting the immediate impression of the upright.

Recent work on training in spatial tasks has not added a great deal to our understanding of the issues raised by Witkin et al. Subjects can benefit from direct training on spatial tasks (Kato 1965; female subjects only, A. Goldstein and Chance 1965), though in an earlier study with fewer practice trials, subjects showed no improvement (Elliott and McMichael 1963[R]). Engineering practice (Blade and Watson 1955[R]) and programmed instruction techniques (Brinkmann 1966[R]) have been shown to enhance spatial visualization performance. However, these studies have not investigated how widely the training generalized, or how long the effects of training lasted. More important for our present purposes, it has not been demonstrated that male and female subjects respond differentially to training. It is reasonable to expect that if the deficit in spatial ability of females results from lack of training, they should begin to catch up with males after additional training; if there were a difference in underlying "ability," however, males might profit more from training than females. At present, the issue is simply unresolved. Goldstein and Chance (1965) did find that, with an extended series of Embedded Figures items permitting extended practice, women improved more; male college students scored better on early trials but there was no sex difference on later trials. If this finding replicates, it will be strong evidence that sex differences in spatial ability are (in large degree) a product of differential training. However, we cannot consider that the issue is resolved on the basis of this single piece of evidence.

What conclusions can be drawn if training on a specific task does not generalize widely to other kinds of performance in the same ability domain? The lack of generalization is probably the rule rather than the exception in the effects of instruction. Math teachers know that different arithmetical operations must be trained individually even though individuals may differ in their general readiness to learn various numerical skills. The point is that lack of generalization does not imply the absence of an underlying "ability."

Furthermore, a generalized "ability" may itself be a product of previous learning. The question whether a given kind of intellectual proficiency (e.g. high math ability) is an additive product of many elements acquired piece by piece, or whether it is related to larger structures that develop in a necessary sequence and are resistant to the immediate impact of specific training, is a widely debated issue, and we cannot contribute much to it here. However, even if one takes the structuralist position, one can argue that there is a heavy impact of experience upon the development of structures. We assume that field independence (which we translate as visual spatial ability), as well as other abilities, is a fairly stable characteristic of an individual upon which any specific training procedures may have only a limited effect, though there are undoubtedly cumulative effects of continued training. Beyond this, we think it likely (as Witkin also does) that early opportunities to learn, and affective aspects of the child's milieu, do have an impact upon the developmental course of these abilities. We turn to a brief consideration of variations in milieu.

Cultural Factors

Cross-cultural work on intellectual abilities (especially as it relates to sex differences) seems to have focused upon the field-dependence field-independence dimension. In their excellent review chapter on cognitive styles, Kagan and Kogan (1970, pp. 1337–40)[R] have summarized the work of Berry, Dawson, and others on field-dependence in people being reared in contrasting cultures. A first point to note is that when "traditional" (nonacculturated) groups are compared with "transitional" people from the same genetic background who are adopting more modern life styles, the "transitionals" have higher spatial scores. The probable role of formal education is evident here.

Taking their lead from Witkin, Dawson (1967)[R] and Berry (1966) have investigated the hypothesis that field-dependence will be more marked in cultures in which there is emphasis upon conformity, reliance upon authority, and restriction of the autonomy of the individual; field-independence, on the other hand, they expect to be more characteristic among individuals growing up in an atmosphere where independence is respected and encouraged. And within cultures, the hypothesis continues, the degree of difference in field-dependence between the sexes should be a function of the degree of sex-role differentiation—the degree to which females are restricted and males allowed independence.

A first point to be noted is that in Berry's work the Embedded Figures Test correlated substantially with three other visual-spatial tests that were also used, and the cluster of measures showed similar cultural and between-sex effects. Hence we can discuss this work in terms of visual-spatial ability rather than field-dependence per se.

Comparisons between African cultural groups that differ in the degree of maternal dominance over children (the Temne vs. the Mende in Sierra Leone, Dawson 1967[R]) have shown that adult males obtain higher scores on spatial tests in the cultures where young children are allowed more autonomy. (Female subjects were not included in this study.) Comparisons between a restrictive African culture and a permissive Eskimo culture have yielded the same relation to adult spatial abilities. Furthermore, when children of both sexes are allowed considerable independence (Eskimo), no sex difference has been found in spatial ability (Berry 1966, MacArthur 1967), whereas substantial sex differences are found when males exercise strong authoritarian control over females (the Temne, as reported by Berry 1966).

Kagan and Kogan point out that it is possible that the lack of sex differences in spatial ability among the Eskimo might result from a specialized gene pool, representing the adaptation of this human subgroup to the special requirements of life in the arctic environment. This possibility cannot be ruled out; we note only that the cross-cultural evidence available to date is consistent with the hypothesis that child-rearing practices, and the social roles assigned the two sexes, affect the degree to which the sexes differ in spatial ability.

Personality mediators. As we have seen above, cultures that allow independence to children tend to produce adults with higher spatial scores than cultures that use more restrictive socialization practices. It would appear that, within cultures, it ought to be true, as Witkin suggested, that the more passive, dependent individuals would have lower scores on spatial tests, with the more assertive, autonomous individuals having higher scores. The direct evidence for this relationship is equivocal. V. J. Crandall and Sinkeldam (1964) observed the free play of children ranging in age from 6 to 12, and recorded instances of dependent behavior toward adults (seeking help, affection, recognition, or approval). Girls who were dependent in this sense had lower-than-average scores on the Embedded Figures Test. However, when IQ was held constant, the correlation dropped to an insignificant level.

Konstadt and Forman (1965)[R], on the other hand, obtained more positive results. They first obtained field-dependence scores for a group of fourth-grade children. Then they observed the children as they worked on another task under conditions of either experimenter approval or experimenter disapproval. The field-independent children were relatively unaffected by the experimenter's attitude, whereas the field-dependent children performed better under approval and worse under disapproval conditions. Thus, if sensitivity to an adult's approval is taken as an index of dependency, the hypothesis is confirmed.

In the earlier review (Maccoby 1966a[R]) it was noted that there were some puzzling findings in which correlations between spatial ability and personality measures ran in opposite directions for the two sexes. Specifically, there was evidence that high spatial ability was associated with "masculine" traits in women, but with *low* masculinity in men. We noted above some evidence relating high body androgenization to low spatial ability among men (p. 122ff). Kagan and Kogan review other evidence on this issue in detail, concluding that the evidence does continue to support the generalization that spatial ability is associated with cross-sex typing, although the relationship appears to be stronger in women than in men. Recently, additional findings have appeared showing very different patterns of correlations between personality variables and measures of intellectual performance for the two sexes. For example, (1) S. Coates (1972) reports a correlation of .41 between aggression and IQ in preschool girls, and a correlation of −.74 for boys; (2) a sense of personal potency (internal locus of control) is positively related to scores on the Embedded Figures Test for girls aged 6–12, but not related among boys of the same age (V. C. Crandall and Lacey 1972); and (3) intellectual achievement striving is positively related to activity level among girls, negatively related among boys (Battle and Lacey 1972). However, a large-scale study with Head Start children (aged 3–6) (Ward 1973[R]) has shown that impulsivity (as measured by low scores on the Motor Inhibition Test) is a negative factor for intellectual performances in *both* sexes. On the whole, the recent correlation evidence supports the earlier contention that different personality constellations are associated with good intellectual performance in the two sexes, and the more bold, assertive girls continue to show greater intellectual abilities and interests than other girls. Evidence is insufficient to reveal whether these personality attributes are more strongly related to spatial than other abilities.

The 1966 Maccoby paper attempted to explain some portion of the sex differences in intellectual performance in terms of sex differences in personality structure. Some of the points made were as follows:

1. For both sexes, independence (autonomy) is positively associated with good intellectual performance, particularly on tests on spatial ability or field-independence. Girls' poorer performance on these tests may stem from greater dependency.

2. Tasks calling for internal serial processing are especially vulnerable to distraction; girls may do poorly on these tasks because they are more oriented toward external, interpersonal cues, and hence more distracted by them.

3. Activity is involved in those intellectual tasks that require restructuring or breaking set. Boys have a higher average activity level, which may give them an advantage on such tasks.

4. Aggression and impulsivity are related to poor intellectual performance in boys but not in girls. It was suggested that a curvilinear relationship may exist between performance on an intellectual task and a dimension running from passive-inhibited to bold-impulsive, such that the midpoint of the dimension is optimal for intellectual performance in both sexes. Boys, being more often at the impulsive end of the scale, profit intellectually from becoming less impulsive; girls, being more often at the passive, timid end of the scale, profit from becoming more bold.

These arguments have not stood up well under the impact of new evidence appearing in the intervening years. As will be seen later, there is now good reason to doubt that girls are more "dependent," in almost any sense of the word, than boys. Hence point 1 is not supported. Point 2 suffers from two weaknesses: there is no evidence (as we have seen in the present chapter) that the sexes differ on tasks calling for serial internal processing; furthermore, girls are not more oriented toward interpersonal cues (see Chapter 5).

With respect to point 3, it is by no means demonstrated that boys do excel on tasks calling for restructuring or breaking set, so that perhaps there is nothing to explain. If there were, activity level is a poor candidate for a personality mediator. We shall see later that the sexes do not differ generally with respect to activity level. There are certain specific stimulus situations under which boys do show elevated activity levels, but these are not the situations that normally prevail while children are performing intellectual tasks; furthermore, high activity level appears to be a *negative* factor among boys for intellectual performance, so that if boys were given ability tests when under high activity arousal, it is doubtful whether this would improve their performance in comparison to girls, even on tasks calling for restructuring.

As for point 4, it is true that different personality factors do seem to promote intellectual competence in the two sexes, but this is not well explained by reference to a dimension running from passivity to impulsiveness. The sexes do not differ in most measures of impulsiveness devised so far, although Mischel does find that boys of preschool age have more difficulty waiting for a delayed reward. The sexes *do* differ with respect to aggressiveness, and on some measures girls are more timid or anxious; perhaps a dimension running from timidity at one end to aggressiveness at the other will be a better candidate for the curvilinear model.

The earlier argument began by assuming the existence of certain sex differences in intellectual performance that have not turned out to be consistently present; it then attempted to explain these on the basis of personality differences that have also proved to be more myth than reality. In view of this, the senior author can do little more than beg the reader's indulgence for previous sins. However, the studies on personality correlates of intellectual performance have continued to suggest that intellectual development in girls is fostered by their being assertive and active, and having a sense that they can control, by their own actions, the events that affect their lives. These factors appear to be less important in the intellectual development of boys—perhaps because they are already sufficiently assertive and have a sufficient sense of personal control over events, so that other issues (e.g. how well they can control aggressive impulses) become more important in how successfully they can exploit their intellectual potential.

CHAPTER FOUR

Achievement Motivation and Self-Concept

We have reviewed what is known about the aptitudes and academic achievement of the two sexes, as these are shown in a variety of standardized tests. However, to have an "aptitude" for learning a particular kind of material, or even to have a good store of already acquired knowledge and problem-solving skill in a given area, is not the same as to do well in school classes or a job, or to seek out opportunities in which one's aptitudes and knowledge may be put to work. Willingness to work, interest in improving one's level of skills, responsiveness to the demands of others to acquire new skills, are all obviously involved.

It has been alleged that the sexes differ in their motivations to achieve. Here is an illustrative assertion: "Girls have different orientations toward intellectual tasks than do boys. Little girls want to please; they work for love and approval; if bright, they underestimate their competence. Little boys show more task involvement, more confidence" (Hoffman 1972[R], p. 130).

Several hypotheses are implied in these assertions. We shall first state the hypotheses concerning sex differences in achievement motivation that have been put forward in these and other writings, and attempt to evaluate each of them in the light of existing evidence. The hypotheses are as follows:

1. Males have a greater need for achievement and are more oriented to achievement for its own sake.

2. Males show greater task involvement and persistence.

3. Males show more curiosity, and engage in more exploratory behavior.

4. Females are motivated to achieve primarily in areas related to interpersonal relations (e.g. to be especially attractive to others; to associate with high-status others, especially men; to have achieving children), whereas males strive to achieve in non-person-oriented areas including intellectual endeavors.

5. Female efforts to achieve are primarily motivated by the desire to please others, so that regardless of the area of achievement (whether in-

tellectual, social, etc.) they care primarily about praise and approval for their performance, whereas males are more motivated by the intrinsic interest of the task.

6. Females have low self-confidence about many tasks. This is sometimes thought to be part of a generalized lack of self-esteem.

We begin with hypothesis 1. One might expect that the simplest, most direct manifestation of a lack-of-achievement motivation would be low achievement. If one takes academic achievement as the criterion, hypothesis 1 is faulted at the outset. It is well known that girls get better grades throughout their school years (see Maccoby 1966b[R], Oetzel summary on pp. 323–51). Table 4.1 shows recent evidence on school performance and interest in school, and supports the earlier conclusion. Girls are more interested in school-related skills from an early age (Baumrind and Black 1967, Barnard 1966), and are less likely to drop out of school before completing high school (Fitzsimmons et al. 1969). Interestingly enough, boys' poorer performance in school does not seem to be a function of any greater feeling of distrust or lack of rapport toward the teacher. In a study of Solomon and Alli (1972), boys showed a more positive perception of the teacher than the girls did (particularly in the early grades) when reacting to taped teacher-child interactions. We will present some evidence later that teachers tend to have more interactions, and longer conversations, with boys in their classrooms. We suggest that boys' poorer school performance is not due to lesser interest in their performance on the part of teachers, or to any greater tendency on the boys' part to dislike the teachers.

We have seen that girls do not obtain higher aptitude or achievement test scores (see Chapter 3), taking all the subject-matter areas together. Hence their better grades must reflect some combination of greater effort, greater interest, and better work habits. Evidently, these school-related motivations are not what is meant when assertions are made about girls' low achievement motivation. Let us turn to research focused more directly on this motivation.

NEED FOR ACHIEVEMENT

The classic work on need for achievement was done some time ago by McClelland and his colleagues. Most of their work was done with male subjects, but they did study women as well, and summarized their findings on sex differences as follows: "1. Women get higher N Ach scores than men under neutral conditions (2 studies). 2. Women do not show an increase in N Ach scores as a result of achievement-involving instructions (3 studies). 3. Women's N Ach scores seem as valid as men's, in that they relate to performance in the same way" (McClelland et al. 1953[R], p. 178). Need for achievement was measured projectively, through a scoring of achievement themes in stories told in response to pictures in the Thematic

TABLE 4.1
School Performance

Study	Age and N	Difference	Comment
R. Bell et al. 1971	2½ (74)	None	Interest in attending nursery school (teacher rating)
Baumrind & Black 1967	3-4 (103)	Girls	Higher interest in preschool skills (observer ratings)
Solomon & Ali 1972	5, 7, 9, 11, 13, 15, 17, 21-25 (294)	Boys & Men	More positive perception of teachers from taped teacher-child interaction
Yando et al. 1971	8 (144)	None	"Classroom achievement" (teacher rating)
Barnard 1966	10 (220)	Girls	Higher positive semantic differential for concepts related to school
C. Johnson & Gormly 1972	10 (113)	Girls	Course grade in mathematics
Achenbach 1970	10-13 (1,085)	Girls	Higher grades, all ages
Buck & Austrin 1971	14-16 (100)	None	Display of positive classroom behavior (teacher rating; black sample)
Monday et al. 1966-67	14-17 (225,402)	Girls	Higher high school grades
Fitzsimmons et al. 1969	15-17 (270)	Girls	Lower dropout rate
Wyer 1967	18 (2,000)	None	First-term freshman grades
Constantinople 1967	18, 21 (353)	None	Perceived instrumentality of college

Apperception Test (TAT). The "achievement arousal" treatment involved having the subjects work on an anagrams task, after being told that the task reflected not only an individual's intelligence but his capacity to organize material and to evaluate situations quickly and accurately—"in short, his capacity to be a leader." After such an "arousal" session, male subjects increased the achievement themes in their TAT responses, but women did not.

It was initially thought that women must have less achievement motivation, since they did not respond to an achievement-arousal condition. However, it may make a difference how the arousal is done—what other motivations it taps. With this question in mind, Field (reported in McClelland et al., p. 179) used a "social" arousal, which involved first of all a discussion concerning the importance of social acceptance by a group as the most important determiner of satisfaction with life, and the claim that the best predictor of social acceptance in a wide range of social situations was acceptance in the present situation. Subjects were then given social acceptance scores that presumably reflected their acceptance by the other members of the group.

In response to this arousal, men's n Ach scores went up somewhat (not significantly), but women's increased considerably more sharply (and significantly). This finding has been a primary basis for the popularity of hypothesis 4 above; it has been assumed that the higher scores for women were due to the emphasis of the Field arousal on social acceptability (an area in which women presumably want to achieve), whereas the previous results with the standard achievement arousal reflected men's interest in intellectual achievement. It should be pointed out that the emphasis on "leadership" introduces a competitive element, and it is difficult to be sure whether the greater increase in women's scores after the Field arousal resulted from omitting the competitive theme, adding the social acceptance theme, or both.

A complication in the measurement of n Ach comes from the use of projective measures, which assume a relationship between projective responses and the subject's own motivations or behavior. It is not uncommon for boys to be given a boys' form of a projective test, in which the central character presented in the story or picture is a male; the girls' form, on the other hand, uses female characters. If girls give fewer achievement themes under these conditions, is this due to their own low-achievement motivation or to their assumption that other girls and women are not achievers? It has been found (Veroff et al. 1953[R], Monahan et al. 1974) that *subjects of both sexes give fewer achievement themes* (and report more negative events) when responding to a story or picture about a female, suggesting that girls' usually lower n Ach scores may not reflect their own motivations but rather their concepts (which they share with men) concerning the usual characteristics of women and girls.

To illustrate the magnitude of this effect, Table 4.2 reproduces mean n Ach scores from groups of high school students.

It should be noted that the achievement-oriented arousal (followed by

TABLE 4.2

Mean Need-Achievement Scores Under Neutral
and Achievement-Oriented Conditions

	Mean n Ach score on picture test			
	Neutral condition		Achievement-oriented condition	
Subjects	Male pictures	Female pictures	Male pictures	Female pictures
Male	1.94	1.72	4.93	1.57
Female	5.76	1.77	5.21	1.92

SOURCE: McClelland et al. 1953[R], pp. 167, 172.

an n Ach test with male pictures) succeeded in bringing the male n Ach scores only up to the level where the female scores already were without arousal. Similar results were obtained in the Field work: women subjects had higher n Ach scores than men under the relaxed conditions, although not so high as relaxed-condition scores obtained in other studies; "social" arousal raised their scores to approximately their usual level, but did not increase the male scores from an initially very low level.

Perhaps a more accurate way of summarizing this early work on achievement motivation would be as follows: when n Ach is measured projectively with male pictures, females in high school and college show a high level of achievement imagery whether given an "arousal" treatment or not; men show a high level only when aroused by reference to assessment of their intelligence and leadership ability. There may be a clue here to boys' lower grades in school—it appears that it takes stronger efforts to motivate them. But the results certainly do not indicate a generally low level of achievement motivation in girls, or that they are motivated only by appeals to their social acceptability. The fact that neither sex shows as much achievement motivation with female pictures is difficult to interpret. We simply do not know whether this reflects the subjects' own motivation to a greater extent for female than male subjects.

Recent work on achievement motivation is summarized in Table 4.3. In studies done with younger children, competition is not stressed. These studies measure achievement motivation from teachers' ratings or observers' reports of the child's efforts to improve some aspect of his performance in relation to an implicit or explicit standard. For example, if a child looks at his own drawing, says "That's not right," and erases what he has done and tries again, the incident is coded as an instance of achievement striving. In three of the four studies with children under six, girls were found to exhibit more "autonomous achievement striving" than boys.

At later ages, there is a shift to questionnaire and projective methods of measurement. The evidence is thin and inconsistent. There were four studies summarized in the 1966 book (Oetzel, pp. 344–45)—one with children and the other three with adults—all using projective measures. Three showed no sex differences. The fourth (McClelland et al., described above) found higher achievement imagery among women under neutral conditions and an increase among men under an intellectual-competitive arousal. More recently, Ramirez et al. (1971) report greater achievement imagery among boys on a projective test in a mixed sample of Mexican American and Anglo adolescents. This study used different forms for the two sexes, presenting own-sex stimulus pictures to each subject, and thus raising the problems of interpretation noted above. Lunneborg and Rosenwood (1972), with a sizable sample of college students, followed up a suggestion by Bardwick, who had found a remarkably low level of achievement-

TABLE 4.3
Achievement Striving

Study	Age and N	Difference	Comment
Baumrind & Black 1967	3-4 (103)	None	Observer ratings: stretches to meet vs. retreats from performance demands; sets easy vs. hard goals to achieve; hazards failure vs. avoids difficult tasks
Wyer 1968	3-6 (70)	None	Preference for easy or difficult games
Klaus & Gray 1968	3-7 (80)	None	Choice of achievement or nonachievement endings to short stories (low SES black; longitudinal)
Callard 1968	4 (80)	Girls	Chose to resume more challenging tasks
Radin 1973	4 (52)	None	Academic motivation (teacher and psychologist ratings)
S. Coates 1973	4-5 (53)	Girls	Autonomous achievement strivings (teacher ratings: Beller Scale)
Emmerich 1971	4-5 (596)	Girls	Classroom observations, early fall and spring: autonomous achievement strivings (black and white, low SES)
	4-5 (415)	None	Classroom observations, early fall and late fall: autonomous achievement strivings (black and white, low SES)
Hatfield et al. 1967	4-5 (40)	None	Observer ratings of child's achievement standards
Lansky & McKay 1969	5-6 (36)	Girls	Autonomous achievement strivings (teacher ratings: Beller Scale)
Masters & Christy 1973	7 (32)	None	Self-reward for easy and difficult tasks
Bandura & Perloff 1968	7-10 (80)	None	Self-imposed performance standards
Battle 1965	12-14 (74)	None	Importance of doing well in math
Battle 1966	12-14 (500)	Boys	Rated importance of doing well in math higher; higher minimal standards of performance (English)
		Girls	Rated importance of doing well in English higher
		None	Minimal standards of performance (Math)
Ramirez et al. 1971	12-17 (600)	Boys	Need achievement, scored from Ss' stories about school-related pictures (Mexican-American, white)
Kimball 1973	13	None	"Fear of success" imagery
	17 (187)	Boys	Less "fear of success" imagery in projective stories (Canadian)
Strickland 1971	14 (120)	Boys	Level of aspiration, Rotter Board (black and white middle SES)
		None	Level of aspiration, Rotter Board (black and white low SES)
Sampson & Hancock 1967	15-17 (251)	None	Need for achievement as measured by Edwards Personal Preference Schedule
Lunneborg & Rosenwood 1972	18-21 (465)	None	Achievement themes in answer to "What makes you happy," "sad?"

oriented responses to the questions "What makes you happy? What makes you sad? What makes you angry?" among a pilot group of college women. Lunneborg and Rosenwood used the same questions with college subjects of both sexes. Points were given toward an achievement score if the individual said, for example, that "success," "a rewarding career," or "getting through school" would bring happiness, or that "doing badly on a test," "inability to explain," or "losing something I should have had a chance at" would make him (her) sad. Although there was a slight trend in the direction of men's giving more achievement responses, the difference was not significant (e.g. 33 percent of men as against 30 percent of women gave "happy" achievement imagery).

Some of the most interesting recent work has focused on the "motive to avoid success" (Horner 1968[R], 1970). Horner argues that traditional measures of achievement motivation do not reflect the conflict situation that particularly affects women, namely that they feel it is acceptable (indeed, expected) to do well at school, but that it is at the same time unladylike to "beat" men at almost any task. This conflict produces a situation in which women want to succeed, but not too much. Horner devised an ingenious method for identifying this conflict. She asked subjects to write stories about highly successful members of their own sex, and scored the stories for all the unpleasant things that were described about ensuing events or the personal characteristics of the successful person. She found that 65 percent of college women described unpleasant events and attributes in discussing successful women, whereas only 10 percent of college men gave such descriptions of successful men. More recently, a more complete design has been used, with adolescent subjects of both sexes being asked to write stories about both successful boys and successful girls (Monahan et al. 1974). *Both* sexes gave more negative responses to stories about successful girls—in fact, boys were even more negative about female success than girls were. Subjects of the two sexes were equally positive about male success.

The work on the fear of success is new and the results are not consistent. Alper (1973)[R] found as much success imagery as failure imagery in women. One study (Kimball 1973) has not found a sex difference in the fear-of-success motive at age 13. A number of other studies (as yet unpublished) have come to our attention in which sex differences in fear of success have also failed to appear. We do not yet know what the age changes may be in the development of the conflict over success, or how the conflict finds expression (if it does) in behavior. But the studies do underline the possibility that a sex difference in "achievement motivation" will be found only (or primarily) in situations in which achievement is assessed in comparative terms. In our culture, achievement tends to be defined in just these terms. All achievements can in principle be rank-ordered, but it may be a mistake to suppose that all achievement is motivated by a concern for rank order.

A recent study by Martin (1973) illustrates nicely how introducing competition into a task has a different effect upon the achievement striving of the two sexes. Martin worked with second-grade children in a beanbag toss game. The subject aimed for one of a series of target areas marked on the floor with each toss. The more distant the target, the more points gained if the toss was successful. Each child played this game alone in one session, and in another session as a member of a same-sex pair taking turns. The rules of the competitive session were that the child with the highest number of points got *all* the points earned by both scorers—or "winner take all." Boys became slightly more conservative in their target choices under competitive conditions, but girls became *much* more conservative, choosing to aim for very near targets. Their aspirations were much lower than those of boys in the competitive condition, but not otherwise. It is true that girls were not as accurate as boys, on the average, in their beanbag throws, so that their conservative behavior under competition may have simply reflected a realistic judgment that this was the only way they were likely to win; however, they were competing against other girls, no more competent than they, and their actual success was not different under the two conditions, so that their loss of self-confidence (if this is indeed what occurred) is not, after all, especially realistic. We shall return to the relation between self-confidence and achievement motivation below.

Is there any inconsistency between the hypothesis that boys are more willing to try to achieve under competitive conditions, and the fact that girls get better grades in school? We think not. We would argue that grades are not generally seen as competitive by children. Grading on the normal curve is not common in the lower grades, and even when it is done, it is probably not well understood by the children. They would not normally believe that an individual's obtaining a high grade on a test would in any way affect anyone else's chances of getting a high grade. It is reasonable, then, that even girls who find overt competition distasteful can work comfortably toward some standard of excellence in the academic sphere. We do not doubt that many girls want to be the "best" in the class, but the competition is indirect, compared for example to sports, and does not involve directly injuring or defeating another specific individual.

RISK TAKING

In a number of the tasks used to measure achievement strivings, a child's willingness to take risks is involved. If he chooses to aspire to a difficult task, he runs an increasing risk of not winning anything at all—or even of losing what he has already won. Slovic (1966) has devised an ingenious task to measure risk taking. The child has a series of nine switches that may be pulled. All except one, when pulled, yield a spoonful of M&M's. One, however, is the "disaster" switch, and when this is pulled, the child loses all the candies previously accumulated. The location of the disaster switch is varied randomly among the nine, so there is no way the child can determine where it is. All he knows is that if he has already pulled several switches, all of which were positively loaded, the chances that the next pull will be a "disaster" have been increased. The subject can pull as many switches as he chooses, and quit with his winnings at any time. Through the age range 11–16, Slovic found boys continuing their play longer (taking more risks), with the result that their total winnings were less than those of girls. He did not find sex differences among children aged 6–10, however. Kopfstein (1973), using the Slovic procedure with 9-year-old children, also found no sex differences. We do not know whether there is a consistent but age-specific tendency for boys to take more risks—replication is needed in the 11–16 age range. In any case, it is evident that the outcome of level-of-aspiration studies may be greatly affected by the degree and kind of risk they involve.

TASK ORIENTATION VERSUS PERSON ORIENTATION

As noted above, one hypothesis about sex differences in achievement motivation is that both sexes are motivated to achieve, but they are oriented toward different *kinds* of achievement, boys being primarily interested in achieving on tasks that deal with inanimate objects or impersonal ideas, and girls on tasks that involve interaction with people. Another related hypothesis is that when the two sexes are working on a task, boys tend to be intrinsically interested in the task itself, whereas girls work primarily for the praise and approval of others (or to avoid their disapproval). As Garai and Scheinfeld put it (1968, p. 270)[R]: "From early childhood on, males appear to have greater achievement needs directed toward successful task accomplishment, while females exhibit greater affiliative or social needs directed toward successful relations with the people in their environment."

Two aspects of task orientation have been studied fairly extensively: task persistence and curiosity (exploration). These studies almost always involve nonsocial tasks, i.e. the child's involvement with objects and materials. The research relevant to these two topics is summarized in Tables 4.4 and 4.5.

In some of the studies reported in Table 4.4, children were assigned tasks by the experimenter, and scores were based either on the child's initial persistence or on his willingness to return to an unfinished task in order to finish it. It could be argued that task persistence in such a situation may have reflected the child's interest in pleasing the experimenter and his docility toward the experimenter's instructions as much as his intrinsic

TABLE 4.4
Task Persistence and Involvement

Study	Age and N	Difference	Comment
J. Kagan 1971	8, 13, 27 mos (180)	None	Number of activity changes, duration of each play activity
Rheingold & Eckerman 1969	9-10 mos (24)	None	Duration of manipulation of toys and other objects
Clarke-Stewart 1973	9-18 mos	Boys	Duration of object involvement (longitudinal)
	10-13 mos	None	Number of prolonged involvements with objects (home observation, longitudinal sample)
	16-17 mos (36)	Boys	Number of prolonged involvements with objects (home observation, longitudinal sample)
Rheingold & Samuels 1969	10 mos (20)	None	Duration of time touched toys or objects
J. Brooks & Lewis 1972	11-15 mos (17 opp.-sex twin pairs)	None	Amount of sustained play or number of toy changes
Wenar 1972	12-15 mos (26)	None	Home observations of initiating and sustaining activities
Jacklin et al. 1973	13 mos (80)	None	Number of toy changes and amount of sustained play
Maccoby & Feldman 1972	2 (64)	None	Duration of longest manipulation of one toy before shifting to another (longitudinal)
	2½ (35)	None	
	3 (38)	None	
Weinraub & Lewis 1973	2 (18)	None	Time spent in sustained play
R. Bell et al. 1971	2½ (74)	None	Interest in obtaining bells, bell-pull situation (teacher rating)
F. Pedersen & Bell 1970	2½ (55)	Girls None	Longer times in single activity before changing Persistence to secure object
Baumrind & Black 1967	3-4 (103)	None	Observer ratings: perseverance in the face of adversity; gives his best vs. expends little effort; does not vs. does become pleasurably involved in tasks
Zunich[R] 1964	3-4 (40)	Girls	Greater number of attempts to solve puzzle box alone
		None	Did not attempt to solve puzzle
Friedrichs et al. 1971	3-5 (50)	None	Time Ss voluntarily pushed pegs down with Experimenter present
Stodolsky 1971	3-5 (16)	Girls	Longer activity segments, fewer activity changes (lower SES black)
	3-5 (19)	None	Same measures as above (middle SES black and white)
	4-6 (38)	None	Same measures as above (middle SES black and white)

(continued)

TABLE 4.4 *(cont.)*

Study	Age and N	Difference	Comment
Wyer 1968	3-6 (70)	None	Perseverance on easy or difficult tasks
Bee et al. 1969	4-5 (114 & mothers)	None	Frequency of toy shifts
Emmerich 1971	4-5 (596)	Girls	Task orientation: behavior observation in nursery school
W. Mischel et al. 1968	7-9 (60)	None	Amount of time worked on maze and number of mazes completed
Stouwie et al. 1970	8-9 (156)	None	Number of seconds attempting to solve difficult EFT
Nakumura & Finck 1973	9-12 (251)	None	Task orientation (questionnaire)
McManis 1965	10-13 (96)	Boys	More persistent in continuing-pursuit rotor task (normal, retardates)
Maehr & Stallings 1972	13 (154)	Girls	Volunteered to repeat task (astronaut aptitude test)
Berger & Johansson 1968	18-21 (144)	None	Number of trials on probability-learning type of task before S expressed desire to quit
Rotter & Mulry 1965	18-21 (120)	None	Number of trials until subjects stopped a matching task with no correct matches

interest in the task. But other studies in the table involved measures of the child's persistence on tasks he had chosen for himself. In both cases, there is no evidence of a sex difference in persistence in the manipulation of objects. The question of whether girls show more "social task persistence" in the sense of sustained interaction with others will be discussed in detail in Chapter 6; anticipating that discussion, in brief it may simply be noted here that girls are not more task-persistent in social tasks.

Research on curiosity and exploration yields inconsistent results. In the 1966 summary, three studies of children aged 3–6 reported greater curiosity in boys, and one study with children aged 9–11 reported no difference. The more recent work shows that under age 3, the sexes are quite similar in their willingness to explore a novel environment. In the age range 3–6, there is a clear trend for boys to show more curiosity and exploratory behavior, although there are several studies finding no difference at this age. For later childhood, the amount of research is limited; some studies show higher scores for boys, some for girls, and some no difference. It appears, then, that there is a tendency for boys to do more exploring and show more interest in novelty, but that this is true only for a fairly narrow age range —the preschool and kindergarten years. The reader may recall that this is the age at which boys were found to be more "impulsive," in the sense that

TABLE 4.5
Curiosity and Exploration

Study	Age and N	Difference	Comment
Rubenstein 1967	6 mos (44)	None	Exploratory visual behavior
Rheingold & Samuels 1969	10 mos (20)	None	Exploratory behavior (mother present)
H. Ross et al. 1972	11-12 mos (8m, 4f)	None	Exploration: novel toy and room
Finley & Layne 1969	1-3 (96)	None	Visual exploration (Indian, white)
Marvin 1971	2 (16)	Girls	"Strange situation": manipulatory exploration; visual exploration (mother-absent episodes only)
		None	Locomotor exploration
	3 (16)	None	Locomotor, manipulatory, and visual exploration
	4 (16)	Boys	Manipulatory exploration; visual exploration (Mo's first departure)
		None	Locomotor exploration
Baumrind & Black 1967	3-4 (103)	Boys	Observer ratings: exploration of environment
		None	Observer ratings: curiosity, enjoyment of new learning experiences
L. Harris 1965	3-4 (32)	Girls	Choice of novel vs. familiar toy
	4-5 (32)	None	Choice of novel vs. familiar toy
Hutt 1970	3-4 (59)	Boys	Exploration in presence of novel toy
		None	Number of manipulations of novel toy, first day
Shipman 1971	3-4 (1,445)	Boys	Choice of unknown (concealed) toy over known (visible) toy
Daehler 1970	4-6 (160)	Boys	Investigatory responses in discrimination task
Yando et al. 1971	8 (144)	Girls	Curiosity: choice of unknown vs. known picture (black)
		None	Curiosity (white)
Maw & Maw 1965	10-11 (914)	Boys	Questionnaire of activity preferences; selection of "outgoing, investigatory activities," 3 studies
Walberg 1969	16-17 (450)	Girls	Greater preference for new, different activities (high school physics students)

they were less able than girls to wait for a delayed, more attractive reward (compared to accepting a smaller immediate reward; see Chapter 3). This is also the age at which sex differences in activity level have most frequently been detected. The relatively uninhibited behavior of the male preschooler, then, has fairly wide implications and affects some aspects of what might be called achievement behavior. It is an open question, however, whether

interest in novel stimuli of the sort implied in the boy's free-ranging activity from age 3 to 6 may properly be considered part of what is usually
meant by "task orientation." Apart from this rather narrow age period,
the sexes are seen in Tables 4.4 and 4.5 to be much alike in their degree
of task orientation and task persistence. We do not see any evidence that
would lead to the conclusion that boys are any more intrinsically interested
in tasks than girls are.

Emmerich (1971 and personal communications) provides some interesting insights into task orientation in young children. Working with large
groups of children in Head Start classes, with repeated behavior observations over a year's time, he obtained large numbers of behavioral measures
and factor-analyzed them. He identified three dimensions, one of which
he labeled *task orientation* vs. *person orientation*. The cluster of behaviors
that characterized the task-oriented children, according to Emmerich, represents "autonomous achievement strivings in which social responses are
subordinated to individualized, task-oriented goals." Task-oriented children are quite capable of being social, he says. However, they direct more
of their social responses to adults; that is, they are likely to ask them for
information and task-related help. "By contrast, the second cluster reflects
affiliative tendencies toward peers in which task requirements and individual achievements are subordinated to interaction processes and goals."
In Emmerich's sample of preschool-aged children, girls were more often
found at the task-oriented end of this dimension. Emmerich notes, however, that there are some developmental trends complicating the picture.
The younger, more immature children tend not to be either very task-
oriented or very person-oriented—they are more withdrawn and inactive.
The oldest, most mature children tend to be *both* person-oriented and task-
oriented. It is only in the middle range of age and competency that the
dimension becomes bipolar and differentiates the sexes. It is as though there
is a point in development where the child cannot take on both kinds of
tasks simultaneously; at this point (at least in Emmerich's sample) girls
tend to concentrate on task-related activities (including using adults as
resources for help in these activities), whereas boys concentrate on social
interaction with peers. But with increasing competence, both sexes can
handle both kinds of activities. Thus sex differences, when they appear,
should be age-specific and transitory. Table 4.4 would certainly sustain
the view that any sex differences in task involvement are transitory. However, the table does not point to any particular age where a sex difference
emerges across different populations and different measures.

"Person orientation" can be considered independently of whether it is
differentiated from "task orientation." As Emmerich has pointed out, they
may occur together. Is there any solid evidence that girls are more "person-
oriented"? Elsewhere (Chapter 6) we review the research on sensitivity

to the cues signifying the needs and emotional states of others and do not find that girls are more "empathic" than boys in this sense. Another approach to the issue is to ask whether, and how, an individual's behavior is affected by the presence of other people. We show (in Chapter 6) that a boy's activity level tends to change when he is with a play group, as compared to when he is alone, while there is no such change for girls. Ryan and Strawbridge (1969) report an experiment involving lever pulling, where boys pulled the lever faster when they were alternating on the task with another boy than when the other boy was merely standing and watching; there was no such effect for girls. McManis (1965) found that boys persist longer at a pursuit-rotor task when another boy is present than when only the experimenter is watching the performance; again, no such effect was found for girls.

Horner (1970), working with college-age subjects, found that men performed better on a task when being observed by peers, whereas for women observation by a peer made no difference in performance. Meddock et al. (1971), on the other hand, found that the effect of presence or absence of an *adult* experimenter during a child's performance on a marble-dropping task did not differ for boy and girl subjects. Thus, it appears that boys are more "person-oriented" only in the sense that they are more influenced by the presence and actions of a *peer*; neither sex seems to be more person-oriented in the sense of being more influenced by the presence or actions of an adult.

This latter possibility can be approached in a different way. Many studies of learning have compared the effectiveness of different reinforcement conditions. In some studies, social reinforcement has been contrasted with material rewards (e.g. candy); in others, positive reinforcement for correct responses has been compared with negative reinforcement for incorrect responses; in still other studies, verbal feedback from the experimenter has been compared with nonverbal (e.g. buzzer), to signal whether a response was correct. And still another design is to compare reinforcement from a liked vs. disliked person. Presumably, a person-oriented subject would find social reinforcement more effective than nonsocial; it is difficult to predict whether positive vs. negative reactions would have a greater impact on such a person, but it is reasonable to expect that verbal feedback would be more effective than nonverbal (nonhuman) information feedback, and that performance would be more affected (for a person-oriented subject) by whether the person delivering the reinforcement is liked or disliked. Table 4.5 shows a large number of studies in which these various comparisons of reinforcement conditions have been made. Of course, many of the studies had positive results in showing that one reinforcement condition was more effective than another across all subjects; but Table 4.6 documents a remarkable unanimity with respect to sex: girls are no more affected than

TABLE 4.6
Sensitivity to Social Reinforcement

Study	Age and N	Difference	Comment
Quay 1971	3-5 (100)	None	Praise or candy in giving Stanford-Binet (black)
K. Hill & Watts 1971	4 (48)	None	Change of preference in response to social reinforcement or nonreinforcement (2-choice learning task)
Meddock et al. 1971	4-5 (64)	None	Supportive or unresponsive E (marble-dropping task)
Spence 1972	4-5 (200)	None	Nonverbal or verbal reward or punishment in picture discrimination task
Crowder & Hohle 1970	5 (64)	None	Praise or information feedback in time estimation task
R. Brooks et al. 1969	5-6 (80)	None	Positive words stated with positive or neutral inflection (marble task)
	5-6 (168)	None	Positive or negative words stated with positive, neutral, or negative inflection (marble task)
Unikel et al. 1969	5-6 (144)	None	Tangible, social, or no reward (discrimination-learning task, low SES)
Yando & Zigler 1971	5-6, 9-10 (192)	None	Imitation of designs projected on screen or drawn by E (normal, retardates)
J. Todd & Nakamura 1970	5-7 (54)	None	Marble sorting in response to positive vs. negative tone of voice, social vs. nonsocial feedback
	6-7 (48)	None	Bead sorting in response to social vs. nonsocial feedback
H. Leventhal & Fischer 1970	5-9 (96)	None	Positive or no reinforcement from E: hole preference, marble insertion rate in marble game
Unruh et al. 1971	6-8 (144)	Boys	Tendency to play marble game longer with social reinforcement
S. Allen et al. 1971	6-7, 10-11 (192)	None	2-choice discrimination task under approval, disapproval, or silence
Spear & Spear 1972	6-7 10-11 (192)	None	Praise, criticism, or silence in discrimination task
Berkowitz et al. 1965	7 (240)	None	Persistence in marble task with intermittent verbal praise
Zimmerman 1972	7 (36)	None	Question-asking training, using praise and no-praise (Mexican-American)
Patterson 1965	7-9 (60)	None	Social disapproval from father or mother in marble game
Babad 1972	8 (40)	Girls	More responsive to deprivation of social reinforcement
Pawlicki 1972	8 (170)	Boys	Contingency and supportiveness of comments influencing performance (marble game)
Zigler & Balla 1972	8, 11 (50)	None	Persistence in marble game with verbal or nonverbal reinforcement (normal, retardates)

(continued)

TABLE 4.6 *(cont.)*

Study	Age and N	Difference	Comment
Montanelli & Hill 1969	10 (108)	None	Change in achievement expectancies or response rates after praise, criticism, or no reaction
McManis 1965	10-13 (96)	None	Performance on pursuit-rotor task under 4 verbal-incentive conditions: neutral, reproof, praise, or competition (normal, retardates)
A. Lott & Lott 1969	14 (100)	None	Performance in visual discrimination task when reinforced by photo of liked, neutrally-regarded, or disliked peer or by card printed with the word "right"
Deci 1972	18-21 (96)	Men	Trend ($p < .07$): spent less time in puzzle task after no verbal reinforcement
		None	Time spent working on puzzle after receipt of verbal reinforcement

boys by social (as compared with nonsocial) reinforcement; and they are not more sensitive to the affective overtones of the feedback provided by an experimenter. Furthermore, neither sex is more influenced by information about the correctness of a response, as distinct from praise. Thus, once more, the hypothesis that boys are task-oriented and girls are person-oriented is not supported.

In previous discussions of this issue, evidence for a linkage between social motives and academic achievement has been sought in correlations between measures of affiliation needs and achievement scores. P. S. Sears (1963)[x] found a significant correlation of .31 between need affiliation (as measured by the TAT) and a composite academic achievement score among fifth- and sixth-grade girls. The correlation for boys was not significant and is not reported; we do not know whether it was significantly different from the girls' correlation, and thus it is not clear whether the finding embodies a sex difference. We have not located other evidence concerning the relationship between social motives and academic performance in the two sexes, and it must remain an open question whether this linkage is stronger in one sex than in the other.

The hypotheses with which this chapter began have not stood up well to the test of accumulated evidence. Males do not appear to have generally greater achievement motivation, although they may show more arousal of this motivation under directly competitive conditions. The task-orientation vs. person-orientation distinction seems to be a poor one from the standpoint of understanding achievement motivation in the two sexes. Boys' greater responsiveness to competitive conditions, and their greater output of energy on a task in the presence of peers, suggest a high degree of person orientation in boys, just as the effectiveness of the "social acceptability" arousal suggests person orientation in girls.

It can hardly be doubted that male adolescents and college students have somewhat different life goals, on the average, than females of the same age. Both have a certain awareness of the kinds of occupations they may realistically hope to enter. Looft (1971), presenting his findings from a study of the vocational aspirations of the two sexes, discusses this point in the following terms: "That girls learn very early the societal expectation for them was perhaps captured most poignantly by the expression of that single girl who initially said she wished to be a doctor when she grew up; when asked what occupation she *really* expected to hold in adulthood, she resignedly replied, 'I'll probably have to be something else, maybe a store lady.'"

So far the impact (if any) of the differences in ultimate occupational goals has not been adequately described; the fact remains that during the long, formative years of schooling, the two sexes have much the same tasks before them and much the same orientation toward achieving on these particular tasks. Do girls' realistic appraisals of their own vocational chances in the present adult society have an impact upon their achievement motivations—and if so, at what point? To understand why this question is difficult to answer, we must return for a moment to the question of the way achievement motivation is measured and what it means. The n Ach measures have been validated in the sense (1) that a correlation has been found between the amount of TAT achievement imagery and performance on selected tasks and (2) that the score is responsive to achievement-oriented "arousal" conditions. It would be unwise, however, to equate the projective measure with the subject's own real-life achievement motivation. Subjects may differ in how thoroughly they project themselves into the storied characters; furthermore the stimulus pictures must necessarily constitute a very limited representation of real-life situations in which achievement strivings might occur. We have not been able to document a sex difference in achievement motivation, as measured in n Ach tests, but it still remains true that in adulthood the achievements of women, in terms of the kind of "success" the world values, are less than those of men. Although the work achievements of the average man spending his life in an average eight-to-four or nine-to-five job may not be especially impressive, a high proportion of the very high achievers in business, science, and the arts are men. We turn now to studies of self-concept, to see whether these post school differences can be traced to any differences in the self-confidence or self-definition of the two sexes.

SELF-CONCEPT

As we have seen, there is some evidence that boys' achievement motivation may be sustained or even stimulated by competitive conditions, whereas girls react in an opposite way. If girls are indeed more vulnerable to competition, is this linked in any way to lack of confidence in their own abilities? Do they suffer from any generalized lack of self-esteem that affects their motivation to achieve a standard of excellence in the tasks they undertake? We shall begin with the question of generalized self-esteem.

When either men or women are asked to rate qualities they associate with an ideal male, they rate them higher than qualities they associate with an ideal female (Rosenkrantz et al. 1968[R]). Both men and women, describing people who succeed in academic settings, depict painful and embarrassing things happening to successful women, good things happening to successful men (Monahan et al. 1974). Both men and women, and high school boys and girls, devalue work labeled as done by women over the same work labeled as normally done by men (H. Mischel 1974[R]). Surely women, knowing that they belong to a sex that is devalued in these and other ways and sharing these values, must have a poor opinion of themselves. We would expect to be able to conclude, with Bardwick, that "women have lower self-esteem than men" (1971, p. 155)[R].

Much research has dealt directly with the question of how people feel about themselves. This question has been approached directly through questionnaires and self-administered scales. It has also been approached indirectly through projective measures, such as the one developed by Brown,* in which the experimenter takes a Polaroid snapshot of the subject child and then asks each subject how the child shown in his own picture feels about his appearance, his academic abilities, his skill in sports, etc. Other studies use ratings made by teachers or other observers, reporting the degree of self-confidence the child seems to display. The majority of studies summarized in Table 4.7 have used self-ratings on standardized self-esteem scales. In such studies, sex differences are seldom found; in the studies that do report a difference, it is as often girls as boys who receive higher average scores. It will be shown in Chapter 5 that girls are somewhat more willing than boys to disclose their weaknesses. Boys obtain higher scores on "lie" scales and "defensiveness" scales that are designed to measure the degree to which an individual disguises his actual evaluation of himself and attempts to present an entirely favorable picture of himself to the researcher. If boys are presenting a more glowing picture of themselves in self-concept inventories than they really feel to be justified, then their scores should actually be somewhat lower than those reported in Table 4.7, and the sex difference would shift in favor of girls' having higher self-esteem.

Studies in which children's self-esteem or self-confidence has been rated by others have had mixed results. Parent ratings of sons do not differ from their ratings of daughters in this respect (Shrader and Leventhal 1968). Teachers sometimes rate girls as having higher self-esteem, even though

* B. R. Brown, Department of Psychology, Cornell University.

TABLE 4.7
Self-Esteem

Study	Age and N	Difference	Comment
Baumrind & Black 1967	3-4 (103)	None	Observer ratings: valuing of self
Shipman 1971	3-4 (1,371)	None	Self-esteem—preschool form of Children's Self-Social Constructs Test (black and white subsample)
Goldschmid 1968	6-7 (81)	None	Ratings of actual and ideal self
Klaus & Gray 1968	6-7 (80)	None	Self-Concept Scale (low SES black; longitudinal)
B. Long et al. 1967	6-13 (312)	None	Self-esteem on Children's Self-Social Constructs Test
Shrader & Leventhal 1968	6-17 (599)	None	Parents' reports of child's self-feelings
Carpenter & Busse 1969	6, 10 (80)	Boys None	Higher self-concept (black subsample) Self-concept (white subsample)
Lepper 1973	7 (129)	None	Negative or positive self-ratings
S. Harris & Braun 1971	7-8 (60)	None	Piers-Harris Self-Concept Test (black)
Herbert et al. 1969	9 (40)	Boys None	Higher self-esteem ratings on Sears Self-Concept Inventory Bledsoe-Garrison Self-Concept Inventory
Bledsoe 1961	9-12 (197)	Girls	Attributed more assets, fewer liabilities to self (elementary form of mental health analysis)
Amatora 1955	9-13 (1,000)	Girls	Higher self-esteem (teacher ratings)
Bledsoe 1967	9, 11 (271)	Girls	More positive self-concepts (adjective checklist)
Coopersmith 1967	10-11 (1,748)	Girls None	Higher self-esteem (teacher ratings) Self-reports of self-esteem
Lekarczyk & Hill 1969	10-11 (114)	None	Revised Coopersmith Self-Esteem Inventory
Coopersmith 1959	10-12 (87)	Girls None	Higher teacher ratings of self-esteem Self-esteem inventory
Carlson 1965	11, 17 (49)	None	Level or stability of self-esteem (longitudinal)
Nawas 1971	18 (125)	Women	Ego sufficiency and complexity scores (projective test; longitudinal)
	26 (125)	Men	Ego sufficiency and complexity scores
Jacobson et al. 1969	18-21 (276)	None	Self-esteem as measured by discrepancy between level of aspiration and expectancy of success
Koenig 1966	18-21 (40)	None	Positive or negative statements about academic self
Nisbett & Gordon 1967	18-21 (152)	None	2 measures of self-esteem

(continued)

TABLE 4.7 *(cont.)*

Study	Age and N	Difference	Comment
Sarason & Koenig 1965	18-21 (48)	Women	More positive self-references (academic self-description)
		None	General description of self
Sarason & Winkel 1966	18-21 (48)	Men	Fewer negative self-references
		None	Positive or ambiguous references
I. Silverman et al. 1970	18-21 (98)	None	Percentage of favorable adjectives checked about self (Gough and Heilbrun's Adjective Checklist)
P. Skolnick 1971	18-21 (114)	None	Level of self-esteem as assessed by questionnaire and self-rating on semantic differential after receiving positive or negative evaluation from confederate
Zander et al. 1972	18-21 (88)	Men	Higher pride-in-self ratings
Bortner & Hultsch 1972	20-88 (1,292)	None	Rating of present status with respect to rating of past status; rating of future status with respect to rating of present status
Kaplan 1973	21 & over (500)	Men	Lower self-derogation scores (subsample of white Ss without a college education)
		Women	Lower self-derogation scores (subsample of black Ss with a high school education or better)
		None	Self-derogation on rating scale (black, white)
Goldrich 1967	25-40 (80)	Women	More optimistic about future professional life, future interpersonal relations, and future self-evaluations
Schaie & Strother 1968	70-88 (50)	None	Burgess Scale of happiness, self-ratings of accomplishments (retired academic and professional workers)

the same boys and girls do not differ when asked to rate themselves (Coopersmith 1959, 1967).

The similarity of the two sexes in self-esteem is remarkably uniform across age levels through college age. We have been able to locate only two studies using post-college subjects. In a study of graduate students, Goldrich (1967) found higher feelings of optimism in women aged 25 to 40, both about their future careers and about their lives in general. In a study of retired professionals, no differences were found in self-ratings or happiness ratings. There are a few discordant notes in the self-esteem picture for women, however. In preliminary inspection of data, to be reported later, on the most recent follow-up of Terman's sample of gifted children, P. S. Sears and M. H. Odom (personal communication, 1974) find that in later middle age women who were gifted as children feel more bitterness and disappointment about their lives than do men who were similarly gifted in childhood. The men, by and large, have had considerably more "successful" lives in terms of personal achievements outside the domestic sphere, and the women tend to look back with some regret on what they now see as missed opportunities. There are two other much smaller-scale longitudinal studies in which measures of self-esteem have been taken. Nawas (1971) reports that among a group studied at age 18 and again at 26, women subjects showed a decrease in ego-sufficiency and complexity scores, whereas men increased in these respects. Engel (1959), working with adolescents, did not find a decrease in self-esteem for either sex over a two-year period. In a study with young adults, Bortner and Hultsch (1972) determined their subjects' current level of self-satisfaction, and then asked them to look back to a period five years earlier and recall how happy they had been with their accomplishments and adjustment to life at that time; the sexes were similar in their self-views, and neither sex reported a loss in self-satisfaction over this time span. Clearly, we do not yet have a consistent picture of how the sexes compare in their self-satisfaction through the adult years. Much must depend on their early-developed talents, on the quality of their marriages, and on the nature of their adult occupations, as well as on wide-impact societal changes (such as depression, war, and technological "progress") that affect the quality of life differently for different generations and different sexes.

So far the work we have summarized on self-concept indicates that when males and females are asked to rate themselves on a series of characteristics, they have equally positive (or negative) self-images, on the whole. One might conclude from this that the two sexes would approach a variety of tasks with equal confidence, but this inference does not prove to be warranted. For example, Carey (1958) found that male college students had a more positive attitude toward problem solving than did female college students. Although almost all the work on self-concept up to college age involves self-ratings, an additional measure of self-esteem has been used with college students. Subjects are asked to participate in a task (or sometimes *imagine* performing a task); they are then asked to predict how well they will do, or following the performance, to describe their satisfaction or pride in their performance. The tasks are sometimes contrived so that a subject's performance is clearly inferior or superior, in terms of some stated norm. Studies asking for confidence measures are summarized in Table 4.8. Clearly, college men are more likely than college women to expect to do well, and to judge their own performance favorably once they have finished their work. Some of the tasks involved are ones in which men characteristically *do* do better (such as work with geometric figures); but many are not. Anagrams are a case in point. Also, women get at least as good grades as men, and often better; yet, when asked what grades they think they will get at the next grading period, men are optimistic in the sense that they think they will do at least as well, and perhaps better, than they have been doing, whereas women are more likely to predict that they will do less well than their past performance would indicate (V. C. Crandall 1969).

There are several possible reasons why women, even though they feel generally as comfortable as men about their own value and competence in the life situations in which they find themselves, should nevertheless express less self-confidence about how they will perform on tasks they are about to undertake. The simplest explanation is that they are more hesitant about bragging, so that though they really feel self-confident they do not say so. However, the confidence measures shown in Table 4.8 are all private (paper and pencil), so no overt bragging is involved. It is difficult to see why reluctance to report favorable things about themselves should affect their task confidence more than their answers to a self-esteem questionnaire.

An obvious possibility is that women do not define themselves in terms of success on these kinds of tasks, and are willing to accept a wider range

TABLE 4.8
Confidence in Task Performance

Study	Age and N	Difference	Comment
V. C. Crandall 1969	7-12 (41)	Boys	Expectancy of success on 6 tasks
	18-22 (380)	Men	Expected grades in relation to past academic record
	18-26 (41)	Men	Expectancy of success on task requiring recall and reproduction of geometric patterns
Montanelli & Hill 1969	10 (108)	Boys	Higher initial expectancy of task success (marble-dropping game)
Battle 1966	12-14 (500)	None	Certainty of reaching minimal goals of school performance in math
Rychlak & Lerner 1965	18-20 (40)	Men	Higher initial expectancy of success on manual dexterity task
Feather 1967b	18-21 (76)	None	Estimate of probability of success on task described as involving luck or skill
Feather 1968	18-21 (60)	Men	Confidence in predicting own performance on anagrams task
Feather 1969b	18-21 (167)	Men	Confidence in predicting own performance, anagrams
Feather & Simon 1971	18-21 (128)	None	Confidence in predicting own performance, anagrams
Jacobson et al. 1970	18-21 (276)	Men	Expectancy of success on the Digit Symbol Test
Julian et al. 1968	18-21 (240)	Men	Confidence in own judgments of timing of light flashes, Asch-type social-influence situation
G. Leventhal & Lane 1970	18-21 (61)	Men	Agree in judging own performance superior when performance is contrived to be superior to partner's
		None	In S's judgments when performance is contrived to be inferior to partner's
S. Schwartz & Clausen 1970	18-21 (179)	Men	Express less uncertainty about what to do in helping with a simulated seizure

of performance as being consistent with a favorable self-image. There is evidence that women are more acceptant of others, despite any weaknesses they may have (Berger 1955[R], Zuckerman et al. 1956[R]), and they may have a similarly more tolerant attitude toward their own performance. Another way of putting this is to say that their aspirations are lower. We have reservations about this hypothesis, in view of the work on achievement motivation discussed above. Girls *do* seem to apply high standards to their own work in the intellectual-academic sphere. Nevertheless, there may be some differences in what aspects of life are deemed important that permit women to feel successful privately, even though they are not seen to be so in the eyes of the world.

TABLE 4.9

Internal Locus of Control

Study	Age and N	Difference	Comment
V. C. Crandall & Lacey 1972	6-12 (50)	None	Intellectual Achievement Responsibility (IAR) Scale
MacMillan & Keogh 1971b	8 (120)	None	Placing blame for interruption of task (normal and retarded subsample)
Walls & Cox 1971	8-9 (80)	None	Internal-External (I-E) Locus of Control Scale (non-disadvantaged)
		Boys	Internal locus (disadvantaged)
V. C. Crandall et al. 1965b	8-10 11, 13, 15, 17 (923)	None Girls	IAR Scale Internal locus (IAR Scale)
O. Solomon et al. 1969	9, 11 (262)	Girls	Acceptance of responsibility for achievement efforts and internal responsibility score (white subsample only)
Dweck & Reppucci 1973	10 (40)	None	Internal locus (IAR Scale)
MacMillan & Keogh 1971a	11 (60)	None	Placing blame for interruption of task
M. Buck & Austrin 1971	14-16 (100)	Girls None	Internal locus (IAR Scale) (adequate-achiever subsample, black) IAR Scale (underachiever subsample, black)
Zytkoskee et al. 1971	14-17 (132)	None	Bialer Locus of Control Scale (black and white)
Benton et al. 1969	18-21 (80)	Men	More self-attribution of responsibility for scores in task (in 1 of 4 conditions only)
Branningan & Tolor 1971	18-21 (333)	Men	Internal score on Rotter I-E Scale
Feather 1969b	18-21 (167)	Men	Internal attribution of performance on anagrams task
Levy et al. 1972	18-21 (110)	None	Rotter I-E Control Scale
Pallak et al. 1967	18-21 (39)	None	Perceived choice in leaving boring task

Another possible reason why women may lack confidence in their performance on a forthcoming task is that they feel less in a position to bring about the ends they strive for—are less in control of their own fates. In recent years, measures have been developed for the "locus of control," and individuals may be characterized on whether they normally feel that the events affecting them are the result of luck or chance (externalizers), or whether they feel that they can control their lives through their own actions (internalizers). As may be seen from Table 4.9, the sexes do not differ consistently on these scales through the grade school and high school years, but in college there is a trend for women to be externalizers. That is, they believe their achievements are often due to factors other than their own skills and hard work.

The greater power of the male to control his own destiny is part of the cultural stereotype of maleness, and is inherent in the images of the two sexes portrayed on television and in print. For example, in a recent study of stories in elementary school textbooks, Jacklin and Mischel (1973[R]) found that when good things happened to a male character in a story, they were presented as resulting from his own actions. Good things happening to a female character (of which there were considerable fewer) were at the initiative of others, or simply grew out of the situation in which the girl character found herself. It is not surprising, then, that young women should be externalizers, by reason of cultural shaping if for no other reason. What is surprising is that the sex difference in this scale does not emerge earlier in life.

In fact, a greater sense of personal strength and potency does emerge among males during the grade school years, if one takes a broader definition than merely the locus-of-control measures. Table 4.10 summarizes a series of studies in which children have been asked to assess their own strength, dominance, or power. Boys and men clearly see themselves as higher on these dimensions. The work on the actual occurrence of dominant behavior of the two sexes is described elsewhere (Chapter 7). For our present purposes, the point of interest is how the sexes perceive themselves, rather than how they actually behave. Omark et al. (1973), using peer ratings to determine a "toughness" hierarchy in a large number of classrooms in several societies, found that boys overestimated their own position in this hierarchy more often than girls did. A boy's position in the dominance hierarchy is a salient aspect of life to him. A girl is normally less concerned about it. But having less feeling of dominance and power might clearly affect a girl's self-confidence in undertaking a task, particularly if she thought she might have to defend her problem solutions in any way.

A boy's tendency to look on the bright side of his own abilities is not confined to the dominance sphere, however. Even with respect to social sensitivity—a presumedly feminine trait—young men seem not to "hear"

TABLE 4.10
Self-Concept: Strength and Potency

Study	Age and N	Difference	Comment
B. Long et al. 1968	6-13 (312)	Boys	Rated self higher on power scale
Fleming & Anttonen 1971	7 (1,087)	Boys	Potency scale on semantic differential self-concept measure
Goss 1968	8 11, 14, 17 (192)	None Boys	Self-ratings of physical strength Self-ratings of physical strength (multiracial)
McDonald 1968	17 (528)	Boys	Described self as higher on dominance (black and white)
Benton et al. 1969	18-21 (80)	Men	Expressed greater feeling of power in contrived role and rated same-sex partner as more powerful
Kurtz 1971	18-21 (40)	Men	Higher potency score on Body Attitude Scale
Cameron 1970b	Adults (317)	Men	Judged self as more powerful and wealthy

comments to the effect that they are insensitive, and their self-ratings of sensitivity are scarcely affected by negative feedback (Eagly and White-head 1972), whereas they do react with improved self-ratings to positive information about their social sensitivity. Young women are responsive to both kinds of information. If this male selective filter operates across a fairly wide range of behaviors, it might help to explain men's greater feeling of potency.

So far, we have found that there is no overall difference between the sexes in self-esteem, but there is a "male cluster" among college students made up of greater self-confidence when undertaking new tasks, and a greater sense of potency, specifically including the feeling that one is in a position to determine the outcomes of sequences of events that one participates in. Is there a "female cluster"? Table 4.11 suggests that there may be one, although the area is amorphous. A number of the studies cited here have used the Carlson adjective checklist. The subject is asked to choose ten adjectives that he believes describe himself, and to circle the five that are *most* descriptive. These five are then weighted more heavily in computing a subject's overall score. The adjectives are scored as either personal or social. Such characteristics as *ambitious, energetic, fair-minded, optimistic,* and *practical* are scored as "personal," while *attractive, cooperative, frank, leader, sympathetic* are coded as "social." There are five studies listed in Table 4.11 that used the Carlson method for scoring individuals on the personal and social dimensions; in four out of five of these, women subjects in late adolescence and adulthood rated themselves higher on the

TABLE 4.11
Social Self-Concept

Study	Age and *N*	Difference	Comment
Walker 1967	8-11 (450)	None	Socialness ratings by self and teacher
P. Katz & Zigler 1967	10 13 16 (120)	Girls Boys None	Social self rated higher Social self rated higher Ss' ratings of social self
Carlson 1965	11 17 (49)	None Girls	Self-description of social orientation Described self as more socially oriented (longitudinal)
Smart & Smart 1970	11-12 18 (267)	Girls None	More socially oriented Social orientation (Asian Indian)
McDonald 1968	17 (528)	Girls	Higher love scores on the Interpersonal checklist: described self as higher (black and white)
Carlson 1971	18-21 (76)	Women	Defined self in social terms
Carlson & Levy 1970	18-21 (202)	None	Social-personal orientation on adjective checklist (black)
Carlson & Levy 1968	18-45 (133)	Women	Defined self in terms of social experiences

social, lower on the personal, adjectives than did men of the same age. These studies reveal something about how the two sexes define themselves; but since the Carlson adjectives are all couched in positive, socially desirable terms, it is not possible to differentiate positive from negative self-images with this scale. Consistent with the Carlson studies is Walberg's finding that girl high school physics students say they have more social interests than their male counterparts. Women consider themselves socially more competent, less shy, more attractive or acceptable to others than men do. The study by McDonald (1968) does report that women believe they feel, and display, more love toward others than men do, but aside from this, our information on the social self is more a matter of definition than of self-esteem. If women do indeed invest themselves more heavily in affiliative relations with other people, it does not follow that they must have higher social self-concepts; indeed, they would be more vulnerable to self-doubt in this very area. It is also true that men's greater involvement with status and power need not imply greater general self-confidence. If they choose to compete for status, they open themselves to many opportunities for failure. There must be numerous bruised egos that are the casualties of competitive encounters. Therefore, although the two sexes may have chosen somewhat different arenas for ego investment, there is no reason to expect any overall difference in self-satisfaction, and indeed, as we have seen, none is found. However, there is some reason to believe that each sex does have a higher sense of self-worth in the area of more central ego involvement.

There is an aspect of the manifestations of self-concepts that is intriguing but hardly explored vis-à-vis sex differences: namely, ego defenses. It has been widely asserted that the "machismo" concept of the male ego is one that leads to the adoption of a variety of defenses: denial of feminine attributes, exaggeration of supermasculine behavior, etc. It seems likely that the young boy's horror of being seen playing with girls is part of this system of ego defense. We have seen that boys exaggerate their own dominance (Omark et al. 1973); also that males are less likely to take in negative feedback about their own performance (Eagly and Whitehead 1972). It is commonly believed that women are more willing to talk about themselves and their frailties—in other words, that they are less defensive about the public presentation of self—but the case is not well documented. Rivenbark (1971) does find that boys do not disclose their thoughts and personal feelings to parents and peers as readily as girls; Williams and Byars (1968) also report that boys are more defensive about whatever level of self-esteem they report than girls are; Bogo et al. (1970) find that boys defend their egos more by turning against a real or presumed external frustrating object, whereas girls engage in more self-blame. All this seems to indicate that girls are more willing to admit weakness, but there is contrary evidence in a study by Hundleby and Cattell (1968)[R], in which girls less often admitted to common frailties than did boys. It is a reasonable hypothesis, based on informal observation, that women defend their egos through dissociation—lack of commitment. They seem less likely to say "I believe" or "I want," and more likely to attribute ideas to others and say "Wouldn't you like to . . ." If an idea or proposal proves unpopular, then the initiator is in a position to dissociate herself from it. We have seen no solid evidence, however, on whether this is actually a form of self-protection more often used by women than men, so it remains hypothesis.

Before closing the discussion of self-esteem and self-definition, we would like to comment on the alleged "narcissism" of females. It is widely believed that women are more concerned than men about having an attractive appearance. Douvan and Adelson (1966)[R] and Coleman (1961)[R] have found this to be the case in adolescent samples. In our review of recent research, we have encountered very little additional evidence for or against this view, except for the isolated fact that girls and women are somewhat more likely to want orthodontic treatment (Lewit and Virolainen 1968). The popular stereotype pictures girls as spending more time in front of the mirror, taking more interest in clothes, daydreaming about being admired, etc. We have learned to be wary of stereotypes, since so many have not stood the test of careful observation. Also, this particular stereotype, if it is valid, probably reflects a sex difference that may be changing rapidly, under the impact of the unisex movement. Men now go to hair stylists and even occasionally suffer the indignities of curlers or driers to achieve the effects they want. Men's clothing styles are much more varied, more colorful, more showy than in the recent past. Still, there is some evidence to support the view that girls continue to be more interested in physical attractiveness than men and boys. Witness the fact that parents, teachers, and peers are more likely to describe girls as concerned about their looks; girls' fantasies and information also reflect this interest (Wagman 1967, Nelsen and Rosenbaum 1972).

However, lest we think of boys as being indifferent to other people's reactions, we must remember the boys' tendency to "show off." Whiting and Pope (1974), in their observations of children in a variety of cultures, recorded "attempts to call attention to oneself by boasting, or by performing either praiseworthy or blameworthy acts with the intent of becoming the focus of another person's attention." They found that boys more frequently engaged in this behavior, and that the sex difference was stronger at ages 7–11 than ages 3–6. In competitive sports, although overt "grandstanding" is frowned upon, there is certainly a large element of self-display. Of course, narcissism is defined as *self*-admiration. In private moments, is a girl more likely to admire herself in the mirror than a boy is to admire his own muscles and daydream self-admiringly about his triumphs? We do not know. We suspect that both sexes are narcissistic, but in somewhat different ways. It is the boy with the most status and power (as well as a reasonable amount of good looks) who can interest the most attractive girls. Traditionally it has been the most beautiful, alluring girl who can interest the highest-status boys. When a girl dresses in an eye-catching manner, or expends a great deal of time on her hair and makeup, she is making a statement to boys about her interest in them, as well as seeking admiration for herself. Similarly when a boy "shows off" to girls, he is signaling to them that he has status and potency; at the same time, he is certainly not free of narcissism. As we have seen, boys tend to believe that their status is greater than it is. We suggest that both sexes admire themselves at the same time that they seek admiration from others and that narcissism is a universal human frailty that is not selective as to sex, though the sexes may admire themselves for somewhat different qualities.

In sum, we have seen that the sexes are quite similar with respect to the aspects of achievement motivation for which evidence is available. They show similar degrees of task persistence. Their achievement efforts are directed toward similar goals; that is, there is no evidence that one sex works more than the other because of intrinsic interest in a task rather than for praise and approval. The two sexes give similar achievement imagery on projective tests under "arousal" conditions. There is some reason to believe that boys' achievement motivation needs to be sustained or stimulated by competitive, ego-challenging conditions, whereas girls throughout the school years seem to maintain their achievement motivation more easily without such stimulation; indeed, at certain ages they may be motivated to avoid competition.

We return to the question of why it is, if males and females have equally good intellectual potential and the two sexes are similar in their achievement motivation throughout the school years, that female achievement in other spheres than the domestic one should drop off so sharply in the years after they have finished their formal schooling. Are there any signs that can be detected earlier than this that would give us grounds for predicting a greater drop-off in women? We investigated the issue of whether there are any differences in self-concept during the school years that might constitute a basis for what happens later. We found that on most measures of self-esteem girls and women show at least as much satisfaction with themselves as do boys and men. During the college years some sex differentiation does occur. At this time, women have less confidence than men in their ability to perform well on a variety of tasks assigned to them; they have less sense of being able to control the events that affect them, and they tend to define themselves more in social terms.

Can women's lesser sense of "internal control" at college age be responsible for lack of achievement during the ensuing years? A first approach to answering this question would be to determine whether "locus of control" measures have been shown to be related to achievement. The answer complicates the picture: among children and young adults high scores on internal locus of control are positively related to school achievement in boys and men, but are unrelated, or only slightly related, in girls and women (Nowicki and Roundtree 1971, Clifford and Cleary 1972[R]). In other words, girls maintain a high level of achievement motivation during the school years whether they have a sense of personal potency or not, whereas boys require this sense for strong achievement motivation. If having a sense of personal control over important events in one's own life is irrelevant to girls' achievement in school, is it irrelevant to achievement after school? Possibly it becomes more relevant during these later years. School is a relatively structured situation, where the tasks to be accomplished are already established. Schools do offer students certain choices, but on the whole, there is an established regimen of courses to be taken and assignments to be completed. Once these tasks are laid out, the two sexes appear to be equally motivated by intrinsic interest in them. But in the post-school world perhaps it is necessary for the individual to seize more initiative in organizing the sequence of actions and events that lead to achievement, and in this situation it may be that a sense of personal potency does make a difference in the achievements of women as well as of men.

However, this is speculation. Whether or not any aspect of the self-concept of the two sexes proves to affect post-college achievement, there are many other factors that differentiate the lives of the two sexes at this point that clearly have an impact. First and foremost are the demands of the domestic duties which have traditionally fallen to women. The struggles of women who have tried to become writers in the face of the daily-life demands normally placed upon women are poignantly described by Virginia Woolf in *A Room of One's Own* (1929)[B]. Until very recently, women have seldom been allowed to be by themselves to do their own work. If a girl does not marry immediately, she is more likely than a boy to live in her parents' home, and more likely to be financially supported by her parents; boys are expected to support themselves (and later their families), which of course acts as a spur to vocational achievement. We should not forget that for many of the greatest creative genuises (e.g. Mozart) their art was the means of earning a living, and they produced abundantly, partly because of the need to support large families and partly because they had jobs that demanded a large output of creative work. Women have seldom had this kind of pressure. Beyond this, most high-level achievement, we believe, comes as the culmination of a long period of training (perhaps including apprenticeship, as in the case of some of the great Italian painters) and ordered steps of promotion. Until recently many of the training opportunities, as well as later steps in the career ladder, have been either closed to women or considerably less open to women than to men.

We do not deny the possibility that there are certain sparks of genius (e.g. potential for mathematical insights) that may occur more frequently among men than women. But until some of the situational factors that have hindered women's nondomestic achievements come to bear more equally upon the two sexes, it is impossible to know whether the initial potential for creative genius is equal in the two sexes or not.

PART TWO

Social Behavior

We have seen that charting the domain of intellectual abilities is not a simple matter. Visual-spatial processes may or may not be involved in the solution of mathematical problems. Verbal processes mediate what are usually classified as nonverbal skills. Even so, the task of organizing the evidence on sex differences in intellectual performance was somewhat simplified by the existence of a body of empirical factor-analytic work, as well as some theorizing, on the "structure" of intellect. This work may not mesh nicely with some of the current thinking about the nature of the cognitive operations that are involved in information processing, but it does nevertheless provide some sort of rationale for topical arrangement of a report on sex differences.

The difficulties of organization are infinitely greater in social behavior. The factorial structure of social behavior has not been clearly delineated —perhaps cannot be. Empirical clusterings change with age, and very probably with the settings in which behavior is observed. The social behaviors that correlate with one another, and that seem to be linked in the sense that they are responsive to similar arousal or eliciting conditions, do not correspond well with the clusters that would be expected on the basis of traditional motivational theories (see Sears et al. 1965[R]). It is sometimes argued that the reason for this disappointing outcome is that we cannot observe motives, only behavior. With this caveat in mind, many social and developmental psychologists have turned to a strategy of identifying a class of behaviors that appears to be behaviorally definable, then searching for the situational or motivational conditions governing the occurrence of these behaviors. The strategy has not always succeeded in avoiding the quicksands of imputing motives to human actions, however. A researcher may set out to study "altruism," for example, or more narrowly "helping behavior," but he will hesitate to classify a person's action in helping someone as altruism if he knows that the actor was attempting to win the con-

fidence of the other person for purposes of future exploitation. Such an action would be referred to the student of Machiavellianism.

We shall attempt, here, to restrict our classifications to the behavioral level, while recognizing that assumptions about needs and motives will influence our decisions about what behaviors "go together" in many instances. We must also deal with the problem of "levels" of explanation. Suppose it should prove true that children of one sex are more likely than those of the other to cry when the mother or father leaves them alone. Are these children more "attached" to the parent or more frightened of being alone? Or do they show more intense attachment behavior because they become frightened more easily? We have encountered frequent instances in which sex differences at an overt level of behavior are attributed to dispositions that are thought to underlie them.

In the chapters that follow, we have attempted first to lay a groundwork by exploring any differences in "temperament" between the sexes (Chapter 5). In Chapter 6 we take up the approach-avoidance dimension of social behavior—the tendency of the individual to seek, or to avoid, contact with other human beings. Included here are the studies of attachment, affiliation, "sociability," empathy, interest in others, nurturance, and altruism, the last two on the grounds that being helpful to another both expresses an attraction and strengthens an affiliative bond. Chapter 7 addresses roughly the cluster of behaviors that deal with power relationships among people—aggression, competition, dominance, compliance, and conformity.

A theme that runs through all three of these chapters on social behavior is the question whether females are in any sense more "passive" than males. Before taking up the specific topics to be discussed, let us first consider what the term passivity means and how it relates to each of the subject-matter areas covered in Chapters 5-7. Some years ago, Helene Deutsch stated the then-current psychoanalytic position as follows (Psychology of Women, 1944, pp. 220ff)[R]: *"If the sexual 'passivity' of the female is generally regarded as typical, it still remains to be seen to what extent other non-sexual manifestations of women's life are patterned after this behavior. The theory I have long supported—according to which femininity is largely associated with passivity and masochism—has been confirmed in the course of years by clinical experience. ... While fully recognizing that women's position is subjected to external influence, I venture to say that the fundamental identities 'feminine passive' and 'masculine active' assert themselves in all known cultures and races."*

What precisely is implied in the assertion that females are more passive than males? In some instances the term refers explicitly to the amount of bodily movement. In other instances the term is seen as reflecting the actions and postures of the two sexes during sexual intercourse: the female is receptive, the male is intrusive; the male is said to be the actor, the female is acted upon. The passivity of the female is thought to show itself in a variety of somewhat more attenuated forms, however, allegedly including:

1. *Submissiveness. The female is thought to invite, or allow, the male to dominate her. In interactions between the sexes, the male is more likely to initiate interactions, the female to respond.*

2. *Lack of aggression. The female withdraws from attack rather than launching a counterattack, and does not initiate aggressive interactions as frequently as the male.*

3. *Dependency. The female is more likely to ask for help, or to cling to others in the face of threat or challenge, while the male engages in active problem solving with or without the mediation of others.*

4. *By extension, the female finds security in the company of others and is therefore more "social" than the male—more oriented toward social stimulation, more responsive to social reinforcement or the danger of losing social approval, more likely to seek proximity to others rather than working or playing independently.*

If the female does indeed submit to dominance attempts, withdraw from threats, and cling to others under stress, this might mean that the female is basically more timid, more easily frightened, than the male. Fear is an arousal state, and although it may be confusing to link it with passivity, the possibility exists that females show immobilization and other "passive" behavior primarily when they are afraid. We begin Chapter 5 by discussing activity level and other manifestations of "arousal" states; we then take up the evidence on the relative timidity of the two sexes.

CHAPTER FIVE

Temperament: Activity Level and Emotionality

ACTIVITY LEVEL

Activity level can be measured in a variety of ways. The traditional method involves the use of a "stabilimeter," which records a shift of weight on different parts of the floor of an animal's cage, or in different portions of an infant's crib or playpen. A method more widely used in recent years involves an observer's recording, either from films or live as the child moves about his environment, of the distance covered per unit time or the number and vigor (or extension) of bodily movements of predetermined kinds. We shall first summarize the animal studies that have been done using measures of these kinds, and then turn to the studies of human children.

Female rats in an activity cage are considerably more active than males (Brody 1942[R]). Most studies have also shown that normal female rats and mice are more active than males in an open-field situation (Gray and Levine 1964[R], Furchgott and Lazar 1969[R], Barrett and Ray 1970[R])—they cross more segments of the floor per unit time. An exception is the work of Wild and Hughes (1972)[R], who did not find a sex difference among rats' activity in exploring a novel space. Administration of male hormones to females neonatally reduces their open-field activity at a later age (Gray et al. 1965[R]). Thus, in the rat, sex differences in activity run counter to what might have been expected, and female sex hormones are associated with high activity levels, male with low.

What about animals closer to man? Harlow reported (1962)[R] that young males engaged in more rough-and-tumble play, whereas females tended to withdraw to the periphery of the play group. Subsequent work (Young et al. 1964[R]) indicates that infant female monkeys, whose mothers have been given injections of male hormones just before the infant's birth, are masculine in a number of respects, including certain aspects of play behavior. Specifically, they engage in more mutual threats and more rough-and-tumble play, and thus they are similar to the normal males that Harlow described. But activity level per se was not measured in these studies. In a recent study with monkeys, Jensen and his colleagues (Jensen et al. 1968[R]) did measure activity. They found that monkey mothers push their male infants away earlier than they do their female infants—perhaps because male infants bite their mothers more and hence are less comfortable to hold (Mitchell 1968[R]). But despite the greater separation from their mothers' bodies, the male infants in the Jensen study were not more active, although the experimenters expected they would be. Preston et al. (1970)[R], working with 7-month-old patas monkeys, also did not find a sex difference in movement in the cage prior to, during, or following separation from the mother.

Sackett (1971)[R], in a study of the effects of early social deprivation on later behavior, tested monkeys at the ages of 4 and 7 years. For our present purposes, the groups of interest are the two control groups—the animals that spent their infancy in a wild (natural) environment, and those born in captivity that were raised with live mothers and peers—in short, those animals that experienced no early social deprivation and that showed normal patterns of social behavior and exploration in adulthood. Among these animals, there were no sex differences in the activity level, as measured by the amount of time spent moving about a test cage. (Females were more active among the socially deprived animals, a fact that Sackett interprets as an indication of greater male vulnerability to depriving environments.)

Mitchell and Brandt (1970)[R], however, observed mother-infant pairs of rhesus monkeys in one side of a cage with another mother-infant pair in the other side; the two pairs were separated by a transparent panel, so they could see but not touch one another. Male infants in this situation climbed longer, ran-jumped more than female infants, and interacted more with the other infant (as far as this was possible) by play-imitating and threatening the other infant. The presence of another infant does appear to stimulate a male monkey infant to greater activity than a female, as part of the rough-and-tumble pattern, but there does not appear to be any general sex difference in activity level apart from this particular eliciting condition.

We turn now to studies of human infants and children. The measurement of activity level in the newborn infant must, of necessity, be a limited affair. In one sense, the infant who spends more time awake is more active than the one with long sleep cycles, so that time spent awake could be considered an index of activity. Other possible indicators are amount of diffuse, spontaneous body movement, breathing rate, height of lifting the head when placed in a prone position, frequency of "startle" response, and amount of body movement in response to specific stimuli. The difficulty regarding these measures as indicators of some underlying quality of the individual that may be labeled "activity level" is that (1) the behaviors are not positively intercorrelated, and (2) most are not stable for individual infants even across brief periods of time. For example, the newborn infant who most frequently shows a startle response also tends to have a relatively *low* level of spontaneous body movement (Wolff 1959[R]). Gordon and Bell (1961)[R] also report that the relationships between activity measures taken within an hour or two of one another show very low, nonsignificant correlations.

Considering prediction over much longer periods of time (R. Bell et al. 1971), we find that newborn boys who appear to be the most active, in the sense that they react most quickly and vigorously when a bottle is removed from their mouths, and who have high breathing rates, tend to be the same children who, as young preschoolers, are passive in the sense that they stand quietly watching other children play rather than becoming involved in active group games. For girls, the predictions are complex: girls who lift their heads relatively high during the first week of life tend to be easily awakened, easily upset, and active as preschoolers; on the other hand, the newborn girls who show a good deal of spontaneous motor movement upon blanket removal show *low* levels of gross body movements as preschoolers. Those neonatal measures that do show some stability in the first few days of life do, in other words, predict certain behaviors several years later, but they do not predict the *same* behavioral qualities; indeed, in a number of instances, the neonatal measures that might be interpreted as indicating a high activity level are associated with later *low* activity levels.

Bell (1960)[R], in reporting a study of a group of male infants, noted that a high neonatal activity level appeared to reflect birth traumas, at least in a number of cases, and he speculated that since boys more often suffer from birth complications, there would probably be a higher proportion of hyperactives among them. When groups of male and female infants are compared, then, the results may depend upon whether or not the samples include children who have undergone complications of pregnancy or delivery of varying degrees of severity. A number of research reports do not describe their selection criteria in detail. Variations in findings of sex differences from one study to another, then, may be partly a function of the proportion of the subjects having birth complications. Some birth traumas have relatively transitory effects; others are long-lasting. Thus sex differences reported from measures taken very early in life are particularly likely to depend upon the number of infants in the research sample with some complications at delivery.

For all the above reasons, we do not regard the available measurements of the behavior of young infants as reliable indicators of any characteristic that can be placed along the activity-passivity dimension, and we have not included the studies of infants under 2 months in Table 5.1. We shall merely mention the possibility that young male infants spend more time awake, although the evidence is not consistent. Based on observations of a group of infants at age 3 weeks and again at 3 months, Moss (1967) reports that the girls slept for a larger proportion of the observation time;

this finding is consistent with a more recent study by Sander and Cassel (1973)[R], who studied a group of 16 infants during their first month of life. The infants were placed in a monitoring crib which recorded movements and permitted distinguishing sleeping from waking states. This study too found that boys sleep significantly less than girls. However, an attempted replication by Moss and Robson (1970) with infants who were observed at 1 month and again at 3 months did not find differential sleep-wake cycles for the two sexes. Results on sex differences in the frequency of startle responses among newborns are similarly ambiguous. Korner (1969) found a tendency ($p < .10$) for boys to startle more frequently while either sleeping or wakeful, but Ashton (1971) found no sex differences in startle reactions. Measures of hand-mouth contacting among newborns may or may not be thought of as legitimate indicators of activity level; in any case, they have not consistently found the behavior to be more frequent in one sex than the other (Korner et al. 1968, Korner 1973, Nisbett and Gurwitz 1970).

Before we review studies of children beyond early infancy, we must consider once again the matter of stability. In a short-term longitudinal study, Maccoby and Feldman (1972) found that activity scores of children aged 2 in an unfamiliar room did not correlate with the activity scores of the same children in a highly similar situation at age 2½ and 3; Escalona and Heider (1959)[R] also found early activity scores to be poor predictors of later behavior; J. Kagan (1971) reports low stability of activity scores for a group of children studied longitudinally at age 8 months, 13 months, and 27 months. Some stability was reported (for boys, but not for girls) by Battle and Lacey (1972) on ratings of "hyperactivity." These ratings were made on the basis of the Fels longitudinal data, for age periods 0–3, 3–6, and 6–10. "Hyperactivity" included impulsive, uninhibited, and uncontrolled behavior, as well as a high frequency of vigorous motor activity. For boys there were significant correlations of hyperactivity scores for adjacent age periods ($r = .42$ and .44), but ages 0–3 and 6–10 were not significantly correlated. An earlier report on the Fels sample (Kagan and Moss 1962[R]) indicated temporal stability (after age 3) for a score called "behavioral disorganization"—again, stability was found for boys but not for girls. Behavioral disorganization referred primarily to episodes of loss of emotional control, and would seem to overlap with the "impulsive, uninhibited, and uncontrolled" aspect of Battle and Lacey's hyperactivity score. We do not know, then, whether the stability reported for boys in the hyperactivity score reflects stability of the "impulsive, uncontrolled" component or the vigorous motor activity component. The latter component would be more comparable to the measures of activity level in the other longitudinal studies.

Walker (1967) found reasonable stability over a one-year period of the

TABLE 5.1
Activity Level

Study	Age and N	Difference	Comment
Lewis et al. 1971b	3 mos (22)	None	Activity changes in response to visual and auditory stimuli
C. Turnure 1971	3, 6, 9 mos (33)	Girls	More limb movement upon presentation of slightly and grossly distorted voice (at 3 mos only); more limb movement in response to mother's normal voice (at 9 mos only)
	3, 6, 9 mos (15)	None	Limb movement in response to mother's and unfamiliar person's voices
L. Yarrow et al. 1971	5 mos (41)	None	Focused exploration of environment (home observation)
J. Kagan & Lewis 1965	6 mos (32)	None	Arm movements in response to a variety of visual and auditory stimuli
	13 mos (30)	None	Number of rectangles traversed during free play period in playroom
J. Kagan 1971	8 mos	None	Number of squares crossed during free play period in playroom
	13 mos	None	Number of squares crossed, playroom
	27 mos (180)	None	Number of squares crossed per unit time (longitudinal)
Rheingold & Eckerman 1969	9-10 mos (24)	None	Locomotor activity in playroom
Clarke-Stewart 1973	9-18 mos (36)	None	Activity level (home observation; longitudinal)
Rheingold & Samuels 1969	10 mos (20)	None	Locomotor activity in observation room with mother present
Goldberg & Lewis 1969	13 mos (64)	Boys	Banging with toys, vigor of play
Messer & Lewis 1972	13 mos (25)	Girls	Number of squares traversed in playroom (low SES sample)
Maccoby & Jacklin 1973	13-14 mos (40)	Boys	Number of squares crossed, playroom, before and after loud noise
	13-14 mos (40)	None	Number of squares crossed before and after loud noise
W. Bronson 1971	15 mos (40)	None	Overall rating of motor activity
Feldman & Ingham 1973	1 (56)	None	Number of squares crossed (Ainsworth "Strange Situation")
Finley & Layne 1969	1-3 (96)	Boys	Number of squares crossed (American and Mexican samples)
Lewis et al. 1971a	2 (60)	None	Arm movements upon presentation of pictures of the human form

(continued)

TABLE 5.1 *(cont.)*

Study	Age and N	Difference	Comment
Maccoby & Feldman 1972	2 (64)	Boys	Number of squares crossed in presence or absence of mother and/or stranger
	2½ (35)	None	Number of squares crossed
	3 (38)	Boys	Number of squares crossed, mo-ch episode
		None	Number of squares crossed, ch-str, mo-ch-str, ch alone episodes
R. Bell et al. 1971	2½ (74)	None	Vigor in play (teacher rating)
Feldman & Ingham 1973	2½ (79)	None	Number of squares crossed ("Strange Situation")
F. Pedersen & Bell 1970	2½ (55)	Boys	Activity recorder, walking
		Girls	"Passive motion" in glider or swing
		None	Tricycle riding, running, rate of tearing down barrier, force exerted to secure object, restless movement
Marvin 1971	2-4 (48)	None	Locomotor exploration
P. Smith & Connolly 1972	2-4 (40)	Boys	Higher overall activity level (observations, indoor and outdoor free play)
Zern & Taylor 1973	2-4 (41)	None	Rhythmic, repetitive body movements, observation in nursery school
Baumrind & Black 1967	3-4 (103)	Boys	Observer ratings of energy levels, and exploration of environment
Shipman 1971	3-4 (1,470)	Boys	Vigor of crank turning
		None	Running speed
J. Schwartz & Wynn 1971	3-5 (108)	None	Motility: observation, first day of nursery school
J. Schwartz 1972	4 (57)	None	Motility: observation in experimental room, alone or with peer
Bee et al. 1969	4-5 (114)	None	Frequency of movement in waiting room from one quadrant to another
Hatfield et al. 1967	4-5 (40)	None	Ratings of activity in laboratory setting
Wolff & Wolff 1972	4-5 (55)	None	Teacher's ratings of gross or fine motor movements
Loo & Wenar 1971	5-6 (40)	Boys	Teacher ratings: activity
		None	Actometer scores (classroom)
Pulaski 1970	5-7 (64)	Boys	Motility during play sessions
J. Kagan et al. 1964	7-8 (76)	None	Restless movement during test-taking at school
Ault et al. 1972	8-10 (29)	Boys	Teacher ratings of hyperactivity (irrelevant talk or play)

(continued)

TABLE 5.1 *(cont.)*

Study	Age and N	Difference	Comment
Walker 1967	8-11 (450)	Boys	Teacher rating "energetic"
	8-11 (406)	Boys	Self-appraisal "energetic"
Achenbach 1969	10 11 (159)	Boys None	Teacher ratings, amount of physical activity
Marks 1968	18-21 (760)	None	Self-report scale, activity level

trait "energetic," as rated inaependently by two successive teachers of a large group of children in the third to sixth grades of school. The stabilities were comparable for the two sexes, and ranged from .37 to .61 (.51 for all grades and both sexes combined).

In general, high or low activity level does not appear to be a consistent characteristic of individual children from one time to another during the preschool years. This fact would lead us to expect that sex differences, if any are found during this period, may be specific to certain ages.

As may be seen in Table 5.1, during the first year of life, results are quite consistent in showing no sex differences in activity level. From the first birthday on, although many studies continue to show no sex differences, those that do find boys to be more active. The only kind of highly mobile behavior that is reported to be more frequent for girls than boys is "passive motion" in a swing or glider (F. Pedersen and Bell 1970).

It is possible that the sex difference in activity level is age-specific, but we cannot be sure from the evidence in Table 5.1. Most studies have been made with children of preschool age. The studies that deal with older children usually shift to new methods—they rely on teacher ratings, rather than systematic behavioral observations. The problems with these methods are seen in the study by Loo and Wenar (1971)—actometers that recorded the amount of gross motor movement a child engaged in did not show boys being more active than girls, whereas teachers reported concerning the same group of children that the boys were more active. Were the teachers simply reflecting sex stereotypes? Or were they reacting to some qualitative difference in the behavior of the two sexes that did not show up in actometer scores? We do not know, but can only point out that with an age-related shift from one kind of measurement to the other, it is not possible to know whether the sex differences in activity level are age-specific or not.

Within a given study, sex differences in activity level are likely to be found with respect to some aspects of behavior but not others. For example, in the Pedersen-Bell report on a group of 2½-year-old children, the two sexes were found to be equally vigorous in tearing down a barrier to obtain a desired object; furthermore, boys and girls did equal amounts of running, tricycle riding, and fidgeting during story time. Boys did do more walking, however, and activity recorders strapped to their backs (which recorded large muscle movements) yielded higher scores.

Evidently there are some situations that elicit high-energy or highly mobile behavior, especially from boys; or, perhaps conversely, there are certain situations that tend to reduce the activity of girls and not boys. Two hypotheses have been considered. The first is that under conditions of stress, girls tend to freeze more than boys do. As a test of this hypothesis, two experiments were done with 13-month-old children (Maccoby and Jacklin 1973). The children were placed on the floor of a room, with their mothers nearby, and the taped sound of a loud, angry male voice was used as a source of moderate stress. In Experiment I, boys remained in one place longer than girls after the onset of the voice—a finding directly contrary to the hypothesis that girls are more likely to become immobile under stress. In Experiment II, the intensity of the sound stimulus was varied. The outcome was that with an intense stimulus both boys and girls moved quickly from the point on the floor where they had been placed (usually moving to the mother); with moderate levels of sound, girls tended (but this time not significantly) to move more quickly than boys. The findings of Experiment II suggest that in the first experiment the girls moved more quickly because they were more frightened—they reacted as they would have to an intensely noxious sound—whereas the boys reacted as they would to a sound that was only moderately intense. Clearly, these results cannot be generalized to other forms of stress; but the experiments provide no support for the hypothesis that it is especially in stressful situations that boys are more active than girls. Other evidence is consistent with this conclusion. As will be seen below, in the studies of attachment in which a child is introduced into a strange room and left alone with a stranger (e.g. Maccoby and Feldman 1972), children of both sexes show reduced activity levels when the stranger enters, but they do so to a similar degree—the girls are not more immobilized than the boys by the strangeness of the environment and the people in it.

A second hypothesis (Maccoby and Jacklin 1971[R]) is that a young male is especially likely to be stimulated to high-energy, high-motoric activity by the presence of other young (or slightly older) males. Halverson and Waldrop (1973) report a further analysis of the actometer data shown in Table 5.1 (Pedersen and Bell 1970) for the NIMH longitudinal sample. They subdivided the records according to whether the children were playing alone or in groups, and found that there was no sex difference in the amount of gross bodily activity when children were playing alone, but that when playing in groups, the girls were approximately as active as they would be while playing alone, while the boys' activity increased markedly. Although Halverson and Waldrop did not have information on the sex of the playmates who made up the play groups, nursery school play groups at this age tend to be sex-segregated, so the findings are consistent with the hypothesis that it was the presence of other young boys that triggered the increased male activity. If this hypothesis proves to be correct, it would help to explain why sex differences tend to appear most frequently after the age of 2, when children begin to interact more frequently with other children. Furthermore, it may account for the great variability in findings from study to study, since the results should depend on the nature of the social situation in which the observations were taken.

To summarize: the studies reviewed have shown a tendency for boys to be more active than girls, but not consistently so for all ages and experimental conditions. During the first year of life, the evidence indicates no sex differences. From this age onward, studies vary greatly as to whether a sex difference is found, but when it is, boys are more active. There appear to be certain eliciting conditions in which boys are more active, and others in which the two sexes are much alike. Very seldom has a greater level of activity among girls been observed. It is well to remember that activity levels have not been studied in situations that might provide elicitors that are especially salient to women and girls. It is clearly possible that there may be a constitutional contribution to the male's tendency to put out more energy, or respond with more movement, to certain stimulating conditions. On the other hand, it is not accurate to describe him as generally more active.

EMOTIONAL UPSETS, FRUSTRATION REACTIONS

In earliest childhood, it is difficult to put a name to a child's state of emotional distress. There have been many efforts to distinguish fear from rage on the basis of physiological indicators. Whatever the success of these efforts with a battery of devices for measuring autonomic reactions, the parent or other observer of the child must usually attempt to infer the nature of the child's emotional state from its sounds and movement, and from the situation that gave rise to the disturbance. Initially, the primary signal of the child's distress is that he cries—sometimes vigorously, with reddened face and thrashing limbs, sometimes in a more subdued fashion. A first index, then, to the frequency of episodes of emotional disturbance in the two sexes is the frequency of crying. As Table 5.2 shows, most of the available information on crying deals with the first year of life. During this time, the two sexes are much alike in the frequency and duration of crying. In Chapter 6, studies of attachment behavior are reported, and some

TABLE 5.2
Crying

Study	Age and N	Difference	Comment
Korner & Thoman 1972	Newborns (40)	None	Crying time
Moss 1967	3 wks, 3 mos (29)	Boys	Less time asleep, more time fussing; higher irritability level (longitudinal)
G. Bronson 1970	1-15 mos	None	Percentage of time infants cried during examination
	4-36 mos (60)	None	Crying in response to novelty (longitudinal)
G. Bronson 1972	3 mos (32)	None	Rating on persistence-of-crying scale
Lewis 1969	3, 6, 9, 13 mos (120)	None	Fret-cry during experimental sessions
R. Caron et al. 1971	3½ mos (98)	None	Crying during conditioning
L. Yarrow et al. 1971	5 mos (41)	None	Frequency of fussing and crying (home observation)
Fourr[R] 1974	6 mos (57)	Boys	Fuss-cry to fear stimuli
Clarke-Stewart 1973	9-18 mos (36)	None	"Irritability" (home observation; longitudinal)
Rheingold & Samuels 1969	10 mos (20)	None	Frequency of fussing (mother present)
B. Coates et al. 1972 •	10, 14 mos (23)	None	Amount of crying before, during, and after separation from mother (2 longitudinal samples)
	14, 18 mos (23)	None	
S. Bell & Ainsworth 1972	1st yr (26)	None	Frequency and duration of crying (home observation; longitudinal)
Goldberg & Lewis 1969	13 mos (64)	Girls	Crying when placed behind barrier
Jacklin et al. 1973	13-14 mos (40)	Girls	Crying behind barrier, if placed near mother in earlier experimental condition
		None	Crying behind barrier, if placed across room from mother in earlier condition
Maccoby & Jacklin 1973	13-14 mos (80)	None	Crying following loud voice (2 trials, 40 in each trial)
Kaminski 1973	1 (48)	None	Frequency of fusses or cries in presence or absence of mother and/or stranger
Feldman & Ingham 1973	1, 2½ (135)	Boys	Crying in "Strange Situation" (in several but not all of the episodes; 2 experiments)
Maccoby & Feldman 1972	2 (64)	None	Crying: child alone or in presence of stranger after separation from mother (longitudinal)
	2½ (35)	None	
	3 (38)	None	

(continued)

TABLE 5.2 *(cont.)*

Study	Age and *N*	Difference	. Comment
Marvin 1971	2-4 (48)	None	Frequency of crying, "Strange Situation"
Dawe[R] 1934	2-5 (40)	Girls	Crying during quarrel with other child
Landreth[R] 1941	2½-5 (32)	Boys None	Crying at home (incident sampling record) Crying at nursery school

of this work has recorded the child's crying when the mother or father leaves the room as an index of attachment. Working with a sample of Australian children, Feldman (1974)[R] found *boys* (aged 1 year) more likely to cry with separation; Marvin (1971) obtained the same result with 2-year-olds, as did Shirley and Poyntz (1941)[R] in an earlier study. On the whole, however, the reactions of the two sexes to separation are quite similar (see Table 6.1).

Early work by Landreth (1941)[R] included records of the frequency of crying among boys and girls of preschool age. The report included 32 children, ranging in age from just under 3 to 5 years of age, and involved observations in the home as well as at school. Boys cried more frequently at home, and the author suggested that this might reflect a greater tendency on the part of boys to become irked with routines and parental restrictions on their activities. The frequency of crying at nursery school was similar for the two sexes in this sample, but the situations that led to crying were different: girls were more likely to cry because of accidental injury, boys from frustration over dealing with a recalcitrant inanimate object or during conflict with an adult. In other words, when boys cried, this was usually part of a frustration reaction, but for girls this was less likely to be the case.

Frustration reactions have not been widely studied, but the work that does exist suggests there may well be a sex difference in these reactions, at least at certain ages. It is not always clear just what should be included as frustration reactions. In Chapter 3 we discussed the studies involving the Matching Familiar Figures test, in which the child must muster the patience to examine a set of highly similar alternatives in detail, rather than quickly make a choice that gets the search process over with (even though speed results in many errors). This test is regarded as a measure of "impulsivity," which is in a sense the inability to tolerate the frustration involved in continued problem-solving efforts. We saw that there was no consistent sex difference in this kind of frustration tolerance. On the other hand, there was a tendency for boys of preschool age to have more difficulty "postponing gratification" on Mischel's test (see p. 101). Furthermore, quick outbursts of temper in frustrating situations may also be more characteristic of boys. Many years ago, F. Goodenough (1931)[R] published a carefully documented study based on diaries kept by parents of 45 young children ranging in age from 7 months to 7 years. For one month, the parents were asked to record each instance of an outburst of anger on the child's part, and to note what events immediately preceded and followed each outburst. Whereas the frequency of anger outbursts was quite similar for the two sexes up to age 18 months, there was a dramatic divergence thereafter: the frequency of outbursts declined to a low level among girls, and declined only slightly among boys, so that during the age range 2½ to 5, boys became angry at least twice as frequently as girls.

Consistent with this early work are the findings of some current (unpublished) work by Van Lieshout (1974)[R]. Sixty-four Dutch children were observed at age 18 months, and again at 24 months. During free play in an observation room, displays of negative emotion were rare. When an attractive toy was taken from the child, however, and placed in a plastic box where it could be seen but not obtained without considerable effort, an appreciable percentage of children at 18 months cried or showed other signs of being emotionally upset. At age 2, the number of girls becoming upset at this instigation had declined considerably, while boys continued to be upset with about the same frequency that had prevailed among them at age 18 months. (The sex difference at 24 months in frequency of "negative emotion" was significant at the $<.01$ level.) We have seen several instances (e.g. Feldman and Ingham 1973, Marvin 1971, F. Goodenough 1931[R], Landreth 1941[R], Van Lieshout 1974[R]) in which boys have shown more negative reactions (including crying) in a situation where they were frustrated. We could add to this list the finding by Maccoby and Feldman (1972) that boys, when left alone by their mothers in a strange room, were more likely than girls to beat or kick angrily upon the door through which the mother had departed, accompanying this activity with loud crying. However, there are some reports in which *girls* have cried more when subjected to frustrating situations. In a widely cited study by Goldberg and Lewis (1969), a child of 13 months is placed behind a barrier, from which he can see desirable toys (and also see his mother, who is seated in the room) but is prevented by the wooden gate or fence from reaching them. Goldberg and Lewis found that girls cried more than boys when placed behind this barrier, while boys more often manipulated the catches at the ends of the barrier, in an apparent effort to get out of their confined position. Maccoby and Jacklin (1973) repeated some aspects of this study; that is, they also used 13-month-old children, and placed them behind a barrier that separated them from the mother and the toys. But this episode was preceded by several events, including a fear-producing stimulus, and a session in which the mother and child played together with the toys on the floor of the experimental room. They compared two groups of children: (1) those who had been close to their mothers at the time of the earlier introduction of the fear stimulus, and (2) those who had been stationed across the room from her. In group 1, the girls cried more than the boys when placed behind the barrier; in group 2, there was no sex difference in crying. In neither group was there any indication that boys were making more efforts to get out from behind the barrier. We cannot tell, in these studies, whether the greater incidence of crying by the girls reflected greater frustration over separation from the toys, greater fear of separation from their mothers, or a choice of crying (instead of pulling at the barrier) as a means of extricating themselves. Possibly vigorous reactions to frustration become channeled into strongly motivated coping behavior rather than crying if the child has the necessary skills and opportunity.

Is it true that boys, when facing impediments, will characteristically make a more vigorous attack upon the barrier instead of crying for help? Pedersen and Bell (1970) studied this question in two situations with children of 2½ years. One test involved showing the child that it was necessary to tear down a paper barrier to reach some attractive toys. The vigor and persistence with which the children attacked this barrier were recorded. In a second task, a row of bells rested upon a table, and had to be picked up individually to be rung. Several of the bells were stuck to the table, and equipped with devices that would measure the strength of the pull exerted to detach them. On both of these measures, boys and girls were quite similar in the vigor of their reactions to the impediments to their actions. Both engaged in vigorous "coping" behavior. In a similar kind of behavioral test, Block (1971)[R] equipped a sliding door in such a way that it would become stuck after being only slightly opened, and the strength and duration of pressure exerted to open it further were measured. The experimenter would approach with an armful of books, and ask the child to open the door. In this situation, boys pushed more intensely (and for a longer time) on the stuck door. There was no sex difference, however, in the children's skill in finding an alternative route to the next room once it became clear that the door would not open.

In summary, what can be said about frustration reactions in young boys and girls? The tendency to show an outburst of negative emotion would appear to be greater in boys after the age of 18 months (see F. Goodenough 1913[R], Van Lieshout 1974[R], Maccoby and Feldman 1972, Landreth 1941[R]). In some cases this takes the form of undirected emotional reactions —what Kagan and Moss (1962)[R] called "behavioral disorganization." In other cases anger is focused upon the frustrating person or object and becomes aggression (see Chapter 7). If boys are more aroused by frustration, does this mean that they attack barriers more energetically, and thus cope more successfully with certain kinds of impediments? The answer to this question is equivocal. The work by Goldberg and Lewis (1969), and that by Block, would suggest that they do. That by Pedersen and Bell, and by Maccoby and Feldman, found the two sexes to be similar in the degree to which they focused their frustration responses toward removing the obstacle.

It is worth noting that the age of the subjects appears to make a considerable difference in the outcome of some of the research cited in this section. The Goodenough and Van Lieshout findings suggest that, if sex differences are found at the age of 2 or later, it is not that boys are increasing in their emotional volatility as they grow older, but that girls are decreasing in the frequency and intensity of their emotional reactions at a faster rate than boys. Why should this be so? Are girls acquiring skills more rapidly that permit them to deal with frustrations before they become too great? Are boys, for some reason, more frequently placed in situations that frustrate them? It is tempting to speculate that girls may be acquiring language faster and that this skill may serve them in good stead in overcoming frustration. But as we saw in Chapter 3, the girls' advantage in language development is slight and, in many samples of children, not demonstrable at all. Furthermore, Brackett (1934)[R] showed many years ago that the amount of crying a child does in nursery school is not related to the level of his verbal productivity. In other words, crying is not outgrown when and because a child acquires sufficient language to express his needs in other ways. As we shall see in later chapters, there is evidence that cooperative behavior in children does not depend upon their verbal skills, and angry, aggressive behavior (more common in boys) frequently takes verbal as well as nonverbal forms. We do not believe that language development is a good candidate to explain why the frequency of negative emotional responses to frustration declines faster in girls than in boys, but are at a loss to suggest an alternative.

FEAR, TIMIDITY, AND ANXIETY

We will not review the animal work on this subject in detail, partly because the parallels to human beings seem quite weak. Concerning rodents, for example, Gray (1971, p. 94)[R] says:

In general, the differences between male and female rodents conform to this pattern: as Maudsley Reactive rat is to Maudsley Nonreactive . . . so male is to female. Thus male rats have been reported to defecate more and ambulate less in the Open Field, to emerge into a novel environment more slowly, and explore it less readily, and to freeze more in response to a novel sound. . . . Ulcer formation as the result of psychological conflict is also more severe in the male than the female rat.

Gray has argued that these sex differences in fear that are found in rodents are reversed in man. But the human evidence cited is either self-report studies (reviewed below) or clinical evidence from doctors' reports of psychiatric symptoms. Fidell (1973)[n] has shown that the same symptoms tend to be diagnosed differently in male and female patients. In cases of ambiguous symptoms (equally ambiguous for the two sexes of patients), doctors more often consider a patient's illness to be psychosomatic if the patient is a woman. Hence we must hesitate to rely upon this source of evidence for information about the prevalence of anxiety states (and their attendant somatic disorders) in the two sexes. We turn now to a search for other sources of information.

The classic work on children's fears was done many years ago by Jersild. In one study involving over 130 families, Jersild and Holmes (1935) asked parents to keep a diary for 21 days, recording all the instances in which their young children showed fear, and giving a detailed description of the situation that appeared to have been frightening to the child. These reports were made for children ranging in age from early infancy through the age of 6. Boys and girls were remarkably similar in the frequency and intensity of fears reported, as well as in the nature of the situations that aroused their fears. Jersild and his co-workers then undertook an experimental study in which they presented children aged 2 through 6 with situations that (judging from parental reports) might be expected to be frightening to at least some children. These situations involved asking the children to approach a snake; approach a large dog; walk across a board elevated several feet above the floor; go into a dark passage to retrieve a ball; obtain a toy from a chair adjacent to a strangely dressed, immobile, and heavily veiled stranger; walk across a slightly elevated runway which tipped when stepped upon; remain alone in an unfamiliar room; and investigate the source of a loud, unexpected noise. There were no differences in the percentages of each sex displaying fear to any of the stimulus situations. However, the intensity of the fear response was higher for girls than it was for boys.

The more recent studies in which children's fear reactions have been directly observed, or in which parents have been asked to make records of their children's emotional reactions, have found few sex differences. Although girls may show a slightly earlier age of onset of stranger fear (Robson et al. 1969), this is not found in all studies (e.g. Bronson 1972) and there is no consistent difference in stranger reactions after the first year. Although Maccoby and Jacklin found in one study that girls of 13 months responded more quickly to a loud sound than boys did, the sex difference did not replicate on a second sample of children. Blayney (1973) did not find a sex difference when testing 4-year-old children's willingness to cross a narrow, elevated plank—a finding consistent with the earlier observation by Jersild. Bandura and Menlove (1968) screened all the children in a large nursery school and identified 32 girls and 16 boys who, by behavioral test, were afraid of dogs. Unfortunately, the recent observational studies have not included a wide range of eliciting conditions, so that it cannot be determined whether some of the sex differences that emerged as especially striking in the Jersild work (stepping on the tipping board, fear of the strange person) would be replicated in present-day groups of children. It would appear that the sexes do not differ in their readiness to enter quickly into nursery school activities when they are first introduced to this new environment (Baumrind and Black 1967, J. Schwartz and Wynn 1971). On the whole, recent observational work does not reveal any consistent tendency for one sex to be more timid than the other. However, there are indications that there may be some specific elicitors that arouse fears more readily in girls than in boys. See Table 5.3.

After children are old enough to read and write, research on fearfulness is done almost entirely with self-reports. Here, as in the case of teacher ratings, a sex difference is sometimes found and sometimes not, but when there is a difference, it is in the direction of greater reported fearfulness among girls. Bandura, in his research on the cure of snake phobias, has on several occasions advertised in local newspapers for subjects who are afraid of snakes and would like to be subjects in a desensitization experiment. The large majority of people responding to such ads have been women (see Bandura et al. 1969[R]). In a few instances, these women were found with behavioral tests to be fully as able to approach and handle snakes as unselected adults who did not describe themselves as being afraid of snakes. And upon discovering that they could actually handle snakes, these subjects were pleased and relieved, feeling that they could now comfortably go on camping trips and enter other situations they had avoided before because of their preconceived snake phobias. Of course, a large number of volunteer subjects *did* prove, behaviorally, to be extremely avoidant of snakes, just as they had thought. However, Bandura and his colleagues have found that their subjects could be fairly readily desensitized to the objects of their fear, so it is difficult to see these fears as in any sense "built in."

How can we distinguish self-attribution of fearfulness from fearfulness itself? This question becomes even more pressing in our efforts to understand the results of studies of anxiety. Whereas studies of fears in early childhood tend to focus on fears of specific objects, work with older subjects shifts to a focus on more generalized anxiety states, and these are usually assessed through self-reports. General "manifest anxiety" scales have been devised for adults and adapted for children (TASC, the Test Anxiety Scale for Children; and GASC, the General Anxiety Scale for Children). In a 1960 summary of their work, Sarason and his colleagues conclude that "the most consistent sex difference we have found is that girls get higher scores than boys on both the TASC and the GASC. The difference between boys and girls on the GASC is greater than on the TASC. This pattern of differences was obtained both in England and America"

TABLE 5.3
Fear and Timidity

Study	Age and N	Difference	Comment
Jersild & Holmes 1935	0-6 (153)	None	Parent report: 21-day diary record of children's fears
Bronson 1972	4, 6½, 9 mos (32)	None	E rating of S's responses to encounter with male stranger
Robson et al. 1969	8, 9½ mos (45)	Girls None	Earlier age of onset of fear of strangers Fear-of-stranger ratings during home visits (longitudinal)
Jacklin & Bonneville[R] 1974	9½ mos (20)	None	Responses to noisy toys, hesitancy to touch buzzing toy, latency to leave mother for attractive toy (2 trials)
Maccoby & Jacklin 1973	13-14 mos (40)	Girls	Shorter latency to move following loud noise
	13-14 mos (40)	None	Latency to move following loud voice
Schaffer & Parry 1972	1 (12)	None	Approach to strange object with flashing lights and bleeps
Kaminski 1973	1 (48)	None	Hesitancy to touch whirring toy
Vernon et al. 1967	2-5 (32)	None	Anxiety following hospitalization, mother questionnaire
Jersild & Holmes 1935	2-6 (105)	Girls	Fear in response to 8 experimentally presented, potentially fearful situations
Baumrind & Black 1967	3-4 (103)	None	Observer ratings: apprehensiveness, at ease vs. ill at ease at nursery school
J. Schwartz & Wynn 1971	3-5 (108)	None	Emotional reaction, first day of nursery school
Blayney 1973	4 (29)	None	Timidity, crossing narrow elevated board mounted on springs
Jersild & Holmes 1935	5-12 (398)	None	Children's reports (in individual interviews) of their fears
Shrader & Leventhal 1968	6-17 (599)	None	Frequency of fears, depression (parent reports)
Yando et al. 1971	8 (144)	Girls	More fearful in interaction with adults (E's rating)
		None	Fearfulness in interaction with adults (classroom teacher's rating)
Walker 1967	8-11 (450)	Girls	Teacher rating, fearfulness
	8-11 (406)	Girls	Self-appraisal, fearfulness
Hannah et al. 1965	18-19 (1,958)	Women	Higher total fear scores (self-rated Fear Survey Schedule)
W. Mischel et al. 1969	18-21 (51)	None	Unpleasantness ratings of hypothetical high and low intensity shocks

(Sarason et al. 1960[R], p. 250). A similar pattern emerged in the Oetzel
bibliography (Maccoby 1966b[R]), and it is again apparent in the evidence
that has been collected since then. Table 5.4 lists studies in which general anxiety scales have been used, and Table 5.5 includes those on test
anxiety. The greater general anxiety of girls and women is fairly consistent
across studies. Measures of test anxiety frequently find no sex difference,
but when there is a difference, girls score higher.

The first question we must ask about these studies is whether the scales
measure "real" fear states of any sort. The anxiety scales have not been
validated against behavioral observations. They have been validated primarily by comparison with teacher ratings, and the correlations are low.
For example, the overall correlation of the TASC with teacher ratings of
children's test anxiety is .20. Secondarily, the value of the anxiety scales
has been proved through their correlation, in predicted ways, with academic performance. This has been an entirely reasonable way to proceed
from the standpoint of the purposes of the developers, who were primarily
interested in the role anxiety plays in taking tests and motivating, or interfering with, school-related tasks. For our purposes, however, the procedure
leaves the question open as to whether girls' higher anxiety scores do reflect genuinely greater fear. Sarason discusses this question in detail (Sarason et al. 1960[R], chap. 9). He notes that boys score higher than girls on
the lie scale, although two studies have found no sex differences on the
lie scale (Cowen et al. 1965, Cowen and Danset 1962). In later work
(Sarason et al. 1964[R], K. Hill and Sarason 1966, Lekarcyzk and Hill 1969),
it has also been shown that boys are more "defensive"—that is, less willing
to admit to weaknesses of various sorts. For example, when asked "Do
you sometimes dream about things you don't like to talk about?" or "When
one of your friends won't play with you, do you feel badly?" a boy is more
likely to say no. On the assumption that these are fairly universal feelings
a denial is interpreted as defensiveness.

Sarason suggests the possibility that girls score higher on self-report
anxiety scales simply because they are more willing than boys to admit
that they feel anxious. It should be noted that Sarason has shown that
even though some children may minimize their own anxious feelings when
completing an anxiety scale, this does not invalidate the scale for purposes
of understanding school-related fears and their effects. This has been
demonstrated by showing that Anxiety scores still correlate significantly
(and negatively) with academic performance, even when Lie Scale and
Defensiveness Scale scores are held constant. However, the sex differences
in anxiety scores might still be a function of boys' greater defensiveness.
It would be possible to analyze for sex differences after having co-varied
out the scores on the Lie and Defensiveness scales, but to our knowledge
this has not yet been done, so the issue remains in doubt.

TABLE 5.4
General Anxiety Score

Study	Age and N	Difference	Comment
Goldschmid 1968	6-7 (81)	None	Children's Manifest Anxiety Scale (CMAS)
Holloway 1958	8 (121)	None	CMAS
Cowen & Danset 1962	9 (132)	Girls	CMAS (French sample)
Cowen et al. 1965	9 (169)	Girls	CMAS
Iwawaki et al. 1967	9 (155)	None	CMAS (Japanese sample)
B. Lott & Lott 1968	9-10 (233)	None	CMAS (white, black)
Barton 1971	9-10 (64)	Girls	Modified form of State-Trait Anxiety Inventory
Grams et al. 1965	9-11 (110)	Girls None	General Anxiety Scale for Children (GASC) CMAS
Palermo 1959	9-11 (470)	Girls	CMAS (white, black)
Penney 1965	9-11 (108)	Girls	CMAS
L'Abate 1960	9-13 (96)	None	CMAS
Hafner & Kaplan 1959	10 (188)	None	CMAS
Baltes & Nesselroade 1972	12-16 (1,249)	Girls	Tense, Cattell's High School Personality Questionnaire (longitudinal)
Templer et al. 1971	13-85 (2,559)	Girls & women None	Death anxiety scores (students, parents of students, upper middle SES apartment dwellers) Death anxiety scores (hospital aides, psychiatric patients)
Hannah et al. 1965	18-19 (1,958)	Women	Higher neuroticism scores (Maudsley Personality Inventory)
Benton et al. 1969	18-21 (80)	Women	Self-report of tension following experiment requiring S to doubt confederate's statements (in high-deceptive-rate condition only)
Kidd & Cherymisin 1965	18-21 (100)	None	Taylor MAS, short version
MacDonald 1970	18-21 (149)	Women None	Self-report, anxiety while waiting for shock; first-borns more likely to drop out of experiment Later-borns, drop out of experiment
Mendelsohn & Griswold 1967	18-21 (181)	Women	Anxiety scale, MMPI
Vassiliou et al. 1967	Adults (400)	Women	Greek translation, Taylor Manifest Anxiety Scale

TABLE 5.5
Test Anxiety

Study	Age and N	Difference	Comment
K. Hill & Sarason 1966	6, 8, 10 (323)	Girls	At ages 8 and 10, higher on Test Anxiety Scale for Children (TASC) (longitudinal)
	9, 11 (347)	Girls	At age 11, higher on TASC (longitudinal)
Feld & Lewis 1969	7 (7,355)	Girls None	TASC (white sample) TASC (black sample)
Solkoff 1972	8-11 (224)	None	TASC
Lekarczyk & Hill 1969	10-11 (114)	Girls	TASC
Entwisle & Greenberger 1972b	14 (566)	Girls	Test Anxiety Questionnaire (black, white)
Sampson & Hancock 1967	15-17 (251)	None	Text Anxiety Scale (Mandler-Sarason)

K. Hill and Sarason suggest (1966, p. 65) that the content of existing anxiety scales may be such as to touch more closely upon the particular anxieties that affect boys, and hence arouse their defensiveness most. Our reading of the General Anxiety Scale for Children leads us to a different conclusion. Some of the items are: "Do you get scared when you have to walk home alone at night?" and "When you are home alone and someone knocks on the door, do you get a worried feeling?" Girls are almost universally warned about the danger of sexual molestation. Sometimes the warnings are vague—girls must avoid strange men, not be out alone at night, lest "something terrible" should happen. We suggest that fears built up in this way would generalize to such settings as a visit to the doctor (usually male), or take the form of a generalized fear of the dark. We count 10 items out of the 45-item GASC that we believe might be weighted toward eliciting fears of these sorts, thus inviting higher scores from girls. There is another set of items (fear of mice, snakes, sharp objects, lightning, being bitten by animals) that could be considered weighted in the same direction if one took a Freudian view of the symbolic meaning of these stimuli. We see very few items in the scale that relate to the boy's special fear of appearing cowardly in the eyes of his age-mate, his fear of public humiliation or failure, etc. Therefore we suggest that girls' higher scores on existing anxiety scales might be just as much a function of the content of the scales as of girls' greater readiness to disclose anxious feelings. Perhaps both factors make a difference.

Where does this leave us, in relation to the question of whether girls are "really" more anxious than boys? It might be possible to reverse the usual sex difference by changing the content of test items. However, the very fact that girls do appear more ready to admit their fears is important. A person who says to himself "I am afraid of snakes" probably really *is* more afraid (in the behavioral sense) than the person who is afraid but denies it to himself. That is, the admission allows the person to act in accordance with his fears and avoid snakes, so that the self-attribution becomes the reality. If this is so, it is less serious that we have so little information on the actual behavior of the two sexes in potentially fear-producing situations.

When one is faced with difficulties in interpreting psychological data, it is always tempting to turn to what seems to be the more objective realm of physiological measures. There have been a number of attempts to relate physiological measures, particularly skin conductance, to scores on the Taylor Manifest Anxiety Scale. They have been largely unsuccessful (Rossi 1959[R], Raphelson 1957[R], Silverman 1957[R], McDonnell and Carpenter 1960[R]). As we have seen, the difficulty may be that the anxiety scales are not measuring "true" anxiety, but even if they were, it might be difficult to obtain a relationship with physiological measures. Lacey (1967)[R], in a review of the work on physiological measures of response to stress (the stress usually being experimentally induced), concludes that no one physiological measure can be related to stress, and that the psychophysiologist's best hope is to look at response *patterns* rather than any individual score. Duffy (1962)[R] discusses sex differences in physiological measures of arousal, and there do seem to be some sex differences. But the relationship of these to fear states has so far not been shown, and we do not have an answer from physiological measures as to whether one sex is more timid or fearful than the other. We would not be surprised if the answer turns out to depend on the stimulus situation. That is, the two sexes may be afraid of somewhat different things, on the average. For the present, however, we can only summarize the state of our knowledge on fear and timidity as follows:

1. Observational studies do not usually show a sex difference in timidity.

2. Teacher ratings and self-reports show girls to be more timid and anxious than boys.

3. Since boys are less willing to admit to fears or anxious feelings (have higher scores on Lie and Defensiveness scales), the sex differences on anxiety scales may be due to this factor.

4. Physiological measures of fear states have not so far clarified differences on psychological measures within and between the sexes.

What are the implications of the findings reported above for the issue of whether girls and women are "passive"? In the studies that reported boys as being more active than girls, it would not be accurate to say that the girls were inactive. In some research, the measure of activity is the amount of space crossed per unit time. When boys were doing somewhat more moving from place to place in a play room, girls were typically settling down to concentrated play with a toy. They did not sit passively doing nothing or stare into space. When teachers rated boys as more "energetic" or "hyperactive," they may have meant that boys made larger or more forceful movements, but there is no implication that girls were unoccupied. In a similar vein, if a boy responds to frustration with an outburst of temper while a girl does not, this may or may not imply that the girl is being "passive" in the sense of giving up and allowing her activities to be impeded by the barrier; perhaps she simply attempts to cope with the obstacle somewhat more calmly. In most studies using behavioral observation, fearfulness is not more common in one sex than the other; when fear is present, it does not appear to immobilize girls more than boys.

So far, then, "feminine-passive" does not appear to be the "fundamental identity" that Deutsch thought it was. It is possible that girls' self-attribution of fearfulness does impose restrictions on their adventurousness in exploring new situations. But it is equally possible that a boy's tendency to lose his temper interferes with constructive, active coping behavior (produces a state of disorganization) that is just as severe an impediment to ongoing activity as timidity would be. Although some provocative (though inconsistent) indications of temperamental differences between the sexes have emerged in the preceding pages, the dimensions have not been defined in such a way as to yield a clear picture of what these dimensions are or what their consequences may be.

CHAPTER SIX

Social Approach-Avoidance

DEPENDENCY

Dependency is one of the two most extensively studied behaviors that are presumed to be sex-typed (the other being aggression). Although W. Mischel (1970, p. 6)[R] indicates that the evidence is not so consistent for dependency as it is for aggression, he does read the existing research as indicating that there is "greater dependency, social passivity, and conformity in females than in males." What is meant when it is alleged that girls are more "dependent" than boys? R. Sears et al. (1965, p. 27)[R] define dependency as "an action system in which another person's nurturant, helping, and caretaking activities are the rewarding environmental events." There are a number of different kinds of actions that a child may engage in in order to obtain "nurturant, helping, and caretaking" activities from another person. Simply remaining near the other person, or touching and clinging to this person, would be examples of dependent supplications. So would noncontact forms of calling attention. So would seeking help, consolation, reassurance, or protection. And even getting attention from another person by being annoying—nagging, whining, disruptive actions—can be interpreted as instances of dependency. All these were indexes of dependency used by Sears and his colleagues (1957, 1965)[R] in their efforts to trace the aspects of family interaction that established dependent behavior in children. A subsidiary interest in this research was to determine whether the sexes differed in the strength of their dependency motivation, or in the frequency of any or all of the behavioral manifestations of this motivation.

Before discussing sex differences in this sphere of behavior, it may be well to underline the currently well-known fact that dependency in the above senses of the word does not represent an identifiable cluster in the social behavior of young children. Sears et al. (1965)[R] reported this lack of clustering among the relevant behaviors. Maccoby and Masters (1970)[R] noted that proximity seeking and attention seeking are part of different clusters which have distinct courses of development and are responsive to different antecedent conditions. They also indicated that the tendency for a child to orient toward adults is relatively independent of the tendency to orient toward age-mates. Two recent studies (R. Bell et al. 1971, Emmerich 1971) have factor-analyzed a large number of measures of young children's behavior, and have identified coherent patterns, but have not found any pattern that can be identified with the hypothesized "dependency" cluster. To complicate the picture, Bell et al. note that the factorial structure of behavior, although largely similar for the two sexes, is different in some rather important respects, so that a given form of "dependent" behavior (e.g. asking for help) might have a different meaning for boys than for girls, depending upon the other behaviors with which it was integrated and the situations in which it tended to occur. Despite these complications, some similar themes emerge from the two studies. Bell et al., studying 2½-year-olds from predominantly white middle-class backgrounds, found that children who showed assertive behavior in response to a barrier and who had good cognitive (especially verbal) skills tended to be oriented toward adults, but "were not dependent in the usual sense." The tendency to orient toward adults was relatively independent of the tendency to orient toward peers. Emmerich worked with a very different sample—disadvantaged children, many of whom were black—with ages ranging from 4 to 5 years. As noted in Chapter 4, "task orientation" (that is, the tendency to persist autonomously in goal-directed efforts) among these children was associated with adult orientation and cognitive interests. Orientation toward other children, on the other hand, was factorially quite distinct and was associated with a good deal of gross motor behavior out-of-doors and with social thematic play (make-believe games).

In view of these findings from cluster analysis, it would be surprising if one sex were to emerge as more "dependent" in all the initial meanings of the word. We may find, for example, that the two sexes are equally sociable, but that one is more oriented toward peers and the other toward adults; or we may find that proximity seeking is more common in one sex, attention seeking in the other. Or it may turn out that the sexes are much alike on the average on all the measures, with a great deal of variation within each sex along the dimensions that have been found to describe stable, consistent individual differences.

In the summaries that follow, sex differences are discussed separately under four categories: (1) proximity seeking, touching, and resistance to separation in relation to child's parents or other adult caretakers; (2) proximity seeking, touching, and resistance to separation in relation to age-mates; (3) social responsiveness, social interests, and social skills in relation to parents or other adults (attention seeking is included here); and (4) social responsiveness, social interests, and social skills in relation to age-mates, or with age of target unspecified. There will be very little information under topic (2).

In a number of earlier studies, global measures of dependency were used, in which instances of help seeking, attention getting, proximity seeking, and touching were combined into a single "dependency" score. In other studies, although distinctions have been made between the various components, scores do not reflect whether the behavior is directed toward adults or age-mates. These studies are not included in the tables, but will be discussed in the text where they seem most appropriate.

Some of the sex differences in other types of behavior have been attributed to a presumed tendency for girls to remain closer to the mother, and cling to her more often, in early childhood. For example, Garai and Scheinfeld say (1966, p. 199)[R]: "The earlier speech development and greater verbal fluency of girls appear to be related to the earlier maturation of their speech organs, their innate tendency toward more sedentary pursuits, *their closer contact with mothers* and their greater interest in people." Table 6.1 presents a summary of the research in which measures have been taken of the physical proximity a child maintains with its mother, and the amount of touching or clinging that has been observed. A few studies with measures of proximity and clinging to fathers are also included. These kinds of behavior are, of course, seen much more commonly in young children than in older ones. It is something of a problem to know whether there are any behaviors in later life that ought to be included here. Our own theoretical bias is no doubt reflected in our decision: we regard early childhood proximity seeking and clinging as the child's response to uncertainty or anxiety about some aspect of the situation he is in, and an indication of the fact that certain crucial individuals in his life are able to reassure him with their close presence. Thus, if a child of 9 or 10 has a bad dream and goes to his parents' room and asks to get in bed with them, this we would see as an instance of perseveration of a pattern established early in life which is seldom manifest at this age; if the same child pesters his father to take him to a ball game, however, we would not regard this as part of the "proximity seeking" behavioral cluster, even though the child is, in a sense, trying to be near his father. With this rather vague criterion in mind, we have included in Table 6.1 only studies of infants and preschoolers, with one exception where the parallel in the behavior of older children seemed very clear.

The studies summarized in Table 6.1 represent a fairly wide range of observation situations and measures. Most commonly, children under age 3 have been observed in a structured situation in which the mother and child have come to a toy-stocked observation room, and the child has been observed in interaction with his mother and the toys, with or without an experimental manipulation of some aspect of the situation. In a few studies, the child's tendency to approach the mother or cling to her has been observed in the home. From age 3 on, a wider range of measurement situations and methods have been used, including records of the child's readi-

TABLE 6.1

Touching and Proximity to Parent, Resistance to Separation from Parent

Study	Age and N	Difference	Comment
Fleener & Cairns 1970	3-19 mos (64)	None	Protest over mother or stranger leaving room
Beckwith 1972	7-9 mos 8-11 mos (24)	None Girls	Percentage of mother initiations to which infant responds with smile, vocalization, or approach (longitudinal)
F. Pedersen & Robson 1969	8, 9½ mos (45)	None	Age of onset and intensity of infant's greeting behavior upon father's return (home observation)
Corter et al. 1972	9-10 mos (10)	Boys	Shorter latency: child follows mother out of room (no toys present)
	9-10 mos (26)	Boys	Shorter latency: child follows mother out of room (1 or 6 toys present)
Rheingold & Eckerman 1969	9-10 mos (24)	None	Child leaves mother to explore adjoining room
Clarke-Stewart 1973	9-18 mos (36)	None	Attachment to mother (home and laboratory observations); "physical" attachment to mother (home observation; longitudinal)
Rheingold & Samuels 1969	10 mos (20)	None	Touching mother during play session in observation room
B. Coates et al. 1972	10, 14 mos (23)	None	Look at mother, vocalize to mother, proximity to mother, touch mother before or after separation
Littenberg et al. 1971	11 mos (24)	None	Vocalize, fret, cry, follow when mother leaves room
J. Brooks & Lewis 1972	11-15 mos (17 opp.-sex twin pairs)	Girls None	Look at mother, remain in proximity to mother Touching mother
Ainsworth et al.[R] 1971	12 mos (56)	None	Proximity to mother, reaction to separation from mother
Goldberg & Lewis 1969	13 mos (64)	Girls	Return to mother after removal from lap. Touch mother, proximity to mother
Messer & Lewis 1972	13 mos (25)	Girls None	Return to mother after removal from lap, touch mother Vocalize to mother, look at mother (low SES sample)
Maccoby & Jacklin 1973	13-14 mos (40)	Boys None	"Trips" to mother Proximity to mother; touching mother; looks to mother
	13-14 mos (40)	None	Proximity to mother; touching mother; looks to mother; "trips" to mother
W. Bronson 1971	15 mos (40)	Girls	Amount of time near mother, structured observation (1 of 3 episodes)
Ban & Lewis 1971	1 (20)	None	Look, touch, proximity, or vocalize to mother or father

(continued)

TABLE 6.1 *(cont.)*

Study	Age and N	Difference	Comment
Feldman & Ingham 1973	1 (19)	Boys	Cry when mother leaves room (Ainsworth "Strange Situation," 1 of 2 episodes)
		None	Proximity to mother
	1 (19)	None	Cry when father leaves room, proximity to father
	2½ (39)	None	Cry when mother leaves room, proximity to mother ("Strange Situation")
	2½ (28)	Boys	Cry when father leaves room ("Strange Situation," 1 of 2 episodes)
		None	Proximity to father
Finley & Layne 1969	1-3 (96)	None	Proximity to mother, contact with mother (American and Mayan Indian samples)
Rheingold & Eckerman 1970	1-5 (48)	None	Distance child roams from mother
Weinraub & Lewis 1973	2 (18)	None	Look, touch, proximity, or vocalize to mother or father
Maccoby & Feldman 1972	2 (64)	None	Proximity to mother, protest over separation from mother (longitudinal) ("Strange Situation")
	2 (20)	None	Proximity to mother, protest over separation in "Strange Situation" (Israeli sample)
	2½ (35)	None	
	3 (38)	None	
Marvin 1971	2 (16)	Boys	"Strange Situation": contact-maintaining behavior (1 of 2 measures), crying following mother's departure; less proximity-avoiding behavior (significant for mother-reunion episodes only)
		None	Proximity-seeking behavior, looks at mother, searches for mother following her departure
	3 (16)	None	"Strange Situation": contact-maintaining behavior, proximity-avoiding behavior, looks at mother, crying, searches for mother following her departure
	4 (16)	Girls	"Strange Situation": contact-maintaining behavior (1 of 2 measures), proximity-seeking behavior, crying following first reunion with mother
		None	Proximity-avoiding behavior, looks at mother, searches for mother following her departure
Blurton-Jones & Leach 1972	2-4 (73)	None	Cry when mother leaves room
Shirley & Poyntz[R] 1941	2-8 (199)	Boys	Upset when separated from mother

(continued)

TABLE 6.1 *(cont.)*

Study	Age and *N*	Difference	Comment
J. Schwartz & Wynn 1971	3-5 (108)	None	Reaction to separation from mother, first day of nursery school
Blayney 1973	4 (29)	None	Reaches for, touches father while on elevated balance beam
Wohlford et al. 1971	4-6 (66)	None	Father-absent lower-class black Ss. Extent of child's involving adult doll in doll play; mother ratings of dependency (clinging)
Guardo & Meisels 1971	8-15 (431)	Girls	Place self-referent silhouette close to parent silhouette while latter praises
		None	Placement of self silhouette while parent silhouette reproves
Ferguson & Maccoby 1966	10 (126)	Girls	Seek parent (or other older people) when sick, alone, or afraid (self-administered scales)

ness to separate from the mother when brought to nursery school. In all, 32 studies report observational data on proximity, touching, or resistance to separation in relation to the mother (or rarely, the father). As Table 6.1 shows, the large majority of these studies find no sex differences. Several studies found no differences for some measures, and differences favoring one sex or the other on other measures. For example, in Maccoby and Jacklin's first study (1973) with children 13 months of age, boys made more "trips" to the mother, but there was no sex difference in the degree of closeness to the mother that the children maintained. In all, there are seven instances in which at least one measure shows greater proximity-seeking behavior in boys, and eight in which there are higher scores for girls. As noted in Chapter 5, higher scores tend to be found for boys in measures of resistance to separation. In several studies, boys cry more when the mother or father leaves the room; and at the early age of 9–10 months, they are more likely to crawl quickly after the mother if she moves into an adjacent room (Corter et al. 1972). In the few instances in which girls obtain higher scores, they tend simply to remain nearer to the mother. However, the number of studies finding no difference in proximity out-number the "girls higher" studies by more than three to one, and hence the picture as a whole is quite clearly one of sex similarity rather than sex difference.

Two reports of studies that were carried out in field situations by anthropologists (Munroe and Munroe 1971, Nerlove et al. 1971[R]) show records sampling how far away from home children aged 3–8 were found during their free time, when they had a choice of where to play. In two different cultures in Kenya, boys customarily played at a greater distance from home. It is difficult to know how to interpret these findings. The behavior does not seem precisely similar to remaining close to the mother when the two are in the same room. Do girls stay closer to home because they want to be able to run to the mother for security in case any threatening situation arises? Have they been given more warnings than boys about the dangers of the outdoor environment? Are the kind of settings they are allowed or expected to participate in located closer to home? We do not know; meanwhile, it would be premature to classify this behavior as "proximity seeking" in the same sense as the behavior in the studies summarized in Table 6.1.

What about children's seeking of security through proximity and clinging to adults other than their primary caretakers? There is evidence that "dependency" (in the proximity-seeking sense) generalizes to nonfamily adults. Rosenthal (1967)[R] has found that instances of remaining near an adult woman experimenter increase with the introduction of fear-producing stimuli (e.g. the taped sound of another child crying). Feldman and Ingham (1973) have similarly found that a child increases proximity to a briefly acquainted baby-sitter upon the entrance of a complete stranger to a strange room. Do girls transfer this security-seeking behavior toward surrogates more readily than boys? A difficulty in answering this question lies in the nature of the measurements available. As Table 6.2 shows, there are eight observational studies of the interaction of children with nonfamily adults (Heathers, Bell et al., Feldman and Ingham, Emmerich, Serbin et al., Zunich, Maccoby and Feldman). Five of these find no sex difference in proximity or clinging. The Feldman and Ingham study with one-year-olds shows boys more likely to remain near a strange adult. The Zunich study, showing higher scores for girls, involved presenting children with a very difficult puzzle—too difficult for them to solve. Their behavior while attempting to cope with this situation was observed. Boys more often showed destructive and emotional responses, more often rationalized their failure, and more often sought help; girls more often sought information relevant to the problem, tried to solve it alone, and *sought contact* with the Experimenter. Their contact seeking, in this case, was part of a pattern of active coping, and would appear to have a somewhat different meaning than the escape from threat that is usually implied in clinging or proximity seeking. In observational studies, then, the picture is one of no established sex difference in proximity seeking to nonfamily adults.

In two of the three studies in which *ratings* have been used, however (Beller and Turner 1962[R], Hattwick 1937[R], Lansky and McKay 1969), girls have been rated more likely to remain close to a nursery school teacher than boys. In our earlier review (Maccoby 1966b[R]) studies using more global measures of "dependency" were summarized, and it was noted that observational studies seldom found sex differences, whereas rating studies fre-

TABLE 6.2

Touching and Proximity to Nonfamily Adult

Study	Age and N	Difference	Comment
Feldman & Ingham 1973	1 (19)	None	Proximity to female stranger when accompanied by mother in "Strange Situation"
	1 (19)	Boys	Proximity to female stranger when accompanied by father in "Strange Situation"
	1 (18)	Boys	Proximity to female stranger when accompanied by adult female acquaintance in "Strange Situation"
		None	Proximity to adult female acquaintance
	2½ (67)	None	Proximity to female stranger when accompanied by mother or father in "Strange Situation"
	2½ (12)	None	Proximity to female stranger when accompanied by adult female acquaintance in "Strange Situation"
	2½ (12)	None	Proximity to female stranger when accompanied by adult female acquaintance in "Strange Situation"; proximity to female acquaintance
Heathers[R] 1955	2 (20)	None	Observation: cling to teacher
	4-5 (20)	None	Cling to teacher (observation)
Maccoby & Feldman 1972	2 (64)	None	Proximity to stranger ("Strange Situation"; longitudinal)
	2½ (35)	None	
	3 (38)	None	
Hattwick[R] 1937	2-4 (579)	Girls	Stay near nursery school teacher (teacher rating)
R. Bell et al. 1971	2½ (74)	None	Frequency of contact with teachers (teacher rating)
Zunich[R] 1964	3-4 (40)	Girls	Seeking contact with adult during puzzle task
Beller & Turner[R] 1962	3-5 (190)	Girls	Seeking physical contact and nearness to teacher (observer rating)
Serbin et al. 1973	3-5 (225 pupils, 15 teachers)	Girls	More often within arm's reach of teacher (nursery school observation)
Emmerich 1971	4-5 (596)	None	"Attachment" to adults in nursery school (observation: remaining near, following, imitating)
Lansky & McKay 1969	5-6 (36)	None	"Dependency," Beller Scales (teacher rating)
B. Long & Henderson 1970	6 (192)	Girls	Projective measure: place "self" figure closer to "teacher" figure
Yando et al. 1971	8 (144)	None	Child positioning self in relation to E

quently reported that girls were more dependent. We can only reiterate now the warning that, although any measurement (including behavior observation) embodies the danger of observer bias, it would appear that ratings are especially susceptible to this problem, particularly where sex differences are concerned. The fact that ratings can be made reliably (in the sense that two raters agree) does not rule out the possibility that the two observers share culturally imposed biases that would lead them to perceive girls as being, on the average, more "clingy" than boys. When rating studies and observational studies conflict, then, in the picture of sex differences they present, we believe it is reasonable to rely more heavily upon the observational ones. In so doing, we conclude that children of both sexes do to some extent transfer to relatively unfamiliar adults their tendencies to seek comfort or security through proximity or clinging, but that there is no consistent tendency for girls to make this transfer any more readily than boys.

It is rare for children to use other children as "security" sources in the same way that they use their parents or surrogate adult caretakers. Harlow (1962)[R] has noted that infant monkeys raised without mothers but in contact with age-mates will cling to these age-mates for comfort in the same way that a normally reared infant clings to its mother. But when an infant monkey has had access both to his mother and to age-mates in early life, it will cling to the mother when frightened but will *not* cling to a favorite playmate, even when the playmate is the only other social object present (Patterson et al. 1974[R]). Though little work has been done on the tendency of human children to cling to one another in fear-producing situations, there is reason to believe that mutual comfort giving is fairly rare, except among children reared together under conditions of maternal deprivation (see Freud and Dann 1951[R]). Infants and young children find other infants and other young children interesting social objects, but the interest appears to be of a different sort, and to serve different functions, than the proximity seeking and physical contacting directed toward adults. The only study we found that reports specifically concerning proximity seeking to other children in a nursery school setting is Emmerich's (1971), in which the tendency to "tag along" after other children, and imitate them, was recorded as "attachment to other children." *Boys* showed this behavior more frequently than girls in the Emmerich sample.

Among adults, of course, any tendency to seek the company of others, or to cling to them, under stressful conditions, is likely to be expressed toward age-mates. The original Schachter work (1959)[R] on affiliation, in which subjects waited for a painful experience (shock) and had a choice of whether to wait alone or in the company of others, included only female subjects, and focused upon individual differences that were related to birth order. Recent work by MacDonald (1970), using a similar anticipation of shock situation and subjects of both sexes, has revealed no sex differences in the tendency to seek closeness to age-mates under this particular stressful condition.

So far, we have discussed separately the child's proximity seeking directed toward the mother, toward other children, and toward nonfamily adults. There is an important body of research that reports physical contact without regard to the identity of the target. R. Sears et al. (1965)[R] recorded touching and holding, and also simply "being near" an adult or child during periods of free play in a nursery school. They found no significant sex differences in such behavior. Whiting and Pope (1974) describe the sex differences that were found in the "Six Cultures" study. Time-sampled observations were made of a group of children in each of six "villages" as the children went about their daily activities. Many of the observations were made when the children were in their own homes or outdoors near their homes (in the "yard," if there was one). Half the children were in the age range 3–6, the other half 7–11. The intent was to obtain multiple observations on 12 girls and 12 boys in each culture, although in two of the societies the sample size fell short of this goal. One of the behaviors recorded was "nonaggressive touching and holding"; this category was scored when the child touched another person, regardless of this person's age, sex, or relationship to the child. In five of the six cultures, girls tended to touch or hold others more frequently than boys, although the sex difference was not significant within any culture. When the six societies were combined, the sex difference was significant, but only in the 3–6 age range, when the behavior was most common. There is some suggestive evidence here, then, that young girls more often make physical contact with a variety of other persons; it is important to be cautious, however, concerning any implications of cross-cultural universality, in view of the small samples and the fact that (perhaps in consequence of the small samples) none of the within-culture differences was significant. Assuming for the moment, however, that the observed differences would be replicated with observations of additional children in these cultures, many interesting questions arise as to the nature of the settings in which the observations took place. In several of these societies, boys are assigned chores (such as the herding of animals) that take them farther away from the house than girls' chores do. Although such chores are normally assigned to older boys, the chances are that boys of 6 or younger may sometimes be allowed to go along; in any case, we do know that boys in several of these cultures are normally found farther away from the house than are girls at any given moment of the day. Their opportunities to seek physical contact with family members is, then, somewhat reduced in comparison to girls'. In most of the studies summarized in Tables 6.1 and 6.2, settings were standardized for the two sexes. This may have been done at the sacrifice of a certain amount of real-life validity, if the sexes differ in the frequency with which they would normally be in settings similar to the ones in which measurements have been taken. In any case, it makes a difference in how results may be interpreted if behavior varies with settings rather than with the use children make of a given setting. In view of the negative outcome of our review of the other studies on proximity seeking (some of which were done in nonindustrial cultures), we regard the Whiting and Pope report as an indication that further cross-cultural observations are needed, and that there may indeed be some cultural settings in which sex differences will consistently emerge; but the fact remains that in the large majority of situations studied so far, they have not emerged.

To summarize so far: the tendency to seek close contact with attachment objects or their surrogates does not appear to be differentiated by sex during the childhood years when this kind of behavior is most apparent; at least, there are no consistent sex differences in the cultural settings where most of the research has been done. Clinging to parents or other caretakers, or remaining near them under conditions of uncertainty or anxiety, is a characteristic of human children that may be observed in all cultures. The ethological view is that this behavior has evolved as a relatively high-potential behavior in young children because of its survival value (Bowlby 1969[R]). From this standpoint there would be no reason why one sex should display the behavior more frequently than the other, unless (a) young children of one sex were more frequently subjected to stressful conditions; or (b) one sex tended to become more frightened with a given degree of objective threat. The sexes were compared in Chapter 5 with respect to their timidity; for the present it need only be said that in the variety of relatively novel situations in which young children have been placed in psychological studies, the two sexes have been remarkably similar in their tendency to seek comfort through proximity to the mother or other familiar adult.

As children grow older, they less and less often seek comfort or protection through closeness to an adult. Their social behavior is more oriented around age-mates, and the functional meaning of proximity changes. That is, if two friends stand quite close together while talking, we suggest that this is not so likely to reflect security needs as is the case with children's proximity seeking toward adults. There is a body of work in which the social interactions of pairs of school-aged children and adults have been studied, and where the focus is on how far from one another the participants in an interaction stand, and whether they face one another directly or turn somewhat away while talking. As Table 6.3 shows, in one study out of five, girls and women stood closer together than boys and men, and in two out of three instances, they faced each other more directly. Furthermore, when projective measures were used—the subject being asked to

TABLE 6.3

Proximity and Orientation Toward Friends

Study	Age and N	Difference	Comment
Langlois et al. 1973[R]	3-5 (32)	Girls	Touch partner, same-sex or mixed-sex pairs (black sample)
		None	Stand close to partner
B. Long & Henderson 1970	6 (192)	None	Projective: distance between placement of "self" symbol and symbols representing other children
Aiello & Jones 1971	6-8 (210 same-sex pairs)	Girls	Stand closer together on playground (white subsample)
		None	Black, Puerto Rican subsamples
		Boys	Face each other more directly (all 3 subsamples combined)
S. Jones & Aiello 1973	6, 8 10 (96 same-sex dyads)	None	Interpersonal distance in conversation
		Girls	Face each other more directly (black, white)
Meisels & Guardo 1969	8-15 (431)	Girls	Closer placement of silhouette "self" to figure described as "best friend"; farther placement of "self" from "stranger," "someone neither liked nor disliked," "someone disliked very much," "someone feared," "strangers," and "feared peers"
		None	Distance between "self" and "friends," "self" and "someone liked very much," and "self" and "an acquaintance"
Guardo 1969	11 (60)	Girls	Closer placement of silhouette "self" and figure described as "best friend," someone you like very much; farther placement, "someone you're afraid of"
S. Jones[R] 1971	Adolescent & adult (220 same-sex dyads)	Girls & women	Face each other more directly during interaction
		None	Interpersonal distance
Dosey & Meisels 1969	18-21 (186)	Women	More affected by sex of other
		None	Closeness of approach to same- or opposite-sex other
Levinger & Moreland 1969	18-21 (96)	None	Placement of figure representing self in relation to silhouettes representing "good friend," "stranger," "dissimilar stranger," and "similar stranger"
Little 1968	18-21 (432)	Women	Doll figures placed close together when discussing pleasant topic, far apart when discussing unpleasant topic (multinational sample)
Argyle & Dean 1965	22-26 (24)	None	Eye contact with confederate during discussion
F. Willis 1966	Adults (755)	Men	Stand close to "friends" (not good friends) during conversation
		Women	Stand close to good friends

place dolls or paper cutouts in relation to one another—girls more often adjusted their placement according to how well acquainted the actors were or how well they liked one another, whereas boys were relatively uninfluenced by these factors in making their placements. In the F. Willis study (1966), the actual proximity of female pairs was similarly sensitive to the degree of friendship between them.

These results are consistent enough to be interesting. They do not appear to reflect any greater general tendency for girls to be "proximity seekers" (see also preceding summaries). It may be that the findings can be interpreted in the light of other aspects of social interests and social behavior, to which we now turn.

It has been alleged that girls are more interested in social stimuli of all kinds, more responsive to the nuances of relationships implied by social cues, and more sensitive to the reactions of others toward one another and toward themselves. Garai and Scheinfeld (1968)[R], for example, say: "In psychological development, from earliest infancy on, males exhibit a greater interest in objects and their manipulation, whereas females show a greater interest in people and a greater capacity for the establishment of interpersonal relations."

As shown in Chapter 2, we were unable to detect any superiority among girls in sensitivity to, or interest in, social cues. That is, there was no sex differentiation in the tendency to fixate faces as compared with nonsocial visual stimuli, or to orient toward voices rather than matched nonsocial sounds. Social responsiveness toward a variety of live people also appears to be undifferentiated by sex during the first two years of life, although there may be some differences in the rate at which certain social responses appear. We see in Table 6.4, for example, that although there appear to be no sex differences in reactions to strange observers at age 3 months (Zelazo) at about 8 or 9 months of age girls show stranger fear while boys do not (Beckwith, Robson et al.). The Robson study is longitudinal, and the authors note that girls developed stranger fear at an earlier age than the boys, on the average. However, in the age range 9–17 months, Clarke-Stewart finds no sex difference in stranger reactions; it may be that the difference detected by Beckwith and Robson et al. simply reflects a sex difference in maturation rate, with boys catching up very shortly after the initial onset of stranger fear in girls at about 8 months. There are slight indications that girls may, in fact, soon begin to be more receptive toward adult strangers—W. Bronson (1971) reports that the girls in her study were most likely to approach a silent and unresponsive stranger than were the boys. Also Maccoby and Feldman (1972) found a somewhat greater incidence of friendly interaction with the stranger among the girls in their longitudinal study (although the difference was not significant at any single age, the direction was consistent at three successive ages). However,

TABLE 6.4
Positive Social Behavior Toward Nonfamily Adult

Study	Age and N	Difference	Comment
Zelazo 1971	3 mos (20)	None	Base rate, smiling at unresponsive E: number of contingently stimulated and elicited smiles during conditioning
G. Bronson 1972	3, 4, 6, 9 mos (32)	None	Response to male stranger (facial expression, vocalizations, gross body movements; Caucasian and Oriental subsamples; longitudinal)
Beckwith 1972	7-11 mos (24)	Boys	Responsiveness to stranger (Rheingold scale)
Robson et al. 1969	8, 9½ mos (45)	Boys	Unsolicited approach to stranger (Boys older at onset of stranger-fear; longitudinal)
Clarke-Stewart 1973	11-13 mos (36)	None	Positive social responsiveness to female stranger (laboratory observation)
W. Bronson 1971	15 mos (40)	Girls	More positive response to silent adult stranger
		None	Reaction to responsive stranger
Feldman & Ingham 1973	1 (56)	None	Positive interaction with female stranger (Ainsworth "Strange Situation")
	1 (18)	None	Positive interaction with female acquaintance ("Strange Situation")
	2½ (79)	None	Positive interaction with female stranger ("Strange Situation")
	2½ (12)	None	Positive interaction with female acquaintance ("Strange Situation")
Maccoby & Feldman 1972	2 (64)	None	Positive interaction with adult stranger ("Strange Situation"; longitudinal)
	2½ (35)	None	
	3 (38)	None	
Fagot & Patterson 1969	3 (36)	None	Help teacher
Baumrind & Black 1967	3-4 (103)	None	Observer ratings: affection toward nursery school staff
M. Yarrow et al. 1971	3-5 (118)	None	Bids for adult attention
Kohlberg & Zigler[R] 1967	3-8 (72)	None	Seeking praise, permission, help, or attention from E during joint task
Ashear & Snortum 1971	3-5, 7, 10, 13 (90)	Girls	Eye contact with female E during interview
R. Sears et al.[R] 1965	4 (40)	None	Seek positive attention from teacher or other adult (behavior observation)

(continued)

TABLE 6.4 *(cont.)*

Study	Age and *N*	Difference	Comment
Emmerich 1971	4-5 (415)	None	Classroom observations, early fall and late fall: adult orientation (black and white low SES)
	4-5 (596)	None	Classroom observations, early fall and spring: affiliation with adults, adult orientation (black and white low SES)
Yando et al. 1971	8 (144)	Boys	Display more positive attention-seeking behavior (teacher rating, white sample only)
		Girls	Display less negative attention-seeking behavior (teacher rating, white sample only)
		None	Display of positive and negative attention-seeking behaviors (E rating, black and white samples)

the bulk of the evidence is that the two sexes are very similar with respect to the amount of friendly interaction with nonfamily adults, including nursery school teachers.

As noted earlier, the amount of friendly interaction with age-mates tends to be factorially quite distinct from proximity seeking or other kinds of interaction with adults. As Table 6.5 shows, the weight of the observational evidence is in the direction of boys being more "sociable" than girls, in the sense that they engage in more positive social interaction with age-mates.

It is difficult to know precisely what to include under this heading—does rough-and-tumble play, for example, qualify as positive social interaction? Such play is frequently exuberantly happy in its affective tone; it can quickly turn into fighting, however, and it is sometimes difficult to distinguish playful rough-and-tumble from aggression. If such play were to be included here, the balance would be even more heavily shifted toward greater "sociability" in boys. Whiting and Pope (1974), for example, report a greater frequency of rough-and-tumble play among boys aged 3–6 in four out of six of the societies they studied, and in five out of the six societies at ages 7–11. The fact that girls less frequently engage in such play, however, does not account for the fact that they emerge as less "sociable" with peers in the studies reported in Table 6.5, since there are many opportunities for girls to interact extensively with age-mates in other kinds of activities and they do not appear to have done so to a degree comparable to the social interactions of boys.

Table 6.6 summarizes the studies in which the tendencies to like and want to be near other people have been measured. We have just seen that boys tend to be more "affiliative" in the sense that they appear to engage

TABLE 6.5

Positive Social Interaction with Peers

Study	Age and N	Difference	Comment
Clark et al. 1969	2-4 (40)	Boys	Have a few close friends, and more children with whom S never plays
		None	Mean number of companions per time interval
McIntyre 1972	2-4 (27)	Boys	Rate of social interaction with peers and adults, observations in nursery school
Anderson 1937	2-6 (128)	Boys	"Integrative" behaviors (i. e. behaviors that show common purpose by work or action) in same-sex or mixed-sex pairs
R. Bell et al. 1971	2½ (74)	None	Friendliness with peers (teacher rating)
Charlesworth & Hartup 1967	3 (37)	Boys	Give affection, acceptance, or submissive types of reinforcements to peers; higher number of different peers reinforced
		None	Give positive attention and approval
	4 (33)	None	Same measures as above
Baumrind & Black 1967	3-4 (103)	Boys	Observer ratings: takes initiative in making friends
		None	Observer ratings: helps (vs. does not help) other children adapt
Barnes 1971	3-5 (42)	None	Frequency of parallel, associative, or cooperative play
Feshbach 1972	4 (104)	None	Child's use of positive reinforcement in teaching task to 3-year-old
Feshbach & Devor 1969	4 (102)	None	Child's use of positive reinforcement in teaching task to 3-year-old
J. Schwartz 1972	4 (57)	None	Time spent looking at or talking to close friend or unfamiliar peer
Emmerich 1971	4-5 (415)	Boys	Classroom observations, early fall and late fall: peer orientation (black and white low SES)
	4-5 (596)	Boys	Classroom observations, early fall and spring: affiliation with peers, peer orientation (black and white low SES)
Anderson 1939	5 (38)	None	"Integrative" behaviors in same-sex or mixed-sex pairs
Feshbach 1969	6 (126)	None	Approach behavior toward same-sex newcomer (2-person groups)
Waldrop 1972	7½ (62)	Boys	Play with group of same-sex peers
		Girls	Play with only one same-sex peer
Walker 1967	8-11 (450)	None	Teacher rating: "socialness"
Benton 1971	9-12 (96)	Boys	More positive evaluation of disliked peer after bargaining over selection of toys
		None	Evaluation of friend or neutrally regarded peer after bargaining session
Hollander & Marcia 1970	10 (52)	Boys	More peer-oriented (vs. self-oriented; questionnaire)

(continued)

TABLE 6.5 *(cont.)*

Study	Age and *N*	Difference	Comment
Feshbach & Sones 1971	12-13 (87)	Boys	Established pairs of same-sex "close friends": shorter latency to speak to a third person (newcomer), higher frequency of incorporating newcomer's ideas, more favorable post-experimental rating of newcomer
		None	Frequency of direct verbal rejection of newcomer's ideas

in more social interaction with age-mates. Girls, on the other hand, are more likely to report that they like the people with whom they interact, even when the other person has not behaved in a rewarding way. A complication in interpreting the two kinds of studies is that the studies of interaction have been observational ones done at early ages, whereas the studies of liking and affiliative feelings are almost always based on self-reports, and have been done with older subjects. Do the different trends appearing in Tables 6.5 and 6.6 reflect an age change, or is it true that girls feel more attraction for others while boys overtly engage in more social interaction?

Our male informants suggest that for much of the interaction that occurs in boys' play groups, liking and disliking one's playmates is essentially irrelevant. The game is the thing. Often there is no choice of who the other participants will be, but if there is, the choice will be made on the basis of game skills. Is it the case that girls are more likely to choose their companions on the basis of personal attraction?

The only information available that is relevant to this question is the size and composition of play groups. Clark et al. (1969), observing children aged 3–4, found that although there was no sex difference in the size of play groups, boys' social relationships tended to be somewhat more intense in that they played consistently with the same other children, and there were certain other children with whom an individual boy would never play. Girls, by contrast, distributed their interactions across a larger number of playmates. R. Bell et al. (1971), reporting on the amount and kind of peer interaction in their longitudinal sample, did not find a sex difference at preschool age, but when these children had reached the age of 7 (Waldrop and Halverson 1973[R]) their patterns of playmate choices had shifted dramatically. Girls were focusing their play in intensive relations with one or two "best friends," while boys played in larger groups of children. We do not know just when the tendency for girls to develop "chumships" and for boys to form "gangs" emerges. Laosa and Brophy (1972) observed these different social patterns for the two sexes among a group of children aged 5–7. Omark et al. (1973) observed it in American, Swiss, and African children in a cross-cultural study discussed in detail in the next chapter.

TABLE 6.6
Self-Report of Liking for Others and Rating of Others

Study	Age and N	Difference	Comment
B. Long et al. 1967	6-13 (312)	Girls	Prefer to do activities in group rather than alone
Mallick & McCandless 1966	8-9 (60)	Girls	Express less initial dislike for confederate who has frustrated them
		None	Dislike of confederate after either (1) opportunity to aggress, or (2) rational explanation of confederate conduct
Walker 1967	8-11 (406)	None	Self-appraisal: "socialness"
Benton 1971	9-12 (96)	Boys	Pairs of nonfriends evaluated each other more favorably
		None	Evaluation of partner, pairs of friends or acquaintances
Ramirez et al. 1971	12-17 (600)	None	Affiliation, projective measure from School Situation Picture Stories Test (Mexican American and Anglo-American Ss)
Rabbie & Howitz 1969	15 (112)	None	Evaluation of own and other group members after rewards were given to only 1 group (Dutch sample)
Benton et al. 1969	18-21 (80)	Women	Less satisfaction at catching same-sex partner in lie
Byrne et al. 1970	18-21 (88)	None	Evaluation of opposite-sex peer after spending 30 minutes with peer (Interpersonal Judgment Scale)
Gallo et al. 1969	18-21 (160)	None	Evaluation of partner's personality (Prisoner's Dilemma game)
Insko et al. 1973	18-21 (300)	None	Liking for same- or opposite-sex stranger after learning some of stranger's attitudes (Interpersonal Judgment Scale)
E. Jones et al. 1968	18-21 (140)	Women	Predicted higher performance for female stimulus person
		None	Ratings of female stimulus person's intelligence
A. Lott et al. 1970c	18-21 (50)	Women	Described liked person in more laudatory terms (adjective checklist)
Lunneborg & Rosenwood 1972	18-21 (465)	Women	Frequent affiliation themes in answer to "What makes you happy?"
Mascaro & Groves 1973	18-21 (33)	None	Attraction to stranger after being informed about stranger's attitudes (Interpersonal Judgment Scale)
Novak & Lerner 1968	18-21 (96)	Men	Rate same-sex partner higher in adjustment and attractiveness
	18-21 (86)	None	Willingness to interact with same-sex partner
Rosenfeld 1966	18-21 (92)	Women	Liking of same-sex partner after contrived interaction
Sampson & Hancock 1967	15-17 (251)	None	Need for affiliation, Edwards Personal Preference Schedule

(continued)

TABLE 6.6 *(cont.)*

Study	Age and N	Difference	Comment
Sarason & Winkel 1966	18-21 (48)	None	Positive, negative, or ambiguous references to others
C. Smith et al. 1967	18-21 (119)	None	Ratings of friendship potential: persons of varying sex, race, and beliefs
Steiner and Rogers[R] 1963	18-21 (100)	Women	Acceptance of peer with conflicting opinion
Touhey 1972	18-21 (250)	Women	Attraction to date selected by computer-dating program (Interpersonal Judgment Scale)
Wagman 1967	18-21 (206)	Women	Higher frequency of affiliative daydreams
Wilson & Insko 1968	18-21 (158)	None	Ratings of confederate on positive and negative personality traits (Prisoner's Dilemma game)
Craig & Lowery 1969	22 (56)	Women	Express more liking for confederate whom they observe being shocked (questionnaire)

Is it accurate to describe girls' friendships as more exclusive, or "deep"? We saw earlier (Table 6.3) that the distance a girl places herself from another person is likely to be a function of how well she knows the person, and that this is less true among boys and men. It is not true, however, that girls are generally more unfriendly to strangers of their own age (see Table 6.6). Studying a large group of Swedish elementary school children, Schaller (1973)[R] inquired about children's reactions to a newcomer to the class. Girls, on the whole, expressed more friendly attitudes toward the hypothetical newcomer. Feshbach and Sones (1971), on the other hand, experimentally formed two-person cohesive groups of junior high school children, and found that boy pairs accepted a newcoming third party more quickly than did girls. It is widely believed that girls establish a considerable degree of intimacy with their best friends, disclosing secrets and otherwise revealing themselves to a friend to a degree that a boy might be unlikely to do. If this were true, it would be understandable that girls would attempt to protect the intimacy of their friendships and be reluctant to accept others into the inner circle, although they might be "friendly" toward newcomers to a classroom. The work on self-disclosure is summarized in Table 6.7. There is little work with subjects under college age. The only study concerned with self-disclosure to age-mates found girls to be more likely than boys to tell secrets to friends. At the adult level, however, a sex difference does not emerge. It is particularly interesting that self-disclosure to one's spouse among married couples seems to be similar for husbands and wives, according to their own reports.

It would appear that there is a qualitative difference in the friendship patterns of the two sexes during childhood and adolescence (reflected in

TABLE 6.7
Self-Disclosure and Trust in Others

Study	Age and N	Difference	Comment
Rivenbark 1971	9, 11, 13, 15, 17 (149)	Girls	Disclosed more to peers
Vondracek & Vondracek 1971	11 (80)	None	Degree of intimacy of self-disclosure to E
Hochreich & Rotler 1970	18-21 (4,605)	None	Interpersonal Trust Scale
Jourard & Friedman 1970	18-21 (48)	Men None	More self-disclosure to male E Self-disclosure, tape-recorded with no E present
	18-21 (64)	None	Time spent in self-disclosure (male E present)
Levinger & Senn 1967	Adults (64)	None	Pleasant and unpleasant feelings described to spouses (self-report)

the size of groupings), but so far we have not been able to identify what lies behind these differences. By definition, girls' friendship patterns are more intimate, by simple virtue of the fact that they are smaller. Yet it is not clearly demonstrated that this "exclusiveness" implies greater hostility to newcomers, or greater self-disclosure, although both these elements may be present.

Another approach would be to inquire whether having only one or two "best friends" implies that a child is especially vulnerable to social pressure from these friends. Is it true that girls attach more weight to peer values and associations than boys do? What happens, for example, when a child must choose between what his peers want him to do and what he himself believes to be right or necessary? What if he must choose between peer values and those of adults (particularly his parents)? The rather limited evidence on this point suggests that it is boys, rather than girls, who are more susceptible to peer influence. In a study by Hollander and Marcia (1970), for example, children were asked to identify classmates in terms such as this: "This is a classmate who goes along with what the other children are doing," "This is a classmate who does what grown-ups think is right," "This is a classmate who does things independently." The subjects also were asked to complete a "dilemmas questionnaire," in which they chose, for example, whether they would go to a camp where their friends were going, even if the activities were not as interesting as those in another camp where they wouldn't know the other campers. On these measures, boys were more "peer-oriented" than girls. That is, more often than girls they chose peer associations and peer values when these conflicted with their own interests and values or with those of adults. This was true of the boys' self-reports about their own probable choices, and also true in their classmates' description of them.

Most of the peer relationships discussed so far refer to same-sex groupings. There is little information concerning the cross-sex attitudes and frequency of spontaneous interaction, although these no doubt change markedly with time. As early as the age of 4, there is evidence that children are more interested in other children of their own sex. That is, R. Sears et al. (1965)[R] found that boys of this age more often attempted to attract the attention of other boys, whereas girls directed their attention-getting attempts toward other girls. No doubt this is relevant to the spontaneous sex segregation of play groups that can be observed during the preschool years. H. Reese (1966) has shown that in the fifth grade, girls like boys better than boys like girls (and we suspect this is even more true at younger ages). At about the age of 10, however, the situation begins to shift: during the fifth-grade year, girls' evaluation of boys remains stable but boys become more favorably disposed toward girls. In grades 6 and 7, the attitudes of both boys and girls toward one another become more favorable, but the boys change at a faster rate. Presumably these attitude changes have some behavioral manifestations, with some spontaneous social groupings becoming less sex-segregated. But the shift in orientation toward the opposite sex does not imply that either sex is becoming more "sociable" than the other.

A picture has emerged, through the last several pages, of boys being more gregarious in terms of the number of peers with whom they interact and of dependence upon the peer group for values and interesting activities. This picture is distant indeed from the view of female personality as involving "greater interest in people, and greater capacity for the establishment of interpersonal relations," unless one regards girls' *intense* (i.e. "best friend") relationships as revealing more such capacity than the more dispersed social relations of boys.

What of the stereotype that girls are more sensitive to the nuances of interpersonal relationships—more "tuned in" to what other people are thinking and feeling—than boys? "Empathy" is a difficult quality to measure. Children's understanding of the motives, feelings, and social relationships of others has usually been studied in two ways: (1) by presenting stories or pictures (or both) that describe social situations, and asking the child to identify how the subjects of the storied incidents feel, what they mean to do, etc.; (2) by experimentally varying the social cues (e.g. tones of voice, supportive vs. neutral statements, friendliness vs. coldness) available to children, and determining the effects of such variation on their behavior.

Table 6.8 summarizes studies using these and related techniques. From these studies, no clear tendency emerges for girls to be more sensitive to social cues. The majority of studies show no differences, and the remainder

TABLE 6.8
Sensitivity to Social Cues: Empathy

Study	Age and N	Difference	Comment
Simner 1971	Newborns (94)	Girls	Cried longer in response to tape of newborn crying (trend, $p < .1$)
	Newborns (155)	None	Duration of cry in response to tape of newborn crying (3 experiments)
Borke 1971	3-8 (20)	None	Skill in identifying others' feelings (selection of faces to match story characters)
Hamilton 1973	3-4, 7, 10 (72)	None	Correct recognition of facial expressions
R. Burton et al. 1966	4 (112)	Boys	Effect of continuous vs. interrupted attention from E on resistance to deviation in marble-dropping task
Shure et al. 1971	4 (62)	None	Preschool interpersonal problem-solving test: alternative solutions to interpersonal problems
Cantor 1971	4-5 (40)	None	Happiness ratings of ambiguous faces
Feshbach & Feshbach 1969	4-5 (48)	Girls	Empathy scores based on response to series of slide sequence (trend, $p < .06$)
	6-7 (40)	None	Empathy scores: response to series of slide sequences
Meddock et al. 1971	4-5 (64)	None	Responsiveness to whether E was supportive or unresponsive in marble-dropping task
Gitter et al. 1971	4-6 (80)	None	Identifying emotions portrayed in pictures (after training) (black, white)
Savitsky & Izard 1970	4-8 (50)	None	Matching photos on basis of facial emotion
J. Todd & Nakamura 1970	5-7 (54)	None	Responsiveness to positive vs. negative tone of voice in marble-sorting task
Solomon & Ali 1972	5-25 (294)	Girls & women	Sensitivity to tone of voice (pleasant, indifferent, displeased) of taped evaluative statements
Whiteman 1967	5-6, 8-9 (42)	None	Understanding of motivations of story characters (black, Puerto Rican)
K. Rubin 1972	5, 7, 9, 11 (80)	None	Egocentrism score, description of nonsense cues to visually separated E
Feshbach & Roe 1968	6 (46)	Girls	Empathy scores: responses to slide sequences utilizing same-sex characters
Madsen & London 1966	7-11 (42)	None	Dramatic acting test (ability to take different roles)
Babad 1972	8 (40)	Girls	Sensitivity to satiation or deprivation of social reinforcement (discrimination task)
Hebda et al. 1972	8 (31)	None	Perception of aggressiveness in faces or expectation of retaliation after hypothetical aggressive act
Pawlicki 1972	8 (170)	Boys	Sensitivity to supportiveness of E's comments (marble-dropping game)

(continued)

TABLE 6.8 *(cont.)*

Study	Age and N	Difference	Comment
Rothenberg 1970	8, 10 (108)	None	Sensitivity to others' emotions (judgments of recorded stories)
Nakamura & Finck 1973	9-12 (251)	None	Sensitivity to social stimuli and/or to potential evaluation by others (questionnaire)
De Jung & Meyer[R] 1963	10-11 (408)	None	Accuracy of guessing how others rate self
Kohn & Fiedler[R] 1961	14, 18, 21 (120)	Men	Make more distinctions among familiar people when rating them on personality dimensions
R. Buck et al. 1972	18-21 (38)	Women	Identification of emotions of televised faces
I. Hilton et al. 1969	18-21 (44)	None	Predictions of behavior in hypothetical situation
Isen 1970	18-21 (30)	None	Attention to confederate's behavior (measured by recall and recognition)
Marlatt 1970	18-21 (96)	None	Effect on discussion of personal problems of interviewer reacting positively, negatively, or neutrally
Craig & Lowery 1969	22 (56)	Women	Rate watching confederates receive shock as more painful
Ekman & Friesen 1971	Children & adults (319)	None	Selection of faces to match emotions of characters in stories (New Guinea sample)

are nearly evenly divided as to whether boys or girls emerge as more skillful in interpreting, or more sensitive in responding to, social cues. A valuable clue to understanding these results is provided by Feshbach and Roe (1968). They showed first-graders pictures designed to embody four different affective situations: happiness, sadness, fear, and anger. Two sets of the same situations were prepared, one set using a female stimulus person, the other a male. The children were asked to report their own feelings upon viewing the pictures, and then to tell how they thought the central character in the picture felt. With the boy as the central character in a scene, boys were more accurate than girls in identifying the probable feelings of the character; on the other hand, when a girl was the central character, girls were more accurate. It is not clear from these results whether children felt more confidence in their judgments about the meaning of a situation when a same-sex person was involved or whether they took more interest in it—both are possible. Although the study standardized the situations in which boy and girl characters appeared, it is probable that the results would be even more dramatic if female central characters were involved in "girlish" activities and boys in "boyish" activities. A child's skill in using social cues probably depends to some extent on his familiarity with the situation in which the people he is evaluating find themselves, as well as upon his feeling of personal identity with them. We might expect, then, that children will be more "empathic" with other children than they are with adults, and more empathic with other children of their own sex especially when the activities involved are sex-typed, so that the observing child is more likely to be familiar with them. A visitor to England, attending his first cricket game, will find it hard to judge whether a particular player on the field is feeling glad or sorry when another player throws or hits the ball in a particular way, although he might be very skillful in making such judgments at an American ball game. What Table 6.6 suggests is that neither sex has greater ability to judge the reactions and intentions of others in any generalized sense, but when activities are sex-typed, so that one sex is likely to know more about a given situation than the other, that sex will have better-developed social judgments. Most men, as well as most women, are in the company of others during a large portion of their waking hours and must learn to take others' reactions into account. It is true that some occupations call for a higher level of social judgment skills than others; it may be that women's usual occupations call for this skill more than men's, although to our knowledge this has not been demonstrated. It would be reasonable to expect, for example, that people with recent experience as parents or nursery school teachers would be more adept at anticipating when a child in their care was about to become emotionally upset than would people inexperienced in child care. Since women are more likely to have daily or even hourly contact with young children, they may be expected, on the average, to have better-developed empathic reactions with young children. On the other hand, because of their greater work experience, men may be better able to "read" the reactions of people at various levels of an organizational hierarchy.

The summaries of earlier research presented in *The Development of Sex Differences* (1966) indicated that women and girls showed more interest than boys in social activities and that their tastes in books and TV programs were more oriented toward the gentler aspects of interpersonal relations and less toward aggression, "action," and science than was true for boys; furthermore, girls developed an interest in the opposite sex at an earlier age, and were more concerned about their personal appearance and attractiveness. To our knowledge nothing in the more recent research contradicts these conclusions. The danger is simply in overgeneralizing from them. Such findings do not warrant any conclusion that girls have a greater "capacity" for social responsiveness. In fact, it is our opinion that the social judgment skills of men and boys have been seriously underrated.

NURTURING OTHERS, MATERNAL BEHAVIOR, AND HELP GIVING

Some time ago, H. A. Murray (1938)[R] used the term "nurturance" to describe the giving of aid and comfort to others; in Murray's terms, nurturant behavior often took the form of a response to "succorance" (bids for help and comfort) from others who were younger, weaker, or for some other reason in a dependent position vis-à-vis the nurturant person. There can be no doubt that women throughout the world and throughout human history are perceived as the more nurturant sex, and are far more likely than men to perform the tasks that involve intimate care-taking of the young, the sick, and the infirm. There is currently considerable interest in this aspect of women's lives, and many questions are being raised concerning whether the assignment of such duties as care of children needs to be a sex-linked thing. To what extend could, or should, boys and men be involved in the care of children? Are there any biological predeterminers that make child-care roles more compatible with "natural" inclinations for one sex than the other?

As a starting point, we shall examine the nurturant behavior of mammals lower than man. If "instinctive" patterns are found in lower animals, we do not think that this implies in any sense that they must be carried over to man. However, we do believe that, since man is a mammal, any biologically based elements in nurturant behavior that man *does* have may represent continuities with those found in subhuman mammals, and we may learn something from tracing their evolutionary history. Furthermore, there have been some rather loose analogies comparing the care of infants in man with that in other mammalian species, and before we consider the validity of such analogies, it is well to be as informed as possible concerning the nature of the behavior in lower animals, its determinants, and its variability.

Let us consider first the role of hormones in animal maternal behavior. A first question is whether the hormones associated with pregnancy and parturition "prime" the female in some way for taking care of the young. Rosenblatt (1969)[R] reports that when blood plasma is taken from female rats that have recently given birth and is administered to virgin females, the latency is reduced for the recipients to show such maternal behavior as retrieving, nest-building, and licking pups. Normally, a virgin female will show such behavior without hormonal treatment when given pups, but the delay in the appearance of the behavior is two or three times as long as when the treatment with maternal plasma has been given. Rosenblatt also finds a gradual increase, during pregnancy, in a female rat's maternal responsiveness to foster pups—an increase that does not occur if she has been ovariectomized. Thus the increase in responsiveness that occurs during pregnancy has a hormonal basis. Moltz et al. (1970)[R] report that virgin female rats will show maternal behavior more quickly and more consistently if they have received a combination of female hormones than if they have not. This, too, points to hormonal control of maternal behavior. It should be noted, however, that the hormonal impetus to maternal behavior gradually declines during the postparturition period. This is shown by continually supplying a postparturient female with young litters; when this is done, her "mothering" behavior diminishes, and the change cannot be attributed to the changes in the appearance of the pups. It is true that young pups are more effective elicitors of maternal behavior than older ones, but when this factor is held constant, there is still a temporal decline in maternal motivation (Rosenblatt 1969[R]).

The hormonal impetus to maternal behavior in rats is superimposed upon a base level of responsiveness that is greater than zero and is *not* hormonally controlled. Both virgin females and males will show maternal behavior toward pups after about five days if a fresh litter of newborns is given to them each day. And this is true even if they have been deprived of the glands that produce sex hormones. A female that has just given birth to pups, of course, is responsive immediately. Rosenblatt has shown (1969)[R] that the stimulation from the pups during the first few days following parturition is crucial in establishing and maintaining maternal responsiveness; if a mother is separated from her pups just after delivery, for a period of two to four days, she will not effectively rear a substitute litter. A similar period of separation at a somewhat later point in time, after maternal behavior has become established, is not so disruptive, and a new litter will normally be effectively cared for. The effect of contact with young is further illustrated in a study by Moltz et al. (1970)[R] in which it was found that ovariectomy and Caesarian section did not interfere with maternal behavior in rats that had borne and cared for previous litters, but it did disrupt maternal behaviors in animals bearing their first litter.

In Rosenblatt's studies, male rats behaved much like virgin females in their responsiveness to pups: such items of "maternal" behavior as licking, crouching over the young, and retrieving them did appear, but only after several days of exposure to the pups. The males did differ in that they were less likely than virgin females to build nests. Rosenberg et al. (1971)[R] have reported that male rats tend to be more aggressive toward pups, and are likely to kill the first litters that are given to them. After several fresh litters have been supplied, however, the male's aggression diminishes and nurturant behavior ultimately appears.

Little is known concerning the possible hormonal basis of maternal behavior in species higher than rodents. To our knowledge, no work has been done relating maternal behavior in apes or humans to the amounts of hormones present in their bodies that are associated with pregnancy and childbirth. A study by Ehrhardt and Baker (1973)[R] does discuss the relevance of *masculinizing* hormones for later "maternal" behavior for girls. A group of girls showing the "adrenogenital syndrome" at birth were studied. These girls received excess androgens prenatally owing to a genetic defect affecting the prenatal functioning of the adrenal cortex, and were born with masculinized genitalia which were subsequently surgically corrected (during the first two years of life). Despite being normal females with respect to internal body structures, and indistinguishable from normal girls externally after surgery, these girls showed a number of "masculine" behavior traits. For our present purpose the point of interest is that they were reported to be less interested in playing with dolls, and less interested in caring for younger children, than a control group composed of their own normal sisters. Unfortunately the source of information is mothers' reports, and the mothers, of course, knew the medical history of the children and hence may not have been unbiased reporters. The magnitude of the differences, however, was striking. If further more objective measures bear out the original findings, this study will indicate that, although the effects of female hormones on maternal behavior are not known in humans, the effects of *male* hormones may be to suppress such behavior.

Whether or not there is a hormonal component underlying maternal responsiveness in humans, it seems that contact with a young infant may be important in maintaining, or activating, this behavior. In saying this, we mean something more than the obvious fact that a person cannot be maternal unless there is an appropriate object to be maternal toward. We mean that it might be true in humans, as it has been shown to be in lower mammals, that there is a critical period immediately following the birth of an infant during which it is important for the mother to have contact with her infant, and that if she does not, at a later time the infant will not elicit as complete maternal behavior from her as it would otherwise do. Investigating this possibility, Leifer et al. (1972)[R] studied maternal responsiveness to premature infants from whom the mothers had been separated during a 3–12-week period when the newborn was hospitalized. The mother-infant pairs were observed after the infant had been discharged from the hospital and returned to the mother's care, and they were compared with full-term infants and their mothers who had not been separated. At one week and four weeks after the infants had left the hospital, observations were made; full-term infants were more often held close to the mother's body, touched affectionately, and smiled at than premature infants from whom the mother had been separated. Of course, it is possible that the mothers were more concerned over the fragility of premature babies, and therefore hesitated to handle them, so the differences in handling cannot confidently be attributed to separation. More crucial information is potentially available from another comparison in the Leifer et al. study. There were two groups of mothers of premature infants. One group had an opportunity to touch and handle their infants during the hospitalization period, and the other group followed the more usual hospital procedure of viewing their infants through a window. Unfortunately the amount and frequency of contact with the infants among the "touch" group were minimal. Even so, there were indications that the mothers in the "touch" group were showing stronger attachment behavior toward their infants than the no-touch group several months after the infants were brought home (Leifer 1970[R]). These findings are consistent with the hypothesis that early contact is important in establishing some aspects of the mother-infant attachment bond in human beings.

It should be noted that in the Leifer et al. study (1972)[R], no group of *fathers* was studied, so we do not know whether contact with a young infant is similarly important in establishing his attachment to a child.

What about the potential of the male for nurturing the young of a species? We noted above that the rat male's initial response to newborns frequently is to attack them, so that it is only after this response has been extinguished that nurturant behavior appears. A similar situation appears to exist in rhesus monkeys. Chamove et al. (1967)[R] used 15 male-female pairs of preadolescent monkeys, aged 18–30 months. An infant monkey, 20–40 days old, was introduced as a stimulus to the juvenile pair. The young females showed four times as much positive behavior toward the infant (including ventral contact, grooming, and play) as did the males; the males exhibited ten times as much hostility toward the infants. In view of this difference in the reactions of the two sexes to an infant, it is understandable that if both sexes of older animals are available, it will normally be a female who "adopts" an orphan. However, Harlow (1962)[R] has reported that if only a male is available, an infant caged with him will persist in its attempts to achieve ventral contact despite repeated rebuffs, and that eventually the male will permit the contact and spend a good deal of time holding the infant close to his body.

The Harlow work, and the work by Chamove et al., has been done with animals raised in captivity, and their behavior may not be typical of animals growing up in the social conditions of a free-living troupe. DeVore (1963[R], Hall and DeVore 1965[R]) studied free-living troupes of cynocephalus baboons in Kenya. In this species, males play a protective role for the troupe as a whole but, aside from this, take little interest in infants. Occasional exceptions occur among high-status males, who may approach a mother with a young infant and attempt to hold or examine the infant briefly, but juvenile males and young adult males who are nondominant were not seen to make such approaches. Juvenile females, by contrast, frequently approached newborns, looked at them intently, touched them, and would hold them if the mother permitted. At a later time, when the infants had moved away from their mothers and formed a play group, they would climb on the adult males and tease them, and the males would permit this up to a point, but did not themselves engage in play or care-taking with the young.

It is well to be aware, however, of how much variability there is in the role of the male among species that are fairly closely related. In another variety of baboon, the hamadryas, for example, the male is much more involved with infants than is the cynocephalus male. Kummer observed these animals in Ethiopia, and reports (1968, p. 301)[x]:

Typical of the hamadryas organization is the high frequency of child care behavior by subadult and young adult males. In the initial unit, the one-year-old female flees into her male's arms when another baboon threatens her, and rides on his back across passages in the sleeping cliff, which she cannot negotiate because of her small size. Such "maternal" tendencies are already prominent in the young subadult hamadryas males. They sometimes pick up a black infant, and hug and carry it at a safe distance from the mother and her leader. The same tendency is later shown by young adult males before they have any females of their own. Five young juveniles of both sexes that we trapped at one cliff and released near another were all caught and mothered in the described way, each by another young adult male. Thus the "maternal" behavior of the male toward his first consort is a continuation of similar behavior at an earlier age. "Child care" motivations in the male are one important root for the formation of the one-male units in hamadryas.

The last point is important. Lest we be tempted to think of the male participation in child care among the male hamadryas as an evolutionary precursor of female liberation, it should be noted that the male hamadryas baboon keeps his females in total subjugation—he isolates them from the rest of the troupe by "herding" them and attacks them if they do not follow him closely at all times. Also, of course, it is still the female who does most of the nurturing of the young.

For our present purposes, the important points to be derived from the behavior of mammalian species other than man are as follows:

1. "Maternal" behavior is to some degree hormonally controlled. Hormonal factors are more powerful during the period immediately following the birth of young, and in untreated animals they diminish strongly toward the end of the "infancy" period.

2. The hormones associated with pregnancy, childbirth, and lactation are not necessary for the appearance of parental behavior. With sufficient exposure to newborns, virgin females and males will show parental behavior, but the behavior is not so readily aroused as it is in a female that has been hormonally "primed."

3. In the males of some species, aggression interferes with responsiveness to the young.

4. Among subhuman primates, there is great variability from one species to another in the degree of male participation in caring for the young.

5. The child-care functions that the two sexes will perform in adulthood are anticipated in the behavior of preadolescents and young subadults. That is, in species in which the adult males do not participate in care of the young, juvenile males do not show positive social interest in infants

(and may even attack them), whereas juvenile females do show such interest; in species in which the adult males are involved in child care, juvenile males show more positive interest in infants.

In view of point 5, it becomes especially important to try to discover whether there is a reliable sex difference among human juveniles in the tendency to be responsive toward infants. We turn now to studies of nurturance in homo sapiens.

Existing research has seldom focused on a child's offering of nurturance to an infant or a younger child—that is, on behavior that might be considered a precursor to later child care. To our knowledge children have not been offered a live baby, or a live kitten or puppy, to care for under conditions where their reactions might be systematically observed. It would be interesting indeed to know whether young boys and girls differ in their response to younger and more helpless beings. Certainly the folklore is that a boy frequently becomes intensely attached to his dog; there is no evidence that either sex is more strongly attracted to *young* animals, as distinct from full-grown ones. The fact that girls more frequently play with dolls from an early age has been taken as evidence of their greater tendency to show spontaneous nurturance. However, considering that girls are more often given dolls, it may be that their nurturant behavior is more frequently *elicited* without there being any underlying difference in "potential" for the behavior. As we noted above, Ehrhardt and Baker (1973)[E] did find that fetally androgenized girls were less interested in dolls than were their normal sisters (according to the mother's report), which suggests a biological component in this behavior.

Parenthetically, in studies of interest in dolls, it might be well to determine to what extent the play with dolls is actually nurturant. It is true that dolls are hugged and tucked into bed, which are nurturant actions by any definition; however, they are also scolded, spanked, subjected to surgical operations, and (in the personal experience of one of the authors) even scalped. If girls choose dolls as a vehicle for acting out a variety of fantasies, this is not in itself evidence that the fantasies are more nurturant than those of boys, although they may be.

What about the potential of adult men and women for nurturant behavior toward animals, infants, and children? This is a topic that is only just beginning to be studied. Extrapolating from what is known about animals much lower than man, it would appear possible that the hormones associated with pregnancy, childbirth, and lactation may contribute to a "readiness" to care for a young infant on the part of a woman who has just given birth. The animal studies also suggest, however, that contact with infants is a major factor in developing attachment and care-taking behavior in the juvenile and adult members of a species, and this is true for both individuals that have given birth and individuals (male or female) that have not.

Even with little experience with infants, however, the human male may have more potential for nurturant reactions than he has been given credit for. In a recent study by S. L. Bem (1974), college students were given the opportunity to interact with an eight-week-old kitten. During one part of the procedure, they were instructed to play with the kitten; during another part of the procedure, kitten play was one of several activities from which the subjects could choose. There was no significant difference between men and women subjects, on the average, in their interest in the kitten, amount of contact with it, and their enjoyment of playing with it.

Recent observations by Parke and O'Leary (1974)[R] bear on the level of interest among adult men in newborn infants. In this study, observations were made in hospital wards. In some instances, the situation involved both the mother and father being present together. The newborn infant was brought in by a nurse, who asked which parent wanted to hold the infant. Records were made of which parent initially took the child, and of the amount of nurturant interaction (looking, touching, rocking, holding, smiling) with the infant that each parent engaged in during the father's visit. With the exception of smiling, fathers engaged in *more* nurturant interaction with the infants than did mothers, when both parents were present. The study also involved observations of fathers alone with their newborn infants (that is, with the mother not being present) and of mothers when the fathers were not present. Here, too, the fathers engaged in as much or more nurturant behavior, by comparison with the mothers. It is of especial interest that Parke used two samples of families. The first was a well-educated group many of whom were especially interested in natural childbirth—half the fathers in this initial sample had attended classes on natural childbirth and many were present at the child's delivery. The second sample was taken in a working-class hospital serving a racially mixed population, and none of the fathers in this group were present at the infant's birth. It is striking that the two groups of fathers, from such diverse backgrounds, should both have shown such high levels of "mothering" behavior toward their newborn infants. The widespread belief that men tend to be uninterested in very young infants, becoming interested only as the children acquire more fully differentiated "personalities," has not been supported by the Parke work. Clearly, detailed information is needed through the growth phases following the newborn period, before it will become clear what truth, if any, there is in the popular belief.

HELPING AND SHARING

We have been discussing nurturant, "maternal" behavior directed toward infants, or other individuals younger and more helpless than the subject. There is a body of research on "altruism" that deals with helpful, supportive behavior that a person may direct toward a variety of other persons, including age-mates. Whiting and Pope (1974), in their observational study of children in six cultures, report the frequency of *offering help*. This category included offering food, toys, or tools, or offering to contribute one's own labor to the joint completion of a task that another person was engaged in. The observers also recorded *offering emotional support*, in the form of consolation, encouragement, physical contact-comfort, or reassurance. Whiting and Pope do not report the ages of the targets of these behaviors—presumably helpful and supportive efforts were sometimes directed at younger children (in which case they would reflect nurturance in the sense discussed above), sometimes toward age-mates, and sometimes toward adults. The authors report that in the age range 3–6, although there is a tendency for girls to show more help-giving behavior than boys, the tendency is not consistent over the six cultures studied, the differences are not large, and they are not significant within any culture or when the cultures are combined. During the ages 7–11, however, girls emerge strongly as the more helpful sex. Offering help is more common among girls in five of the six societies at this age, and the overall sex difference is significant ($p < .01$). The giving of emotional support shows even stronger results: girls aged 7–11 give more in all six of the cultures studied, and the difference for the combined data is significant at the .001 level.

It should be noted that the giving of help by girls in the six cultures studied by Whiting and Pope was accompanied by a form of dominance called "suggesting responsibly." This category included instances in which a child would attempt to control another child in the interests of that other child's well-being or safety. (Warning another child not to go near a dangerous cliff and insisting that the child come in to a meal would be cases in point.) It would appear that girls, in a variety of cultures, are more likely than boys to adopt the role of being responsible for the welfare and conduct of others. It is reasonable to suppose that this stems from the more frequent assignment of girls to baby-sitting responsibilities (Whiting and Pope 1974, Barry et al. 1959[R]).

Aside from the Whiting and Pope report, research is rare that involves observations of young children's giving of comfort and assistance to one another in naturalistic situations. Hartup and Keller (1960)[R], observing children aged 3–5, found no sex difference in giving affection to other children, giving praise or help, or giving reassurance and comfort. It is worth noting that the children who most often gave help and affection to others were the same children who most often *asked* for help and affection from others—in other words, helpful behavior was part of a reciprocal system. The nurturance-giving children, however, were significantly *unlikely* to engage in the more passive forms of proximity seeking—that is, simply remaining close to others. Help giving, then, is distinctly not a passive process, even though it is associated with forms of seeking positive social contact that have sometimes been labeled "dependency."

R. Sears et al. (1965)[R] did time-sampled observations of the free play of 40 four-year-olds, and reported the frequency with which children behaved nurturantly. Their definition was "voluntarily guiding or assisting another with the intent of being helpful or performing a service," and included offering comfort to another child who was upset as well as offering task-oriented help. They found such behavior to be rather rare among children of this age, and the frequency did not differ significantly between the sexes. In the same study, projective doll-play measures of nurturance were also obtained. In this procedure, a child was presented with a one-story roofless dollhouse and a family of five dolls: a mother, father, boy, girl, and baby. The child was invited to act out domestic scenes or "stories" of his own invention. Again, helpful behavior by one member of the doll family toward another was a fairly infrequent occurrence; however, girls more frequently than boys showed the dolls engaging in such behavior.

Recent research on altruistic behavior has involved setting up experimental situations in which there are opportunities for the subject to go to the assistance of someone who appears to be in distress. These studies (along with the naturalistic ones on help giving) are charted in Table 6.9. Many of the experimental studies are done with college students or adults. It may be seen that there is no consistent tendency for one sex to offer help more readily than the other. In those studies where a sex difference does appear, there is reason to believe, at least in some instances, that situational elements make helping easier for one sex than the other. For example, in the Gaertner and Bickerman study, the subject was required to phone a garage mechanic to get help for the person in distress. A garage mechanic could be expected to be male. Presumably, women, on the average, are more reluctant to initiate interaction with a strange man than a male subject would be.

The major exception to the no-difference trend in Table 6.9 is the cross-cultural work of Whiting and Pope. Either girls are more consistently trained to be help givers in other cultures than our own, or the major experimental studies of help giving have not sampled the situations in which female helpfulness would be most apparent. Despite the cross-cultural findings, the conclusion reached from our examination of findings on helping behavior is that a person's helpfulness is not consistently related to his sex.

The same is true of other manifestations of altruism. Tables 6.10 and 6.11 chart the studies in which subjects are given the opportunity to donate to charity, and those in which the willingness to share toys, candy, or other valued items is measured. The large majority of these studies show no sex differences. Where a difference is found, the direction somewhat more frequently favors girls and women, but the number of no-difference findings requires us to conclude that no trend toward greater female altruism has been shown.

TABLE 6.9
Helping Behavior

Study	Age and N	Difference	Comment
Hartup & Keller[R] 1960	3-5 (41)	None	Giving help, praise, reassurance, affection to age-mate
Whiting & Pope 1974	3-6 7-11 (134)	None Girls	Offers help, gives support (overall 6 cultures) Same measure
R. Sears et al.[R] 1965	4 (40)	None	Guiding or assisting another
Staub 1971a	5 (64)	None	Helping other child in distress
Staub 1971c	5 (75)	Girls None	Helping child in distress (1 of 4 groups) Helping adult pick up paper clips
Staub 1970	5, 6, 7 9, 11 (232)	None	Helping child in distress
Dlugokinski & Firestone 1973	10, 13 (164)	None	Amount of money donated to charity
I. W. Silverman 1967	11 (199)	None	Minutes volunteered for later experiment
Staub 1971b	12 (40)	None	Responses to distress cues from adjoining room
Nemeth 1970	15-17 (120)	None	Completing survey or getting other to complete survey
Aronson & Cope 1968	18-21 (80)	None	Number of phone calls made as a favor
Bickman 1972	18-21 (423)	None	Helping behavior in response to phone call
	18-21 (300)	None	Helping behavior in response to letter
	18-21 (298)	None	Helping behavior in response to person present
J. Darley & Latané 1968	18-21 (72)	None	Speed in reporting fictitious epileptic seizure
Gruder & Cook 1971	18-21 (104)	None	Number of questionnaires stapled as a favor
Isen 1970	18-21 (30)	None	Helpfulness to confederate carrying armload of items
S. Schwartz & Clausen 1970	18-21 (179)	None	Speed of helping victim believed to be having a seizure
		None	Response to tape-recorded cries of victim with 4 other bystanders present
		Men	Responded more quickly when one of 4 bystanders is medically competent
		Women	Responded more quickly when no other bystanders are present
		None	Number of Ss who did not respond (all 3 conditions combined)

(continued)

TABLE 6.9 *(cont.)*

Study	Age and *N*	Difference	Comment
Thalhofer 1971	18-21 (192)	Women	Offering time or money to help fictitious boy (1 of 2 conditions)
Gaertner & Bickerman 1971	Adults (1,109)	Men	Made phone calls to a garage when asked to over the phone by a confederate (black and white sample)
Piliavin et al. 1969	Adults (4,450)	Men	First to help in staged collapse on subway train
Wispé & Freshley 1971	Adults (176)	Men None	Helped pick up dropped groceries (black sample) Picking up dropped groceries (white sample)

TABLE 6.10
Donating to Charities

Study	Age and *N*	Difference	Comment
Staub 1971c	5 (75)	Boys	Donating candy to needy children (1 of 4 groups)
Bryan et al. 1971	7-8 (96)	None	Donating rewards to charity
B. Moore et al. 1973	7-8 (42)	None Girls	Mean pennies contributed Median penny contributions higher
J. Grusec 1971	7, 11 (88)	None	Donating rewards to charity
J. Grusec 1972	7, 11 (100)	None	Donating marbles to poor children
J. Grusec & Skubiski 1970	8, 10 (80)	None	Marbles to poor children
Rosenhan & White 1967	9-10 (130)	None	Gift certificates to charity box
G. White 1972	9-10 (210)	Girls None	2 days later, donation of gift certificates Immediate donating behavior
Fouts 1972	10-11 (40)	None	Donating pennies to charity
Dlugokinski & Firestone 1973	10, 13 (164)	Girls	Donate more money to charity (trend, $p < .1$)
Regan 1971	18-21 (81)	None	Donating behavior

In summary, our survey of research on attachment, affiliation, and positive interactions of all kinds has shown surprisingly little sex differentiation. To be sure, we have woefully little information on some topics (such as nurturance), and on other topics (such as empathy) we must remain dissatisfied with the way the disposition in question has been measured. Nevertheless, the picture that has emerged is one of high "sociability" in both sexes. There may be a qualitative difference in the nature of the social relationships most sought by the two sexes. The fact that boys travel in

TABLE 6.11
Sharing Behavior

Study	Age and N	Difference	Comment
Masters 1968	3-5 (40)	None	Token sharing with partners
I. Lane & Coon 1972	4-5 (80)	None	Rewards to self and partner
Masters 1971	4-5 (120)	None	Tokens to absent partner
Masters 1972a	4-5 (80)	None	Token sharing after model absent
G. Leventhal & Anderson 1970	5 (144)	Boys	Took more rewards than girls did when told performance was superior to fictitious same-sex partner
		None	When told performance was same or inferior to fictitious same-sex partner
Dreman & Greenbaum 1973	5-6 (120)	None	Candy sharing to known and unknown recipients (Israeli sample)
Elliott & Vasta 1970	5-7 (48)	None	Sharing candy or pennies after observing models
Presbie & Coiteux 1971	6 (64)	None	Sharing marbles after observing models
Hapkiewicz & Roden 1971	7 (60)	Boys	Shared viewing time of peep show with same-sex partner
Slaby 1973	8-9 (66)	None	Pennies shared
M. Harris 1970	9-10 (168)	None	Sharing game winnings
Kahn 1972	18-21 (120)	Women	Shared more money in an underpay condition
		None	Amount of money shared in the equal and overpay conditions
I. Lane & Missé 1971	18-21 (128)	Women	Shared more of game rewards
G. Leventhal & Lane 1970	18-21 (61)	Women	Shared monetary reward more equally

larger groups whereas girls more often establish close friendships in twos (or sometimes threes) probably has considerable significance. We suspect that the size of social groups has a great deal to do with dominance patterns. Large groups cannot so easily function without a dominance hierarchy as can small groups; is the small size of girls' social groups in part a reflection of their reluctance to enter into dominance hierarchies and compete for positions in such hierarchies? This question takes us squarely into the area of power relationships in social groupings, the topic to which we now turn.

CHAPTER SEVEN

Power Relationships

In the history of humankind, group efforts to seize territory, possessions, or governments by force have been the province of men. So have efforts to resist the incursions of others. Societies are rare indeed that have placed women in the front ranks of their armies. Forceful person-to-person power struggles (duels, jousting, boxing), whether for blood or "sport," have also been almost exclusively male endeavors. Why should this be so? In the present chapter, we shall ask whether it is all forms of power assertion or only the directly aggressive ones that characterize the male. We shall be concerned with the developmental course that power relations take within and between the sexes as children progress through childhood and adolescence. Especially interesting is the question of the female response to male aggression—is the female submissive, compliant, yielding? In asking these questions, it will be necessary to consider both biological and social factors that may affect sex differentiation.

AGGRESSION

The word "aggression" refers to a loose cluster of actions and motives that are not necessarily related to one another. The central theme is the intent of one individual to hurt another. But attempts to hurt may reflect either the desire to hurt for its own sake or the desire to control another person (for other ends) through arousing fear. Modes of expressing hostile feelings vary greatly—in some instances, the intent to hurt never gets beyond the stage of vindictive daydreams; in others the expression is overt but highly disguised; direct physical attack is rare among adults, though sharp words and other kinds of hostile actions are ubiquitous. Most important of all, a person who is known for a readiness to fight under some circumstances will be meek and gentle under others, and this is true among animals as well as among human beings. For example, Kuo (1967)[a] has studied chow dogs, and reports that they will attack cats in one setting and interact with them in a friendly fashion in others. So even the presence of a consistent "stimulus" does not yield consistent behavior.

Given this variability, there is no reason to expect that any one group of individuals will be consistently more "aggressive" than another. It is surprising, then, to find that males do appear to be the more aggressive sex, not just under a restricted set of conditions but in a wide variety of settings and using a wide variety of behavioral indexes. This generalization was documented some years ago by Terman and Tyler (1954)[R] in their review of the research of the 1930's and 1940's. A similar picture emerged from the 1966 summary by Oetzel (Maccoby 1966b[R]). More recent studies (plus several omitted from the earlier listing) are shown in Table 7.1. The major fact highlighted by the table is that males are consistently found to be more aggressive than females. Even the exceptions, when examined in detail, prove not to be strong. For example, Blurton Jones (1972) reports that his sample of 25 children appears to be atypical, and when an associate (Burke) did further observations on a larger sample, including the original Blurton Jones group of 25 children, the usual higher level of aggression in boys was found.

The behavioral sex difference is found in a variety of cultures. For example, the cross-cultural work reported by Whiting and Pope (1974) involved time-sampled behavior observations in seven cultures. (Only six of the cultures are included in their tables, and the seventh is discussed in the text.) Two age cohorts were observed in each culture: children from 3 to 6, and another group from 6 to 10. In all the cultures studied, direct physical assault of one child upon another was rare, and the data base was insufficient to test for sex differences. However, boys engaged in more "mock fighting" (rough-and-tumble play); they exchanged more verbal insults; and a boy was more likely than a girl to counterattack if aggressed against in either verbal or physical form.

Omark, Omark, and Edelman (1973)* have reported extensive time-sampled observations in three societies: the United States, Switzerland, and Ethiopia. In each culture, children were observed on the school playground. Aggression was defined as pushing or hitting without smiling; a greater incidence of this behavior was found among boys in all three societies.

The bulk of the psychological research done on aggression with subjects beyond the preschool years has involved standardized eliciting situations. Modeling studies are numerous; the subjects observe models performing a variety of actions, some aggressive and some nonaggressive, and the subjects' subsequent behavior is observed. Studies measuring aggression follow-

* The work by Omark et al. forms part of a larger cross-cultural project initiated by Daniel G. Freedman (1971)[R]. A report of the project, "The Development of Social Hierarchies," was presented at the meetings of the World Health Organization, Stockholm, 1971.

ing exposure to a model have been included in Table 7.1. Boys consistently exhibit more aggression following exposure to a model; this conclusion applies to both directly imitative and nonimitative aggression (see Table 7.1). Another large body of research involves giving the subject the opportunity to administer shocks to an age-mate. The situation is presented as one in which the subject is helping teach something to the target person and is administering the shock as punishment for wrong responses. (The "victim" is a confederate who does not receive real shocks—a fact that the subject learns after the experimental session is over.) The subject may choose the duration and intensity of shocks to be administered. The findings of a number of studies are consistent in showing male subjects to be more likely than females to administer high levels of shock and to hold the shock button down longer.

It is possible that the sexes differ in aggressiveness not only quantitatively but qualitatively. E. Goodenough (1957) noted this possibility in reporting the comments of parents whom she interviewed. The parents were asked to describe their children's personalities. Goodenough discussed their comments as follows (p. 302):

Parents' comments about aggression or activity in their children seem to imply in boys a force barely held under control, "dynamic," "a bomb shell," "bold," "belligerent." These mothers felt that the cup was running over: "a great deal of unnecessary energy," "so much energy he doesn't know what to do," "so much energy he can't use it all up." Differentiation in this category is significant largely because of the abundant physical energy ascribed to boys, and because aggression seems closely associated with physical force. Parents of girls seem more likely to equate aggressiveness with the personal reaction of anxiety and confusion, rather than with a release of uncontrollable gross motor energy.

We saw in Chapter 5 that boys were likely to be more active than girls in precisely those situations where aggression may also be observed—namely, during play with other boys. It seems quite possible, then, that aggression and activity may be linked in boys in much the way that parents believe it is, although whether intense activity arises from the arousal of aggressive impulses or vice versa, we do not know. It would be interesting indeed to know whether aggression and activity level co-vary more among boys than among girls, but for the present the question must remain open.

There have been a number of suggestions in previous writings on sex differences to the effect that the two sexes may be equally aggressive in the sense of their underlying motivation to hurt others, but that the two sexes characteristically show their aggression in different ways. The hypothesis takes two different forms:

1. The two sexes are reinforced for different forms of aggression. Girls are allowed to show hostility in subtle ("catty") ways, but not physical

TABLE 7.1

Aggression

Study	Age and N	Difference	Comment
		Observational Studies	
F. Pedersen & Bell 1970	2-3 (55)	Boys	Observation of aggressive behavior in indoor free play with peers
McIntyre 1972	2-4 (27)	Boys None	Physical aggression, classroom observation Verbal aggression
P. Smith & Connolly 1972	2-4 (40)	Boys None	Rough-and-tumble play, play noises Aggression
Blurton Jones 1972	2, 3-4 (25)	Boys	Wrestling and hitting (during rough-and-tumble play when the slide was not available)
		Girls	Rough-and-tumble at age 2 (no difference in older age group)
		None	Aggressive play
Berk 1971	2-5 (72)	None	Offensive-combative response to interference with desired activity
Vernon et al. 1967	2-5 (32)	None	Observer ratings of aggression while child goes through standard hospital admission procedures
Fagot & Patterson 1969	3 (36)	None	"Throw rocks, hit with an object, push" (nursery school observation)
Baumrind & Black 1967	3-4 (103)	None	Becomes hostile (vs. does not become hostile) when hurt or frustrated (observer ratings)
Serbin et al. 1973	3-5 (225)	Boys	Frequency of aggressive responses, observation of free play in nursery school
Whiting & Pope 1974	3-10 (57)	None	Rough-and-tumble play (Kenya)
	3-11 (134)	Boys	Behavior observation in 6 cultures: counteraggression in response to aggressive instigation by other (in 7-11-year-old age group only), rough-and-tumble play, verbal aggression
		None	Number of physical assaults (trend: boys, but n. s.)
Langlois et al.[R] 1973	3, 5 (32)	Boys	Hit with objects, 2-child play session (black suburban sample; first 2 sessions only)
Emmerich 1971	4-5 (415)	None	Defiance-hostility, classroom observations, early fall and late fall (black and white low SES)
	4-5 (596)	None	Defiance-hostility, classroom observations, early fall and spring (black and white low SES)
Hatfield et al. 1967	4-5 (40)	Boys	Verbal and fantasy aggression during mother-child interaction (trend, $p < .1$); physical aggression
		None	Direct, indirect aggression to mother
Omark et al. 1973	4-8 (450)	Boys	Playground observation, frequency of hitting or pushing without smiling (American sample)
	5-9 (250)	Boys	Playground observations (Swiss sample)
	8-10 (250)	Boys	Playground observations (Ethiopian sample)

(continued)

TABLE 7.1 *(cont.)*

Study	Age and N	Difference	Comment
	Experimental Studies		
Rosekrans & Hartup 1967	3-5 (36)	None	Aggression toward toys, following modeled aggression
Feshbach 1972	4 (104)	Boys	Negative reinforcement administered by preschool-aged "teacher" to younger child (black, white; low, middle SES)
Feshbach & Devor 1969	4 (102)	None	Negative reinforcement administered to younger child
Larder 1962	4 (15)	Boys	Percent of trials, choice of aggressive toy
C. Madsen 1968	4-5 (40)	Boys	Imitation of filmed aggression, nonimitative verbal aggression
		Girls	Nonimitative physical aggression directed at Bobo doll
		None	Imitative verbal aggression
Parton & Geshuri 1971	4-5 (112)	Boys	Imitation of videotaped aggressive responses toward toys and dolls
Rau et al. 1970	4-10 (79)	Boys	Emotionally disturbed children; aggression toward mother and toys, observation session
M. Martin et al. 1971	5-7 (100)	Boys	Total and imitative aggression toward doll after observing male model
J. Nelson et al. 1969	5-7 (96)	Boys	Aggression toward objects, nonaggressive modeling
		None	Aggression toward objects after aggressive modeling
D. Hicks 1968	5-8 (84)	Boys	Imitative aggression with toys after exposure to filmed male model and hearing male E evaluate model's acting
Liebert & Baron 1972	5-6, 8-9 (136)	Boys	Aggressive play with knife, gun, and doll (observations following exposure to films)
		None	Willingness to hurt unseen peer
J. Grusec 1973	5, 10 (60)	None	Aggression to Bobo doll after exposure to female model and hearing female E evaluate model's behavior
N. Feshbach 1969	6 (126)	Boys	Session 1, aggressive responses to Bobo doll
		None	Session 1, direct, indirect aggression to partner
		Girls	Session 2, indirect aggression to newcomer, first 4 minutes
		None	Session 2, indirect aggression to newcomer, last 12 minutes; direct aggression to newcomer; direct and indirect aggression displayed by newcomer
Bandura et al. 1966	6-8 (72)	Boys	Imitation of model performing aggressive and non-aggressive behaviors
Hapkiewicz & Roden 1971	7 (60)	Boys	Aggression toward peers after viewing aggressive cartoon, nonaggressive cartoon, or no cartoon
J. Grusec 1972	8-9 (54)	Boys	Imitative aggressive responses (trend, $p < .1$)
		None	Nonimitative aggressive responses

(continued)

TABLE 7.1 *(cont.)*

Study	Age and N	Difference	Comment
Mallick & McCandless 1966	8-9 (48)	None	Number of "shocks" administered to same-sex confederate
	8-9 (60)	None	Impede confederate's progress on task
	8-9 (60)	None	Impede confederate's progress on task
Slaby 1973	8-9 (60)	Boys	Delivering "punches" to unseen peer by pressing button
M. Moore 1966	8, 10, 12, 14, 16, 18 (180)	Boys	Amount of violence perceived, simultaneous stereoscopic exposure to violent and nonviolent scenes
Shortell & Biller 1970	11 (48)	Boys	Deliver a higher intensity of noise to unseen peer
Ditrichs et al. 1967	12-13 (150)	Boys	Constructed more sentences using hostile verbs, following vicarious reinforcement
Titley & Viney 1969	17 (40)	Boys	Shock delivered to confederate
Buss 1966	18-21 (240)	Men	Intensity of shock to confederate
Epstein 1965	18-21 (40)	Men	Intensity of shock to confederate "learner"
Knott & Drost 1970	18-21 (80)	Men	Shocks to confederate after receiving shock: "masculine" men higher than "feminine" men, "masculine" women, and "feminine" women
Larsen et al. 1972	18-21 (213)	Men	Intensity and duration of shocks to male victim, following aggressive modeling (no difference in total voltage administered)
		None	Duration of shocks, maximum and total voltage administered: control, female learner, conformity, high model conditions
D. Leventhal et al. 1968	18-21 (80)	None	Shocks given to male confederate
Paolino 1964	18-21 (84)	Men	Intensity and frequency of aggressive episodes in dreams
Shomer et al. 1966	18-21 (64)	Men	More threats to partner, in effort to achieve cooperative game strategy
Shuck et al. 1971	18-21 (40)	Men	Intensity of shock given to confederate
Taylor & Epstein 1967	18-21 (24)	Women	Increase in intensity of shocks with increased provocation from opponent
		None	Intensity of shocks given to confederate
Youssef 1968	18-21 (120)	Men	Intensity of shocks delivered to confederate
Hokanson & Edelman 1966	18-24 (28)	None	Shock to confederate following shock to S

(continued)

TABLE 7.1 *(cont.)*

Study	Age and *N*	Difference	Comment
Deaux 1971	Adults (123)	None	Speed of honking at driver blocking intersection
Doob & Gross 1968	Adults (74)	Men	Speed of honking at slow driver at intersection

Ratings, Questionnaires, Projective Measures

Study	Age and *N*	Difference	Comment
Vernon et al. 1967	2-5 (32)	None	Aggression toward authority (mother questionnaire following child's release from hospital)
Manosevitz et al. 1973	3-5 (222)	Boys	Number of fights (parent report)
Santrock 1970	4-6 (60)	Boys	Doll play aggression (disadvantaged black sample, half father absent)
		None	Aggression (mother interview)
Wohlford et al. 1971	4-6 (66)	Boys	Intensity and frequency of aggression in doll play (black, low SES, father absent)
		None	Frequency of intense aggression, mother interview
Klaus & Gray 1968	6 (88)	None	Peer nominations (low SES black sample)
Semler et al. 1967	8 (567)	Boys	Peer ratings, aggressive behavior items
Semler & Eron 1967	8 (863)	Boys	Peer ratings, aggressive behavior items
Walker 1967	8-11 (450)	Boys	Teacher rating, aggressiveness
	8-11 (406)	Boys	Self-appraisal, aggressiveness
Ferguson & Maccoby 1966	10 (126)	Boys	Self-report, antisocial aggression
Devi 1967	16-24 (220)	Men	Asian-Indian students; self-reports, overtly aggressive reactions to frustrating situations
		None	Self-reports, suppressive aggressive reactions to frustrating situations
Barclay 1970	18-21 (55)	Men	Aggressive TAT imagery following arousal by hostile female E
Brissett & Nowicki 1973	18-21 (80)	Men	Self-rating, Child and Waterhouse Frustration Reaction Inventory
Harmatz 1967	18-21 (50)	Women	Pre-test, hostility scale
		None	Post-test, hostility scale, following verbal conditioning
Pytkowicz et al. 1967	18-21 (120)	Men	Aggressive content, attitude questionnaire. Increase in hostility following insult
		None	Sarason Hostility Scale (change in scores after being insulted)
Wagman 1967	18-21 (206)	Men	Higher frequency of aggressive and hostile daydreams
Youssef 1968	18-21 (120)	Men	Hostility Scale (Cook-Medley's, Siegel's)
Zillmann & Cantor	18-21 (40)	None	S's ratings of the humorous content and novelty of aggressive jokes and cartoons

ways. Physical aggression is thought appropriate for boys, whereas catti-ness is not. Behavioral differentiation follows different socialization pres-sures for the two sexes in these two directions.

2. Aggression in general is less acceptable for girls, and is more actively discouraged in them, by either direct punishment, withdrawal of affection, or simply cognitive training that "that isn't the way girls act." Girls then build up greater anxieties about aggression, and greater inhibitions against displaying it; the result is that their aggressive impulses find expression in displaced, attenuated, or disguised forms.

In both forms of this hypothesis, then, it is argued that the sexes do not differ in "real" aggression but only in behavioral forms or modes of show-ing aggression. S. Feshbach (1970, pp. 192–93)[R] states the position as fol-lows: "These data [on acceptance of newcomers; see below] along with evidence that girls are higher in pro-social forms of aggression and also have more conflict over aggression and greater aggression anxiety than males suggest that the difference between boys and girls in aggression does not lie in the strength of aggressive drive, but in the mode of behavior by which aggression is manifested. The evidence is compelling that boys are more physically aggressive than girls, yet a different pattern of results is obtained when more indirect, non-physical forms of aggression are eval-uated."

This point of view has been based on several pieces of evidence. First, some studies (e.g. Bandura et al. 1961[R]) indicated that, although there was a greater incidence of direct, physical aggression among boys, there was no sex difference in verbal aggression. However, other reports have not sustained this generalization. R. Sears et al. (1965)[R] found that boys displayed both more physical and more verbal aggression than girls during free play with peers in the nursery school. Hatfield et al. (1967), reporting on the same sample of children, presented data on observations of mother-child interaction. Physical aggression was rare, though somewhat more common for boys than girls ($p < .10$). The sex difference in verbal aggres-sion was greater, with boys having a significantly higher rate. Whiting and Pope (1974) report that, in seven cultures, both verbal and physical ag-gression was more common among boys. McIntyre (1972), on the other hand, found boys to be more aggressive only with respect to physical, not verbal, forms of behavior. In free play among children, it is often the case that fights are preceded or accompanied by verbal taunts, threats, or insults (see Whiting and Pope). At least in some situations, then, the two types of aggressive behavior may be expected to co-vary, rather than being alter-native "outlets." However, this is by no means a universal finding. McIntyre, for example, found verbal and physical aggression to be positively corre-lated for girls, negatively for boys! For the present, the most that can be said is that if there is a sex difference in the forms aggression takes, the verbal-physical distinction does not accurately describe the difference.

A second piece of evidence for the "different modes" hypothesis is a study by Feshbach (1969) with first-graders, which has been widely cited as showing that girls are less accepting (more hostile) toward a newcomer than boys. In this study, children were first formed into two-person (same sex) "clubs," with badges and attractive equipment to promote cohesion. Then at a subsequent meeting a third child was introduced into the group; in some instances, the newcomer was of the same sex as the original pair, in others, of opposite sex. Responses to the newcomer that were coded as Direct Aggression included Physical Aggression, Verbal Aggression, and Expressive Aggression (sneering, threatening gestures). Ignoring, Avoiding, Refusals, and Excluding were coded as Indirect Aggression. The results were as follows:

| | Average total response in 16 minutes | | | |
| | By boy pairs toward: | | By girl pairs toward: | |
Type of aggression	Boy newcomer	Girl newcomer	Boy newcomer	Girl newcomer
Direct	1.3	.5	.4	.6
Indirect	1.7	1.4	2.4	2.2

Boys were somewhat more directly aggressive toward a newcomer than were girls, but this was confined to male targets, and the difference was not significant. The girls did show a significantly higher rate of ignoring, avoiding, and excluding during the first four minutes of the interaction, but this was temporary, and the interactions "warmed up," with sex differences becoming insignificant. As in all indirect measures of aggression, there is room for argument about whether the initial lack of acceptance by girls toward a newcomer is properly called "aggression." As will be discussed more fully below, girls normally congregate in smaller groups than boys. Their initial exclusiveness, then, may be related to their normal social patterns and have little relation to aggression. There is no evidence in the Feshbach work that the girls' initial avoidance or ignoring represented efforts to hurt or derogate the newcomers; on the other hand, it *may* have involved this quality. The fact that the sex difference was transitory, however, and the fact that boys showed somewhat more direct aggression toward a male newcomer (and the fact that boys, as newcomers, significantly more often displayed aggression toward the established pair) would not permit us to conclude that there is more hostility involved in "breaking into" an established group of girls than into one of boys.

There is a third kind of evidence that has led to the conclusion that sex differences in aggression are more apparent than real. This is the work on modeling. As Table 7.1 shows, boys normally do more spontaneous copying of modeled aggression than do girls. Bandura (1965)[R], however, showed that if children were offered a reward for performing as many of the model's aggressive responses as they could remember, sex differences were greatly reduced (though not eliminated), and it became apparent that girls had noticed and remembered more of the modeled aggression than they displayed in their spontaneous behavior. Mischel (1970, p. 42)[R] discusses this experiment in the following terms: "Boys and girls may be similar in their knowledge of aggressive responses, but they usually differ in their willingness to perform such responses. These differences presumably reflect differences in the sex-determined response consequences that boys and girls obtained and observed for such behavior in the past, and that they therefore expect in the future." The term "disinhibition" is used by Bandura in discussing the findings, and both Mischel and Bandura suggest that girls would show very nearly as much aggression as boys if they were not inhibited by fear based upon negative socialization experiences.

A first point to note in interpreting the Bandura results is that, although he has shown a large part of the sex difference in imitative aggression to be found in performance rather than acquisition, there probably are some differences in acquisition as well. Girls do not notice and retain the details of modeled aggression to the same extent that boys do. In the Bandura experiment, even under the incentive conditions, girls recalled less. In an early study of memory for film content, Maccoby and Wilson (1957)[R] found that girls recalled less of the aggressive content. In the work by M. Moore (1966), children in the age range 8–16 were shown pairs of pictures in a stereoscope, one picture showing a violent scene, the other a nonviolent one. Boys more often reported seeing the violent scene. Kagan and Moss (1962)[R] found that, in tachistoscopic presentation of aggressive scenes, girls required longer exposure times than boys to recognize the picture. Thus, whether as a result of anxiety and "perceptual defense" or not, it would appear that girls do not add aggressive actions to their repertoires of potential behaviors as readily as boys do through observing aggressive events.

Nevertheless, it is clear that girls do have a great deal of information about aggression that they never put into practice. The question is whether their failure to perform aggressive actions is to be attributed to anxiety-based inhibition that has been developed as a result of negative socialization pressure in the past. This is an extraordinarily difficult hypothesis to either falsify or confirm. There is reason to believe that girls do experience (or, at least, report) more anxiety about aggression than boys. R. Sears (1961)[R] developed a self-report scale on aggression anxiety, and found that girls obtained higher scores. Rothaus and Worchel (1964)[R] found evidence of greater aggression anxiety in women's TAT responses. However, we do not know whether these anxiety differences are present as early in life as sex differences in aggression may be detected. As will be documented in Chapter 9, young boys receive as much punishment for aggression as girls, or more, and on the basis of punishment alone, they would be expected to have as much fear of performing aggressive acts. Even if a difference in anxiety about aggression could be documented for the early years, the existence of more anxiety among girls need not be taken as the only, or even the major, reason why they are not so greatly influenced by aggressive models. The vast majority of actions that individuals observe being performed by others in their presence are not imitated at (or near) the time they are observed. In some instances the observer would be afraid of the consequences if he did imitate, but there are other much more common reasons. The observed action may be incompatible with the ongoing, organized stream of the observer's own actions and motives; it may not be consonant with the observer's self-concept; the observer may have a different, habitual response already established for the situation; or the observer may simply lack any motivation that would make imitation rewarding. The Bandura study has demonstrated that girls may know nearly as much as boys about how to go about hurting others; it has *not* shown that the major reason they do not make behavioral use of this knowledge is fear of the consequences, although of course such fear may be present in many instances.

To our minds the attempt to interpret sex differences in aggression in terms of anxiety-induced displacement or attenuation of aggressive responses is equally unsatisfactory. As we noted earlier, high levels of anxiety about displaying aggression should lead to attenuation of the response. Surely, one form of attenuation would be to convert hostile feelings into mock fighting—to act out, "in play," aggressive impulses that would be unacceptable in "real" form. Yet one of the best established sex differences is the much greater incidence of mock fighting (rough-and-tumble play) among boys. Boys, rather than girls, seem to express aggression in attenuated form. Another similar instance may be found in aggressive fantasies, which are presumably "safe" forms of aggression, and are nevertheless consistently reported more frequently among boys. What about displacement of aggression to safe objects—teasing of animals, bullying of younger children? We have little evidence on this point. Titley and Viney (1969) did investigate the question of whether "helplessness" in a victim increased or decreased aggression (in the form of shocks) displayed toward him. They found that males delivered more intense shocks to a victim who appeared to be physically disabled than they did to a normal victim; for female subjects, the reverse was true. A related finding by Aronson and Cope (1968) is that men who overheard someone being harshly treated developed a dislike for the victim, while women felt positively emotionally drawn to the victim of another's attack. Thus, if either sex could be said to be "displacing" aggression toward safe targets, it was the men, not the women, who were doing so. Of course, it could be argued that girls and women have such deep, strong anxiety about aggression that it operates to suppress (to some extent) initial perception of aggressive events, aggressive fantasies, aggressive behavior toward any target no matter how helpless, and even the mildest, most attenuated forms of aggression (horseplay, practical jokes). But if this is so, it becomes impossible to distinguish strong aggressive tendencies accompanied by strong inhibition from weak aggressive tendencies. We would like to urge serious consideration of the possibility that the two sexes are not equal in initial aggressive response tendencies. Whether the early sex differences in aggressive tendencies have a biological base, or spring from greater social encouragement of this behavior in boys, is a question to which we return below.

An interesting feature of the research on aggression is the sex difference in targets, or victims, of aggression. In three of the experiments in which subjects of college age were asked to administer shocks to learners (Buss 1966, Taylor and Epstein 1967, Youseff 1968), the sex of the victim was systematically varied. In all three, women "learners" were given milder shocks, and fewer of them, than male "learners." In another study with 11-year-olds (Shortell and Biller 1970), subjects used a loud noise as "punishment" for another child and, again, girls were given less punishment than boys. Patterson et al. (1967)[R], in their observational study of aggression in two nursery schools, found that girls were less frequently aggressed against. This study showed that there was a positive correlation between being a victim and being an aggressor; thus victimhood is part of being involved in dyadic aggressive interchanges that are more characteristic of boys than girls.

The tacit assumption that girls will not be aggressed against is further revealed in a study by Sandidge and Friedland (1973). Children aged 9–10 from relatively impoverished homes were shown cartoons of a child (either a boy or a girl) speaking aggressively to another child of the same or opposite sex. The subjects were asked to respond as they believed the other child would. The responses of boy and girl subjects were very similar: both gave more aggressive responses (that is, retaliated more strongly) if the cartoon aggressor was a boy. An interesting sidelight on this study is that subjects of both sexes responded more aggressively if they were answering for a girl. This finding would be consistent with the interpretation that, since girls are not supposed to be attacked, when they *are* attacked, they are seen as justified in retaliating as strongly as possible.

In a study by Langlois et al. (1973)[R], children were brought in pairs to a playroom stocked with toys, and their interactions recorded. Some of the subjects were observed in same-sex pairs, others in mixed-sex pairs. At age 3, there was little sex difference in aggression, though both boys and girls aggressed somewhat more often (not significantly so) against a female playmate. At age 5, however, the situation was clear: boys were more aggressive, but only toward a male playmate. This applied both to hitting the other child directly and hitting with an object. Thus, the differentiation of targets did not occur in this sample until age 5, but it did occur.

The single exception in the "victim" data comes from one study of honking at other drivers at an intersection. Deaux (1971) placed either a man or woman driver in a car at an intersection. When the light turned green, the driver deliberately stalled his (or her) car and did not move forward through the intersection. Observers recorded how soon other drivers began to honk. Other drivers honked more quickly at a woman driver than at a man driver. This work suggests that the prohibition against aggression toward women does not extend to a mild form of aggression toward an unfamiliar person with whom one is not in a face-to-face encounter. Another interpretation is that others feel freer to try to influence the behavior of an unknown woman than that of an unknown man—that is, that women are seen as more proper objects of dominance attempts. This issue will be taken up later in the section on dominance.

Although the studies are few, the results are quite consistent: girls and women are less often the objects, as well as the agents, of aggressive action. This same phenomenon has been observed among monkeys and apes.

Males aggress primarily against each other, and seldom against females. One may speculate about the biological utility of this. For the survival of a bisexual species, it is more important for a higher proportion of females than males to survive to maturity; hence a low level of aggression toward them by the more powerful male would have value from an evolutionary standpoint. Pointing to biological utility, however, does not explain behavior. We still need to know what the process is that leads to a lower level of victimizing females.

There may be a clue in the work of Cairns (1972)[R]. Working with mice, Cairns first isolated male mice (a treatment shown to increase aggressiveness when they are subsequently placed with a partner), and then used drugs to vary the "state" of the cage-mate with whom they were placed. If placed with a placebo-treated male cage-mate, the isolated animal would attack. But if the cage-mate was sedated, attacks against him were much less frequent. Cairns's observations were that aggressive interchanges did not occur full-blown, but that there were preliminary exploratory "probes" by one animal of the other; if one animal nosed or licked the other vigorously and the other reacted with equal vigor, the first animal would then respond with increased vigor, and so on in a circular escalating process until violent fighting ensued. This cycle could be interrupted simply by nonreactivity of one of the partners.

Patterson et al. (1967)[R], too, found evidence of an escalation process, though the role of a victim's passivity is ambiguous. They charted the reactions of the victim to each initiation of aggression by another child and then coded them as either positively or negatively "reinforcing" to the aggressor:

Positively reinforcing. Target does not respond, withdraws, gives up toy, cries, assumes defensive posture (e.g. covers head), protests verbally.

Negatively reinforcing. Target tells teacher, recovers the property that aggressor took, retaliates (e.g. hits back).

They found first of all that most aggressive acts were positively reinforced in a nursery school setting. Furthermore, when a child was positively reinforced for an act of aggression, he was likely, subsequently, to repeat the same action toward the same victim. If he was negatively reinforced, the likelihood of a repetition decreased. Thus we see a process of conditioning of aggressive behavior at work.

If one considers these results jointly with those of Cairns, an interesting dilemma appears: Patterson et al. indicate that a "passive" response by the victim (i.e. nonresponse or withdrawal) supports the aggressive tendencies of the aggressor, making him more likely to attack this same victim again. Cairns, on the other hand, finds that if the victim is experimentally made passive so that he does not respond to an attack, the aggressor does not continue his attack. Is it possible that one kind of response by the victim governs the immediate continuation of the encounter, and another governs the probability of recurrence of the behavior on future occasions?* However this question may be answered, it would appear that a victim's crying or showing other signs of distress will stimulate the aggressor to continue the attack; but under some circumstances, so will resistance. Perhaps the only way for the victim to turn off an attack is either to "play dead" or to counterattack with enough force to drive the attacker away.

When it comes to explaining sex differences, however, the findings of Cairns and those of Patterson et al. leave many unsolved puzzles. Girls do not "play dead," nor do they counterattack. Patterson et al. considered the possibility that girls were less often victims of aggression because they did not positively reinforce aggression when it was directed toward them. However, the findings were that girls were no more and no less likely than boys to cry or yield in response to an aggressive attack. Thus they were less frequent victims despite the fact that they provided the same contingencies for aggressors' behavior.

Whiting and Pope (1974) also found that girls do not provide more positive reinforcement for aggression—that is, they are no more likely to withdraw or yield when attacked. Whiting and Pope do report that boy victims are more likely than girls to retaliate actively against an aggressor —to provide negative reinforcement. It appears, then, that boys are more

---

* This question was raised in a personal communication from Gerald Patterson.

frequently selected as the victims of aggression despite the fact that the consequences to the aggressor are more likely to be aversive.

Another possibility considered by Patterson et al. (1967)[R] was that individual differences in frequency of aggression and of being victimized might be accounted for by vigor, or activity level. It seemed reasonable that the more active, vigorous children might get into more social encounters of all kinds than less active ones, and the Cairns work underscores the importance of the reactivity of the victim in producing escalation of initial encounters into fights. Patterson et al. measured activity level in three ways: the amount of distance covered per unit time; the vigor of physical activity; and the vigor of verbal activity (high vigor-screaming, loud crying, or shouting). Surprisingly, the correlations between aggressiveness and the first two measures were low and insignificant (.23 and .10, respectively). Only the correlation between aggression and verbal vigor was significant (.66). Thus the hypothesis that general activity level is related to the aggressor-victim cycle received only weak support. The authors say (p. 35):

The highly aggressive child seemed to be interacting at a high rate. Initially, this was thought to reflect little more than the general activity level of the child. However, upon closer examination, it would seem likely that amount of social interaction is more than just a function of activity level. The child who interacts at a high level with his peers is not only an active child but he is also an individual who has been conditioned to be highly responsive to peer-dispensed reinforcers.

The reader will note the assumption by Patterson et al. that a child who is highly responsive to peer-dispersed reinforcers must be so because of prior conditioning. They may be right, but the possibility of biological factors should not be overlooked. If prior conditioning is the key, we must ask why boys, rather than girls, should have been more thoroughly conditioned to this particular variety of social responsiveness. In any case, the work of Patterson et al. is relevant to the question of sex differences in that it focuses attention upon the nature of the reactivity of children to one another during social interaction. They report that certain children in their study, when they were aggressive, seemed, for some reason not clear from the data, to obtain more reinforcement from other children than the average child's aggression receives. (Whether this means that some children find a given set of reactions to an attack more exciting, or that some children's attacks produce stronger reactions, we do not know.)

It was shown in the preceding chapter that, although boys and girls do not consistently differ in general activity level, boys tend to be more active in the company of their peers and seem to engage in interaction with a larger number of peers. We suggest that when a young boy makes a tentative "probe" of another boy, he is more likely to get an exciting reaction than if the probe is directed toward a girl. What precisely makes a reaction exciting, or why some children produce more excitement in others so that an interaction is prolonged and escalated, we do not know. Evidently, classifying the responses of the other into "positive" and "negative" reinforcers does not capture the behavioral quality that is important for sex differences, although it *is* important for the acquisition of aggressive behavior when children's behavior is charted without regard to sex. Exciting reactions to initial approaches are no doubt a central feature of rough-and-tumble play, a form of "mock aggression" that is consistently more common among male than female play groups. Detailed observations are needed, perhaps drawing upon the methods of ethology, to provide further insights into the nature of "exciting reactions." It will be especially important to take note of signs of submission or distress on the part of the victim, and the effect these have upon the aggressor. This may be an aspect of interaction wherein the sexes differ, but there is no evidence to date on whether this is the case. G. R. Patterson reports (personal communication) that when a victim cries, the aggressor is likely to hit again. Thus, if girls did cry more when attacked (which they probably don't), this would not explain their being under-chosen as victims. There must be something else that they do or fail to do when attacked that interrupts the circular process, but exactly what it is has not yet been identified.

One suggestion: perhaps girls are more skilled at eliciting responses from others that are incompatible with aggression. Could it be that they inspire affection or sympathy? Or make the attacker feel guilty? Or divert the attention of the aggressor from themselves? Clearly, the continuation of an aggressive sequence can only be understood if consideration is given to the alternative forms of response that are available to the parties to a quarrel; it would also be useful to know the conditions that govern an aggressor's or victim's turning to these alternatives.

So far, we have argued that the higher level of male aggression probably cannot be accounted for by learned fear of aggression among girls, or by any tendency for girls to reinforce the aggression of boys. It is time to consider whether the sex difference in aggression has a biological foundation. We contend that it does. This is not to say that aggression is unlearned. As can be seen from the work of Bandura (1973)[R] and Patterson et al. (1967)[R], there is clear evidence that aggression *is* learned. But the learning process calls for a form of reactivity that is not well understood, and with respect to which the sexes may have different degrees of preparedness. Let us outline the reasons why biological sex differences appear to be involved in aggression: (1) Males are more aggressive than females in all human societies for which evidence is available. (2) The sex differences are found early in life, at a time when there is no evidence that differential socialization pressures have been brought to bear by adults to "shape" aggression differently in the two sexes (see Chapter 9). (3) Similar sex differences are found in man and subhuman primates. (4) Aggression is related to levels of sex hormones, and can be changed by experimental administrations of these hormones.

Let us provide some documentation for the fourth point. We shall not attempt to summarize the extensive body of research that has accumulated in recent years concerning the relationships between sex hormones and behavior. The reader will find several existing reviews useful for more complete coverage of these issues: Hutt 1972[R], Hamburg and Van Lawick–Goodall 1973[R], Lunde 1973[R], Levine 1971[R], Money and Ehrhardt 1972[R]. We shall simply present here some of the well-established generalizations with a few selected references.

1. Male hormones (androgens) function during prenatal development to masculinize the growing individual. Genetic females exposed to abnormally high (for females) levels of androgens prenatally are masculinized both physically and behaviorally, including elevated levels of threat behavior and rough-and-tumble play.

Young, Goy, and Phoenix (1964)[R] demonstrated this fact experimentally by administering testosterone to pregnant monkeys; the female offspring of these animals not only had masculinized genitalia but showed malelike play patterns, including elevated levels of rough-and-tumble play. There are a few parallel cases in human development, in which genetic females receive excess amounts of male hormones prenatally. (This can result from abnormal activity of the fetus's adrenal glands as well as from maternal injection of masculinizing hormones during pregnancy.) The most thorough study of girls of this kind has recently been reported by Ehrhardt and Baker (1973)[R]. They studied 17 fetally androgenized girls, and compared them with their 11 normal sisters. As we noted in Chapter 5, the androgenized girls underwent surgical correction of their masculinized external genitalia, following which they could not be distinguished physically from normal girls. Their behavior, however, continued to be masculinized, by comparison with their sisters, in the following ways: they much more often preferred to play with boys; they took little interest in weddings, dolls, or live babies, and preferred outdoor sports. Initiation of fighting was somewhat more common among these girls, but not significantly so by comparison with their normal sisters. A cautionary note is needed about this work: the initial abnormality of the experimental subjects was caused by a prenatal malfunctioning of the adrenal gland. The subjects all required continued treatment with cortisone, through childhood, to correct the adrenal deficiency. The cortisone treatment was designed to bring their cortisone concentrations to a normal level, and, hence, after treatment, this level should not be different between them and their normal controls; however, there may be side effects of artificial restoration of a deficient hormone level that have not yet been detected and may have led to some of the behavioral characteristics of the treated girls. Further-more, as we noted earlier, the behavioral evidence comes from mother interviews. Although we do not doubt that mothers are in a better position than anyone else to know many details of their children's interests, prefer-ences, and habitual activities, the mothers' expectations for the girls' be-havior and their own responses to them might have been influenced by prior knowledge of their daughters' medical problems.

It is primarily in their consistency with the animal experimental work on early-administered hormones that the findings with human subjects become especially compelling. Specifically with respect to aggression, it has been shown that administration of testosterone to infant female rodents increases their fighting in adulthood (Edwards 1969[R]), whereas neonatal adminis-tration of the female hormone estradiol *reduces* adult fighting (Bronson and Desjardins 1968[R]).

These studies and many others with animals indicate that sex hormones present before birth or just at the time of birth sensitize or "program" the individual so as to affect behavior in childhood and adulthood. This is true in spite of the fact that the sexes are not very different in their levels of sex hormones from birth until puberty. The primary effect of prenatal an-drogens is frequently referred to as the production of a "male brain." Al-though accurate, this terminology may be misleading, in that it may imply to the lay reader that the major effects are upon intellectual functioning. Actually, what is meant is that the brain's functions (or, more specifically, the functions of the hypothalamus) in controlling the production of hor-mones are "set" in a different way for the two sexes early in development, and that this setting depends on the amount of testosterone present at a crucial period of prenatal growth. The timing of the crucial period varies between species. In any case, it now appears to be demonstrated that the amounts of sex hormones present prenatally and perinatally affect two things: the amount of certain behavior (including fighting, rough-and-tumble play, and threat behavior) during childhood, and the way sex hor-mones produced at adolescence and adulthood will affect the individual. Thus, administration of androgens in adulthood to a fetally untreated fe-male will not fully masculinize her sexual behavior; but it will do so if she was also subjected to the influence of unusually high (for a female) levels of male hormone prenatally (Levine 1966[R]).

2. Male hormones increase aggressive behavior when they are admin-istered postnatally even without prenatal sensitization. A study by Joslyn (1973)[R] illustrates the kinds of effects that can be produced. The subjects were three male and three female rhesus monkeys that were separated from their mothers at 3–4 months of age. Beginning at age 6½ months, regular injections of testosterone were begun for the three females, and continued to the age of 14½ months. The males were untreated. There were

three time periods during which the animals were placed together for 30 minutes a day in an observation cage and their social behavior recorded. The three time periods were ages 5–9½ months, ages 13½–16 months, and ages 25–27½ months. The main focus of the study was on social dominance, a topic that will be discussed more fully below. Aggressive responses were studied as part of the establishment of dominance relations. The findings were that initially, before the testosterone treatment of the females began, the males were dominant and showed more aggression than the females. After the onset of testosterone treatment, the frequency of aggression by the females increased; it was approximately equal to that of the males by the end of the first observation period (age 9 months). During the early portion of the second observation period, two of the females attacked and subdued the two most dominant males. These two females continued to be dominant throughout the second observation period (after hormone treatment had been discontinued) and also maintained their dominance through the third observation period, almost a year after the cessation of hormonal treatment. At this time, aggression was infrequent within the group, and there was an increased frequency of social play, but the amount of rough-and-tumble play among the males was considerably reduced by comparison with normal males, as was their sexual behavior. The androgen treatment of the females did not significantly increase the incidence of rough-and-tumble play among them or the incidence of malelike sexual behavior; it only reduced these behaviors in their untreated male cage-mates! During androgen treatment, the females developed a more luxuriant growth of hair, and gained weight to the point that they outweighed the males, but the weight difference disappeared after the termination of the treatment. The female who gained the most weight was the one who did *not* attack the males and move up the status hierarchy during the second observation period. However, after the cessation of treatment, when she had lost some weight, she then began to dominate the two initially dominant males. Thus the ability of one animal to subdue another in a fight was not solely a matter of their relative weights, although this was undoubtedly involved.

The reader will recall that the male animals in this experiment were untreated. What has been shown in the studies cited so far is that dosages of male hormones will increase fighting (or rough-and-tumble) in females. Will dosages of androgens elevate the already higher levels of these behaviors in males? There is little research relevant to this question. Ehrhardt did find that fetally androgenized *boys* were not behaviorally very different from their normal brothers, suggesting that there may be a certain minimum level of prenatal male hormone needed to masculinize an individual's behavior, and that once this level has been reached, further amounts will have little effect. However, the data from a species far distant from man

—chickens—suggest a different conclusion. Andrew (1972)[R] administered varying amounts of testosterone to chicks, and measured the frequency of their attacks upon the experimenter's hand. The treated males were more aggressive than untreated males. Among females, however, although the testosterone did bring about comb growth, there was no increase in attack behavior as a result of hormone treatment. It is an open question whether, among human beings, variations in the amount of testosterone present prenatally are associated with individual differences in aggressive behavior during the growth cycle.

3. More aggressive males tend to have higher current levels of androgens. Rose et al. (1971)[R] have measured the plasma testosterone levels of the members of a monkey troupe, and found higher androgen levels among the dominant animals. Although little is known about the relation between adult androgen levels and behavior among human males, a study by Kreuz and Rose (1972)[R] is suggestive. Plasma testosterone measures were taken from blood samples of a group of 21 young men in prison. Verbal aggression and fighting in prison did not correlate with blood scores, but the men with higher testosterone levels had committed more violent and aggressive crimes during adolescence.

It is important to be cautious in interpreting the "effects" of testosterone levels from correlations. Rose et al. (1972)[R] have shown that if males low on the dominance hierarchy among their male cage-mates are placed with females whom they can dominate and with whom they can have an active sex life, their testosterone levels rise markedly and remain high. After an animal is defeated in a fight, however, his testosterone level goes down and remains low. Thus hormone levels constitute an open system. A testosterone level is not something that an individual "has" independently of experience, even though in a stable social situation a given individual's score is quite stable. At the present state of our knowledge, it would appear that a high testosterone level can be both a cause and a result of aggressive behavior.

So far we have been discussing the effects of male hormones (particularly testosterone) upon behavior in the two sexes. What about female hormones? Here our knowledge is meager indeed, but what is known is sufficient to make clear that the action of female hormones is by no means simply opposite to that of male hormones. For example, in a study with rats, Bronson and Desjardins (1968)[R] found that neonatal administration of estradiol decreased the later aggressiveness of males, but *increased* this behavior in females. Levine and Mullins (1964)[R], also working with rats, found that neonatal dosages of estradiol interfered with adult sexual behavior in both sexes—it did not make the females more "female," but less so. Thus it would appear that estrogens "mimic" androgens in females but not in males. The anti-androgenic effects in males are further indicated in the research of Work and Rogers (1972)[R]. They identified a stable dominance hierarchy among six male rats, and then administered an estrogen to each of the three animals highest in the hierarchy. On the seventh day of treatment, a new stable hierarchy emerged, with the three treated rats now occupying the lowest three status positions in the hierarchy. Following the termination of treatment, the original hierarchy gradually reappeared. The effect of estrogens upon human beings, or even upon animals close to man, remains essentially unexplored.

We have been presenting a fairly detailed case for a biological contribution to the sex difference in aggression. It seemed incumbent upon us to establish this case as explicitly as possible, since many readers will no doubt address the issue initially with an assumption that any psychological difference between human groups is entirely a result of differences in experience and training. It is time to restore some balance to the discussion. We have been emphasizing male aggression to the point of allowing females to be thought of, by implication, as either angelic or weak. Women share with men the human capacity to heap all sorts of injury upon their fellows. And in almost every group that has been observed, there are some women who are fully as aggressive as the men. Furthermore, an individual's aggressive behavior is strengthened, weakened, redirected, or altered in form by his or her unique pattern of experiences. All we mean to argue is that there is a sex-linked differential readiness to respond in aggressive ways to the relevant experiences.

The aggressiveness of the male has been thought to express itself in a number of ways other than in interpersonal hostility. Competition and dominance, for example, are both thought to have an aggressive element. Indeed, as has been seen above, in some of the animal research, aggression has been studied in the context of the establishment and maintenance of dominance hierarchies. We now examine competition, dominance, and compliance to see whether we can determine how close the similarity is between aggression and these behaviors with respect to sex differentiation.

COOPERATION AND COMPETITION

There is little doubt that the human male is more interested in competitive sports than the human female. Although the two sexes may be said to compete equally for grades during their school years, much academic achievement striving does not appear, to the individual concerned, to involve defeating another person. That is, as we have pointed out earlier, it is possible for a student to strive to improve upon his record of grade performance or to compare himself with an objective standard of achievement without feeling subjectively that he is striving to be better than someone else, and without being competitive in the narrower sense of the word. The old-fashioned spelling bee is a thing of the past in most classrooms, and defining academic success in competitive terms is quite deliberately avoided by many teachers. Still, children do rank-order themselves and others with respect to a variety of skills. The degree of competitive motivation that is involved in academic achievement striving is something that can vary widely from one achieving student to another. As we have seen in Chapter 4, girls work hard for grades, but especially during adolescence they frequently try to avoid the implication of being "better" than boys.

In the daily activities of adult life, men more frequently than women find themselves in open competition with others for jobs, promotions, contracts, clients, etc. In the traditional occupations of women, competitive pressures are notably less. It would be interesting to know whether the competitive interests and behavior of the male are merely a derivative of the social roles assigned to him, or whether there is a built-in element, linked to the patterns of aggression and dominance that have already been identified. But before this question is addressed, let us review the results of the research on competitiveness, as compared with cooperativeness, in the two sexes.

Much of the work with children has involved experimental procedures developed by Madsen and his colleagues. The procedure used by Szal (1972) with nursery school children, for example, used the Madsen marble-pull game. This game involves a marble holder that will slide back and forth across a table. Two children play, each standing at one end of the table holding a string attached to one end of the marble holder. If one child pulls while the other releases his string, the marble holder can be pulled over to one end of the table, where the marble will drop into a player's cup. If both players pull at once, the marble holder comes apart, and the marble rolls into a trough and is not "won" by either player. The players are told that the objective of the game is for both players to get as many marbles as they can. Subjects in the Szal study included boy-boy pairs, girl-girl pairs, and mixed-sex pairs. In this situation, the boy-boy pairs obtained few marbles; each player seemed unwilling to let the other player gain a point, and the marble holder was frequently pulled apart. Girl-girl pairs, by contrast, usually arrived quite quickly at a turn-taking strategy. The experimenters expected that in mixed-sex pairs the boys might dominate the play, getting most of the marbles while the girl yielded, but this did not happen. The two sexes were quite similar in the number of marbles obtained, and girls became more competitive, boys more cooperative, than they were when playing against a same-sex partner.

There are few other studies of competition in young children that have been designed to test for sex differences. The Nelson-Madsen study (1969), also done with four-year-olds, involved a two-person "cooperation board" in which the object was to pull strings in such a way that a pointer would move across a target. Cooperation between the two players was necessary for the pointer to be moved to the desired places. The payoff arrangements were varied, in one case involving joint rewards, in the other individual rewards (each player having his own target spot). The time taken to achieve the necessary degree of cooperation and the amount of turn-taking were not significantly related to the sex composition of the pairs, but the experiment was not designed with such a test in mind and the sex groupings were uneven, with only seven boy-boy pairs being included in the study.

Other studies reporting cooperative and competitive behavior among subjects of varying ages have not yielded consistent results where sex differences are concerned. About half the studies find no sex differences. Among those that do, boys are most frequently found to be more competitive, although there is a reversal in a Mexican-American subsample in one of the Madsen studies (S. Kagan and Madsen 1972a). On the whole, it may be said that boys tend to be more competitive, but the behavior is evidently subject to situational and cultural variations to a considerable degree.

With older children and adults, cooperation has been studied most frequently through the use of the Prisoner's Dilemma game. In this game, two players must simultaneously choose A or B (see diagram).

Player 1

		A	B
Player 2	A	5,5 AA	10,1 BA
	B	1,10 AB	1,1 BB

The payoff arrangements are such that if both choose A, both get a moderate reward. If both choose B, both get a minimal reward. If Player 1 chooses B while Player 2 chooses A, 1 gets a large reward while 2 gets a small one, and the reverse situation applies if it is Player 2 who chooses B while Player 1 continues with an A (cooperative) choice. An illustrative set of rewards is shown above. The nature of the payoff matrix can, of course, be varied, as can the nature and amount of communication between the two players. An early study by Rapoport and Chammah (1965) reported male pairs as being more cooperative on this game than female pairs (although there was no difference in number of cooperative choices between the members of a male-female pair). Since that time a large number of studies have used variants of the Prisoner's Dilemma game, and, as may be seen from Table 7.3, the results of the studies taken as a whole are remarkably consistent in finding little or no sex difference.

The picture that emerges from Tables 7.2 and 7.3 is not entirely consistent with the view that males are the more competitive sex, although in Table 7.2 there is a trend in this direction. Clearly, the issue must be raised whether these studies of "competition" really are studying anything reflecting the behavior that is labeled "competitive" on the sports field or among

TABLE 7.2
Competition (Contrasted with Cooperation)

Study	Age and *N*	Difference	Comment
Lapidus 1972	3-4 (30)	None	Taking marbles out-of-turn while playing marble-pull game with mother
L. Nelson & Madsen 1969	4 (72)	None	Cooperation board, group and limited reward conditions: solution time, turn-taking (white, black)
Hatfield et al. 1967	4-5 (40)	None	Direct, indirect aggression to mother (observer ratings of mother-child interaction)
Szal 1972	4-5 (40)	Boys	Low cooperation, Madsen (boy-boy pairs vs. girl-girl pairs)
S. Kagan & Madsen 1971	4-5, 7-9 (320)	None	Performance on cooperation board after receiving either cooperative, competitive, neutral, or no instructions (Anglo-American, Mexican-American, and Mexican samples)
S. Kagan & Madsen 1972b	5-6, 8-10 (96)	Boys None	Rivalrous in choice of division of marbles with age-mate, 1 out of 4 conditions (American sample) Number of rivalrous choices (Mexican sample)
Stingle 1973	5, 8, 11 (126)	None Boys None	Age 5, 8, cooperation task Age 11, competitive behavior on cooperation task: time per trial Age 11, number and type of rewards achieved
Shapira & Madsen 1969	6-10 (80)	Boys None	Cooperation board, competition was adaptive (urban sample only) Cooperation board, cooperation was adaptive (Israeli sample, half urban and half kibbutz)
S. Kagan & Madsen 1972a	7-9 (128)	None	Frequency of taking partner's present, frequency of letting partner keep present (circle matrix board, Mexican and American samples)
	7-9 (64)	None	Willingness to block partner from obtaining prize (circle matrix board, Mexican and American samples)
	7-11 (160)	Boy-boy pairs Girl-girl pairs None	Open box requiring simultaneous use of 4 hands more slowly (Mexican sample, trial I) Open box more slowly (American sample, trial I) Trials II-V (both samples)
M. Madsen & Shapira 1970	7-9 (144)	None	Group vs. individual reward: difference in performance between conditions on cooperation board (multiracial sample)
	7-9 (156)	None	Cooperation board, individual reward condition (Mexican and multiracial American sample)
A. Miller & Thomas 1972	7-11 (96)	None	Cooperative board, group and individual rewards (Indian and Canadian samples)
Shears & Behrens 1969	8, 9 (316)	Boys	Higher frequency of "exploitative" behavior when in most powerful position in 4-player game requiring the formation of alliances

(continued)

Power Relationships   251

TABLE 7.2 *(cont.)*

Study	Age and N	Difference	Comment
Marwell et al. 1971	18-21 (186)	Women	Frequency of taking from other player's winnings (in 2 out of 5 experiments)
		None	Number of pairs of Ss who reached state of steady cooperation
Shomer et al. 1966	18-21 (64)	Women	Slower to achieve cooperative state in non-zero-sum game

junior executives who covet the same higher job. In these real-life situations, competition is the path to real individual gains. In most of the Madsen studies, competition is maladaptive. The same is true of most versions of the Prisoner's Dilemma game. Players must develop a cooperative strategy, and come to trust one another, if both are to maximize their individual gains; furthermore, each is in a position to prevent the other from succeeding by using a noncooperative strategy. Madsen's point is, of course, that people in modern Western cultures are so thoroughly trained to be competitive that they continue to be so even in situations that are carefully arranged so that cooperation would be more individually functional. A "cooperative choice" in the Madsen games may reflect either enlightened self-interest, a player's altruistic interest in gratifying his partner, or both. Procedural variations are needed to distinguish these motives from one another, and to distinguish both of them from actions designed to diminish the rewards to one's partner, apart from gains or losses to oneself. McClintock and his colleagues (1972, 1973)[x] have devised a set of problems that will yield the necessary distinctions. First, the subject is offered a simple choice between two peanuts (or candies, or marbles) and one. The subject, of course, chooses the larger number. Then the subject is asked to choose for himself and another person simultaneously: in option A, when the subject chooses three peanuts, the other person receives four; in option B, when the subject chooses two peanuts, the other person receives one. If the subject chooses three for himself, the other player gets more than he does; the only way he can "beat" the other player is to accept a smaller reward for himself. The choices can be varied in such a way that the player can increase the other's reward without either sacrifice or gain to himself, etc. Using a series of such choices, McClintock can distinguish pure competitive motivation (that is, the desire to "defeat" the other) from self-interest and generosity. At the time of this writing, McClintock had not completed the work, using same-sex and mixed-sex pairs, that will make it possible to contrast the sexes on the three motivations. When these results are in hand, they should help to resolve the discrepancies among previous studies as to whether boys or girls were shown to be more competitive. They may

TABLE 7.3
Cooperation: Prisoner's Dilemma Game

Study	Age and N	Difference	Comment
Ware 1969	6, 9, 12 (216)	Girls None	Cooperation in same-sex dyads Cooperation in mixed-sex dyads
Tedeschi et al. 1969a	8, 9 (96)	Girls	More cooperative choices, fewer jointly competitive choices, more trusting, more forgiving
		None	Number of jointly cooperative choices, trustworthiness, repentance
Lindskold et al. 1970	10, 11 (144)	Boys	Cooperative choices, simulated same-sex partner
Oskamp & Kleinke 1970	14-17 (100)	Boys	Cooperative choices, same-sex pairs
Bedell & Sistrunk 1973	18-21 (90)	Men	Male-male dyads and mixed-sex dyads made more cooperative responses and rewarded partners more than female-female dyads
Crowne 1966	18-21 (76)	Men	Cooperative choices; same-sex pairs, Ss having entrepreneurial fathers
		None	Ss having bureaucratic fathers
Gallo et al. 1969	18-21 (160)	None	Cooperative choices, same-sex pairs
Gallo & Sheposh 1971	18-21 (200)	None	Cooperative choices, same-sex pairs
Grant & Sermat 1969	18-21 (48)	None	Cooperative choices, simulated same-sex and opposite-sex partners
Horai & Tedeschi 1969	18-21 (90)	None	Cooperative choices, simulated partner
Kahn et al. 1971	18-21 (40)	None	Cooperative choices, same-sex pairs
	18-21 (80)	Men	Cooperative choices (cooperative response optimal)
		Women	Cooperative choices (competitive response optimal)
		None	Cooperative choices, mixed-sex pairs
Kershenbaum & Komorita 1970	18-21 (96)	None	First competitive response, same-sex pairs, with cooperative instructions and controlled feedback
Komorita 1965	18-21 (72)	Women	Cooperative choices: simulated same-sex partner whose responses made competition optimal
	18-21 (40)	Men	Cooperative choices, simulated same-sex partner whose responses made cooperation optimal
Komorita & Mechling 1967	18-21 (64)	None	Cooperative choices following betrayal by partner; same-sex pairs

(continued)

TABLE 7.3 *(cont.)*

Study	Age and *N*	Difference	Comment
McNeel et al. 1972	18-21 (144)	Mixed-sex pairs	More cooperative responses in modified Prisoner's Dilemma game than either male-male or female-female pairs
		Like-sex pairs	Cooperative choices
R. Miller 1967	18-21 (120)	None	Modified Prisoner's Dilemma, same-sex pairs
Pilisuk et al. 1968	18-21 (176)	None	Cooperative responses (modified Prisoner's Dilemma game)
Pruitt 1967	18-21 (100)	None	Cooperative choices, same-sex pairs (standard-modified versions)
Rapoport & Chammah 1965	18-21 (420)	Men	Cooperative choices on later trials, same-sex pairs
		None	Cooperative choices in mixed-sex pairs
Speer 1972	Adult married couples (120)	None	Cooperative choices
Swingle 1970	18-21 (60)	None	Percentage of exploitative responses in non-zero-sum game
Tedeschi et al. 1968b	18-21 (64)	Women	Cooperative choices, first 10 trials of a 100-trial game with a simulated partner
		None	Cooperative choices, overall
Voissem & Sistrunk 1971	18-21 (96)	None	Cooperative choices, with or without communication, same-sex pairs

also yield results more consistent with known sex differences in interest in competitive games and occupations. In future work, it will not be surprising if "competitiveness" is found to serve a complex cluster of motivations. A track star may be primarily interested in setting a new world's record; he measures his own performance against an abstract record. Another runner, however, may be trying to win a particular race, judging his own performance by comparison with that of the other runners. In either case, he may not care particularly about humiliating the other runners. In other sports, the damage to the egos of other players is an important part of the victor's pleasure in winning. Some sports, which seem to the spectator to be viciously aggressive, may have more the quality of rough horseplay to the participants, and a game may be followed by a convivial beer party including both teams (this is not uncommon in soccer games, for example). On the other hand, real hatred can develop during a game, hatred that continues outside the sports arena and leads to continual brawls and individual acts of revenge. Much depends, of course, on the nature of the prize that is offered for winning.

Team sports are intensely competitive between teams, but call for close cooperation within the team and a considerable degree of subordination of the individual player's desire to star. Internal team discipline is often maintained through a tough dominance hierarchy that is not especially friendly (Fiedler 1954[R]), but the result is more effective cooperation and subordination of the individual. In one-to-one sports, however (tennis, boxing), the individual can both compete intensely against the opponent and "show off" individually. In other words, competition involves varying degrees of aggression and varying degrees of simultaneous cooperation. In view of what is known about sex differences in aggression, we would expect men to be more competitive than women in those situations in which aggression toward the opponent plays an especially strong role. However, it is quite possible that males are both more competitive *and* more cooperative (via a dominance hierarchy) in those situations calling for both qualities.

It should be stressed that the intensity of competition depends on the identity of the opponent. In a recent study (Peplau 1973[R]), dating couples of college students competed under two conditions: against each other, or as a team competing against another couple. The task was a verbal skill task (anagrams). Girls who had traditional attitudes about women's roles, and who feared success (in Horner's terms), performed considerably less well when competing against their boy friends than when joining them to compete against others. For women with more "liberated" attitudes, the identity of the competitor made little difference in performance. Evidently, many women feel that to compete against a man with whom they are emotionally involved will make them less attractive. It would seem that competition, for them, implies that they are either aggressing against, or attempting to dominate, the opponent; for other women in this situation, either competition does not have this implication or they are not afraid of being seen as dominant.

The contrasting behavior of men in these two competitive situations is interesting. There was one group of men who, in an independent measurement, gave "threatened" or hostile responses to stories of achievement by women. These men *increased* their performance when competing against their girl friends, by comparison with their performance in team competition. Men who did not feel threatened by female achievement, on the other hand, performed better in the team competition situation (J. Pleck, cited in Peplau 1973[R]). It would appear the implications of competition are very different for some couples than for others: for some men, competition with a woman is seen as a challenge to male dominance, whereas for others it is not. We now turn to dominance within and between the sexes.

DOMINANCE

Like competition, efforts by one individual to dominate another can serve a number of motives. In some cases, one individual is attempting to use another as an instrument to achieve his own ends, regardless of the consequences for the other person. In other instances, dominance attempts are part of an individual's efforts to assume leadership so as to organize a group to strive cooperatively for a mutually rewarding goal. Sometimes, the dominating individual may simply want the perquisites that go with leadership. On some occasions, dominant behavior would be more accurately called "counterdominance"—in the sense that it represents a refusal to be guided or controlled by another—and is thus a means whereby the individual defends his right to his own freedom of action. Finally, there are instances in which dominant behavior seems primarily intended to humiliate another, and in such cases it is hardly distinguishable from aggression. Table 7.4 details the recent studies of dominance.

The writing about dominance in the two sexes has been much influenced by ethological work with primates. (The reader is referred to *Primate Behavior*, 1965, edited by DeVore[R], for documentation of some major generalizations below.) In primate troupes, as well as among lower mammals, it has been clearly shown that a fairly stable dominance hierarchy exists among the males of certain groups, although these hierarchies are more stable in some species than others. Among chimpanzees, for example, a stable "pecking order" among the males is not always identified (Reynolds and Reynolds 1965[R]), though some troupes do show it; among baboons a dominance hierarchy has always been found.

In observational work, a dominant animal is defined as one whose threats result in withdrawal by other animals; who prevails in conflicts over females, food, sleeping places, etc.; toward whom submissive gestures are made; and who is likely to be followed by other members of the group when he moves away from the group. The adult male dominance hierarchy evolves out of both real fights and playful rough-and-tumble encounters among juveniles. In adulthood, although threatening, chasing, and harassment occur fairly frequently among the males of a primate troupe, serious fighting is fairly rare, and occurs primarily when a long-established dominance hierarchy is being threatened. It is thought that the dominance hierarchy has functional importance in that it reduces the necessity for constant fighting. A wounded animal easily falls victim to predators, and thus it is important for survival that fighting should be rare after the males acquire their large teeth (or horns, or whatever fighting equipment the species provides) and can inflict real injury on one another.

In some primate troupes, coalitions among males have been observed, and in some instances the dominant male functions in the leadership role only so long as his "lieutenant" is present. DeVore notes (1965[R], pp. 61–62): "A male's dominance status was a combination of his individual fighting ability and his ability to enlist the support of other males."

Dominance hierarchies among female primates exist, but they are less well documented than the male ones. There is reason to believe that the female hierarchies are less stable. A female's status tends to change when she is in estrus, and to reflect the status of her male consort while she is in the mating phase of her cycle. At other times, she resumes her place in the female hierarchy. Perhaps because of these movements in and out of the female hierarchy, there tends to be rather frequent aggression among the females, but this is mild in degree and does not result in disabling damage being inflicted, hence it is not dangerous to the survival of the troupe. However, there are certain females who do succeed in exercising unchallenged dominance toward other females over long periods of time.

During the time when they are establishing their dominance hierarchy, juvenile males tend to withdraw from the company of females and congregate in groups of five, six, or more. Males at this age generally do not attempt to dominate adult females, and they avoid dominance attempts from them. In adulthood, the males generally dominate the females, although there is some overlap in the two status hierarchies in some species. In others, there is not. A record of the dominant interactions of pairs of individuals in a troupe of chimpanzees is reported by Jane Goodall (1965)[R] as follows:

	Adult male	Adult female	Adolescent male	Adolescent female	Juvenile
Adult male dominates	16	11	14	8	7
Adult female dominates	0	6	3	5	—

Beginning with the assumption that human beings ought to be similar to lower primates in the biological origins of dominance behavior and in the social functions this behavior serves, Omark et al. (two 1973 papers) have looked for similar patterns of social behavior among human children. They have worked in several cultures, using behavior observation of children aged 4–10 in free play, and a "hierarchy test," in which they asked each child to rate each pair of children in the classroom group in terms of "which is tougher." The child included himself in the comparative ratings. In order to make sure that the children understood what was meant by "tough," the subjects were asked to give another word for "tough"; if the subject had difficulty expressing the concept verbally, he was asked to "do something tough," whereupon he would usually double up a fist and make a threatening gesture. Younger subjects were given pictures of class members as aids to memory while they were making their ratings, and responded orally in an individual session; older children worked with paper-and-pencil forms. The stability of a dominance hierarchy within a classroom group was determined by the amount of agreement (a) between the two members of a pair and (b) among the class as a whole, concerning the relative toughness of the class members.

The major findings from these studies are as follows:

1. Beginning at about first grade, boys congregate in larger groups than girls. Girls play together in twos or threes, boys in "swarms."

2. The play groups are very largely sex-segregated, but a few girls are found in the largest boys' play groups, and these tend to be the girls who are at the top of the girls' toughness hierarchy.

3. There is more rough-and-tumble play among the boys.

4. Boys are rated as tougher than girls as early as nursery school age, though there is some overlap, with the toughest girls being tougher than the least tough boys.

5. There are dominance hierarchies for both sexes, but the boys' hierarchy tends to be more stable (that is, more agreed upon) than the girls' hierarchy. Highest agreement is reached on boy-girl pairs, where other children, and the two participants themselves, usually agree that the boy is tougher.

Omark et al., then, have shown a remarkable degree of consistency between the dominance relations found among certain primates and those found among young human beings, when dominance is defined as toughness. The matter of definition is important. The fact that males are the more aggressive sex has been amply documented (see Table 7.1). If toughness is merely a synonym for aggression, the Omark work does not add a great deal to what is already known, other than to show that there is a stable rank-order of aggressiveness *within*, as well as between, the sexes. Is it true that the position an individual establishes in the toughness hierarchy, largely through his fighting ability, forms the basis for a more generalized dominance status, so that the toughest child also dominates others in situations where aggression is not especially relevant? As a test of this question, Omark and Edelman (1973) set pairs of children (American sample, nursery school through third grade) to work on a "Draw a picture together" task, in which each child was given a crayon of distinctive color and the pair were asked to make a joint picture. Dominance could be measured by seeing which child's color established the main outline of the resulting picture, and which child's color occupied more of the available space (territorial dominance). In mixed-sex pairs, boys dominated girls at every grade except kindergarten. In same-sex pairs, the consonance with the toughness hierarchy was not clearly established. Although it was true that outline dominance was achieved by a somewhat higher proportion of tough children (as determined by the "hierarchy test") at each grade, the relationship was significant only in two grades out of five. Thus there is some tendency for toughness scores to predict dominance in cooperative situations, but the point is not fully established.

In the cross-cultural report of Whiting and Pope (1974), a useful distinction is made between "egoistic dominance" and "suggesting responsibly." If an older child warns a younger one to stay away from the fire,

TABLE 7.4

Dominance

Study	Age and N	Difference	Comment
Parten 1933a	2-4 (34)	None	Directing group activities
Anderson 1937	2-6 (65)	Girls None	More dominance behavior in same-sex pairs Dominance behavior in mixed-sex pairs
Baumrind & Black 1967	3-4 (103)	None	Not easily (vs. easily) intimidated or bullied, bullies (vs. avoids forcing will on) other children, permits self to be dominated vs. will not submit (observer ratings)
Sutton-Smith & Savasta 1972	3-4 (17)	Boys None	Engage in more attempts to influence other children's behavior Number of attempts to influence adult's behavior (nursery school observation)
Gellert 1962	3-5 (55)	None	Teachers' rank orderings of children's dominance
Whiting & Pope 1974	3-11 (134)	Boys None Girls None	"Egoistic dominance" (attempt to control other for own ends) at ages 3-6 "Egoistic dominance" at ages 7-11 "Prosocial dominance" (offer responsible suggestions) at ages 3-6 "Prosocial dominance" at ages 7-11
Emmerich 1971	4-5 (415)	None	Classroom observations, early fall and late fall: submissiveness vs. dominance (black and white low SES)
	4-5 (596)	None Boys	Classroom observations, early fall and spring: submissiveness vs. dominance, attempts to control peers Attempts to control adults (black and white low SES)
Szal 1972	4-5 (60)	None	Number of commands, marble-pull game (same- and mixed-sex pairs)
Omark et al. 1973	4-8 (450) 5-9 (250) 8-10 (250)	Boys Boys Boys	Position in "toughness" hierarchy, peer ratings (American sample) Toughness (Swiss sample) Toughness (Ethiopian sample)
Omark & Edelman 1973	4-8 (436)	Boys	Dominate in the "Draw a Picture Together" test at ages 4, 6, 7, and 8; no difference at age 5 (mixed-sex pairs)
Anderson 1939	5 (38)	Boys None	More dominance behavior in same-sex pairs Dominance behavior in mixed-sex pairs
Feshbach 1969	6 (126)	None	Number of orders given to same-sex partner, or to same- or opposite-sex newcomer
C. Harrison et al. 1971	6-11 (649)	None	Teacher's report: child chosen as a leader by peers

(continued)

TABLE 7.4 *(cont.)*

Study	Age and N	Difference	Comment
Zander & van Egmond 1958	7, 10 (418)	Boys	In mixed-sex, 4-person groups: influence attempts (both successful and unsuccessful), demands
		None	Suggestions, evaluations of others
Bee 1964	9 (36)	Boys	Speak first in problem-solving interaction with parents
Braginsky 1970	10 (225)	None	Children's Machiavellianism Scale
	10 (96)	None	Success in persuading other child to eat bitter crackers; strategies of persuasion employed
Christie 1970b	11 (72)	None	Children's version of Christie's Likert-type Mach Scale
Nachamie 1969	11 (72)	None	Kiddie Machiavellianism Scale, success in bluffing in a dice game
Baltes & Nesselroade 1972	12-16 (1,249)	Boys	"Dominance," Cattell's personality questionnaire
Sharma 1969	18-20 (293)	None	Asian Indians: self-ratings, dominance-deference scale
Arkoff et al. 1962	18-21 (252)	Men	Caucasian American and Japanese samples, self-ratings on dominance-deference scale
		None	Japanese-American sample
Christie 1970a	18-21 (1,596)	Men	Scores on Machiavellianism Scales, Likert-type and forced-choice versions, (white sample)
	18-21 (148)	Men	Scores on Likert-type Mach Scale (black sample) Scores on forced-choice version of Mach Scale (trend, $p < .1$)
Denmark & Diggory 1966	18-21 (308)	None	Fraternity and sorority members' reports of their leaders' use of authoritarian practices
	18-21 (19)	None	Fraternity and sorority leaders' reports of their leadership styles
Gardiner 1968	18-21 (199)	None	Thai sample: self-ratings, dominance-deference scale
Markel et al. 1972	18-21 (72)	Men	Greater speaking intensity when addressing female E
		None	Speaking intensity when addressing male E
Strongman & Champness 1968	18-21 5M, 5F	None	Eye contact, directed gaze, speech with gaze upon introduction to new acquaintance

for example, this is a form of dominance, but it is quite different in quality from the behavior of the child who attempts to make another child run an errand for him. In each of the seven cultures studied, girls were more likely to attempt to control the behavior of another person in the interests of some social value or in the interests of that other person's welfare. Boys, on the other hand, showed more "egoistic dominance" in five of the six societies reported.

In the Whiting and Pope work the age ranges are broad, and we do not have a clear picture of the starting age for the greater frequency of male dominance attempts in the various cultures studied. It should also be noted that the target of "egoistic dominance" was not specified—we do not know whether boys were issuing dominant directives primarily to one another, to girls, or to adults. Since boys congregate primarily in all-male play groups, it would appear likely that most of their dominance attempts are directed toward one another. If this were true, it would be consistent with the observations of primate groups.

Although the evidence is scanty, it would also appear that boys make more attempts to dominate adults than do girls. The studies by Berk (1971), Emmerich (1971), and Bee (1964) all indicate that boys take more initiative vis-à-vis adults, in the sense of trying to establish the form that the interaction will take, and hence more often run into conflict with what the adult wants done (Berk). See Table 7.4.

Although the Omark and Edelman (1973) work indicates that boys dominate girls in the sense that both know which is tougher, it is not clear whether this implies that boys issue directives to girls any more frequently than the other way around. Feshbach (1969) found that pairs of girls slightly more frequently issued directives to a boy newcomer than did pairs of boys to a girl newcomer, but the frequency of this behavior toward a stranger was low and the sex difference was not significant. Szal (1972) did not find that either sex succeeded in dominating the other in the Madsen marble-pull game. Thus the existence of a dominance hierarchy in the Omark and Edelman sense does not imply a unidirectional flow of controlling acts from one sex to the other. See Table 7.4.

These findings suggest that perhaps being tougher does not imply a generalized dominance among human children. If dominance is thought of as successful efforts by one person to control or manipulate the behavior of another, it is clear that there are many ways to do this other than through physical force or the threat of it. The work of Christie and his colleagues (1970a,b) on Machiavellianism makes this point. An individual may be accommodating and even submissive as part of a plan to influence another's behavior; if he succeeds, he has, in one sense, succeeded in dominating the other. A "Mach" scale has been devised, to measure the extent to which an individual uses exploitative and manipulative behavior in interpersonal relations. High scores on this scale have been shown to be related to success in bargaining with others for desired outcomes. Much of the work on Machiavellianism has not looked for sex differences. In the adult studies that do analyze for sex differences, men have generally proved to be more Machiavellian than women (Christie 1970a, p. 32). However, using a children's form of the Mach test, Nachamie (1969) did not find a sex difference. Braginsky (1970) also adapted the Mach scale for use with children; she compared the scores of 10-year-old boys and girls on this scale, and also observed the performance of the children toward one another in a situation calling for Machiavellian behavior. On the children's form of the

Mach test, the sexes did not differ, although there was a good deal of variation among children within each sex in their willingness to take a manipulative stance toward others. In the behavioral test, the subject child was offered money for every unpleasant-tasting cracker (soaked in quinine solution and then dried) that he could get another child to eat. Boys and girls were equally successful in "dominating" other children in the sense of being able to persuade them to eat the bitter crackers. High-Mach boys were more directly coercive in their methods, and told more direct lies to their victims; high-Mach girls were more indirect and were more likely simply to omit unpleasant truths. However, these results were reversed in the low-Mach groups: low-Mach girls were coercive, low-Mach boys were indirect. Thus there were no overall sex differences in the strategies employed to influence the other children. This study, then, does not reflect a greater dominance by one sex than the other, or even, surprisingly, the use of different strategies of persuasion, at the age of 10.

What can be said concerning dominance relations between the sexes during adolescence and adulthood? Many studies have been made of leadership in small adult groups; but because most of the groups studied have been homogeneous as regards sex, cross-sex dominance patterns have not been revealed. However, some of the major findings of leadership studies may be relevant to cross-sex dominance. Leadership studies have shown that very few individuals seem to be endowed with a general personal quality of leadership such that they can assume leadership in different groups having different objectives. Other things being equal, dominance in a group will be exercised by the person whose formal status assigns him to leadership (e.g. the ranking officer in a military group). When a group is first formed, and where no formal statuses have been assigned (as in the case of a jury beginning its deliberations), the group will usually choose its formal leader on the basis of preexisting status indicators such as education, occupation, age, and sex. But expertise in the subject-matter areas related to the group's objectives is also important in dominance patterns in informal groups, and this is a major factor that limits the ability of an individual to transfer his leadership status to a new group.

Collins and Raven (1968)[8] summarize research on dominance within groups; they make the point that, whereas among animals there seems to be a simple rank-ordering of power that generalizes across situations, this is less true in groupings of human children, and becomes progressively less true the older the members of the group and the more complex the social setting in which they function. This warns us that it is unwise to infer, from having identified some similarities between dominance in children's play groups and dominance among groups of subhuman primates, that dominance patterns among human adults can be easily described in the same terms.

On the issue of dominance relationships between the sexes in adulthood, perhaps the studies of marriage partners are the most relevant. Here, it becomes difficult indeed to identify the dominant partner, at least in American families. Parsons (1955)[R] attempted to describe family influence patterns in terms of the differentiation of two kinds of leadership: "instrumental" leadership, directed toward the organization and completion of joint tasks, and normally exercised by the husband; and "expressive" leadership, aimed at creating, restoring, and maintaining bonds of emotional solidarity among family members, a form of leadership (Parsons thought) normally assumed by the wife. Later work did not find, however, that the roles actually assumed by the members of functioning families correspond to this description (see Leik 1963[R], Burke 1972[R]). In a large number of families, power over decision making seems to be either exercised jointly or divided according to the individual competencies of the members, and husband and wife influence one another in a variety of direct and indirect ways, with no one person being consistently "in charge." Collins and Raven say (p. 160): "In the analysis of husband-wife interaction, the power structure shows even greater variability and multidimensionality [than in other groups], with dominance varying according to task domain, and changing with time." They point out that wives become relatively more dominant (or more equal in dominance) the longer the marriage continues (see also Wolfe 1959[R]).

In many interactions between adult men and women outside marriage, dominance relations are dictated by formal status, as in the case of the male employer and his female secretary. Judging from the work on leadership, it would be likely that, even when formal status requirements are not present, a man's generally higher status would lead him to adopt a dominant role, and a woman to accept or even encourage this, in the early stages of group formation. An item of evidence is that men are chosen as jury foremen much more frequently than their numbers alone would warrant (Strodtbeck and Mann 1956[R]). With continued association, the relative competence of the individual group members in skills that are important to the group's objectives should weigh more heavily, so that whenever a woman group member possesses these skills, her dominance should increase, if lack of formal status does not prevent it. An interesting illustration of how stereotyped sex roles affect initial group formation, but do not necessarily hold up with increased acquaintance among the individuals involved in a continuing relationship, is found in the work of Leik (1963)[R]. When Leik formed strangers into simulated families, the men and women involved took up traditional role relationships toward one another (the man taking instrumental leadership, the woman assuming "expressive" functions). In actual families, however, this role differentiation did not occur.

It becomes important to know how stable the dominance patterns are that have been established on the basis of preexisting status considerations. If leadership is initially assumed by someone who has less relevant knowledge or skill than someone else in the group, how easily does the dominance pattern shift? This issue has been the subject of research by Cohen and Roper (1973)[R] with interracial groups of schoolchildren. They have found that it is necessary not only that the black children in such a group should *have* greater knowledge, but that both the black and white children in the group should be explicitly aware that they do, before the black children will assume (or be allowed) leadership. It is likely that a similar situation prevails between the sexes, although the matter has not yet been studied systematically.

A final point should be made concerning the relation of aggression and dominance. Dominance among groups of primates or young boys is largely achieved by fighting or threats, although we should remember that, even among apes, the ability to maintain coalitions with other animals is important. In human groups, particularly as humans move from childhood into adulthood, they begin to outgrow their reliance upon aggression as the chief means for achieving dominance. When children identify other children who, they say, can "get them to do things," the characteristics of these "influential" children often include "toughness," particularly when the influential child is a boy. Girls stress, in addition, however, that they can be influenced by someone who is polite and pleasant (Gold 1958[R]). In an early study of disturbed, aggressive children from deprived environments (Polansky et al. 1950[R]), the children whose behavior was imitated by others, and who directly influenced other children, tended to be good athletes, physically strong, and independent of social pressure from others. In a study of normal adolescents, however (Marks 1957[R]), male clique leaders were boys who were interested in social activities, were popular, and were "acceptable," though athletic prowess was important. A boy's popularity or prestige at this age seems to be much less based upon fighting prowess than it once was, at least among middle-class children. Among girls in the Marks study, leadership was exercised by girls who were attractive, popular, and style-setters, but also by girls who had either strong scientific interests or athletic skills. Leadership qualities, then, have become quite diverse, and adolescents who are able to dominate other adolescents, in the sense of achieving leadership status, can no longer simply be described as tough. By college age, there is some reason to believe that male leaders employ more authoritarian methods of leadership and control within their own groups than women do within their groups (Denmark and Diggory 1966), and athletic ability still plays a role in some groups (though not in many others); but maintaining a leadership position depends above all on being effective in achieving the group's goals. This is increasingly true as individuals go into adult social groups of greater complexity.

Effective leadership does call for toughness of a certain kind, but interpersonal aggression is usually not needed; indeed, it is detrimental to many aspects of group functioning and must be strictly controlled if a group is to stay together and function effectively. Dominance in adulthood (in the sense of influencing others) may be exercised by nonaggressive Machiavellian means (flattery, bribery, deception), or it may depend upon subject-matter competency and supportiveness toward other group members.

It is true that dominance in some adult human relationships still depends upon brute force. A report from the *Manchester Guardian* on wife-beating in midsummer 1973 provides an illustration:

One day, for instance, he came home from work and it was five o'clock and he said "Why aren't the children in bed?" and I said it was too early and he beat me and said "None of your lip." So I put them to bed and he said "Hit him," meaning my son and I did. Then he said "Hit him again, he's not crying loud enough." I wouldn't, and he hit me and broke my nose and laid my face open so that I needed stitches in it. I ran out on him and went to the police and tried to take him to court, but I still had to live at home, and in the end he forced me to withdraw the summons.

The report of the *Guardian* revealed that this was not an isolated instance, and that brutality of husbands to wives occurred in a range of social classes (the above report comes from a family with a good income). The reader will note that this kind of violent imposition of one person's will upon another can occur among members of the same sex; the potentialities for it are greater, however, between the sexes because of their unequal strength. Although incidents of this kind exist as an ugly aspect of marital relations in an unknown number of cases—an aspect that tends to be unseen, or deliberately ignored and denied, by outsiders—there can be little doubt that direct force is rare in most modern marriages. Male behavior such as that described above would be considered pathological in any human (or animal!) society and, if widespread, would endanger a species. But the question is, how much does the *potentiality* for direct force affect the relationship between normal adult men and women? We have seen, in the section on aggression, that there is a consistent prohibition against the expression of aggression by men toward women. It may be that there is a reciprocal restraint on the part of women, which operates to protect them from the aggressive potential of men, and takes the form of their seldom producing the behavior that will stimulate male aggression, and turning off an aggressive sequence once it has begun (perhaps simply by refusing to respond to a provocation with a counterprovocation), so that the circular escalating process described by Cairns (1972, pp. 71–81)[8] does not occur. The above account describes the relationship between human males and females as an ethologist would see it, with emphasis on cross-species similarities. There are important differences between the human condition and that of animals, however. We shall discuss more fully below the social conditions that we believe limit the use of aggression as an instrument of dominance between the sexes; for the present, let us simply say that we believe any man-woman pair usually forms a coalition in which, in the interests of maintaining the mutually rewarding aspects of the relationship, aggression is deliberately minimized. When this has happened, it is by no means clear that one sex usually succeeds in dominating the other. We have seen that males tend to be the more dominant sex in the sense of directing more dominance attempts toward one another, toward authority figures, and perhaps toward females as well; it does not follow that females are submissive. It is possible, in fact, that dominance-submission is not a single continuum. We shall now consider the evidence on submission (compliance, conformity), and we shall then return later to the role of aggression in the maintenance of hierarchical relationships between the sexes.

COMPLIANCE, SUBMISSION, SUGGESTIBILITY

Among animals, as we have seen, males direct more of their dominance attempts toward one another, although they do dominate females when conflicts occur. Among human children, partly because of the sex segregation of play groups, it is again true that the higher rate of dominance attempts by males is largely a within-sex matter. Whereas everyone agrees that boys are "tougher," it is not clear that in direct encounters between the two sexes boys use more direct power assertion or that girls submit to it. It is necessary to examine directly the evidence on compliance and submission.

As may be seen in Table 7.5, there is considerable evidence that young girls (of preschool age or younger) are more likely than boys to comply with an adult's directions. Minton et al. (1971) made home observations of instances in which children of 2½ did something that called for maternal intervention, and noted the outcome of such interventions. A higher number of incidents occurred with boys; when they did occur, girls more often complied immediately with the mother's first directive to stop or change the behavior. With boys it was more often necessary to repeat the direction, or increase pressure, to get compliance. A similar situation was observed by Serbin et al. (1973) in interactions between nursery school teachers and their pupils. Hertzig et al. (1968), recording lower and middle SES children's behavior while taking an intelligence test, found that in the lower SES group, girls were more likely to make a serious, sustained effort to follow the tester's directions, the boys to ignore or forget them. Studies are not completely consistent in their findings, however: Landauer et al. (1970) compared children's willingness to obey when asked by their own mothers (as compared with other children's mothers) to pick up a

TABLE 7.5

Compliance with Adult Requests and Demands

Study	Age and N	Difference	Comment
D. Stayton et al. 1971	9-12 mos (25)	None	Compliance to mother's verbal commands
Minton et al. 1971	27 mos (90)	Girls	Comply immediately with mother's suggestion or command
F. Pedersen & Bell 1970	2-3 (55)	Girls	Conform to adult models during rest period: lie down
R. Bell et al. 1971	2½ (74)	Girls	Teacher ratings: cooperate with teacher's suggestions to change activities
Hertzig et al. 1968	3 (116)	None	Attempt to follow instructions during administration of IQ test (middle SES U.S. sample)
	3 (60)	Girls	Attempt to follow instructions (low SES Puerto Rican sample)
Baumrind & Black 1967	3-4 (103)	None	Observer ratings: disrespectful vs. courteous demeanor with adults, provokes vs. avoids conflict with adults, responsible vs. irresponsible about following nursery school rules, conforming vs. willing to risk adult disapproval
Landauer et al. 1970	3-4 (33)	None	Obedience to own mother's or other mother's command
Serbin et al. 1973	3-5 (225)	Girls	Ignore teacher's requests less often
Blayney 1973	4 (29)	None	Agree to follow father's instructions
Hatfield et al. 1967	4-5 (40)	Girls	Observer ratings: obedience to mother during experimental session (trend, $p < .1$)
London & Cooper 1969	5-16 (240)	None	Hypnotic susceptibility
Sgan 1967	6 (72)	Girls	Change preference to agree with E's preference (low SES sample)
		None	Middle SES sample
C. Madsen & London 1966	7-11 (42)	None	Hypnotic susceptibility
Bronfenbrenner 1970	12 (353)	Girls	In conflict situation choose more alternatives acceptable to adults

large number of objects. Children complied more readily with the requests of a strange mother than with those of their own mothers, but there were no sex differences in compliance. In studies of "resistance to temptation" (see Table 7.6), children are instructed by an adult experimenter not to touch an attractive toy while the experimenter is out of the room. In two studies with American children (Stouwie 1971, 1972), girls obeyed for a longer time, although in a study with Brazilian children (Baggio and Rodrigues 1971) no sex difference was found. On the whole, the bulk of evidence favors the girls being more "obedient" to adults in the early years.

The situation is different with respect to compliance to pressure from age-mates. In the Whiting and Pope (1974) work, time-sampled behavioral

TABLE 7.6
Resistance to Temptation

Study	Age and N	Difference	Comment
Hartig & Kanfer 1973	3-7 (261)	None	Comply with E's request not to look at attractive toys, and other instructions
R. Burton 1971	4 (60)	Boys	Cheat less in beanbag game, rules established by adult E
Mumbauer & Gray 1970	5 (96)	None	Comply with adult-established rule during E's absence, beanbag game
W. D. Ward & Furchak 1968	5-7 (24)	Girls	Comply with E's request not to touch attractive toys, temptation situation
Slaby & Parke 1971	5-8 (132)	Girls	Comply with E's request not to touch toy; 1 experimental group (2 of 3 measures)
		None	Comply with E's request not to touch toy; 5 experimental groups
Parke 1967	6, 7 (80)	Girls	Comply with E's request not to touch toy
Biaggio & Rodrigues 1971	7 (39)	None	Brazilian sample: conform to E's prohibition against touching toy
Stouwie 1971	7-8 (120)	Girls	Conform to E's instruction not to touch toy: longer latency, less time spent playing with toy
Stouwie 1972	7-8 (112)	Girls	Less time spent playing with forbidden toy
		None	Latency to touch forbidden toy
Rosenkoetter 1973	8-12 (48)	None	Compliance with adult command in temptation situation after exposure to deviant or nondeviant model
Keasey 1971a	11 (108)	Boys	Complied in resistance to temptation situation
Jacobson et al. 1970	18-21 (276)	Boys	Not cheating on test, temptation situation

observations were analyzed for the occurrence of "dominance instigations" from others directed at the subject child, as well as for the subject child's responses. Although dominance instigations by peers and by adults were not separated, most of the time-samples occurred while the children were not under direct adult supervision, but were in either child play groups or child work groups. Most of the dominance instigations, then, must have come from peers. In none of the six cultures studied did girls prove to be significantly more compliant when others attempted to dominate them; the trend was in this direction for three of the cultures, but boys showed a higher incidence of compliance in two cultures. Overall, then, neither sex was more compliant.

Another form of compliance to peer pressure may be seen in the so-called Asch situation, in which the subject must make a judgment in a perceptually ambiguous situation (e.g. degree of autokinetic movement) when his own judgments differ considerably from those of a group of peers and all the judgments are public. In this situation, some subjects adjust their judgments to those of the group members; others do not. The majority of studies show no sex difference in this situation. When differences are found, it is more often girls and women who are more "suggestible," although there are three studies in which males are more susceptible to social influence. On the other hand, the reader will recall that in a study by Hollander and Marcia (1970; discussed in Chapter 6, p. 210) ten-year-olds were asked to nominate the members of the class who "go along with what the other children are doing." On this measure, as well as by self-report, boys were more conforming to peer group values.

Studies on the effects of persuasive communication have a more consistent outcome. In pioneering work by Janis (Hovland and Janis 1959[R]) female subjects were found to be more "persuasible." Since this original work, an enormous literature on attitude change has developed. Following are some generalizations that have emerged: an individual is more likely to change his views following a persuasive communication if he is either uninvolved or uninformed concerning the issue the communication deals with; individuals with generally low self-esteem are more persuasible, which may be only another way of saying that people who *believe* they are poorly informed about an issue will change their minds readily, whether or not they actually are less well informed than others. Sex differences in persuasibility, then, ought to depend upon the nature of the issue under consideration, and how interested and informed the two sexes are concerning it. We did see in Chapter 4 that women of college age lack confidence in their performance on a variety of new tasks; it would be reasonable to expect, then, that there might be a general tendency for women to be more subject to social influence in a variety of situations. On the other hand, women did not prove to have a generally lower sense of self-esteem, and on those grounds no overall difference in susceptibility to social influences would be expected. In any case, as Table 7.7 shows, none is found.

In the relatively impersonal situation that is involved in persuasive communications, neither sex is more suggestible than the other. In face-to-face encounters, when an individual must openly disagree with the opinions of others, as is the case in the Asch situation, women somewhat more often conform to others' judgments, but inconsistency of the findings and the frequency of sex similarity are striking. So far we have not been able to find a common theme in the studies that find a sex difference as compared with those that do not. Perhaps there is a clue in the study by Sitrunk and McDavid (1971): men complied with group judgments when the subject matter was "feminine"—that is, when they would have reason to lack confidence in their own judgment. The Asch situation frequently involves judgments of the lengths of lines. Since this is a visual-spatial task, do women lack confidence in their ability to be accurate and hence defer to others on only this type of task? Most of the studies in which women are

TABLE 7.7
Conformity, Compliance with Peers, Susceptibility to Influence

Study	Age and *N*	Difference	Comment
Baumrind & Black 1967	3-4 (103)	None	Observer ratings: submits to group consensus vs. takes independent stand, suggestible vs. has mind of own
Whiting & Pope 1974	3-11 (134)	None	Withdrawal from aggressive instigations, compliance with prosocial and egotistically dominant instigations (6 cultures)
Samorajczyk 1969	6 (60)	None	Barber Suggestibility Scale
V. Allen & Newtson 1972	6, 9, 12, 15 (366)	None	Asch-type conformity to adult and peer pressure; 3 types of stimuli
Bishop & Beckman 1971	7-11 (144)	None	Conformity to confederates' judgments of line length
Costanzo & Shaw 1966	7-9, 11-13 15-17, 19-21 (96)	None	Conformity to confederates' judgments of line length
H. Hamm & Hoving 1969	7, 10	Girls	Conformity to partners' judgments, auto-kinetic effect
	13 (192)	None	Conformity to partners' judgments, auto-kinetic effect
N. Hamm 1970	7, 10, 13 (216)	Girls	Conformity to peers' judgments (1 of 3 tasks)
Mock & Tuddenham 1971	9-11 (280)	Girls	Conformity to same-sex peers' visual-spatial judgments (white, black)
Sistrunk et al. 1971	9-10, 13-14 17-18, 20-21 (80)	Girls / Boys None	Conformity to other's judgments of line length, Brazilian sample, ages 9-10, 20-21 / Brazilian sample, ages 13-14, 17-18 / American sample
Carrigan & Julian 1966	11 (96)	Girls	Match own story choice to "popular" choice
N. Dodge & Muench 1969	11 (122)	None	Conformity to peers' perceptual judgments
Bronfenbrenner 1970	12 (353)	Boys	In conflict situations, choose more antisocial alternatives urged by peers (Soviet Russian sample)
LeFurgy & Woloshin 1969	12-13 (53)	None	Conformity to same-sex peers' moral judgments
Schneider 1970	12-13 (96)	None	Judgments of area of geometric figures (white, black)
Landsbaum & Willis 1971	13-14, 18-21 (64)	None	Length judgments of lines, Asch-type social influence situation
Gerard et al. 1968	14-17 (154)	Girls	Conformity to group judgments in Asch situation
Wyer 1966	14-17 (80)	None	Conformity to fictitious group norms, quantitative judgments

(continued)

TABLE 7.7 *(cont.)*

Study	Age and N	Difference	Comment
Sistrunk & McDavid 1971	14-21 (270)	Girls & women	Conformity to masculine opinion items (3 of 4 experiments)
		Men	Conformity to feminine opinion items (2 of 4 experiments)
		Boys & men	Conformity to neutral opinion items (1 of 4 experiments)
Sampson & Hancock 1967	15-17 (251)	Boys	Conformity to fictitious group norms
Sistrunk 1971	16-17 (32)	Girls	Conformity to fictitious group response (black sample)
	16-17 (32)	None	White sample
Stricker et al. 1970	16-18 (190)	None	Conformity to fictitious group norm; conformity to group judgment in Asch situation
Beloff 1958	18-21 (60)	None	Change in response set (Thurston-Chave War Scale) after exposure to simulated group report
T. Cook et al. 1970	18-21 (63)	Women	Accept legitimacy of experimental deception
Dean et al. 1971	18-21 (161)	None	Attitude change following persuasive communication
Dillehay & Jernigan 1970	18-21 (90)	None	Influence of biased questionnaire on recommendations of severity of punishment
Eagly & Telaak 1972	18-21 (118)	None	Attitude change after exposure to discrepant communication
Endler 1966	18-21 (120)	Women	Agreement with contrived consensus following positive or negative reinforcement for agreement or disagreement
Endler & Hoy 1967	18-21 (120)	None	Conformity to simulated group opinion
Frager 1970	18-21 (139)	None	Conformity to peer judgments, Asch situation (Japanese sample)
Glinski et al. 1970	18-21 (56)	None	Conformity to majority opinion in social influence situation
Greenbaum 1966	18-21 (100)	None	Attitude change after speaking in defense of counterattitudinal topic
Hollander et al. 1965	18-21 (112)	Women	Conform to inaccurate perceptual judgments of same-sex others
Insko 1965	18-21 (70)	None	Influence of telephone caller's approval or disapproval on S's opinion
Insko & Cialdini 1969	18-21 (152)	None	Responses to opinion statements after positive or negative reinforcement
Julian et al. 1968	18-21 (240)	Women	Conform to erroneous judgments of same-sex others
Linder et al. 1967	18-21 (53)	None	Attitude change following writing essay taking position opposed to S's own

(continued)

TABLE 7.7 *(cont.)*

Study	Age and N	Difference	Comment
Marquis 1973	18-21 (52)	None	Attitude change after exposure to persuasive communication
Nisbett & Gordon 1967	18-21 (152)	None	Effect of persuasive communication
Osterhouse & Brock 1970	18-21 (160)	None	Acceptance of discrepant communication
Rosenkrantz & Crockett 1965	18-21 (176)	None	Charges in S's recorded impressions of a confederate after hearing others' impressions
Rule & Rehill 1970	18-21 (90)	None	Attitude change following persuasive communication
I. Silverman 1968	18-21 (403)	None	Effect of persuasive communication
I. Silverman et al. 1970	18-21 (98)	None	Responsiveness to implicit demands or persuasibility
R. Willis & Willis 1970	18-21 (96)	None	Conformity to partner's judgments of aesthetic value
Worchel & Brehm 1970	18-21 (73)	None	Attitude change following persuasive speech
Wyer 1967	18 (128)	None	Conformity to fictitious group norms, quantitative judgments

more likely than men to yield to group pressure do indeed involve spatial stimuli; however, there are numerous instances in which spatial stimuli have been used and the sexes have not differed in conformity. All that can be said at this point is that the results are inconsistent, and that when Asch experiments are considered in conjunction with other conformity studies, neither sex shows an overall tendency to be more susceptible to social influence from peers.

Another indicator of readiness to be influenced by others is spontaneous imitation. As we have seen in Chapter 2, in the section on modeling, there is no sex difference in the ability to learn from a model when given the instructions to use the model's behavior as a guide for one's own performance. However, spontaneous imitation may indicate something deeper in the way of a person's reliance upon others, or lack of confidence in himself. Table 7.8 summarizes the studies in which the occurrence of imitation has been tabulated, and where task instructions did not specifically call for imitation. There appears to be no generalized sex difference in imitation. Any differences that occur are usually related to the nature of the modeled behavior. We saw earlier, in Table 7.1, that when the model behaves aggressively, boys are more likely to imitate; girls imitate more when the model is showing affectionate behavior; and for many modeled behaviors, there is no sex difference.

TABLE 7.8
Sex Differences in Spontaneous Imitation

Study	Age and N	Difference	Comment
F. Pedersen & Bell 1970	2-3 (55)	Girls	Copy posture, follow game, with adult model
Fryrear & Thelen 1969	3-4 (60)	Girls	Imitation of filmed female model's affectionate behavior Imitation of filmed male model's affectionate behavior (trend, $p < .1$)
Bandura & Huston 1961	3-5 (48)	None	Imitation of novel action displayed by female model
W. Mischel & Grusec 1966	3-5 (56)	None	Imitation of novel aversive and neutral behaviors
S. Ross 1971	3-5 (48)	None	Imitation of peer-modeled storekeeper mannerisms
Yarrow & Scott 1972	3-5 (118)	None	Imitation of neutral, nurturant, and nonnurturant responses
Hamilton 1973	3-4, 7, 10 (72)	None	Spontaneous imitation of facial expressions to happy and sad films
Dubanoski & Parton 1971	4 (90)	None	Imitation of object manipulation after viewing filmed model
C. Madsen 1968	4-5 (40)	None	Imitation of toy rejection
Masters 1972a	4-5 (80)	None	Imitation of neutral behaviors displayed by male and female models
Hetherington & Frankie 1967	4-6 (160)	None	Imitation of parent's novel responses
Rosenblith[R] 1961	5 (80)	Girls	Tend to imitate model's color choice ($p < .1$)
Portuges & Feshbach 1972	8-10 (96)	Girls	Imitation of incidental gestures and remarks of filmed female teacher

We have seen, then, that girls are not generally more compliant, conforming, or suggestible than boys across all subject matters and sources of influence. They do not change their minds more readily following persuasive communications; they do not usually yield more to group pressure in the Asch-type experiments. When play is observed, girls are not more often seen to yield when age-mates attempt to coerce them. One consistent sex difference has been uncovered in our analysis of compliant behavior, however: girls do tend to conform more readily than boys to directives from parents and teachers. This fact has implications for the demands that continue to be made on girls. Whiting and Pope (1974) note that boys in several of the societies they studied showed a higher frequency of self-initiated acts; they comment that this probably reflects the fact that girls are more frequently interrupted in their activities by the demands of others. Not surprisingly, a person who wants a service done is more likely to choose as a target for his new request someone who has responded positively to previous requests.

The possibility should not be overlooked that girls' greater readiness to comply with adult requests stems from the way the requests are delivered. If adults make a demand upon a girl with a greater sense that they have the *right* to make the demand, and a greater confidence that it will be obeyed, there may be some subtle expression of assurance in the manner of delivery that increases the chance of success.

Considering the findings on dominance and compliance jointly, the conclusion seems to be that boys are more dominant than girls, in the sense that they more frequently attempt to dominate others, but their dominance attempts are *primarily directed toward one another*. Girls are more compliant, but *primarily toward adults*. It is possible that girls form a coalition with the more dominant adults as a means of coping with the greater aggressiveness of boys, whose dominance they do not accept. Perhaps this complex interplay of forces is one of the reasons for the spontaneous sex segregation of children's friendship and play groups. This suggests that it is girls who avoid playing with boys; there is every reason to believe, however, that spontaneous sex segregation occurs at least as often at the initiation of boys.

In adulthood, new forces come into play. If we ask whether, in a dating couple or a married pair, it is usually the man or the woman who is more likely to accommodate to the wishes of the other, we are asking a question that probably has no general answer. It seems evident that an individual's susceptibility to being influenced by another person or group will depend crucially upon two things: (1) the importance to the individual of maintaining the relationship involved; and (2) his freedom to leave the relationship if it ceases to be satisfying. There is no reason to expect a sex difference with respect to these factors over all the situations in which the sexes encounter one another, and the evidence to date suggests that no overall pattern of dominance and submission exists between the two sexes. Within certain prescribed social arrangements, however—notably, marriage—there may well be an imbalance. Traditionally, maintaining a marriage has been more important to a woman, because she has fewer alternatives for economic support, cannot so easily find sexual satisfaction outside the marriage (because of the sexual double standard), and because the rearing of children, although important to both, is usually more central to her life than her husband's. Under these conditions, a woman would be more likely to accept her partner's dominance within a marriage than vice versa. However, the more important fact is that both partners to a long-standing man-woman relationship derive benefits and satisfactions from the relationship and both are reluctant to give it up. This fact imposes strict limits on the degree to which either party can dominate the other in any coercive sense.

SUMMARY

The evidence is strong that males are the more aggressive sex. In this chapter, we have considered the widely held view that the two sexes are actually equivalent in aggressive motivation but that girls are conditioned to be afraid of displaying their aggressive tendencies openly, showing them instead in attenuated forms. We have argued that this position is a weak one, inconsistent with much that is known about the nature and development of aggression in the two sexes. We have argued that the male is, for biological reasons, in a greater state of readiness to learn and display aggressive behavior, basing the argument in part on studies of the relationship between sex hormones and aggression. The evidence for greater male aggressiveness is unequivocal; a different picture emerges from the research on competitiveness and dominance, although these behaviors have been assumed to be directly linked to aggression. Male competition in real-life settings frequently takes the form of groups competing against groups (as in team sports), an activity that involves within-group cooperation as well as between-group competition, so that cooperative behavior is frequently not the antithesis of competitiveness. Most research on competition has been conducted in contrived situations that fail to take account of this fact and that do not correspond well with the naturalistic conditions under which competitiveness is most intense; hence, the failure to find consistent sex differences in existing studies of competition has not closed the issue. Studies of dominance have revealed a greater tendency among males to attempt to dominate one another, and during childhood a boy's aggressiveness has a considerable bearing upon his ability to dominate other boys. There is little evidence, however, on whether boys successfully dominate girls during childhood. Their unstructured encounters are relatively few, since the sexes usually segregate themselves during play. In adolescence and adulthood, aggression declines as the means for achieving dominance (or leadership). As the power to influence others comes to depend more and more upon competencies and mutual affection and attraction, rather than simple power assertion by force, equality of the sexes in power-bargaining encounters becomes possible. The relation of the outcome to the social-institutional settings in which the encounters occur will be taken up in the final chapter.

PART THREE

On the Origins of Psychological Sex Differences

In the preceding chapters, we have presented and summarized a large body of evidence concerning how the sexes differ psychologically, and how psychological sex differentiation changes with age. We have discussed possible explanations of specific differences at a number of points. For example, hormones and brain lateralization were explored in connection with sex differences in spatial ability; and in the analysis of aggressive behavior, studies of hormonal effects were reviewed, and parallels were drawn between sex differentiation in human beings and that in the lower animals, with the implication that cross-species biological factors were at work. So far, however, the social shaping of sex-typical behavior has only been lightly touched upon, and it is to these processes that we now turn.

We believe social shaping to be of the utmost importance in children's acquisition of sex-typical behavior. We also believe this acquisition is related to certain sex-linked biological predispositions, but to say so is not to deny the importance of social learning. The question is: what form does social shaping take? Given that adults and other children have expectations concerning how a boy or girl ought to behave, how are these expectations conveyed and how precisely do they operate to influence the child's behavior? Obviously one means of communication to the child is for the adults responsible for his care to deliver rewards and punishments to the child, contingent on whether his behavior is sex-appropriate. Another means is by example: if it can be shown that children imitate people of the same sex as themselves, then the demonstration of appropriate behavior by the same-sex models should be a powerful source of influence upon the nature of the sex-typed behavior that children adopt. We have chosen to take up the second topic first, because we believe that the answer to the question of whether children do in fact consistently imitate same-sex models determines how much weight we must place upon alternative explanations. We begin Chapter 8 with a brief résumé of the evidence on the age *at which children show sex-typing in the narrower sense: how early they come to prefer the toys and activities that are stereotypically "masculine" or "feminine." We then turn to the question of whether the early development of this kind of sex typing can be attributed to the imitation of same-sex models. In Chapter 9, we take up the direct socialization pressures brought to bear upon children, and attempt to determine what the differences are in the way boys and girls are treated. We ask whether differential parental behavior reflects (1) direct attempts to shape children toward what is thought to be sex-appropriate behavior; (2) the fact that children of the two sexes have different initial behavior tendencies that result in their eliciting different behavior from their parents; (3) parents' views about what the two sexes are like (rather than what they should be like); or (4) simple transfer into the family situation of behavior that the two parents have learned previously in their relationships with people of the same or opposite sex. The four processes are not, of course, mutually exclusive, but they might produce quite different outcomes in the way of parental actions toward sons or daughters.*

Chapter 10 summarizes the major findings of the survey of factual evidence detailed in Chapters 2–9, listing what appears to be "myth" and what "reality" among the widely believed generalizations about sex differences. It also summarizes the weaknesses of the two most popular theories concerning the origins of psychological sex differentiation, and considers alternatives to them.

CHAPTER EIGHT

Sex Typing and the Role of Modeling

In the narrower sense, sex-typed behavior refers to "role behavior appropriate to a child's ascribed gender" (R. Sears et al. 1965[R], p. 171). It is difficult to determine what behaviors are, and what are not, linked to sex roles. The mere existence of a behavioral sex difference does not constitute evidence of such linkage. For example, it may eventually be substantiated that infant girls are more sensitive to touch and pain than infant boys; if this were so, however, it would not necessarily be the case that an infant girl would be thought "unfeminine" if she were relatively insensitive to touch and pain. In a similar vein, spatial ability is not central to the usual concepts of masculinity and femininity, although it does differentiate the sexes. But there are some aspects of behavior that are clearly labeled "masculine" or "feminine." In the present chapter, we begin by tracing the differentiation of the sexes with respect to such behavior.

SEX-TYPED INTERESTS AND ACTIVITY PREFERENCES

By what age do children's interests and activities become differentiated into "masculine" and "feminine" patterns? Is this a gradual process, with more differentiation occurring year by year, or are there certain crucial points in development where fairly radical changes may be seen in the degree of sex typing that children's interests show?

We begin with studies of toy preferences. A number of studies have been done with children just over a year old in which a child is brought with its mother to a play room stocked with toys. The child is allowed to explore, and records are made of the amount of time spent with each toy. There is evidence that boys and girls do make somewhat different choices even at this early age, but the toy attributes responsible for the choices are obscure. W. Bronson (1971) found that girls spend more time with a stuffed animal, and Goldberg and Lewis (1969), who obtained the same result, thought that girls might be especially interested in any toy with a face (as a manifestation of their greater social interests). This hypothesis, however, is not consistent with later findings. Jacklin et al. (1973) found that the two sexes spent equal amounts of time with stuffed animals, but that the boys preferred toy robots—which also had faces. Furthermore, Kaminski (1973) found that boys of 13 months played with dolls more than did the girls; she suggested that this might reflect the fact that more girls than boys had dolls at home, so that dolls were more novel, and hence more interesting, to boys. In any case, "faceness" is evidently not the factor that accounts for early sex differences in toy preference. Another possibility is that it is the soft tactual quality of stuffed animals that attracted the girls in the Bronson and Goldberg and Lewis studies. Kaminski, however, provided several toy trucks for 13-month-olds (along with a variety of other toys), one truck being covered in rabbit fur, one in aluminum foil; the girls did not prefer the furry surface, nor did the boys prefer the metallic one, so it is doubtful that it is the tactual quality of the surface that is important. Nor is the "manipulability" of the toy related to sex differences in preference. In the Kaminski study, the most manipulable toys were the most attractive to children of both sexes and there were no sex differences in their use. The same was true in two studies by Jacklin et al. Goldberg and Lewis found boys to be more interested in door knobs, floor tiles, and electric outlets, girls in blocks and pegboards; both sexes manipulated the objects of their choice, and there seemed to be no relationship to the number of moving parts. It would be interesting to be able to find developmental links between the early toy preferences and the choices of more clearly "masculine" and "feminine" toys that may be discerned from age 2 onward, but the elements that differentially attract one-year-old boys and girls are not well enough understood to permit identifying the continuities that may exist. The point is of some interest, because it is possible that societies begin to label as "masculine" those toys that differentially attract boys even if there is no relationship of the toy to a masculine role. For example, blocks are thought of as "boyish" toys even though they are not related to adult male occupations in the sense that a fireman's hat or a toy truck is. In a similar vein, there is no obvious reason why preschool girls should be spending more time in painting, drawing, cutting paper, or manipulating play dough (since few modern mothers make bread, and professional artists are frequently male). If these activities become labeled as more appropriate for one sex, then, it seems possible that it is because children of one sex choose to do them rather than vice versa. However, by preschool age, differentiation may be seen that does clearly relate to adult sex-typed activities: girls sew, string beads, play at housekeeping; boys play with guns, toy trucks, tractors, and fire engines, and do carpentry. Based on adult judgments of what activities are feminine and what masculine, a number of investigators have used picture tests for preferences in toys or activities. Clear tendencies for girls to choose stereotypically feminine activities, boys masculine ones, have been found as early as such tests have been used (R. Sears et al. 1965[R]), with 4-year-olds. In developing their "area usage" test for sex typing, Sears and his colleagues also found that 4-year-old boys spent more time in the portion of a large nursery school play room where blocks, wheel toys, and carpenter tools were to be found, whereas girls spent more time in the area having the dress-up clothes, the cooking equipment, and the doll houses. That other aspects of sex typing are also developing in the preschool years is indicated by the responses of children| aged 4–6 to questions about whether they will be "mommies or daddies" when they grow up (S. Thompson and Bentler 1973). With only a single exception, all the children in this study answered this question sex-appropriately. Furthermore, very few thought they could be the opposite-sex parent if they wished. Although Emmerich (1971), agreeing with Kohlberg's (1966)[R] earlier contention, finds that children of 4–6 do not have well-developed "sex constancy" (i. e. they believe that it is possible for a pictured person's sex to change with a change in dress and hair style), it would appear that they do have a fairly clear, stable concept of their own sexual identity and the fact that this implies certain adult functions that are not arbitrary or subject to change. Table 8.1 shows the evolution of sex-typed interests as children grow older. The early tendency of boys to engage in more large-muscle or "gross motor" activity appears later in the form of greater interest in both organized and informal sports. The games that girls prefer during the elementary school years (jacks, jump rope) are not so clearly related to their artistic and manipulative activities of the preschool years, but the dress-up theme can of course be seen in their greater interest in, and knowledge about, styles and appearance during adolescence (Nelsen and Rosenbaum 1972).

Given that boys show "masculine" and girls "feminine" interests from the preschool years onward, can it be said that one sex is more fully sex-typed than the other? Does either sex have more inhibitions about performing activities normally associated with the opposite sex?

Efforts to measure the degree of sex typing of the two sexes have frequently involved use of the "It" test (Brown 1956[R]). This is a projective test in which a cut-out doll, referred to as "It," is offered the opportunity to choose among a variety of sex-typed activities. Commonly, girls have It engage in feminine activities, and boys choose masculine activities for It. Early reports indicated that, with this measure, boys appeared to develop sex-typed choices at an earlier age, and that in fact there might be a decline in sex typing among girls between the ages of 5 and 10. However, these results were called into question by the possibility that the It doll in widest use objectively resembled a boy more than a girl (N. Thompson and McCandless 1970), so that girls were making realistic choices for the sex that they perceived the doll to be, rather than making choices projectively for themselves. Not all studies, however, showed a "masculine bias"

TABLE 8.1
Toy and Activity Preferences

Study	Age and N	Difference	Comment
J. Brooks & Lewis 1974	11-15 mos (17 pairs of twins)	None	Stuffed animals, pull-toys
Kaminski 1973	12 mos (48)	None	Baby doll, young child doll, pick-up trucks, ring stack toy, merry-go-round
		Boys	Both dolls (combined score)
Goldberg & Lewis 1969	13 mos (64)	Boys	Play with "non-toys."* Bang with toys rather than manipulate them
		Girls	Play with blocks, pegboard, stuffed dog, and inflated plastic cat; manipulation of combinations of toys
		None	Play with pail, toy lawnmower, mallet, wooden bug (pull-toy), quoits
Messer & Lewis 1972	13 mos (25)	None	Blocks, pail, toy lawnmower, stuffed dog, inflated plastic cat, mallet, pegboard, quoits, wooden bug, non-toys; bang with toys (low SES sample)
Jacklin et al. 1973	13-14 mos (40)	Boys	Amount of time playing with robots
		None	Amount of time spent manipulating toys; play with stuffed ("cuddly") animals, toy work bench, toy ferris wheel
W. Bronson 1971	15 mos (40)	Girls	Play with small toy dog
Bridges 1927	2-3 (10)	Boys	Most frequent activities: building with large bricks, fitting cylinders into holes, color pairing, naming objects in postcards, cube construction
		Girls	Most frequent activities: fitting cylinders into holes, threading beads, writing on blackboard, fastening buttons
F. Pedersen & Bell 1970	2-3 (55)	Boys	Manipulate physical objects (e. g. blocks, toys); gross motor activity
		Girls	Play with clay or dough; play on swing or glider
		None	Ride tricycles
Clark et al. 1969	2-4 (40)	Boys	Play with blocks and push-toy; drink milk
		Girls	Play with dolls; paint, cut, glue, crayon, sew
		None	Play with toy cars and trucks, puzzles, old car parts, plasticine, sand, clay, and musical instruments; play house; saw and hammer; climb up and play in balcony
Parten 1933b	2-4 (34)	Boys	Trains, kiddie cars, blocks; play with boys
		Girls	Swings, paper, beads, painting; play with girls
		None	Play house (doll play excluded)

*Non-toys include structured features of a room, such as doorknobs, floor tiles, and electric outlets.

(continued)

TABLE 8.1 *(cont.)*

Study	Age and N	Difference	Comment
Fagot & Patterson 1969	3 (36)	Boys	Blocks, transportation toys
		Girls	Painting, artwork
		None	Puzzles, tinkertoys, marbles, beads, design board; hammering; engaging in musical activities; playing with live or toy animals; dressing up in costumes; using tools; playing on swing, teeter-totter, or slide
Rabban[R] 1950	3 (60)	None	Choices among masculine and feminine toys
	4-8 (240)	Boys	Guns, steamrollers, trucks, racing cars, fire engines, cement mixers, soldiers, knives
		Girls	High chair, buggy, crib, beads, dishes, purse, doll, bathinette
Moyer & Von Haller 1956	3-5 (87)	None	Time playing with blocks, number of structures built
Vance & McCall[R] 1934	3-6 (32)	Boys	Woodwork, large blocks, equipment requiring large muscle activity
		Girls	Housekeeping materials; materials for "passive play"
Farrell 1957	3-7 (376)	Boys	Play with blocks
Whiting & Pope 1974	3-11 (134)	Boys	Feed and pasture animals
		Girls	Domestic chores, food preparation
J. Schwartz 1972	4 (57)	Boys	Frequency of firing toy gun
R. Sears et al.[R] 1965	4 (40)	Boys	Choice of masculine toys and pictured activities
		Girls	Choice of feminine toys and pictured activities
Emmerich 1971	4-5 (415)	Boys	Gross motor activity, fantasy activity
		Girls	Artistic activity
		None	Cognitive and fine manipulative activity (early-fall, late-fall observation sessions)
	4-5 (596)	Boys	Gross motor activity, fantasy activity
		Girls	Artistic, cognitive, and fine manipulative activity (early-fall, late-spring observation sessions)
Fauls & Smith 1956	4-5 (38)	Boys	Choice of pictured "masculine" activity
		Girls	Choice of pictured "feminine" activities
Wohlford et al. 1971	4-6 (66)	Boys	Masculine choices, picture activities test
		Girls	Feminine choices, picture activities test
DeLucia 1972	5-6 (24)	Boys	Picture preference test: prefer wheel toys, tool set, airplane, Erector set, football
		Girls	Prefer cosmetics, doll buggy, doll wardrobe, broom set, dish cabinet
Farwell 1930	5-7 (271)	Boys	Prefer building with blocks
		Girls	Prefer sewing
		None	Preference for modeling and painting materials

(continued)

TABLE 8.1 *(cont.)*

Study	Age and N	Difference	Comment
Laosa & Brophy 1972	5-7 (93)	Boys	Masculine choices, measures of sex-role orientation, preference and adoption
		Girls	Feminine choices, same measures as above
W. D. Ward 1969a	5-8 (32)	Boys	Preference for masculine toys, pairs of pictured toys
		Girls	Preference for feminine toys, pairs of pictured toys
DeLucia[R] 1963	5-9 (226)	Boys	Masculine choices, picture toy preference test
		Girls	Feminine choices, picture toy preference test
Liebert et al. 1971	6-8 (40)	Boys	Prefer toys said to be "boys' toys"
		Girls	Prefer toys said to be "girls' toys"
Looft 1971	6-8 (66)	Boys	Name larger range of occupations in answer to "What would you like to be?" Order of preference: football player, policeman, doctor, dentist, priest, scientist, pilot, astronaut
		Girls	Occupational preferences in order: teacher, nurse, housewife, mother, stewardess, salesgirl
Ables 1972	7-12 (128)	Boys	Wish for material possessions and money
		Girls	Wish for another person
		None	Wish for pets, activities, specific skills or attributes, or for some identity
Rosenberg & Sutton-Smith (1960)	9-11 (187)	Boys	Prefer games: forceful physical contact, dramatization of conflict between male roles, propulsion of objects through space, complex team games
		Girls	Prefer games: dramatization of "static activity," verbal games, ritualistic non-competitive games, choral and rhythmic games, and games with central role for 1 player
Maw & Maw 1965	10-11 (914)	Boys	Self-report: choose outgoing investigatory activities
Honzik[R] 1951	11-13 (468)	Boys	In constructing "scene from exciting movie," use blocks, vehicles, persons in uniform
		Girls	Use persons in ordinary dress and furniture
Nelsen & Rosenbaum 1972	12-17 (1,916)	Boys	Know more terms related to money, autos, motorbikes
		Girls	Know more terms related to clothes, style, appearance, boys, popularity
T. Hilton & Berglund 1971	12, 14, 16 (1,859)	Boys	Read scientific books and magazines at ages 14 and 16; indicate more interest in math courses at ages 14 and 16; talk about science with friends and parents at ages 14 and 16
Walberg 1969	16-17 (1,050)	Boys	Cosmological activities, tinkering
		Girls	Participation in nature study, application of science to everyday life

(continued)

TABLE 8.1 *(cont.)*

Study	Age and N	Difference	Comment
Monday et al. 1966-67	18 (238,000)	Men	Prefer engineering, agriculture, technology
		Women	Prefer social, religious, educational fields
Thomas 1971	18-21 (60)	None	Student activism, political participation
Constantinople 1967	18, 20 (353)	Men	Achieving academic distinction, preparing for a career that requires postgraduate study
		Women	Important college goals: acquiring an appreciation of ideas, establishing own values, developing relationship with opposite sex, finding a spouse, developing ability to get along with different kinds of people, preparing for a career beginning immediately after college
		None	Learning how to learn from books and teachers, contributing in a meaningful manner to some campus group, becoming self-confident, achieving personal independence, gaining many friends

of this sort (see Kohlberg 1966[R], Hartup and Zook 1960, Brown 1962[R], Lansky and McKay 1969). There followed a series of studies in which the original It doll was replaced by a "concealed It" (a cut-out in an envelope) or a "blank It" (a card replacing the doll), or in which the subject makes choices directly for himself rather than for a projective figure of any sort. The reader is referred to Fling and Manosevitz (1972) for a brief review and list of references to these studies, which yielded conflicting results. With the masculine bias of the test eliminated, Fling and Manosevitz find that among children of 3–4 years, both boys and girls make sex-typed choices, but neither sex is significantly more likely to make sex-appropriate choices than the other, though there was a nonsignificant trend in this study for boys to be more sex-typed.

Other kinds of measures have been used in the attempt to discover whether one sex is more clearly sex-typed than the other. R. Sears and his colleagues (1965)[R] asked 4-year-old children to carry out a "pretend" telephone conversation with their mothers; each child was asked, in turn, to pretend to be the "mommy" or the "daddy" talking to a child, and was then asked to pretend to be either a boy or girl talking to a parent. Some children refused to adopt the role of an opposite-sex child or parent, others did so easily. However, no sex difference was found in the willingness of boys and girls to adopt an opposite-sex role.

Hartup, Moore, and Sager (1963)[R] did find a sex difference in willingness to engage in cross-sex activities. They offered children of nursery school age two toys: one a rather unattractive sex-neutral toy, and the other an attractive toy that was clearly suitable for the other sex. They found that boys were more likely to avoid the sex-inappropriate toy than were girls. The boys' avoidance of feminine toys was especially marked when an experimenter was present, suggesting that the boys expected adult disapproval for playing with girlish things. The girls, on the other hand, showed interest in boys' toys whether an adult was present or not. S. Ross (1971) found that among 3-5-year-olds playing shopkeeper, boys were more concerned than girls that their customers in the play store (a same-sex peer) choose a sex-appropriate toy. In Chapter 9 we shall discuss the evidence for differential pressure being brought to bear on the two sexes for sex-appropriate behavior. For the present, the point of interest is that in this particular respect, existing research using behavioral (rather than projective) measures indicates that boys of preschool age are more fully sex-typed than girls.

Working with children aged 4-7, W. D. Ward (1968) found that boys made more sex-appropriate toy choices than did girls; Pulaski (1970), putting children aged 5 and 6 into a play room with a variety of toys available, found that boys played consistently with masculine toys while girls were more likely to choose some boyish and some girlish toys. Wolf (1973) allowed children aged 5-9 to observe a model playing with a toy inappropriate for the subject's sex, and found that following such exposure, girls were more willing to play with a sex-inappropriate toy than were boys. And, finally, a study by Ferguson and Maccoby (1966), involving measures of sex-role acceptance, found that at the age of 10 boys preferred the activities associated with their own sex role more than did girls. There is some evidence that the greater preference by males for the activities associated with their own sex continues into college age. S. Bem (personal communication, 1974) found that men choose masculine activities over feminine ones even when they would be paid more for performing feminine activities. This result is especially striking, considering that when choosing among sex-appropriate tasks, men choose so as to maximize monetary reward considerably more than women do. But their desire for money notwithstanding, they avoid stereotypically female tasks, whereas women's choices of activities are more sex-neutral. Recent research, then, is consistent with earlier work (DeLucia 1963[R], Hartup and Zook 1960, Rabban 1950[R]) in showing that (a) at nursery school age, both sexes are sex-typed, and (b) starting at approximately the age of 4, boys become increasingly more sex-typed than girls, in that they are more likely to avoid sex-inappropriate activities, and more likely to accept (prefer) the activities associated with their own sex role.

In earlier chapters, we have seen that the behavior of young boys and girls is differentiated along sex lines in some respects but not in others. Some of the stereotyped views about how the sexes differ, such as the greater aggressiveness of boys, have been borne out. Some, such as the belief that girls are generally more dependent or sociable, have not. We have now seen that preschool boys and girls do differ, on the average, in a number of their preferences for activities and toys; furthermore, it is true that children tend to choose same-sex playmates, although there is great variation in these matters among children of the same sex. In presenting the evidence on sex differences, we have touched upon some of the reasons why differential development might occur, including some aspects of genetic involvement and hormonal influences. We now turn to some of the social processes that have been thought to underlie sex differences.

HYPOTHESES CONCERNING THE ROLE OF MODELING

The major summarizing papers and chapters on sex typing (Kagan 1964[R], R. Sears et al. 1965[R], Kohlberg 1966[R], Mussen 1969[R], Mischel 1970[R]) all emphasize the role of imitation and identification in the acquisition of the child's sex-typed behavior. Although treatments and emphases differ considerably, certain major themes may be found in the arguments presented.

1. *Differential reinforcement alone would not account for the rate and breadth of sex-role acquisition; imitation must be involved.* "Gender roles are very broad and very subtle. It would be difficult to imagine that any kind of direct tuition could provide for the learning of such elaborate behavioral, attitudinal and manneristic patterns as are subsumed under the rubrics of masculinity and femininity. Furthermore, these qualities are absorbed quite early and are highly resistant to modification" (R. Sears et al. 1965[R], p. 171). Bandura and Walters describe how children in other cultures acquire sex-role activities: the girls stay with their mothers, watching and imitating the mothers' domestic activities; the boys accompany the fathers and are given child-size tools so that they can copy their fathers' work activities. The parents offer very little direct tuition. The authors say (1963[R], p. 48):

While playing with toys that stimulate imitation of adults, children frequently reproduce not only the appropriate adult-role behavior patterns but also characteristic or idiosyncratic parental patterns of response, including attitudes, mannerisms, gestures, and even voice inflections, which the parents have certainly never attempted directly to teach. . . . Children frequently acquire, in the course of imitative role-playing, numerous classes of inter-related responses *in toto*, apparently without proceeding through a gradual and laborious process of response differentiation and extinction or requiring a lengthy period of discrimination training.

2. *Because parents are (a) highly available, (b) nurturant, and (c) powerful, they are the models most likely to be copied in the acquisition of sex-*

typed behavior, particularly in the preschool years (see especially Mischel 1970[R], pp. 28–37). Some writers stress the hypothesis that the child's love, admiration, and respect for his parents cause him to take one or both parents as "ego ideal," and to establish enduring motivation to emulate them.

3. *Children are more frequently exposed to models of their own sex than to cross-sex models.* Therefore, through imitating whatever model happens to be available, they will tend to acquire more sex-appropriate than sex-inappropriate behavior. Since children of both sexes initially spend more time with the mother than the father, both will initially acquire feminine behavior; at a later age, boys will begin to be in the presence of male models for an increasing proportion of their time, and hence will increasingly acquire masculine behavior.

4. *Same-sex models will be imitated more than opposite-sex ones because the child tends to imitate models whom he perceives as similar to himself.* Mischel (1970)[R] amplifies this point as follows (p. 38):

From the viewpoint of social learning theory, the greater attentiveness to same-sex models, especially when they are displaying appropriately sex-typed behavior, probably reflects that people generally are reinforced throughout their histories more for learning the sex-typed behaviors of same-sex models than those of cross-sex models. It certainly seems likely that children are much more frequently rewarded for watching and imitating same-sex models (rather than cross-sex models), especially when the models display sex-typed behaviors. Boys do not learn baseball by watching girls and girls do not learn about fashions from observing boys.

We should note that points 1 and 2 above would not jointly be sufficient to explain the acquisition of sex-typed behavior through modeling. It has been clearly demonstrated that children will imitate the more dominant powerful figure when more than one model is available; furthermore, children will choose to imitate a more nurturant model, other things being equal (Bandura and Huston 1961, Hetherington 1965[R], and Hetherington and Frankie 1967). Within a given family, then, if the mother is the more nurturant figure, children of both sexes should imitate her for this reason; if the father is the dominant figure, children of both sexes should imitate him for this reason. These processes would not make boys masculine and girls feminine. Freud, in his discussions of the psychosexual development of the two sexes, stumbled over this issue and attempted to solve it by simply saying that the boy identifies with the aggressor, whereas the girl's identification with her mother is "anaclitic"—that is, based upon nurturance and dependency. This "solution" is merely a restatement of the problem. It does not provide a reason why the power of a model, or the nurturance of a model, should affect the two sexes differentially. It simply asserts that this is the case.

It was noted above that the "model availability" hypothesis (point 3) leads to the assumption that a boy's first primary model is his mother, and that he must shift his identification at some point from his mother to his father and to other male models in order to become masculine. This same point is stressed by writers who emphasize the role of nurturance in early identification. The first and strongest attachment figure for both sexes is likely to be the mother. Because of this attachment, children of both sexes are alleged to form an initial identification with the mother, and in the case of the boy, this identification must be disrupted and replaced if the child is to be adequately sex-typed, whereas the girl may simply continue identification with her initial model. Hence, the development of sex typing of girls is thought to be simpler, more consistent, and capable of consolidation at an earlier age than that of boys. The most recent exponent of this position is Lynn (1969, especially p. 23)[R]. The view that boys must shift from one primary model to another has been thought to imply two things: (1) that in the early preschool years, a boy will resemble his mother more than his father, with father-son similarity appearing at age 4 or later—the precise age depending upon the mechanism that is thought to bring about the shift from one model to the other; (2) that the boy may make his shift in choice of model with respect to some attributes and not others; he may continue to identify with his mother with respect to aspects of his behavior and personality that are not directly linked to sex typing, while adopting his father's behavior where masculinity is an issue. Another possibility, particularly if the father is not a strong identification figure, is that the boy will be like his mother with respect to "latent" aspects of sex typing but masculine with respect to the more obvious, or superficial, aspects of his sex identity, and may show signs of conflict over his sex role.

Kohlberg (1966)[R] argues that if age-related shifts do occur in any aspect of a boy's or girl's "identification" with the mother or the father, these shifts can hardly be attributed to characteristics of the model such as their nurturance or power: "The power theories of identification cannot account for . . . age shifts in terms of family structure variables as such, because the family's power structure does not change regularly according to the age of the child." Kohlberg's statement alerts us to the fact that if there is a shift at a particular age in any aspect of sex-role adoption, it is necessary to consider not only whether there has been a corresponding shift in the availability of the appropriate-sex model, but whether there has been a shift in the nurturance or power assertion directed by each parent to the same-sex child. Kohlberg believes that no such age-related shift occurs in the internal dynamics of family relationships, but the question is an empirical one.

To recapitulate: the fact that observational learning occurs is not in doubt. It is also clear enough that children learn many items in their behavioral repertoires through imitation of their parents. The problem is why children of the two sexes should learn *different things*—sex-typed things.

Two explanations have been offered: (1) that the same-sex model is more available, and (2) that children select same-sex models, among those that are available, on the basis of perceived similarity between themselves and the model.

Let us first consider the issue of model availability.

AVAILABILITY OF SAME-SEX MODELS

The identity (and sex) of the individuals with whom the child spends most time is highly culture-bound. Among the Rajput in India, for example (Minturn and Hitchcock 1963[R]), women are confined to a courtyard; children also spend most of their time in the courtyard when they are very young, while they are still dependent upon the care-taking of their mothers and other female relatives; but as soon as they are old enough to escape from the courtyard, they can go to the fields with their fathers, and spend time with men and older boys at the men's sleeping platform. Although girls can leave the courtyard before they officially go into purdah when they are married, they have less freedom of movement and are less likely to go to the men's platform or accompany men during their work in the fields. The view that both sexes of children initially have primarily female models available, but that with increasing age each sex is exposed more and more to same-sex models, seems to fit this culture very well.

The matter is by no means as clear in most segments of American society. Children of both sexes tend to be primarily in the care of female adults during the preschool years. Mothers may make a special effort to see to it that their children have same-sex playmates—or the children may *choose* same-sex playmates—but this would hardly provide an explanation of sex typing, since other children would presumably have been exposed to the same kind of primarily female modeling as the subject child. Fathers do not normally take their children to work with them; hence there is no opportunity to give their sons any greater exposure to the world of masculine work. When the children are quite young, their primary exposure to their father comes when the father is at home after work and on weekends. It is an open question whether a young boy sees more of his father at home than does the young girl. F. Pedersen and Robson (1969) report that when the father is at home he spends as much time playing with a 9-month-old daughter as he does with a son of the same age. There is little evidence of how the situation develops during the years from 2 through 5. Is a father more likely to take a son with him on an errand? Ask him to help with masculine chores? Chat with him and take an interest in his activities and concerns? It may be that this is the case, and in one study (R. Sears et al. 1965[R] and personal communications) fathers of kindergarten-aged children did say in an interview that they spent more time with sons than daughters. However, as will be shown later, there are special elements of tension between father and son, and of attraction between father and daughter, that might imply at least as much interaction (at least *supportive* interaction) between fathers and girls. It has not been demonstrated that fathers are more "available" as models to their sons than their daughters during the preschool years; indeed, we do not consider it likely that there is any substantial difference in availability in the sense of sheer amounts of time the child spends in the father's presence. At later ages, of course, fathers will no doubt be more likely to take their sons to ball games and into primarily male settings, but this differentiation occurs, we suggest, *after* the child has already developed sex-typed interests, and may be a result rather than a cause of this development.

Parents, of course, are not the only sex-typed models. What about the differential availability of other same-sex models to boys and girls? Children spend enormous amounts of time watching television, but both sexes see the same models until such time as they select different programs on the basis of their previously developed sex-typed interests. In school, it is frequently the case that the teachers are women and the principals are men, but these two kinds of models are equally available to children of the two sexes. Older siblings of the two sexes are equally available as models to young boys and girls. The fact that children play primarily with same-sex peers does not appear to be a function of which peer is *available*, but which sex peer is *chosen*—again, an outcome, rather than a cause, of sex-typed interests. It seems reasonable to assume, then, that at least in most segments of American culture, models of the two sexes are available to boys and girls to a similar degree. There are settings where models of only one sex are primarily available, but young children of both sexes tend to be exposed to such settings equally often.

Regardless of the *relative* frequency of exposure to male and female models, both boys and girls do have *frequent* exposure to models of both sexes, though not in all settings. American children seldom have the opportunity to see their fathers at work, and therefore their initial concepts of the adult world of work, and the different roles played in it by men and women, are likely to come from other sources, such as television. Such sources may provide more stereotypic views about these roles than the child would acquire if he did have more direct exposure to the work of his parents or other personally known models. Nevertheless, we are suggesting that models of both sexes are plentifully available to both boys and girls, and that children can learn from their actions what behavior is considered appropriate for each sex.

SELECTION OF SAME-SEX MODELS

When models of both sexes are available, do girls more often attend to, and/or imitate, the female model, and boys the male model? There is some evidence that in adulthood such selection does occur. In an early study, Maccoby et al. (1958)[R] monitored the eye movements of college-aged subjects as they viewed two standard Hollywood films. In the scenes in which both the male and female leads were on screen (and no other characters were present), male viewers spent proportionally more time watching the male leading character while female viewers spent proportionally more time looking at the female lead. Less direct evidence of model selection is found in a study (Maccoby and Wilson 1957[R]) that tested children of junior high school age on their recollection of the details of the actions, and stimuli to actions, of various filmed characters. Boys remembered more detail from the aggressive incidents depicted in the film, *provided that the agent of the action was a boy rather than a girl*; similarly, the girls recalled more of the social and romantic content, provided that the agent of the action was a female character in the film. Mischel (1970, p. 39)[R] summarizes a series of studies, all done with adults or children aged 12 or older, in which some models were objectively more similar to the viewer than others, or a perception of similarity was induced by telling the viewer that a given model shared some of his tastes and attributes whereas another model did not. In these studies it was repeatedly demonstrated that viewers are more likely to match some aspect of their behavior to a model's if that model is perceived as similar to themselves. We may extrapolate from these findings to the probability that an adolescent or adult will imitate a same-sex model rather than an opposite-sex model whenever the fact of shared sex is relevant to the situation. Mischel adds the proviso that imitation is more likely to occur when learners have little information—when their own past experience provides little guidance to what behavior is appropriate.

The subjects in the experiments cited above were old enough to be fairly sophisticated about perceiving similarities between themselves and others. What about younger children? Are they likely to take note of the fact that another person is of the same sex as themselves, and govern their imitation accordingly? Kohlberg (1966)[R] argues that selective imitation on this basis ought not to occur until children have established a fairly stable concept of their own sex. He says that such a concept depends, in part, upon the achievement of "gender constancy"—the understanding that a person's sex is not changed by changing clothes or hair styles, but remains as a constant attribute of the person throughout life.

Some work in progress by R. G. Slaby and his colleagues at the University of Washington (personal communication, 1974) bears upon the relationship between gender constancy and model selection. Using subjects aged 3–5 years, Slaby assessed gender constancy through questioning the children concerning whether they believed they could be a different sex if they wished to, etc. Each child then viewed a split-screen videotape.

One side of the screen showed a man, the other a woman, both engaged in the same activities; the child could see only one side of the screen at any given moment—which side was a matter of the subject's choice. Although there were no overall sex differences in choice of model, the children who measured high on gender constancy watched the same-sex model more than the children who did not show gender constancy. This finding is consistent with Kohlberg's contention, for although Slaby did not study imitation, selective attention to a model's actions would presumably facilitate later imitation of the model.

We have seen that some aspects of sex typing (such as the preference for same-sex playmates and certain sex-typed toys) occur at ages 3 and 4; but Kohlberg argues that a more general tendency to group all males together and "identify" along sex lines does not occur till later. In discussing age changes in the development of sex identity, Kohlberg says:

[A boy's] preference for same-sex peers is established before his preference for same-sex parent figures. The cognitive-developmental theory suggests two reasons for this discrepancy. The first is that the boy's classification of adult males in the common category "we males" is a more cognitively advanced achievement, and therefore comes later than his classification of other boys in that category. It is not until about age five-six, when the child begins to sort objects predominantly on the basis of similar attributes, that he forms groupings which include same-sex figures of diverse ages. The second consideration is that the boy's affectional tie to his mother is deep, and it takes time before the boy's self-conceptual or sex-role identity considerations can lead him to subordinate it to the development of a tie to the father.

If Kohlberg is right that the tendency to imitate selectively the same-sex parent, or other same-sex adults, does not occur earlier than age 5 or 6, then assumptions concerning such modeling would obviously be a weak explanation of any sex typing in behavior that occurs before this time.

To evaluate the Kohlberg position on age changes, as well as the positions of the previously cited social learning theorists concerning the importance of modeling, information is needed concerning the occurrence of same-sex imitation and the ages at which it may be demonstrated to occur. There are two approaches to this issue, one indirect and the other direct. If it can be demonstrated that children show clear and detailed resemblances to the same-sex parent, this fact would be consistent with the hypothesis that the child has imitated that parent. Clearly, the existence of the resemblances would not constitute proof of modeling—a resemblance might have come about through differential reinforcement or even sex-linked inheritance. However, the likelihood of a modeling explanation is increased if the matched behavior is of the sort—such as speech inflections—that is seldom subject to direct socialization pressure from parents. Furthermore, if parent-child resemblances are weak or absent, a modeling explanation of the acquisition of sex-typed behavior is jeopardized. We first present what little evidence is available on parent-child resemblance, and then turn to direct studies of imitation of same-sex and cross-sex models.

PARENT-CHILD SIMILARITIES

Before the studies and their findings are discussed, a word about method may be useful. Parent-child similarities can be studied in terms of mean level of a given attribute. For example, the number of hours spent in outdoor sports could be recorded for a set of fathers, mothers, sons, and daughters. The fathers would no doubt be found to spend more time in such activity than the mothers. And the boys would probably be spending more time in sports than the girls. The boys' mean scores for the total number of hours spent, then, would be more similar to the fathers' than to the mothers' mean scores, and girls' more similar to the mothers' than to the fathers'. These facts reveal little, however, about whether the tendency to be interested in sports is a product of modeling the behavior of the same-sex parent. Boys and men might both be more interested in sports for some biological reason, such as greater physical strength or a higher metabolism rate; or boys might simply have accepted sports as part of the cultural definition of masculinity, regardless of the behavior of their own fathers. What is needed is a determination of whether it is the boys whose *own* fathers are most active in sports who become especially interested in sports, and the sons of the more sedentary, cerebral fathers who are also sedentary and cerebral. In short, within-sex correlations are needed.

Studies reporting within-family correlations find, in general, that children are not notably similar to their own parents. Furthermore, when there is a correlation between parent and child scores, the correlations are not stronger between same-sexed parent and child. An early study by Lazowick (1955)[R] involved having college students and their parents rate a set of concepts on the semantic differential. The concepts to be rated included "myself," "man," "woman," and "family." All the correlations between parent and child scores were low. Daughters were no more like their mothers than they were like their fathers. Sons were slightly more like their fathers than their mothers, but they were no more like their own fathers than they were like a randomly selected set of other people's fathers.

Roff (1950)[R] summarized the research that had been done prior to 1950 on parent-child similarity in social and political attitudes and on personality traits as measured by personality inventories. Most of the studies were done with adolescents or young adults and their parents. His conclusion from the survey was as follows: "For any particular variable, there is either no difference or little difference between father-son, mother-son, father-daughter, and mother-daughter correlations." In other words, for aspects of beliefs and personality that are not specifically related to sex typing, there is little evidence that people tend to resemble the same-sex parent, at least by the time they have reached young adulthood. More recent work by Troll et al. (1969)[R] reveals a number of correlations between college students and their parents with respect to values and personality traits, but, again, no consistent tendency was found for students to resemble the same-sex parent more than the opposite-sex parent.

What has been found with respect to more clearly sex-typed attributes? In a study by Rosenberg and Sutton-Smith (1968)[R], college women from 2-child families were given the Gough Femininity scale. The scale was also administered to the subjects' mothers, fathers, brothers, and sisters. Correlations were computed for all the within-family pairs. The male siblings' scores correlated to a small degree with the parents' scores, but equally with mothers' and fathers' scores. The girls' scores—those of the college girls who were the primary subjects and their sisters—did not correlate significantly with the femininity scores of either parent. The work of Troll et al. yields a consistent result: correlations between generations with respect to stereotypic sex-role behavior are near zero and nonsignificant.

Perhaps it is true that by the time the children have reached adolescence, their sex-typed behavior is subject to so much peer pressure that daughters of especially feminine mothers are no longer especially feminine, and that a boy's masculinity is not clearly related to his father's masculinity. But perhaps the within-family similarities could be detected at an earlier age, when the children's mothers and fathers were the children's primary models. Again, the existing studies do not support the hypothesis of parent-child similarities. Hetherington (1965)[R] reports that the femininity of girls aged 3–6 is unrelated to their mothers' femininity. In a similar vein, Mussen and Rutherford (1963)[R] found that the femininity of first-grade girls, as measured in the It test, was unrelated to the femininity of their mothers' activities and interests, and that boys' masculinity scores were unrelated to either their fathers' masculinity or their mothers' interests. Boys whose mothers especially enjoyed cooking and sewing did not choose feminine activities of this sort for the It doll. Thus there is no evidence in this study either that the young boy is acquiring his masculine behavior and interests through modeling from his father, or that he is being hindered in his sex-role development by modeling feminine behavior from his mother.

The findings of Fling and Manosevitz (1972) point to a similar conclusion. Mothers' and fathers' It test scores were not significantly related to the It scores of their preschool sons or daughters.

IMITATION OF SAME-SEX MODEL

Perhaps the problem is that the measurements are too indirect. The measures in the studies of parent-child similarity we have discussed up till now are either projective measures or paper-and-pencil personality in-

ventories of uncertain validity for comparing the behavior of two generations. Perhaps to determine whether girls acquire their sex-typed characteristics by copying their mothers, and boys by copying their fathers, it
would be more satisfactory to obtain direct observations of the phenomenon by putting children in a position to imitate their parents and seeing
whether they do so. More specifically, the question is whether, when offered the opportunity to imitate one parent rather than (or more frequently than) the other, the child chooses the same-sex parent as primary
model. Ideally, studies are needed in which children have been observed
with their own parents, and their imitations recorded. Hetherington (1965)[R]
has done three such studies. The first involved children ranging in age
from 4 to 11. The children saw each of the parents express aesthetic preferences, and subsequently had an opportunity to make aesthetic choices
of their own from the same stimulus materials. Hetherington was interested primarily in the relationship between parental dominance (and other
parental characteristics) and childrens' imitations. She obtained powerful
results with respect to these objectives. For present purposes, however,
the important finding is that at every age level the subjects failed to show
any consistent tendency to imitate the same-sex parent. In a second experiment with children aged 4–5, selective imitation of the same-sex parent was
found, significant for girls and of borderline significance ($p < .10$) for
boys. In a third study, with subjects ranging in age from 3 to 6, prefer-
ential imitation of the same-sex parent did not occur.

Most of the research on imitation does not involve the child with his
own parents, but exposes the child to unfamiliar models—either peers or
adults—or, in some cases, makes use of doll play. Hartup (1962), for example, used doll play incidents in which a mother doll would perform one
action and a father doll another; the subject was then given a child doll
and asked to show which one of the two actions the child doll would perform. With this technique, Hartup found that children of nursery school
age imitated the same-sex parent. Kohlberg and Zigler (1967)[R] used a
similar technique with children aged 4, 5, and 7, but in their analysis combined imitation of same-sex parent doll with measures of attachment to
same-sex parent (e.g. "Whom does the boy doll want to put him to bed
and say goodnight?"). The combined score was called "parent orientation,"
and the subjects did show, on the average, greater orientation toward the
same-sex parent. The contribution of imitation (as distinct from attachment) to this score is not known. These same children did *not* show sex-
typed imitation when they could either copy the paper cut-out done by a
male or female experimenter or make one of their own design.

We have located over 20 studies in which children were exposed to models of both sexes, and their imitation of same-sex vs. cross-sex models compared. The studies are show in Table 8.2. An entry of "No" in the table

means that there was no significant interaction between sex of child and sex of model. A significant interaction could be of two kinds: selective imitation of same-sex models by each sex, or selective imitation of cross-sex models. The table specifies, whenever an interaction exists, which kind it is. In instances in which subjects of both sexes chose primarily one sex of model (i.e. when there was a main effect for sex of model) the table entry is "No."

Table 8.2 indicates that there is little consistent tendency for children of preschool or grade school age to select same-sex models. The studies in which children copied indiscriminately from male or female models included imitation of affection from filmed models, imitation of aggression, imitation of toy choices, aesthetic preferences, self-reinforcement, and a variety of relatively novel actions. The studies that do report a same-sex model choice tend to have subjects over the age of 5, so there may be an age trend; however, other factors are present in these studies that make any conclusions about age trends risky. For example, in the two Wolf studies, the models were of the same age as the subjects and were shown playing with toys that would be inappropriate for the subject's sex. In the first experiment, male subjects saw a model (either a boy or a girl) playing with an oven with a kettle on it, and girls saw the model playing with a truck with a tire on it. The subject later had an opportunity to choose between these two toys to play with. In the second experiment, the sex-typed toys were a doll and a fire engine. A boy was found to be more likely to play with the toy stove or the doll if he had previously seen a boy playing with these toys; seeing a girl play with these toys did not serve to encourage a boy in sex-inappropriate play. The same was true, in mirror image, for girls, who in general played more freely with boys' toys than boys did with girls' toys, but who were even more likely to do so after viewing another girl play with the truck or the fire engine. Thus it appears to be true that when a child already has built up inhibitions against playing with a given toy, a same-sex peer can symbolically "give permission," or make the situation seem safe, to play with the normally forbidden toy. But the Wolf studies do not indicate that the initial preference for same-sex toys was acquired through selective imitation of same-sex models. On the whole, it simply cannot be said that young children spontaneously imitate people of their own sex more than people of the opposite sex. This is true of imitations of parents as well as of models who are unfamiliar to the child.

Table 8.2 does not show findings separately for boys and girls, and hence does not permit us to evaluate the hypothesis that boys initially tend to imitate their mothers and then switch to their fathers as a primary model. In fact, however, the studies give little support for such a hypothesis. There are a number of studies in which both boys and girls imitate male models

TABLE 8.2

Imitation of Same-Sex or Cross-Sex Models

Study	Age and N	Interaction	Comment
Fryrear & Thelen 1969	3-4 (60)	No	Imitation of filmed M and F model's affectionate behavior
Bandura et al.[R] 1963a	3-5 (96)	No	Imitation of aggressive behavior from live and filmed adult models
Bandura et al.[R] 1963b	3-5 (72)	No	Imitation of novel responses of M or F E who either controlled or consumed resources
Hartup 1962	3-5 (63)	Same-sex	Imitation of action of Mo or Fa doll
McDavid 1959	3-5 (32)	No	Imitation of adult M or F model's choice of door for candy search (S had no knowledge of model's success)
D. Hicks[R] 1965	3-6 (60)	No	Imitation of aggressive responses from filmed adult and peer models
Kohlberg & Zigler[R] 1967	3-8 (72)	No	Imitation of M and F E's paper cutouts
Leifer[R] 1966	3, 5, 7 (108)	No	Imitation of filmed preadolescent model's novel actions and choice of sex-neutral toys
Cook & Smothergill 1973	4 (154)	Same-sex	Imitation of M and F model's picture choices
Hetherington[R] 1965	4-5 (72)	No	Imitation of parents' aesthetic preferences
	6-8 (72)	No	Imitation of aesthetic preference of Mo or Fa
	9-11 (72)	No	Imitation of aesthetic preference of Mo and Fa
Masters 1972a	4-5 (80)	No	Imitation of neutral stylistic behaviors
Hetherington & Frankie 1967	4-6 (160)	Same-sex (n.s. for boys)	Imitation of novel game behaviors of Mo and Fa
DuHamel & Biller	5 (63)	Same-sex	Imitation of child doll of Mo and Fa doll's judgments of traits of human figures
Rickard et al. 1970	5 (40)	No	Forced imitation, 5-word strings
Rosenblith[R] 1959	5 (120)	No	Imitation of adult M or F E's color choice
W. D. Ward 1969a	5-6 (16)	No	Imitation of M or F placing bets in a game of chance
	7-8 (16)	Same-sex	Same as above

Note: M and F designate male and female models other than the parents. Mo and Fa designate mother and father.

(continued)

TABLE 8.2 *(cont.)*

Study	Age and N	Interaction	Comment
Wolf 1973	5-9 (140)	Same-sex	Imitation of televised M or F peer model, duration of play with sex-inappropriate toy
	7-11 (60)	Same-sex	Imitation of live peer model playing with sex-inappropriate toys
Bandura & Barab[R] 1971	6-7 (16)	No	Imitation of modeled motor responses (sample includes 4 retardates)
Bandura & Kupers 1964	7-9 (160)	No	Imitation of standard-setting and self-reinforcement in bowling game

more (Bandura et al. 1963a,b[R], Hicks 1965[R], Rosenblith 1959[R] and 1961[R]). In two of these studies, the response to be imitated is aggression, and Bandura has suggested that a response is more likely to be imitated (by a child of either sex) if it is displayed by a model for whom the behavior seems appropriate to the child. But over the range of behaviors represented in the studies in Table 8.2, it is not true that both sexes of children initially prefer female models; there is simply little selection on the basis of the model's sex.

It should be noted in addition that if boys initially imitated their mothers and then switched, girls should be more fully sex-typed than boys, at least during the preschool years. As was shown at the beginning of this chapter, the opposite is the case.

Earlier in this chapter, we noted the fact that research to date has not demonstrated the existence of within-sex parent-child similarities on any of the dimensions that have been measured. Roff's (1950)[R] early summary of the work on social and political attitudes did reveal that adolescent children have attitudes that are related to those of their parents, but that children's attitudes are no more closely related to those of the same-sex than the cross-sex parent. These findings are reasonable in the light of the research on imitation: children do imitate models, but they do not systematically imitate a same-sex model. Hence, they ought to resemble both their parents, not particularly the same-sex one. When it comes to measures of sex typing, the results are puzzling. Children's scores on sex typing are not correlated with those of the same-sex parent. In the light of the fact that we know children do imitate their parents with respect to many things, we should expect them to resemble both parents with respect to sex-typed behavior as well, even though they do not imitate the same-sex parent more than the opposite-sex parent. Why should they resemble neither parent? Clearly, the methods used to measure sex typing are relevant here. Assume, for example, that a little girl is copying behavior from both parents; every time she copies feminine behavior from her mother she achieves a point toward a score that might produce a positive correlation with her mother's femininity score; but whenever she copies a bit of masculine behavior from her father, she not only reduces her own femininity score but moves toward obtaining a negative correlation with her mother's femininity score. If bisexual modeling is what is actually going on in the home, then zero-order correlations between the parent and child M-F scores would be the result.

Unfortunately, this solution to the problem is too glib. Children do not develop androgynously. As has been shown above, the results of many studies are quite unequivocal on this score: by age 4, children on the average prefer toys and activities that are considered by the adult society to be sex-appropriate. Children of each sex prefer to play with other children of their own sex, although this is more pronounced for boys. These preferences can be demonstrated projectively with the It test, and they can also be demonstrated in straightforward choices that the child makes on his own behalf in toy preference tests; in addition, the preferences may be observed in the child's behavior when his activities are time-sampled and enumerated during the free play periods at nursery school. The children are clearly sex-typed; but their degree of sex typing is unrelated to that of the same-sex parent; furthermore, in experimental situations when children have choices of models, they do not consistently select same-sex models. It would appear, then, that their sex typing does not originate through modeling.

Before this conclusion is accepted, there are some other possibilities that must be considered. Perhaps the problem is that when "masculinity" or "femininity" is measured in an adult, different things are measured than when the presumably similar characteristics are measured in childhood. A mother's M-F score reflects interests, activities, and attributes that her daughter may not even perceive, much less be able to copy. Perhaps little girls *are* learning their sex-typed behavior by imitating their mothers, but perhaps they are imitating behaviors that are not normally included in the measures of the mother's femininity. For example, most of the toy preference tests rely heavily upon dolls as indicators of feminine interest. The toy preference test used by R. Sears et al. (1965)[R], modeled after Rabban's test, included a baby doll, a doll crib, a doll bathinette, a doll feeding chair, and a doll buggy. The only feminine items not related to dolls were a set of dishes and two purses. The masculine toys offered for choice were more varied. Perhaps a girl who gets a highly feminine score is imitating her mother's care-taking with younger siblings. But the mother's femininity score does not include items that would reveal whether she is frequently engaged in this activity or not. If same-sex imitation were at work, we would expect to find that when a girl saw her mother taking care of a baby, the girl would spend a good deal of time playing with dolls. The boy, on the other hand, should be less affected by whether he sees his mother caring for a baby, since the mother is not his primary model. We have not been able to find published data bearing upon this matter. Sears has provided us with doll-play data from the 1965 study *Identification and Child-Rearing.* In this study, girls showed significantly more nurturant responses to the baby doll than did the boys. Sears' new analysis (personal communication, 1974) involves separating the children who have younger siblings from those who do not, to see whether the child's responses to the baby doll are influenced by opportunities to see the mother take care of a younger child. When the sample is subdivided by both sex and ordinal position, the number of cases in each group is small, and the results are only suggestive, but they are interesting nonetheless: girls tend to be nurturant to the baby doll whether they have younger siblings or not; boys tend to show nurturance *only* when they have younger siblings. Thus it is boys, rather than girls, who seem to be copying the behavior they have observed in their mothers!

On the basis of this rather fragmentary evidence, we are inclined to believe that our earlier conclusion was justified: that early sex typing is not a function of a child's having selectively observed, and selectively learned, the behavior of same-sex, rather than opposite-sex, models. Furthermore, it would appear that the lack of parent-child similarity in sex typing is not just a function of the fact that the wrong things are being measured in the two generations. It has been noted before (R. Sears et al. 1965[R], p. 186) that masculine and feminine behavior at age 4 is a qualitatively very different thing from masculinity and femininity in adulthood. When a little girl shows flirtatious behavior toward her father, this behavior is not a carbon copy of what she sees her mother doing. What the little girl sees might be the father coming home from the office, a quick kiss or brief hug between the mother and father, the mother flashing some smiles at her husband as she gets dinner, the exchange of conversation such as "How was your day, honey?" etc. This is not the kind of behavior fathers are referring to (see p. 329) when they say that their daughters are "little flirts," "soft and cuddly," etc. If the daughters are imitating their mothers, the match is not close, and the model's behavior has been filtered through childish eyes and the imitative actions are a function of a childish body and a childish level of behavior organization. This brings us to a very central point about imitation. The developmental psycholinguists have shown us that when a child is asked to repeat a grammatically complex sentence, the child will simplify it. In many instances the child reprocesses the sentence so that most of the meaning is retained, but uses a structure that expresses the child's level of grammatical competence. It would not be surprising if this same kind of process goes on in social behavior. If the little girl perceives that her mother is being affectionate toward the father, and sets out to copy this behavior, the behavioral output will have to be constrained by the child's already developed behavioral capabilities, at least to a degree, and the result will be childlike affection-showing. We recognize that it is hazardous to suggest that a child will sometimes copy the "meaning" of an action rather than the action itself; it is extraordinarily difficult to be operational about the "meaning" of action. And, in any case, the possibility of transformational imitation does not seem to help in understanding the issue before us. If a young child were imitating the meaning of the same-sex parent's behavior, then it ought to be true that the little girls who are most feminine in a childish way have mothers who are especially feminine in an adult way, and we have seen that this does not appear to be true.

Our analysis of the arguments concerning the role of modeling in sex typing and our review of the research on selective imitation have led us to a conclusion that is very difficult to accept, namely that modeling plays a minor role in the development of sex-typed behavior. This conclusion seems to fly in the face of common sense and to conflict with many striking observations of sex-typed role playing on the part of children. For example, here is an excerpt taken from Minturn and Hitchcock's report of the play of Rajput children in India (1963, p. 334)[R]:

Both sexes have their own type of fantasy play which is modeled on adult work. The little girls play at cooking and the boys at farming. One child in the sample was particularly fond of playing at cooking. She had a set of toy dishes, and she would build herself a hearth out of three stones and go through the exact motions of making bread. She used either mud or potsherds for her bread, rubbed oil in the frying pan, patted the breads, fried them on the fire underneath the pot to let them puff, took them out, flattened them, and stacked them on a dish beside her. It was an exact copy of the motions that an adult woman goes through in making bread. When she finished she washed the dishes and stacked them, and washed the floor in the place where she had cooked.

When the boys play at farming, they sometimes make rather elaborate imitations of fields, and then irrigate them. More often the play is somewhat simpler, as in the following observation: A group of boys were playing at sowing. They had long sticks and were pretending to plow. They said, "Let's grow wheat." Some of the boys started scattering dust like seed. They were following boys who were "plowing" the ground with sticks. They said "burr," "burr," "burr," which is what the men say to the cattle. They leveled the ground with a stick by rolling it along the ground.

In the face of observations of this kind, how can we possibly say that modeling is not of crucial importance in the acquisition of sex-typed behavior? We must note that Rajput culture is highly sex-segregated, because of the custom of purdah for women; it is possible that in this culture girls are primarily exposed to female models and boys to male models, and that their play reflects this fact. We are inclined to doubt, however, that the matter of model availability is the primary explanation. American children, too, display sex-typed imitations of adult work when they play. But when they are offered models of the two sexes in controlled experimental situations, their imitations are usually indiscriminate as to sex. Clearly, the discrepancy between acquisition and performance that Bandura and Walters (1963)[R] and Mischel (1970)[R] have espoused so vigorously must be involved. Note that someone *had given the little Rajput girl a set of dishes.* Having the dishes in her hands, she knew what to do with them, on the basis of previous observational learning. We suspect that if someone had given such a set of dishes to a small Rajput boy, he too would be quite capable of displaying the detailed motions involved in making bread.

What are the reasons, then, a child might not perform actions that he has in fact learned how to do through observational learning? A first reason is the one we have just suggested: the necessary eliciting conditions do not occur. A second is that the child has reason to believe the action is inappropriate for him. He knows there are many actions permitted to an adult that are not permitted to a child; e.g. adults may handle sharp objects, drive cars, etc., whereas a child may not, and a child must wait for a considerable time to put into practice many of the actions that are in one sense already in his repertoire (Maccoby 1959[R]). In a similar vein, he comes to know that certain actions are appropriate for a person of his own sex, and others are not. This factor, we believe, is paramount. To be as explicit as possible, we suggest that (a) the modeling process is crucial in the acquisition of a wide repertoire of potential behaviors, but this repertoire is not sex-typed to any important degree; (b) knowledge of what behavior is appropriate is crucial in the selection of what items will be used in performance out of the repertoire of potential actions.

There is a reservation to point (a): the repertoire itself might become sex-typed if the person does in fact come to seek exposure to, or selectively attend to, same-sex models. If a girl decides to take sewing lessons, she is likely to go to a woman teacher, and thus add to her repertoire some specific female-role skills that a boy will not possess because he did not expose himself to this modeling. Furthermore, it is possible that when both sexes of models are available for a particular skill that a child wishes to acquire, the child will normally choose to copy whichever model might be expected, on the basis of sex, to be more proficient in the activity. But this is a shaky assumption. Cooking, for example, is a female activity; yet if offered the choice to imitate a housewife cooking dinner or a male chef cooking at a restaurant, the chances are that children of both sexes would copy the latter. The prestige of model can override the sex-appropriateness of the activity. In any case, if children do operate on the assumption that one sex is likely to be a better model for certain kinds of skills, we suggest that selective imitation based on such assumptions is a relatively late development; we saw little evidence of it in the studies of imitation in children under 10, though most of the studies cited were not designed with this particular issue in mind. In any case, seeking out a same-sex model implies that the seeker has already developed sex-typed interests; hence, such selection cannot be an explanation of the development of such interests.

Like other writers on the subject, we have stressed the distinction between acquisition and performance, and have argued that, at least in early childhood, *acquisition* of behavior through modeling is not sex-typed. The sex typing of behavior that may be observed at these ages is then held to be a function of performance factors. What are these factors? Two general classes have been proposed: Mischel's position is that the reinforcement history of the individual, and his observations of the reinforcements delivered to models, will determine which actions a child selects out of his repertoire for performance. Sex typing, then, according to this view, would be a product of direct reinforcement (to self or others) for sex-appropriate behavior. The alternative point of view is Kohlberg's: that it is the child's growing understanding of his own sexual identity, coupled with his growing understanding of the content of the sex roles prescribed by the culture around him, that determine the child's behavioral choices. In this view, sex typing is dependent upon certain aspects of cognitive growth. A child's inferences concerning what behavior is sex-appropriate are partly based, of course, upon the instances of differential reward and punishment, and in this sense Kohlberg's theory is not distinct from Mischel's. But in the cognitive-developmental view, differential reinforcement is only one of the sources of information a child uses to construct the concept of sex-appropriate behavior that he uses to guide himself.

It becomes important to know as precisely as possible what different patterns of reinforcement contingencies *are* experienced (directly or vicariously) by the two sexes. It is to this topic that we now turn.

CHAPTER NINE

Differential Socialization of Boys and Girls

A scene from the early musical "Carousel" epitomizes (in somewhat car-icatured form) some of the feelings that parents have about bringing up sons as opposed to daughters. A young man discovers he is to be a father. He rhapsodizes about what kind of son he expects to have. The boy will be tall and tough as a tree, and no one will dare to boss him around; it will be all right for his mother to teach him manners but she mustn't make a sissy out of him. He'll be good at wrestling and will be able to herd cattle, run a riverboat, drive spikes, etc. Then the prospective father realizes, with a start, that the child may be a girl. The music changes to a gentle theme. She will have ribbons in her hair; she will be sweet and petite (just like her mother), and suitors will flock around her. There's a slightly dis-cordant note, introduced for comic relief from sentimentality, when the expectant father brags that she'll be half again as bright as girls are meant to be; but then he returns to the main theme: she must be protected, and he must find enough money to raise her in a setting where she will meet the right kind of man to marry.

Despite recent changes in social attitudes, this rendition no doubt still contains more than a kernel of truth about the way mothers and fathers feel about the two sexes. It is widely assumed that these parental attitudes and feelings must translate themselves into differential behavior on the part of parents toward sons and daughters. Parents, it is thought, must bring to bear direct or indirect pressure to make their children fit sex stereo-types. The theory that sex typing in children's behavior is brought about through direct "shaping" by socialization agents is probably the most per-vasive point of view in writings on the subject. Even theories that stress modeling tend, as shown in Chapter 8, to depend upon prior occurrence of differential socialization, so that children of the two sexes are motivated to select different models. The role of direct socialization appears to be crucial, then, not only in its own right but also in establishing the founda-tion upon which later self-socialization is based. The objective of the pres-ent chapter is to determine whether, and in what ways, boys and girls are treated differently by parents and other socializing agents. In addition, we shall consider the following questions: To what extent is the differential treatment consistent with the characteristic behavioral differences between children of the two sexes? Are there any aspects of family dynamics that transcend the simple preference among parents that their boys shall be masculine and their girls feminine, and that lead to differential treatment of boys and girls?

A search of the literature for studies of differential socialization reveals an interesting phenomenon. Most work on sex-role socialization has been done within sex, not between sex. Most researchers have been interested in the question of what makes some boys more masculine than others, or some girls more feminine than others. Tables of correlations are presented, for a given sex, showing the relationship between socialization practices and some measure of masculinity or femininity; the correlations are shown separately for boys and girls. There is an assumption underlying this practice, only sometimes made explicit, that if we know what makes some boys more masculine than others, we will automatically have discovered what makes most boys more masculine than most girls.

There are some pitfalls in this assumption. For example, Sears et al. (1965)[1] found that parental punitiveness feminized both boys and girls. Then, according to the usual assumption, it might be inferred parents must be more punitive toward girls, on the average, and this must be one factor that makes girls more feminine than boys. In fact, as we shall see, parents are probably more punitive toward boys. We must recognize the possibility that boys are more "masculine" than girls (in some sense of this term) *despite* what their parents are doing, not because of it. We do not mean to imply that there are different laws of learning, or different laws of human behavior, for the two sexes. However, it does seem clear that if we want to understand the role of differential socialization, there is no substitute for direct comparisons between the parents of boys and the parents of girls; inferences from within-sex correlations are simply not sufficient.

A second trend that emerges when one reviews the studies of parent-child interaction and its effects is that the large majority of the studies deal with children under school age. We suspect this age bias stems from several implicit assumptions. A major one is the assumption that the influence of the parents declines when the child enters school, while that of teachers and age-mates increases. Beyond this, there is the assumption that the impact of external socialization agents is greatest in the younger years because of changes in the psychological dynamics of the child. The young child is sometimes thought to be more pliable because he is more dependent—he needs the attention and affection of his parents more than an older child does and is therefore more willing to conform to their demands. A second reason for emphasizing the importance of early socialization is, of course, the concept of identification and its consequences: once a child has "identified" with his parents, he spontaneously accepts their values and, to a major degree, thereafter socializes himself (primarily by imitation). A related view, that of the cognitive-developmental theorist, is that once the child has achieved a fairly stable self-concept (including a stable sex identity) he will select models accordingly, and socialization will become a more and more autonomous process. A Skinnerian view, on the contrary, would argue that there is no reason why external contingencies should not continue to shape and reshape the individual; this view would not point to any developmental change in the relevance of external socialization forces. Unfortunately, the existing body of research, concentrating as it does upon the early years, does not provide a basis for an appraisal of these contrasting points of view.

In the sections that follow, a set of hypotheses will be set forth concerning possible processes that might underlie differential treatment of children of the two sexes; then findings of existing studies will be summarized; and finally the hypotheses will be evaluated in the light of this evidence.

HYPOTHESES

Hypothesis 1. Parents treat children of the two sexes so as to shape them toward the behavior deemed appropriate for their sex. This hypothesis leads to the prediction, for example, that boys would be rewarded for being tough and competitive, girls for being compliant and nurturant, and that each sex would receive negative reactions for sex-inappropriate behavior. It need not be true, of course, that this parental behavior is deliberate; it may be quite unintended from a subjective point of view. Furthermore, in the case of sex-typed behavior that is deemed undesirable by the parent, it may simply be opposed with less vigor in the sex for which it is consistent with a sex-role stereotype. That is, there may be differential withholding of negative reinforcement as well as differential reward.

Hypothesis 2. Because of innate differences in characteristics manifested early in life, boys and girls stimulate their parents differently and hence elicit different treatment from them. Furthermore, the same parental behavior may produce a different response in a boy than a girl, again because of innate sex-linked characteristics. In short, the child "shapes" the parent rather than vice versa, and a circular pattern of interaction becomes established based upon an individual child's demands and the parent's discovery of what works with that child. The nature of the child's demands, and the nature of the parental actions that will be effective, will differ initially to some degree for the two sexes.

Hypothesis 3. Parents base their behavior toward a child on their conception of what a child of a given sex is likely to be like. Whether innate temperamental differences exist or not, many parents believe they do, and parents govern their socialization practices accordingly. This adaptation may take one or more of three forms:

3a. Parents devote special attention to training children to overcome what they believe to be their natural weaknesses. If parents believe, for example, that boys are naturally more aggressive than girls, they may make stronger efforts to control and counteract aggressive behavior in sons than daughters. With girls, their efforts might be more directed toward helping them to overcome their assumed natural timidity.

3b. Parents accept as inevitable, and do not attempt to change, any behavior they believe to be "natural" for a given sex.

3c. Parents have a perceptual adaptation level that is different for the two sexes. *They tend to notice, and react to, whatever behavior is seen as unusual for a child of a given sex.*

Hypothesis 4. A parent's behavior toward a child will depend, in some degree, upon whether the child is of the same sex as himself. We suggest three possible mechanisms underlying cross-sex and same-sex parent-child relationships:

4a. Each parent expects and wants to be a model for the same-sex child. He will be especially interested in teaching that child the "lore" that goes along with being a person of their shared sex.

4b. Each parent transfers to his children some of the behavior he is accustomed to displaying toward adults of the two sexes. In some cases this amounts to outright sexual attraction and seduction of the opposite-sex child. In addition to cross-sex attraction, there are cases on record of a homosexual parent who seduces a same-sex child. Most commonly, of course, there are simply discreet elements of flirtation with the opposite-sex child, and elements of rivalry with the same-sex child. Dominance-submission relationships, as well as sexual ones, may generalize to children. If a woman is accustomed to taking a submissive stance toward her husband and other adult men, the hypothesis says that she will be more likely to behave submissively toward a son than a daughter. Clearly there are instances in which the role demands of parenthood (especially motherhood) are not consistent with habitual male-female interaction patterns. It would be reasonable to expect that the simple generalization of a parent's own habitual behavior toward adult males or females would be more likely to occur with older, rather than younger, sons and daughters.

4c. Parents will tend to identify more strongly with a same-sex child. Specifically, the parent will see more similarities between himself and a same-sex child, and will have stronger empathetic reactions to that child's emotional states. A given parent's relation to a same-sex child will depend, then, to some degree on the parent's self-attitudes. A parent with low self-esteem will be frequently made anxious by the things a same-sex child does; this parent will be preoccupied with the things the child might do wrong or the ways he might get into trouble, and will tend to assume that other people are reacting negatively to the child. A self-confident parent will have confidence in a same-sex child. Rothbart (1971) suggests that this "counteridentification" of parent with the same-sex child is particularly strong for firstborn children, and rather weak with later-borns.

All four of the kinds of processes we have hypothesized may be at work in the interactions in a given family. Sometimes the processes are not entirely compatible with one another. We now turn to an examination of what is known about parental behavior toward children of the two sexes, to see to what extent these themes may be detected and how they are orchestrated and balanced when they create conflicting pressures within a family.

Total Parent-Child Interaction

The amount of interaction between the parent and the young child does not consistently depend on the sex of the child. Among studies that do report a sex difference, there are more studies that find greater interaction with boys, but the majority report no difference (see Table 9.1). Some of the studies cited report interaction in terms of the amount of time the parent spends in specific activities with the child; others use scores based on detailed time-sampling of specific behaviors, such as touching or eye contact with the child; the conclusion reached by the study, however, does not seem to depend in any systematic way upon the nature of the measure used.

Most of the studies, of course, report interaction between the *mother* and the child. The studies that do report father data are inconsistent. Gewirtz and Gewirtz (1968) find that Israeli fathers tend to stay longer with infant sons than daughters when they visit their children in the children's house. Consistent with this, though at a later age, is the R. Sears et al. (1965)[R] finding (from father interviews) that fathers have more interaction with sons than daughters of kindergarten age. (Note that this is the same sample of children as that reported by Hatfield et al. 1967.) F. Pedersen and Robson (1969), however, did not find a sex difference in the amount of time fathers spent caring for, and playing with, their 8-9-month-old infants, and in Tasch's study (1952)[R], fathers who were interviewed said they had been more involved in the care-taking of their daughters than their sons.

Turning to more specific classes of parental behavior, we do find a consistent trend for parents to elicit "gross motor behavior" more from their sons than from daughters (see Table 9.2). This parental behavior takes several forms. Lewis (1972) reports that mothers are more likely to respond to a son's large-muscle movements than to those of a daughter; Moss (1967) and L. Yarrow et al. (1971) report that parents "stress the musculature" of male infants—meaning, presumably, that they are more likely

TABLE 9.1
Total Interaction (Social Stimulation)

Study	Age and N	Difference	Comment
Parke et al.	0-2 days	Boys	Mother and Father touch infant
1972	(19)	None	Mother and Father hold, kiss, feed, rock, explore infant
Tasch[R]	0-17 yrs	Girls	Father participation in daily care
1952	(85)		(father interview)
Thoman et al.	2 days	Firstborn boys	Time spent breast-feeding
1972	(40)	Later-born girls	
Leiderman et al.	1, 4 wks	None	Mother holds infant (full-term and
1973	postdischarge		premature samples)
	(66)		
Moss	3 wks	Boys	Mother attends infant
1967	(29)	None	Mother holds, feeds, looks at infant
	3 mos	None	Mother holds, feeds, attends, looks
	(25)		at infant (longitudinal)
Lewis	3 mos	Boys	Time mother holds infant
1972	(32)	None	Mother touches, looks, smiles, rocks, plays with infant; total time of interaction; ratio of mother-child interaction to infant action
Gewirtz & Gewirtz	4 mos	Boys	Amount of time spent feeding
1968	(8m, 4f)	None	Duration of mother's visits to children's house (kibbutz)
	8 mos	Boys	Time spent feeding
	(8m, 4f)	Boys	Duration of father's visits to children's house
L. Yarrow et al.	5 mos	Boys	Variety and level of social stimulation from caretaker (black sample)
1971	(41 & primary caretakers)		
		None	Caretaker proximity
Beckwith	7-11 mos	None	Mother touching
1972	(24 adoptive mo-inf. pairs)		
Clarke-Stewart	9-18 mos	None	Total amount of mother-child-interaction; amount of social stimulation from mother; mother's response to infant's distress and demand behaviors; mother's response to infant's social signals (home observation; longitudinal)
1973	(36)		
F. Pedersen &	9½ mos	None	Father caretaking, emotional involvement, time spent in play, level of play stimulation (assessed by interviewing mother; firstborn)
Robson 1969	(45)		
Minton et al.	27 mos	Boys	Total mother-child interactions
1971	(90)		

(continued)

TABLE 9.1 *(cont.)*

Study	Age and N	Difference	Comment
Biber et al. 1972	4 (225)	Girls	Amount of teacher's instructional contact with child (videos of classroom)
Radin 1973	4 (52)	None	Total mother-child interaction (behavior observation during mother interview; multiracial, low SES)
Bee et al. 1969	4-5 (114)	Both	Maternal interaction during child's problem solving (boys, white middle SES; girls, black and white lower SES)
Hatfield et al. 1967	4-5 (40)	None	Mother involvement and attentiveness during structural mother-child interaction
Sears et al.[R] 1965	4-5 (40)	Boys	Amount of father interaction (father interview)
Rothbart 1971	5 (56)	Girls	Mother's "anxious intrusions" during supervision of child's performance on 5 tasks

TABLE 9.2
Stimulation of Gross Motor Behavior

Study	Age and N	Difference	Comment
Tasch[R] 1952	0-5 yrs 6-17 yrs (160)	None Boys	Father interview: report of father-child rough-and-tumble play
Moss 1967	3 wks (29)	Boys	Mother stimulates, arouses; stresses musculature
	3 mos (25)	None	Mother stimulates, arouses; stresses musculature (longitudinal sample)
Lewis 1972	3 mos (32)	Boys	Mother "responds proximally" (touch-hold) to gross motor movement of infant
L. Yarrow et al. 1971	5 mos (41 & primary caretakers)	Boys	Caretaker encourages gross motor responses (black sample)

to handle them roughly and pull their arms and legs vigorously. In an interview conducted by Tasch (1952)[R] with fathers of children of a wide range of ages, the fathers reported engaging in more rough-and-tumble play with their sons than with their daughters. The form of the motor stimulation undoubtedly changes drastically with the age of the child, but the continuing theme appears to be that girls are treated as though they were more fragile than boys. F. Pedersen and Robson (1969) report that

TABLE 9.3

Verbal Interaction and Stimulation

Study	Age and N	Difference	Comment
Parke et al. 1972	0-2 days (19)	None	Mother and father vocalizations to infant
Thoman et al. 1972	2 days (40)	Girls	Mother talks to infant during breast-feeding (firstborns)
		None	Later-borns
		Girls	Mother talks to infant during nonfeeding activities (trend, $p < .1$)
Leiderman et al. 1973	1, 4 wks postdischarge (66)	None	Mother laughs and talks to infant (longitudinal)
Moss 1967	3 wks (29)	None	Mother imitates and talks to infant
	3 mos (25)	None	Mother imitates and talks to infant (longitudinal)
Lewis 1972	3 mos (32)	Girls	Mother vocalizes to infant
Lewis & Freedle 1972	3 mos (40)	Boys	Mother responds to infant vocalization
		Girls	Mother vocalizes to infant
J. Kagan 1971	4 mos (180)	Girls	Distinctive vocalizations from mother (upper-middle SES only)
		None	General vocalizations from mother
L. Yarrow et al. 1971	5 mos (41)	None	Mother's contingent response to infant vocalization
Goldberg & Lewis 1969	6 mos (64)	Girls	Mother talks to infant during experimental session
Beckwith 1972	7-9, 8-11 mos (24 adoptive *mo*-inf pairs)	None	Mother vocalizes to infant
Phillips 1973	8, 18, 28 mos (57)	None	Mother's verbalizations to child
Clarke-Stewart 1973	9-18 mos (36)	None	Verbal stimulation by mother, home observation (longitudinal)
Minton et al. 1971	2 (90)	None	Mother reasons with child, questions child
Halverson & Waldrop 1970	2½ (42)	Girls	Number of mother's statements and words to child while administering tasks
Lapidus 1972	3-4 (30)	None	Mother's verbalizations to child while teaching cooperation game
Serbin et al. 1973	3-5 (225 & 15 teachers)	Boys	Teacher holds extended conversation with child
Blayney 1973	4 (29)	None	Father's verbalizations to child while child performs on elevated balance beam
Bee et al. 1969	4-5 (114)	Both	Mother gives information to child in waiting room (boys, black and white lower SES; girls, white middle SES)
		None	Mother asks question, makes suggestion to child in waiting room

(continued)

TABLE 9.3 *(cont.)*

Study	Age and *N*	Difference	Comment
Hatfield et al. 1967	4-5 (40)	None	Mother reasons with child (observation)
Rothbart 1971	5 (56)	Girls	Mother questions child ($p < .1$)
		None	Amount of information mother gives to child about tasks; amount of time mother spends in conversation or explanation; complexity of mother's explanations
Greenglass 1971a	9-10, 13-14 (132)	None	Mother's communication during joint problem solving (Canadians and Italian-Canadians)
M. Hoffman & Saltzstein 1967	12 (270 & available mothers & fathers)	Girls	Both parents' use of induction, father's more pronounced (child report, middle SES)
		None	Mother's and father's use of induction (parent report)
	12 (174)	Girls	Father's use of induction (child report, low SES)
		None	Mother's use of induction (child report)

fathers are more apprehensive about the physical well-being of infant daughters than infant sons at the age of 9 months; Minton et al. (1971) detect a similar trend somewhat later, at age 27 months, when mothers express more worry about physical danger to daughters than sons. However, few studies have measured either roughness of handling or fears about injury to the child, so it is too early to say whether this is a consistently sex-typed aspect of parental beliefs and behavior.

Amount of Verbal Interaction

As noted in Chapter 3, recent evidence does not clearly indicate that girls undergo more rapid verbal development in the first few years of life. Earlier evidence did point to such a conclusion, however, and it has sometimes been assumed that a female head start in verbal ability might be a function of girls' receiving more verbal stimulation or reinforcement from their caretakers. As may be seen from Table 9.3, the evidence on this subject is inconsistent. The majority of studies show no difference in the amount or kind of parental vocalizations to sons as compared with daughters. In a number of instances when differences are found, it is only for a portion of the sample. For example, Thoman reports mothers talking more to daughters when the child is a firstborn, but not for later-born infants. Kagan finds that well-educated mothers use more distinctive vocalizations (that is, vocalizations when in face-to-face orientation to an infant and unaccompanied by any other form of stimulation) with daughters than with sons, but this difference is not found among mothers with less education, and there is no difference in the total amount of maternal vocalization directed by mothers toward infants of the two sexes. Furthermore, although well-educated mothers are somewhat more likely to respond to a female infant's vocalization within 10 seconds, less-well-educated mothers are somewhat more likely to respond to a *son's* vocalizations within this short time. The significance of these differences was not tested. Bee also found, with older children, that whether a mother vocalizes more to a son or daughter is a function of the social class of the families. J. Kagan (1971, p. 106) makes the point that it is probably the direct and immediate interaction with an infant, accompanied by eye contact, that serves to build the child's vocalizations. It may be that much of the evidence summarized in Table 9.3 is not sufficiently refined to reflect important interactional properties of this kind that might be differential for boys and girls. But on the basis of existing evidence, it can only be said that results are highly variable across sample subgroups, and that the bulk of the evidence does not add up to any clear trend for mothers to provide more verbal stimulation to daughters than sons. A number of studies found no sex differences, and those that did are inconsistent in the direction of the difference found.

Parental Warmth

Perhaps the most widely studied dimension of parent-child relationships is the warmth-hostility or warmth-rejection dimension. In the early 1950's, in an interview study with mothers of 5-year-old children (R. Sears et al. 1957[R]), the mothers were asked to recall how much time they had spent playing with the child when it was an infant, and how much they had cuddled it. The current level of affectional interaction with the child was also assessed. Summary ratings of "mother's warmth to infant" and "mother's warmth to child currently" were made; the mothers of daughters recalled somewhat warmer interaction with their infants than did mothers of sons, but no difference in the amount of warmth to the two sexes was reported at the age of 5. Since that time there have been many observational studies as well as additional interview studies, and the work has even been extended to subhuman primates. Observations of rhesus monkey mothers and their infants (Mitchell and Brandt 1972[R], Mitchell 1968[R]) have revealed that mother monkeys embrace and clasp an infant more if it is a female. After about the age of 3 months, there is an increase in the amount of rejection and threat behavior the mother shows to male infants, but not to females. Mothers bit the male infants more frequently than the female infants (sometimes in response to being bitten). On the other hand, mixed with threats toward male infants were seemingly contradictory bits of behavior: the mothers occasionally played with their male infants, but almost never with their female infants; and the mothers of the males more often lip-smacked to their male infants (a conciliatory gesture), presented sexually to them, and were more often seen submitting to rough treatment from them. Similar differential treatment of infant males and females by adult male monkeys of some species has been reported (see Mitchell and Brandt 1972[R] for a review). It is difficult to know what precisely it is about an infant's appearance or behavior that permits a monkey mother to "recognize" its sex, but it is evident that infants of the two sexes do stimulate their mothers differently and establish a different pattern of relationships with them. The interactions become more differentiated with the infant's increasing age, and one result is a higher level of nonpunitive physical contact between a mother and a female infant.

With human infants, however, no clear-cut pattern of differential treatment emerges from the nine observational studies now available (see Table 9.4). Six of these report no difference in the amount of affectional contact between mother and infant in the first two years. Leiderman et al. (1973), working with a group of infants some of whom were premature, found that during the first week after the infants were discharged from the hospital, mothers did tend to hold daughters in a ventral-ventral position more often; however, the total amount of holding and other affectionate contact did not differ for male and female infants. When these mother-infant pairs were observed one month postdischarge, the girls were still receiving more ventral-ventral holding, but now the boys received more total affectionate touching. Lewis (1972) found that among a group of 3-month-old infants, the boys were held more; Goldberg and Lewis (1969), however, report concerning a group of 6-month-old infants that the girls were more frequently touched than the boys. At nursery school age, Radin (1973) finds mothers showing more affection to daughters; but three studies (Baumrind 1971, Hatfield et al. 1967, and Allaman et al. 1972) find no differences in maternal affection. In these studies, observations of parental behavior are available, as well as interview data in some instances. Both Baumrind and Hatfield et al. do report tendencies for fathers to show somewhat more hostility toward sons at this age, but the trends do not reach statistical significance.

When children themselves, at older ages, are questioned on how much affection they have received from their parents, girls are likely to report receiving more affection (Siegelman 1965, Hoffman and Saltzstein 1967, Droppleman and Schaefer 1963[R], Bronfenbrenner 1960[R]). Since observational studies of parent behavior when the children are younger do not usually report differential parental warmth to children of the two sexes, the differences reported by the children themselves may either reflect selective perceptions on the children's part or indicate that differentiation in parental warmth to the two sexes does develop but only some time after the children reach school age.

TABLE 9.4

Warmth, Nurturance, and Acceptance

Study	Age and *N*	Difference	Comment
Allaman et al. 1972	0-6 yrs (95)	None	Mother affectionateness (observation)
	0-10 yrs (65)	None	Mother affectionateness, intensity of contact (observation)
Sears et al.[R] 1957	"infancy" (379)	Girls	More warmth by mother to infant (mother recall)
	5 yrs (379)	None	Warmth to child (mother interview)
Leiderman et al. 1973	1, 4 wks post-discharge (66)	Boys	Mother affectionately touches infant (4 wks)
		Girls	Mother and infant in ventral contact (observation; 1, 4 wks)
		None	Mother holds, smiles, touches infant affectionately (1 wk); mother holds, smiles at infant (4 wks)
Moss 1967	3 wks (29)	None	Mother smiles, rocks, gives affectionate contact
	3 mos (25)	None	Mother smiles, rocks, gives affectionate contact (longitudinal)
Lewis 1972	3 mos (32)	Boys	Mother holds infant
		None	Mother rocks, touches, smiles at infant
Kagan 1971	4 mos (180)	None	Physical affection from mother
L. Yarrow et al. 1971	5 mos (41 & primary caretakers)	None	Expression of positive affection by caretaker (black sample)
Goldberg & Lewis 1969	6 mos (64)	Girls	Mother touches infant (observation)
Clarke-Stewart 1973	9 mos (36)	None	Mother's positive attitude toward child (interview)
	9-18 mos	None	Physical contact with mother (home observation; longitudinal); mother's positive attitude toward child (observer rating)
	18 mos	Boys	More positive attitude toward child (questionnaire)
D. Stayton et al. 1971	9-12 mos (25)	None	Mother's acceptance (vs. rejection) (observer ratings)
Baumrind 1971	3-4 (293 parents)	None	Mother is rejecting, father is rejecting (observer ratings)
Baumrind & Black 1967	3-4 (95 parents)	None	Warmth: presence of loving relationship, demonstrativeness, approval, empathy, sympathy (mother and father interviews)
Sears et al.[R] 1953	3-5 (40)	None	Mother's nurturance when child is upset or mother busy; father's nurturance (mother interview)
		Boys	Mother's bedtime nurturance

(continued)

TABLE 9.4 *(cont.)*

Study	Age and N	Difference	Comment
Serbin et al. 1973	3-5 (225 & 15 teachers)	None	Teacher hugs child in response to dependent behavior
		Boys	Teacher hugs child in response to appropriate participation in classroom activities
Kagan & Lemkin[R] 1960	3-6 (67)	Girls	Child perceives father as affectionate
Blayney 1973	4 (29)	None	Father expresses affection or approval to child
Hilton 1967	4 (60 & mothers)	None	Number of overt expressions of love and/or support while child attempts series of puzzles
Radin 1973	4 (52)	Girls	Mother's nurturance (observation; trend, $p < .1$)
Hatfield et al. 1967	4-5 (40)	None	Mother's warmth toward child, mother's responsiveness to child (observer ratings)
Sears et al.[R] 1965	4-5 (40)	Girls	Father's satisfaction with child's socialization (father interview)
Laosa & Brophy 1972	5-7 (93)	Boys	Mother and father equally nurturant (child questionnaire)
		Girls	Mother more nurturant than father (child questionnaire)
Siegelman 1965	9-11 (212)	Girls	More affective reward, less expressive rejection from father (child questionnaire)
		None	Nurturance, instrumental and affiliative companionship from father; affective reward, expressive rejection, nurturance, instrumental and affiliative companionship from mother
Armentrout & Burger 1972	9, 10, 12 (635)	None	Parental acceptance, child report (working-class sample)
	11, 13	Girls	Greater parental acceptance, child report (working-class sample)
Cox 1970	11-13 (100)	Girls	Perceive fathers as more loving, less rejecting
		None	Perception of maternal love and rejection
Droppleman & Schaefer[R] 1963	12 (165)	Girls	More love and nurturance from both parents (child interview)
M. Hoffman & Saltzstein 1967	12 (270 & available mothers & fathers)	Girls	More affection from mother, father; child report (middle SES)
		None	Parental affection (mother and father interviews)
	12 (174)	Girls	More affection from mother, father; child report (lower SES)
T. Miller 1971	13 (35)	Girls	More empathy, genuineness, and positive regard from mother (inner city black; mother questionnaire)
	13 (99)	None	Empathy, genuineness, and positive regard from mother (white suburban sample; mother questionnaire)

(continued)

TABLE 9.4 *(cont.)*

Study	Age and *N*	Difference	Comment
Bronfenbrenner[R] 1960	15 (192)	Girls	Tendency for more affection, especially from father (child questionnaire)
Wyer 1965	18 (889)	Women	Acceptance by mother (mother ratings of child)
		None	Father's acceptance (father ratings of child)

Restrictiveness

Another child-rearing dimension of some importance is the restrictiveness (vs. autonomy-granting) dimension. Mitchell (1968)[R] found that mother rhesus monkeys restrained their female infants more than their male infants. In a number of factor analyses of the behavior of human parents, the restrictiveness dimension has emerged as relatively distinct from the warmth-hostility dimension. Furthermore, those who assume that there is a sex difference with respect to the amount of independent or exploratory behavior children show attribute the difference sometimes to parental tendencies to allow children of one sex more freedom than is allowed to the other. In the early study by Sears et al. (1957)[R], sex differences were not found in this area of parental behavior. Mothers placed similar limits on boys and girls with respect to how far away from the house they were allowed to go. The mother checked on the child's whereabouts equally often when the child was out of sight, and allowed no more freedom to one sex than to the other when it came to making noise or being rough with household objects. Similarly, mothers held similar expectations for daughters and sons with respect to the kind of self-help they should be capable of: demands were similar for being able to dress themselves, take care of their own clothes, and wait on themselves at the table. Nakamura and Rogers (1969) have made a useful distinction between what they call "assertive autonomy" and "practical autonomy." The former refers to a child's acts of independence that do not have labor-saving value for the mother; the latter, by contrast, involves the child's being helpful to the mother by waiting on himself. As we have noted above, the Sears study found no sex differences in granting autonomy of either kind. The bulk of more recent studies have had similar results (see Table 9.5). The studies that have identified any differential treatment of boys and girls have more often found greater independence-granting to girls than boys. For example, in Radin's (1973) recent work with parents of 4-year-old children, both interview data and direct observations of parent-child interaction have been collected. Scores are summarized into an overall restrictiveness

TABLE 9.5
Restrictions, Low Encouragement of Independence

Study	Age and N	Difference	Comment
White House Conference[R] 1936	0-12 mos (4,100)	None	Restriction of play area (mother interview)
Allaman et al. 1972	0-80 mos (95)	None	Mother restrictiveness; coerciveness of mother's suggestions (home observation)
	0-10 yrs (65)	None	Same measures as above
Tasch[R] 1952	0-17 yrs (160)	Girls	Father concerned about child's safety (father interview)
Beckwith 1972	7-11 mos (24 adoptive mo-inf pairs)	Boys	Mother's restrictiveness, particularly mother with only high school education
F. Pedersen & Robson 1969	8, 9½ mos (45)	Girls	Father apprehensive over infant's well-being (mother interview)
D. Stayton et al. 1971	9-12 mos (25)	None	Maternal control over child (home observation)
Clarke-Stewart 1973	9-18 mos (36)	None	Mother's restrictiveness and directiveness (home observation, longitudinal sample)
Minton et al. 1971	27 mos (90)	Boys	Mother gives "simple" prohibition to child (trend, $p < .09$)
		Girls	Mother concerned about physical danger to child; gives "directive" prohibition (home observation)
Block 1972	3 (90)	Boys	Father: "I have firm rules for my child"
		None	Mother: "I have firm rules for my child"
		Boys	Father does not encourage child to be independent of him
		None	Mother: "I encourage my child to be independent of me"
Nakamura & Rogers 1969	3 (39)	Boys	Low expectations for "assertive autonomy" by father
		None	Low expectations for "assertive autonomy" by mother
		Girls	Low expectations for "practical autonomy" by mother
		None	Low expectations for "practical autonomy" by father
Baumrind 1971	3-4 (293 parents)	Boys	More firm enforcement for father and trend ($p < .1$) of more firm enforcement from mother
		None	Mother's and father's encouragement of independence and individuality, directiveness; father values conformity, father authoritarianism (home observation)
	3-4 (415 parents)	None	Mother and father: firm enforcement, authoritarianism, early maturity demands, value of conformity, promotion of nonconformity (parent interviews)

(continued)

TABLE 9.5 *(cont.)*

Study	Age and N	Difference	Comment
Baumrind & Black 1967	3-4 (95)	Boys	Father's restrictions on child's initiative (no difference–mother)
		Girls	Mother's demands for obedience, strictures about neatness (no difference–father)
		None	Mother and father: maturity expectations (permissiveness for exploration, rewarding of self-sufficiency), strictness (care of family property, aggression toward other children, television, responsibilities about orderliness), encouragement of independence (contact with other adults, introduction to new experiences) (parent interviews)
Blayney 1973	4 (29)	None	Father's protectiveness, restrictiveness (observation)
Callard 1968	4 (80)	Girls	Lateness of age recommended by mother for independence granting
Newson & Newson 1968	4 (700)	None	Level of restrictions and demands vis-à-vis bedtime, table behavior, neatness, physical mobility (mother interview)
Radin 1973	4 (52)	Boys	Mother's restrictiveness (observation of mother-child interaction during mother interview; low SES, multiracial sample)
Bee et al. 1969	4-5 (114)	None	Mother's use of control statements
Hatfield et al. 1967	4-5 (40)	Boys	Mother restricts, punishes independence; directiveness $(p < .1)$
		Girls	Mother's concern over water play (structured observation)
		None	Mother's pressure, reward for independence; pressure for obedience; concern over neatness, orderliness
Rothbart 1971	5 (56)	Girls	"Anxious intrusions" by mother while child performs task (structured observation)
Sears et al.[R] 1957	5 (379)	None	Level of restrictions and demands; neatness, TV watching, household tasks, bedtime, table manners, physical mobility (mother interview)
J. Gordon & Smith[R] 1965	6-7 (48)	None	Maternal strictness (mother interview)
Armentrout & Burger 1972	9-13 (635)	Boys	Greater parental psychological control (child's report)
		None	Firmness of parental control (child report, lower-middle SES)
Thomas 1971	18-21 (60 parent-child pairs)	Women	Low "permissiveness" (parent and S interview, politically conservative sample)
		None	Permissiveness (liberal sample)

scale. Radin finds (personal communication) that mothers are significantly more restrictive with boys than with girls. Baumrind (1971) finds that both mothers and fathers use firmer enforcement with sons than with daughters —that is, once a direction has been given, they are more likely to follow it up to make sure that a boy has complied with it. Baumrind also finds, however, that boys and girls are given equal encouragement for "independent individuality." In the Hatfield et al. (1967) study, mothers were more likely to restrict the independent movements of sons—and more likely to punish independence—than of daughters. When it came to the kinds of independence that were helpful to the mother, mothers did exert pressure for the child to be independent, and rewarded independence, but sons and daughters were treated equally in these respects.

The Newson and Newson study in England (1968) found no sex differences in the range of movement inside and outside the home that was allowed to the child at age 4, or in the demands the mother made for the child to do things by himself rather than asking for help. Their study is a longitudinal one, and they have collected socialization data at successive points in the child's development. At the time of this writing, the data for age 7 are being analyzed. At this age, for the first time in the Newsons' study of this large group of families, a substantial difference has begun to emerge in the treatment of sons and daughters. Daughters are receiving more of what the Newsons call "chaperonage." For example, mothers are much more likely to meet a daughter after school and escort her home. Although the chaperonage difference is very clear, this does not imply that girls are restricted with respect to all aspects of independent behavior. Girls are allowed to make as many decisions as boys about where they wish to go and what they wish to do. It is only that their whereabouts must be known and that they are more often in the company of an adult. Probably the greater chaperonage of girls stems directly from the greater danger of molestation—a danger that, although often elaborated in maternal fantasies, is also quite real. Possibly there is also some anticipation of whatever chaperonage the parents will deem suitable when their daughters reach adolescence. It is interesting that this particular difference in the socialization of boys and girls occurs so late. During the preschool years, of course, both of the sexes are watched and accompanied and their whereabouts are carefully monitored, so that in a sense the issue does not yet arise.

To summarize: during the preschool years, there is a trend in some measures toward greater restriction of boys, but the findings from study to study are not consistent, and the bulk of the evidence is that there is little or no difference in the socialization of boys and girls when it comes to independence-granting.

Reactions to the Child's Dependency

The term "dependency weaning" has sometimes been used to describe the process whereby a parent who has consistently given help or affection whenever the child wanted it begins to detach the child by ignoring such demands, guiding the child into more independent actions, or sometimes actively pushing the child away. Do parents begin dependency weaning at an earlier age if the child is a son? Do they become more irritated over a son's dependency demands? Mischel (1970^R, p. 49) says: "In regard to dependency, the average difference between the sexes . . . seems consistent with the widely assumed greater permissiveness for dependency by females as opposed to males in our culture." There is evidence that reward for dependency is indeed associated with high (or increased) levels of dependent behavior in children (see Maccoby and Masters 1970^R, pp. 141–42). But as Mischel notes, the prevalent view that the amount of reward by socializing agents for this behavior is a function of the child's sex is usually an *assumption*—little evidence is cited from direct observation or parent interviews concerning how parents do in fact handle dependency bids from sons as compared with daughters. Table 9.6 summarizes studies that do report data on this subject.

There are four observational studies cited. Two of these (Clarke-Stewart 1973, Baumrind 1971) report no difference in the way parents respond to dependency supplications from sons and daughters. In the Serbin et al. (1973) study, children and their teachers were observed in nursery school. Boys and girls equally often solicited help from their teachers, but teachers responded to a higher proportion of boys' solicitations. The teachers' response to children's seeking of proximity, on the other hand, was not differentiated as to sex. The girls more frequently sought proximity, but the probability of a teacher response, once a child did seek proximity, was similar for boys and girls. (We do not know to what extent male teachers would make similar differentiations.) In the Hatfield et al. study (1967), boys were more frequently punished by their mothers for dependency bids, but, as noted in the previous section, they were also more frequently punished for *independent* behavior. It appears, then, that these maternal reactions are part of the more general picture of greater punitiveness to boys (discussed below); they do not appear to reflect any specific shaping of dependent, as distinct from independent, behavior.

Two of the studies cited in Table 9.6 involve the use of tapes of a child's voice, identified to some parents as the voice of a boy, and to others as the voice of a girl. The parent was asked to say what his reaction would be if his own son (or daughter for those hearing the girl's voice) said the things that had been taped. Some of the remarks made by the child's voice

TABLE 9.6
Reward (Permissiveness) for Dependency

Study	Age and N	Difference	Comment
Clarke-Stewart 1973	9-18 mos (36)	None	Mother's responsiveness to infant's social signals (home observation; longitudinal)
Block 1972	3 (90)	Girls	Father feels it important to comfort child when upset (questionnaire; trend, $p < .1$)
		None	Importance to mother of comforting child when upset (questionnaire)
Baumrind 1971	3-4 (293 parents)	None	Mother and father discourage emotional dependency and infantile behavior (home observation)
	3-4 (415 parents)	None	Mother and father discourage infantile behavior (parent questionnaire)
Rothbart & Maccoby[R] 1966	3-4 (98 mothers, 32 fathers)	Boys	Mother's permissiveness and positive attention to comfort seeking (mother's written response to tape of child's voice)
		Girls	Father's permissiveness and positive attention to comfort seeking (father's written response to taped voice)
		None	Mother's and father's response to help seeking
Serbin et al. 1973	3-4 (225 children, 15 teachers)	Boys	Rate of teacher response to child's solicitation of attention
		None	Rate of teacher response to child's proximity seeking
Baumrind & Black 1967	4 (95)	Boys None	Mother rewards dependency (interview) Father rewards dependency (interview)
Hatfield et al. 1967	4-5 (40)	Girls	Less punishment of dependency (observation; trend, $p < .1$)
		None	Mother rewards dependency
Sears et al.[R] 1957	5 (379)	None	Reward, permissiveness, punishment for dependency (mother interview)
Lambert et al. 1971	6 (73)	Girls	Parental compliance to comfort-seeking requests
		None	Parental compliance to requests for help (mother's and father's response to tape of child's voice)
Levitin & Chananie 1972	6-7 (40 teachers)	None	Teacher's approval of dependent behavior in hypothetical boy or girl (questionnaire)

represented dependency supplications—demands for help or nurturance. The Rothbart and Maccoby (1966)[R] study found that mothers were more permissive toward such demands from boys, and fathers from girls. In the Lambert et al. (1971) study, both French-Canadian and English-Canadian mothers and fathers, when hearing a child's demand for comfort for a minor injury, were more likely to say they would withhold comfort if they believed the child to be a boy. There was no significant difference, by sex of child, in the tendency to give help of other kinds when demanded by the child.

Interview studies have also produced mixed results. In the Baumrind and Black study (1967), mothers of boys were more likely to report that they responded positively to the child's dependency than were mothers of girls. In the Sears et al. study (1957)[R], mothers were asked about their handling of the child's help seeking, attention seeking, and clinging. Mothers of boys and mothers of girls were highly similar in their permissiveness for such behavior, and in the amount of reward and punishment they reported administering for it. In the Block study (1972), fathers reported feeling that it was more important to give comfort to a girl when she was upset than to do so for a boy, but mothers made no such distinction.

Recent work by Osofsky and Oldfield (1971)[R] shows clearly that when a girl behaved dependently, her parents changed their behavior toward her. A structured observation situation was arranged including two tasks, one of which required the child (age 4–6) to seek the parent's help, while the other permitted independent functioning. During the time when the daughter was behaving dependently, both mothers and fathers talked to her more and became more controlling; perhaps more interesting is the fact that fathers, but not mothers, reacted positively to their daughters' increased dependency. It would be interesting to see this same procedure repeated with male subjects. Judging from the Rothbart and Maccoby (1966)[R] findings, it is possible that mothers would react more positively to the dependency bids of sons than daughters. But this remains to be seen. For our present purposes, the salient point is that the Osofsky and Oldfield study did not include subjects of both sexes, so no comparison can be made between the treatment of sons and daughters.

Considering the evidence as a whole, there has been no clear demonstration that one sex received more reinforcement for dependency than the other. As further evidence accumulates, it appears likely that the answer to the initial question will depend upon a much more fine-grained analysis of child behavior—that "dependency" is much too broad a category. If any sex differences do emerge, it appears that the degree and even the direction of such differences may depend both upon the sex of the *parent* and upon what particular aspect of dependency is involved. A good hypothesis is that instrumental dependency (help seeking in pursuit of some goal other than affectional contact itself) will not be rewarded more in girls; in fact, the reverse may be the case (see Serbin et al. 1973). Possibly a supportive, positive response to a child's display of feelings of all sorts, including a positive response to clinging (whether it is activated by fear or love), is an aspect of socialization that will eventually be more evident in parental responses to girls. At present, however, the evidence does not exist to support such a generalization. It is well to remember that there is very little difference between the sexes in the frequency or intensity with which dependent behavior occurs (see Chapter 4); hence, it should not be surprising that patterns of differential reinforcement have not become apparent.

Reactions to the Child's Aggression

It is commonly asserted that parents are more likely to permit or encourage aggression in boys than in girls, and that this is one of the reasons boys are more aggressive. Frequently cited in support of this view is the early report by Sears, Maccoby, and Levin (1957)[n] that mothers of boys said they allowed their children to show more aggression toward neighborhood children (particularly in self-defense) than did mothers of daughters. Furthermore, mothers of boys reported themselves as being more permissive than mothers of girls when a child was aggressive toward its parents, although the two sexes received approximately equal amounts of punishment for such behavior. More recent research calls for reevaluation of the question of differential parental reinforcement of aggression in the two sexes.

Lambert et al. (1971), in their study of French-Canadian and English-Canadian parents, found that both mothers and fathers reacted more harshly to a show of temper from a boy than to the identical behavior from a girl (see Table 9.7). Minton et al. (1971), observing 2-year-olds and their mothers at home, found that boys were more likely to be reprimanded for aggression toward the mother than were the girls. The observational study by Serbin et al. (1973) in nursery school classrooms showed not only that boys were more likely to commit an aggressive or destructive act, but that, once such an act had occurred, the probability of the teacher's responding to it was greater if the actor was a boy. The nature of the teacher's response also differed for the two sexes. When girls were aggressive, the teacher usually "softly reprimanded" them. When boys were aggressive, the teacher's response was more often a loud reprimand, restraint, or talking to the child and giving directions concerning desired behavior.

In a study of 40 preschoolers and their families, involving both behavior observation and parent interviews, Sears et al. (1965)[n] found no sex differences in the permissiveness of the parents toward a child's display of aggression toward the parents. Nor did the amount of punishment for such behavior differ by sex of child. Surprisingly, the parents in this study also said they did not press their sons, more than their daughters, to hit back when attacked by a neighbor child. In a similar vein, with a much larger sample studied in England through mother interviews, the Newsons (1968) found no differences between the mothers of sons and the mothers of daughters in their reactions to the children's aggression. Parents of boys

TABLE 9.7

Permissiveness (Reward) for Aggression (or Competitiveness)

Study	Age and N	Difference	Comment
Tasch[R] 1952	0-17 (85)	Boys	Father expects more aggressiveness; worried if unaggressive
		None	Father worries over disobedience (father interview)
D. Stayton et al. 1971	9-12 mos (25)	None	Frequency of discipline-oriented physical interventions by mother (home observation)
Minton et al. 1971	27 mos (90)	Girls	Less often reprimanded for aggression toward mother (home observation)
Block 1972	3 (90)	Boys	Mother and father believe competitive games are beneficial (questionnaire)
		Girls	Father allows anger toward himself (questionnaire)
Baumrind & Black 1967	3-4 (95)	Boys	Mother tolerates verbal protest, believes in less control of parent-directed verbal and/or physical aggression (interview)
		None	Father's tolerance of verbal protest, belief in control of parent-directed verbal and/or physical aggression (interview)
Lapidus 1972	3-4 (30)	Boys	Mother makes self-deprecatory statements during game
		None	Mother lets child win, encourages cooperation (observation)
Rothbart & Maccoby[R] 1966	3-4 (98 mothers, 32 fathers)	None	Mother's and father's reaction to other-directed aggression (written response to tape of child's voice)
		Boys	Mother permits aggression toward herself
		Girls	Father permits aggression toward himself
Sears et al.[R] 1953	3-5 (40)	None	Mother's responsiveness to aggression (interview)
Serbin et al. 1973	3-5 (225 pupils, 15 teachers)	Girls	Lower likelihood of teacher response to child's aggressive or destructive ($p < .08$) behavior; fewer loud reprimands for disruptive act
J. Gordon & Smith[R] 1965	3-4, 6-7 (48)	None	Permissiveness for aggression (mother interview)
Newson & Newson 1968	4 (700)	None	Mother does not intervene in children's quarrels; encourages, permits aggression toward parents (English sample)
Sears et al.[R] 1965 and pers. communication	4-5 (40)	None	Permissiveness of aggression toward parents Demands aggression toward peers (parent interview and observation)
Sears et al.[R] 1957	5 (379)	Boys	Mother more permissive of aggression toward parents and peers; mother's encouragement to fight back if attacked (interview)
		None	Punishment for aggression

(continued)

TABLE 9.7 *(cont.)*

Study	Age and N	Difference	Comment
Lambert et al. 1971	6 (73)	Girls	Parental acceptance of show of anger (parent response to taped hypothetical situations, English-Canadian and French-Canadian samples)
		None	Parental acceptance of insolence
		Boys	Mother's acceptance of insolence (French-Canadian sample only)
		Girls	Father's acceptance of insolence (French-Canadian sample only)
		None	Parent's reaction to argument between child and baby, and between child and baby after child is hurt
		Boys	Mother sides more with child in argument between child and guest (French-Canadian sample only)
		Girls	Father sides more with child in argument between child and guest
Levitin & Chananie 1972	6-7 (40 teachers)	None	Teacher approval of aggressive behavior in hypothetical boy or girl (questionnaire)

and girls were equally likely to say that they allowed their children to settle their own quarrels with neighbor children or siblings; equally likely to tell a boy or girl to hit back when attacked; and equally unwilling to permit a child to be insolent or "cheeky" toward the parents. In the Baumrind and Black (1967) study, however, the mothers of boys did say, during interviews, that they were more tolerant of resistive behavior (protests, aggression toward the parents) than did the mothers of girls.

Taken together, the series of studies summarized in Table 9.7 certainly does not present a consistent picture of greater permissiveness toward boys' aggressive behavior. The observational studies of parents' reactions to their children's aggression have all been done in the home or in a contrived experimental situation where other children are not present; thus information is available from these studies only on socialization pressures directed toward the child when he is aggressive toward the parents or toward siblings. Only interview data are available concerning what a parent does when children fight with other children outside the home. Observations are needed of the way that parents, when they supervise a play group, handle aggressive behavior among children. And data concerning father reactions would be especially useful; it may be that fathers, but not mothers, encourage their sons to fight. Still, it is in the area of aggression more than any other sphere of behavior that we find evidence for cross-sex effects, with fathers being especially severe toward boys. Rothbart and Maccoby (1966)[R] found that mothers were more willing to accept angry behavior toward themselves from sons than from daughters, whereas fathers reacted in the reverse manner, being more permissive of aggression from daughters than from sons. Lambert et al. (1971) replicated this cross-sex effect, finding that fathers would accept "insolence" from daughters more readily than from sons, and that if a child got into an argument with a guest, the father would tend to take his daughter's side but take the guest's side against a son. Mothers, on the contrary, accepted insolence more readily from sons, and sided with their sons against the guest, but not with their daughters. Block (1972) found that fathers of boys were more likely than fathers of girls to say: "I don't allow my child to get angry with me."

The Sears et al. (1965)[R] and Newson (1968) findings concerning parents' attitudes about allowing a child to fight with other children are puzzling, especially in view of Tasch's report (1952)[R] that fathers, during an interview, say that they tend to worry if a son is unaggressive (unwilling to defend himself), whereas they feel little such concern over an unaggressive daughter. Some of the inconsistency in the data no doubt stems from different understandings of what is implied by "aggression." At least in middle-class families, with which most of the research has been done, parents attempt to train children of both sexes to solve their interpersonal problems through reasoning and negotiation rather than physical force; especially as children grow older, they are unlikely to draw much parental approval for physical fighting. At the same time, parents do not want their children to be the victims of other children's aggressions, and many do value a kind of competitive toughness in their children, which presumably parents prefer to see expressed in sports and in forms of dominance behavior short of physical force.

Is competitive toughness more encouraged in boys than in girls? It seems a good hypothesis that this would be so. Observational work on parental encouragement of competitive behavior is very scarce. Lapidus (1972) did observe mother-son pairs and mother-daughter pairs while the mother was teaching a cooperative marble game to her nursery-school-age child (see Chapter 6 for details of the procedure). The game was designed in such a way that individual players could earn "points" only if the other player allowed him to. The hypothesis of the study was that mothers would let their sons win, thus encouraging them in competitive behavior, whereas they would insist on taking turns with their daughters. The results did not sustain the hypothesis. Although boys did get somewhat more points than girls in competition with their mothers, the difference was not significant. Mothers quite uniformly encouraged cooperative behavior with both sons and daughters. Mothers did not explicitly allow boys to take marbles out of turn more often than girls, or show approval when they won a point. The only significant sex difference was that mothers were more likely to make self-deprecatory comments to sons than to daughters. For example, a mother would occasionally say to a son: "I don't play this game very well," or "I must be doing something wrong." Such remarks were very seldom made to daughters. Preliminary data from a study by Williams (1973)[n] on fathers' encouragement of a son's or daughter's competitive behavior suggest that fathers too do not differentiate in this respect.

This kind of study does not reveal whether the parents are encouraging their children's competitiveness toward other children; it is quite possible that a mother would encourage cooperative behavior when the child is interacting with her, but do so less consistently when it came to cooperative or competitive behavior with age-mates. A more critical problem is that the Madsen marble game is designed so that competitive behavior is self-defeating; in many real-life situations, rewards are a scarce commodity that can be obtained only by defeating another person. Parental encouragement of competitiveness needs to be studied in relation to such situations. The primary implication of the Lapidus study is that in a situation where cooperativeness is a productive strategy, mothers are as likely to try to teach this strategy to a son as to a daughter.

Encouragement of Sex-typed Activities

To what extent do parents actively support the development of sex-typed activities and interests in the two sexes? Although quantitative reports are not available, it would appear obvious that when Christmas or birthdays approach, parents are likely to buy dolls or toy cookstoves for their daughters and trucks or electric trains for their sons. Whether these choices occur because the parents are responding to already developed preferences expressed by the children, or whether their purchases precede and guide the development of such preferences, we do not know—it is likely that the influence works in both directions. Parental sex-typing pressures need to be studied in the earliest portions of children's lives, and little such observation has been done. In two recent experiments (Jacklin et al. 1973), a variety of toys was available in a playroom, and records were made of mothers' choices of toys to offer to their 13- and 14-month-old children during a free-play session. The toys included stuffed animals, robots, a toy workbench, and a musical ferris wheel. There was no evidence that the mother chose different toys to offer to a son, as compared with a daughter. The children's toy choices differed by sex, but the mothers' did not. However, the available toys did not include some of the most highly sex-typed ones, and we do not doubt that many parental toy choices are sex-typed, and that children are actively discouraged from playing with sex-inappropriate toys. When parents buy sex-typed toys for their children, this of course can have a long-term effect, since the toys remain part of the child's daily environment for a considerable period.

It is interesting to consider whether boys have been more heavily conditioned than girls to avoid opposite-sex interests and activities. Intuitively, it seems that a boy would be subject to more disapproval for being a "sissy" than a girl would for being a tomboy. As reported earlier, Hartup, Moore, and Sager (1963)[R] found boys were more likely to avoid the sex-inappropriate toys than were girls. The fact that boys' avoidance of feminine toys was especially marked when an experimenter was present suggested that the boys had previously been subjected to more socialization pressure than were the girls to adopt appropriately sex-typed activities. Direct evidence on the relevant parent behavior is available from two studies.

Lansky (1967) presented parents of preschool children with hypothetical situations in which a boy or girl chose either a masculine or feminine activity. When a girl chose a boyish activity, neither mothers nor fathers seemed especially concerned. When a boy chose girlish activities, however, both parents reacted quite negatively, and this was especially true of fathers. Fathers were also somewhat more likely to show positive reactions when a boy chose boyish activities than when a girl chose feminine ones. But the primary sex differences were found in negative parental reactions to cross-sex activity choices by boys. Similar results have been obtained by Fling and Manosevitz (1972). They studied families with nursery-school-age children, asking the parents to make "It test" choices for their children and, in an interview, inquiring about parental guidance of the children toward or away from certain sex-typed activities. Parents were asked how strongly they would object to their children's engaging in any of the activities they had omitted in their choices for It. Scores were derived that represented the extent of their discouragement of a child's sex-inappropriate activities. Both mothers and fathers chose more sex-appropriate activities for their sons in the It test than they did for girls. Both parents much more strongly discouraged sex-inappropriate behavior in sons than daughters. Positive encouragement for sex-appropriate activities was not so clearly biased toward heavier pressure on the boys; mothers of girls encouraged their daughters somewhat more than their sons in this respect. On the whole, the results of the two studies clearly sustain the Hartup and Moore interpretation of their findings: more social pressure against inappropriate sex typing is directed at boys than at girls.

Fathers' emotional reactions can be powerful, as illustrated by the comment made by a father who was asked in an interview whether he would be disturbed by indications of "femininity" in his son: "Yes, I would be, very very much. Terrifically disturbed—couldn't tell you the extent of my disturbance. I can't *bear* female characteristics in a man. I abhor them" (E. Goodenough 1957, p. 310). In view of the strength of these feelings, it is not surprising to find fathers playing an active role in guiding their sons away from "sissy" behavior. In addition, however, a father's reactions are important in developing the femininity of his daughter. There are certain subtle ways in which he shows interest in and appreciation of his daughter's femininity. Some clues to this are to be found in comments by fathers reported by Goodenough. She asked parents to describe their children's personalities. Most of the children being described were 2 or 3 years old. The parents began by describing the things that seemed most salient to them in their children's personalities. Then they were asked: "Is your child more masculine or more feminine in personality? Give some examples of what you mean." Here are some of the things that fathers said about their little daughters: "A bit of a flirt, arch and playful with people, a pretended coyness." "Soft and cuddly and loving. She cuddles and flatters in subtle ways." "I notice her coyness and flirting, 'come up and see me sometime' approach. She loves to cuddle. She's going to be sexy—I get my wife annoyed when I say this." Ten out of 20 fathers of girls described their daughters in similar terms.

These comments no doubt reflect to some degree what the little girls' behavior was really like; but they also reflect the fathers' perceptions. The point of interest here is that the fathers appeared to enjoy being flirted with by their daughters; furthermore, the mothers in the Goodenough study reported instances in which their husbands had put pressure on them to dress their daughters in dresses rather than pants, to keep their hair long, etc., when the mother would not have considered it especially important for their daughters to look dainty and feminine at this young age. Fathers appear to want their daughters to fit their image of a sexually attractive female person, within the limits of what is appropriate for a child, and they play the masculine role vis-à-vis their daughters as well as their wives. This may or may not generate rivalry between mother and daughter, but there can be little doubt that it is a potent force in the girl's development of whatever behavior is defined as "feminine" by her father.

Parental Responses to Children's Sexuality

In most cultures, there is a double standard of adult sexual morality. Women are expected to be modest and, to some degree, chaste. Men are allowed (or even expected) to have a more active sex life and engage in more sexual exploration. In encounters between the sexes, men are expected to take the initiative. These cultural definitions of the role to be played by the two sexes are central to the meaning of "masculinity" and "femininity" in any culture where the definitions exist. It might certainly be expected that the treatment of children would reflect them. We do not know precisely how early in a child's life the socialization for his adult role in courtship and sex might be expected to begin, but it would not be surprising if, even in early childhood, parents emphasized the importance of modesty more with daughters, and were less permissive toward them in dealing with overt displays of sexual activity and interest.

This is an area of socialization, of course, in which direct observation of parent-child interaction yields little information. For the most part the child's sexual behavior occurs either when the child is alone (and is revealed only when the mother "catches" him), when he is with other children and adults are not present, or in the intimacy of bathtime and bedtime. We must rely upon parental reports of such instances and their outcomes for our information on how sexual behavior is socialized.

Three interview studies have obtained data on socialization as it is directed toward childhood sexuality. The first is the Sears, Maccoby, and Levin study of a group of 379 families in the Greater Boston area (1957)[R]. The second is the small-sample study by Sears et al. (1965)[R] done in a suburban community in California. The third is the study of 700 English families living in or near Nottingham, conducted by the Newsons (1968). In each of these studies, detailed information was obtained concerning the parents' reactions to their children's masturbation and to any instances of sex play with other children. Parents were also asked what kind of information they gave their children on sexual matters, and whether children were allowed to be seen, or to see other family members, in the nude. In both England and the United States, working-class parents were considerably less permissive toward children's sexuality than were middle-class parents. But in none of the studies did any difference whatever emerge in the treatment of boys and girls. Parents were equally severe in their reactions to masturbation, whether it occurred in a son or daughter; they were equally likely, or unlikely, to allow the child to be seen in the nude by other family members; they were equally likely to give the child information about sex; and they reacted similarly to instances of sex play with neighbor children, regardless of the sexes of the children involved.

It is possible, of course, that there are counteracting tendencies involved here. According to the Sears hypotheses, discussed below, both parents ought to be made more anxious by sexuality in a boy, and hence they should insist more firmly on his being modest. On the other hand, since modesty is going to be more important for a girl later in life, they ought to begin training her more consistently for this behavior than they would a son. If both factors are at work, they might cancel one another and yield what has been found—no difference in the training of the two sexes. In any case, no positive evidence has emerged that parents are engaging in specific sexual socialization that prepares children differentially for "double standards" of adult sexual life. Of course, the sex information that is given to both boys and girls—that babies grow inside the mother and that the father plants the "seed" for the baby—fosters the development of the children's sex-role concepts, but this development does not stem from differential treatment of the two sexes with respect to information-giving.

Physical Punishment and Other Negative Sanctions

There are some fairly clear differences in the amount and kind of discipline directed at boys and girls. As Table 9.8 shows, with few exceptions

TABLE 9.8
Physical Punishment (Power Assertion)

Study	Age and N	Difference	Comment
Tasch[R] 1952	0-17 (85)	Boys	Use of physical punishment (father interview)
Minton et al. 1971	2 (90)	Boys	Maternal use of physical punishment (home observation; trend, $p < .1$)
Block 1972	3 (90)	Boys	Father believes "physical punishment is best way of discipline" (trend, $p < .1$)
		None	Mother believes "physical punishment is best way of discipline"
		Boys	Mother does not "find it difficult to punish child"
		None	Father "finds it difficult to punish child"
J. Kagan & Lemkin[R] 1960	3-6 (67)	Girls	Child perceives father as punitive
J. Gordon & Smith[R] 1965	3-4, 6-7 (48)	None	Physical punishment (mother interview)
Baumrind & Black 1967	4 (95)	Boys	Physical punishment by father (father interview)
		None	Physical punishment by mother (mother interview)
Newson & Newson 1968	4 (700)	Boys	Mother's use of physical punishment (mother interview)
Sears et al.[R] 1957	5 (379)	Boys	Use of physical punishment (mother interview)
Simpson[R] 1935	5-9 (500)	Boys	Father spanking (child interviews)
		Girls	Mother spanking (child interviews)
		Girls	Father spanking (child's stories to pictures)
Siegelman 1965	9-11 (212)	Boys	Physical punishment by mother and father (child report)
Zussman 1973	10 (44)	None	Parental use of power assertive techniques (mother, child report)
M. Hoffman & Saltzstein 1967	12 (270 + available mothers & fathers)	Boys	Power assertion from mother and father (child report, middle SES sample)
		None	Parental use of power assertion (mother and father interviews)
	12 (174)	None	Power assertion from mother and father (child report, lower SES sample)
Bronfenbrenner[R] 1960	15 (192)	Boys	Physical punishment received from both father and mother (child report)

boys receive more physical punishment than girls do. This finding is consistent over a wide range of ages, and is found in both interview and observational studies. Boys also appear to receive more of what M. Hoffman and Saltzstein (1967) have called "simple power assertion"; this may take the form of physical punishment, but there are other forms of direct coercion, such as picking the child up and moving him from an undesired activity toward a desired one. Feshbach (1972) tabulated aversive maternal behaviors of all sorts in a mother-child interaction session in which the mother was attempting to teach her 4-year-old child to solve a puzzle. The sample included middle- and lower-class mother-child pairs, and each of these social-class groups was composed of two racial groups. Boys received more "negative reinforcement" in each middle-class racial group. Minton et al. (1971), observing 27-month-olds with their mothers at home, report that the boys receive somewhat more physical punishment, and that when they do something disapproved (or seem about to do so) their mothers are more likely to prohibit the action by simply saying "No!" With girls, prohibitions are softened or deflected with suggestions of something else the girl might do instead. In a large-scale study done in England, the Newsons (1968) found very few differences indeed in parental treatment of boys and girls up to 4 years old. An exception occurred with respect to physical punishment: boys were "smacked," as the English say, more frequently than girls, and this is consistent with the findings of the earlier American study by Sears, Maccoby, and Levin.

Why do boys receive more physical punishment? The work of Taylor and Epstein with college students (1967) is interesting in relation to this question. They tested the willingness of subjects to administer shocks to other college students who were behaving in a deliberately uncooperative, irritating way. Both male and female subjects showed much greater reluctance to shock a confederate they thought was a girl. There seemed to be a deep-seated prohibition against inflicting physical pain on girls. Consistent with this is Block's (1972) finding that mothers report they find it more difficult to punish their daughters than their sons. We may speculate about why this reluctance to hurt girls exists: is it because they are believed to feel pain more intensely? Because they are physically weaker and less able to defend themselves against attack? Because they are potential child-bearers? It would be interesting to know how cross-culturally universal the prohibition is, and under what conditions it breaks down.

There is another explanation for the more frequent spanking of boys. Perhaps they simply "need" it more! Minton et al. (1971) have done a sequential analysis in which they find that mothers tend to escalate their pressures according to the demands of the situation. The mother begins a sequence with a simple command to the child to do something or to stop doing something. If the child complies, the sequence ends there. If the child does not comply, the mother raises her voice, or forces compliance by physically moving the child out of harm's way, or spanks (this latter rarely). As noted in Chapter 6, Minton et al. find that girls obey the first command more frequently than boys, and hence the later escalating steps tend not to occur for girls. Furthermore, one instance of compliance or noncompliance affects subsequent episodes. In the Minton study, if a child did not obey one command from the parents, the next time an issue came

TABLE 9.9
Nonphysical Discipline

Study	Age and *N*	Difference	Comment
Minton et al. 1971	27 mos (90)	Boys	Mother's simple prohibitions (observation; trend, $p < .09$)
		Girls	Mother's directive prohibitive
		None	Mother totally prohibitive
Fagot & Patterson 1969	3 (36)	None	Criticism by female nursery school teachers (observation)
Baumrind 1971	3-4 (293 parents)	None	Mother's and father's willingness to express anger or displeasure to child; father authoritarianism (home observation)
	3-4 (415 parents)	None	Mother's and father's anger with child, mother and father authoritarianism (questionnaire)
Baumrind & Black 1967	3-4 (95)	Boys	Mother uses deprivation of privileges (mother interview)
		None	Father uses deprivation of privileges (father interview)
		Girls	Mother uses withdrawal of love (mother interview)
		None	Father uses withdrawal of love (father interview)
		None	Frightening the child (mother, father interview)
Serbin et al. 1973	3-5 (225 pupils, 15 teachers)	Boys	Teacher uses loud reprimands
		None	Teacher uses soft reprimands
Feshbach 1972	4 (104)	Boys	Mother uses negative reinforcement in teaching child to solve puzzle (black and white, middle SES sample)
		None	Black and white, low SES sample
Bee et al. 1969	4-5 (114)	Boys	Mother expresses disapproval of child's action in waiting room (black and white, lower SES)
		None	Mother gives negative feedback during problem-solving interaction (white middle SES)
Sears et al.[R] 1965	4-5 (40)	Boys	Severity of toilet training and child's reaction (mother questionnaire)
Rothbart 1971	5 (56)	None	Mother criticizes, says child is incorrect during problem solving
Sears et al.[R] 1957	5 (379)	Girls	Mother's withdrawal of love (mother interview)
Davis 1967	6-7 (238)	Boys	Negative comments from teacher (child interview)
Hermans et al. 1972	9-10 (40)	None	Mother and father give negative task-oriented or negative person-oriented reinforcement while child performs 4 tasks (Dutch)

(continued)

TABLE 9.9 *(cont.)*

Study	Age and N	Difference	Comment
Armentrout & Burger 1972	9-13 (635)	Boys	Parental psychological control (child report, lower-middle SES)
Zussman 1973	10 (44)	Boys	Parental use of love-withdrawal techniques (mother, child report)
		Girls	Parental use of teaching techniques (reasoning, discussion, role-taking; mother report)
		None	Parental use of teaching techniques (child report)
W. Meyer & Thompson 1956	11 (78)	Boys	Frequency of teacher disapprovals (classroom observation); receive teacher disapproval (peer nomination, 2 of 3 classrooms)
M. Hoffman & Saltzstein 1967	12 (444)	Girls	Father uses induction (child report, both middle and low SES)
		Girls	Mother uses induction (child report, middle SES only)
		None	Mother and father use love withdrawal (child report, both subsamples)
	12 (129 mothers)	None	Mother uses induction, love withdrawal (interview with middle SES mothers)
	12 (75 fathers)	None	Father uses induction, love withdrawal (interview with middle SES fathers)

up and the parent made a new demand, the parent was likely to move to coercive methods more quickly than he would if his previous demand had had a more satisfactory outcome. Thus a series of episodes in which a child has taken a restrictive posture has cumulative impact, involving increasing amounts of scolding and punishment. Minton et al. (1971) observed children and their mothers in an experimental situation two weeks after their observations in the home; they report that the children who had been punished at home remained a greater distance away from their mothers in the experimental room. Thus parent avoidance may enter into the developing circular process and make it more difficult for the parent to influence the child with the gentler pressures that he might otherwise use.

The observations by Serbin et al. (1973) of teachers and children in a nursery school setting also point to a circular process. Boys more often than girls ignore a teacher's direction. Boys also receive more negative control: they receive more reprimands of all sorts, especially loud reprimands, and they are more likely to be physically restrained (see Table 9.9). But perhaps the most interesting feature of the analysis is that when the frequency of the child's resistive behavior is controlled for, there is still a greater incidence of negative control (per instance of resistive child behavior) directed toward boys. It appears quite possible that this greater tendency of teachers to scold or restrain boys when they do something that calls for teacher intervention may be a product (as in the Minton study) of a history of interactions in which weaker forms of intervention were ineffective.

Praise, Reward, and Positive Feedback

Table 9.10 presents the studies in which the amount of praise, reward, or other positive feedback to the child has been studied. The picture is a mixed one. A number of studies found no sex differences, but those that did usually report that boys receive more positive feedback than girls. Several studies have reported that boys receive both more positive and more negative feedback than girls. In the Serbin et al. (1973) study, nursery school teachers were shown, as noted above, to use more negative feedback with boys, but, as Table 9.10 shows, they also used more praise and longer conversations in response to an action of the child's, and Table 9.4 shows that they hug the boys more often. At an older age, W. Meyer and Thompson (1956) found that boys received both more praise and more disapproval from teachers during class than did girls. Bee et al. (1969) found that lower-class mothers gave their sons more positive feedback during a problem-solving task than they did their daughters, but at the same time they expressed more disapproval of boys' actions while mother and child were in a room waiting for a session to begin. It is clear enough, first of all, that positive and negative feedback are not to be thought of as opposite ends of a single continuum. But beyond this perhaps obvious point, it is more interesting for our present purposes that boys seem to be more often the objects of this dual input system than girls. As we noted on p. 307, it is not clear that parents and teachers have any greater total amount of interaction of all kinds with boys than with girls. The present findings do point to the possibility that parents have more of a certain kind of interaction with boys—how shall this relationship be described? As evaluative? As a relationship of surveillance? Perhaps the fact is that the data on total interaction deal more with the first two years of a child's life, whereas the data on positive and negative discipline tend to come from studies of nursery-school-age children or older. In some situations, boys appear to be more attention-getting, either because they do more things calling for adult response or because parents and teachers see them as having more interesting qualities or potential.

Achievement Pressure

We saw in Chapter 4 that there was little consistent sex difference in the achievement orientation of the two sexes, although there was a tendency for girls to maintain a higher level of interest in academic achievement through the school years. It would be interesting to know whether either sex is subject to more parental pressure for school achievement. The evidence is scanty. Table 9.11 shows observational studies in which mea-

TABLE 9.10

Praise and Reward (Positive Feedback)

Study	Age and N	Difference	Comment
Fagot & Patterson 1969	3 (36)	None	Total reinforcement by female teachers (observation)
Charlesworth & Hartup 1967	3-4 (70)	Boys	Reinforcement from same-age boys (observation)
		Girls	Reinforcement from same-age girls
Serbin et al. 1973	3-4 (225 children, 15 teachers)	Boys	Amount of praise by teacher for participation in appropriate classroom activities
Baumrind & Black 1967	4 (95)	Boys	Father's use of tangible reward (father interview)
		None	Mother's use of tangible reward (mother interview)
Biber et al. 1972	4 (225)	Girls	Teacher gives positive reinforcement during instruction: Montessori and "enrichment" preschools
		None	Positive reinforcement from teacher in "structured academic" preschools
Blayney 1973	4 (29)	Girls	Father demands that child assume self-direction (1 of 3 experimental phases)
		None	Father requests child to assume self-direction
			Father presents child with challenging situation
Feshbach 1972	4 (104)	None	Mother gives positive reinforcement while teaching puzzle to child (black and white, low and middle SES sample)
Hamilton 1972	4 (24)	Girls	Amount of social reinforcement received from adults in nursery school (observation; trend, $p < .1$)
Bee et al. 1969	4-5 (114)	Both	Mother gives positive feedback during problem solving (boys, black and white lower SES; girls, white middle SES)
		None	Mother gives child approval in waiting room situation
Rothbart 1971	5 (56)	None	Amount of praise, number of times mother says child is correct during problem solving
Sears et al.[R] 1957	5 (379)	Girls	Mother's praise (mother interview)
Hermans et al. 1972	9-10 (40)	None	Mother and father give positive task-oriented or positive person-oriented reinforcement while child performs 4 tasks (Dutch)
Meyer & Thompson 1956	11 (78)	Boys	Receive teacher praise (observation: 1 of 3 classrooms)
		None	Receive teacher approval (peer nomination)

TABLE 9.11
Achievement Demands, Pressure.

Study	Age and N	Difference	Comment
Allaman et al. 1972	0-6 yrs (95)	None	Amount of praise or criticism for intellectual performance; standards held by mother and father for intellectual performance
Tasch[R] 1952	0-17 yrs & older (160 & 85 fathers)	Boys	Father's expectation for child to go to college (father interview)
Minton et al. 1971	27 mos (90)	Girls	Mother's pressure for competence (home observation, upper-middle SES only)
Baumrind 1971	3-4 (293 parents)	None	Parents' expectation of household help (home observation)
Callard 1968	4 (80)	None	Achievement-inducing scale (parent questionnaire)
I. Hilton 1967	4 (60)	None	While children attempted to solve a series of puzzles: amount of direct help and number of task-oriented suggestions, critical or supportive statements (observation)
Hatfield et al. 1967	4-5 (40)	Boys	Mother's pressure for achievement (observation)
Rothbart 1971	5 (56)	None	Maternal pressure for success on memory task; mother's expectations of child's performance on picture and puzzle tasks
		Girls	Mother's "anxious intrusions" into child's task performance
Sears et al.[R] 1957	5 (379)	Boys	Mother expects child to go to college
Greenglass 1971a	9-10, 13-14 (132)	None	Mother's demands during joint problem solving (observation)
Buck & Austrin 1971	14-16 (100)	Girls	Mother's concern with child's intellectual achievements, high expectancy levels, high minimal academic standards (black sample)
T. Hilton & Berglund 1971	14-16 (1,859)	Boys	Mother wants college-prep child to continue education beyond high school (child questionnaire)
		Boys	Father wants college-prep child to continue education beyond high school (significant for age 16 only; child questionnaire)
		None	Vocational sample, same measures as above

sures have been taken of the amount of pressure a mother puts on a young child for competent task performance; there is no consistent tendency for either sex to be singled out for such pressure. When it comes to expectations for the child to go to college, however, it is clear that parents more often hold such an expectation for sons than daughters. Whether the belief that a son will, and should, go to college is accompanied by greater pressure on him to prepare himself academically is something that existing studies do not reveal. One problem in interpreting data is that when parents are asked such questions as "How important is it to you for your child to do well in school?" or "How concerned are you about your child's grades?" the parent may answer in terms of worry over the child's doing poorly, rather than in terms of insisting that the child shall be an outstanding student. More information is needed concerning such things as parents' reactions to report cards, and the extent to which they monitor the homework of sons and daughters during grade school and especially high school years.

EVALUATION OF HYPOTHESES

Sex-typed Shaping

Having summarized the research on differential socialization, we return to the hypotheses with which this chapter began. The first issue is whether parents (and other socializing agents) treat children of the two sexes so as to shape them toward behavior deemed appropriate for their own sex. Do parents reward sex-appropriate behavior and punish or otherwise negatively sanction inappropriate behavior? The question of what kind of behavior is considered by parents to be sex-appropriate perhaps deserves brief discussion here. Traditionally this concept encompasses a wide range. In previous centuries not only the way a person dressed, but also the kind of work he could engage in, the places he could go, and the kind of recreational activities he engaged in were almost completely determined by his sex. This has changed radically in recent years, but the rate of change varies among cultural groups, and, for many parents, "ladylike" behavior still implies many constraints on bodily movements (such as the requirement to sit in a modest position), the maintenance of an appealing quality in her social approaches, particularly toward men, and many assumptions concerning appropriate activity and the kind of life a girl will lead when she is grown. The definitions of masculine behavior, of course, also vary enormously among parents, with a core of culturally agreed-upon features. The way a parent goes about socializing a child with respect to the sex typing of behavior must depend on his own definitions and values. In some cases the parent may rather deliberately attempt to prepare the child for a role the child is expected to play as an adult; in other instances, the parent's reaction to something the child does will not depend upon the parent's conception of the ultimate consequences of the behavior for the child's adult sex role, but will represent an immediate response to something that is seen as sex-inappropriate for the child at the time the behavior occurs. In other words, not all sex-typing socialization is *anticipatory* socialization.

It is widely assumed that parents do a great deal during the child's early life to define for the child what sex-appropriate behavior is, and to guide the child directly toward the adoption of this behavior. Our survey of the research on socialization of the two sexes has revealed surprisingly little differentiation in parent behavior according to the sex of the child. However, there are some areas where differential "shaping" does appear to occur. First, there is the obvious matter of dressing the two sexes differently. We hypothesize that parents are uncomfortable if others misidentify their children. If a child's sex is not clearly discernible from body build or hair style, parents may be expected to add an item of dress that will convey the necessary information.

There is evidence that parents encourage their children to develop sex-typed interests, in part through providing sex-typed toys for them. Even more strongly, they *discourage* their children—particularly their sons—from engaging in activities they consider appropriate only for the opposite sex. We may ask why it is that parents are more upset when a boy wants to wear lipstick or put on high heels than they are when a girl wants to paint a false moustache on her face or wear cowboy boots. Although the dynamics underlying this parental reaction are not clear, it would appear that feminine behavior in a boy is likely to be interpreted as a sign of possible homosexual tendencies, and, as such, it is a danger signal to parents and triggers powerful anxieties in them—perhaps especially in fathers. Following an analysis of parental sex anxiety in relation to the parent's care-taking interactions with infant sons and daughters, Sears comments, "Sex anxiety is essentially heterosexual in females, but is essentially homosexual in males" (Sears 1965[R], p. 159). Both parents, in other words, are likely to find their own sex anxieties more stimulated by the sexual qualities of a son than by those of a daughter, and hence will avoid too intimate physical contact with him. Furthermore, if the Sears interpretation holds, it is easy to see why a father would react more strongly against any possible signs of homosexuality in a son than in a daughter. It is less easy to see why a mother should do so. Perhaps we are simply dealing here with a realistic parental appraisal of the fact that homosexuality is considerably more common among males than females; if the likelihood of later development of this widely disvalued behavior is in fact greater for boys, then it becomes especially important for parents to nip early signs of it in the bud.

Whatever the underlying determiners, we have seen that in the area of sex-typed behavior as narrowly defined, parents do press their children toward the adoption of sex-appropriate behavior. There are other aspects of the children's behavior that the parents do not regard as relevant to masculinity or femininity, and they do not socialize differentially for these behaviors, even though the sexes may actually differ with respect to them. Even more interesting, however, are the behaviors that parents do consider relevant to masculinity and femininity but that they do not appear to treat differently in boys and girls. An interesting case in point is aggression. We have not found that parents reward boys more for aggressive or competitive behavior, or punish girls more for these behaviors. To some degree, the reverse may be true: boys receive more punishment for aggression. One might argue that punishment will actually serve to stimulate the child's aggressiveness by providing aggressive models, but even though this may be true, it involves a different mechanism of learning than what is normally meant by a "shaping" process. There is evidence that parents believe boys naturally are more aggressive than girls, on the average. They usually do not value the behavior in either sex, and one of the primary concerns of parents and children of preschool-aged children is to help them control their tempers and teach them socially acceptable ways of getting what they want, without grabbing, hitting, or pulling, and without being destructive toward valued objects. The frequency of temper outbursts and fights does decrease dramatically between the ages of 3 and 6. Since a low level of aggressiveness is actually desired by parents for both boys and girls, positive reinforcement for it will be rare. Although it is undoubtedly true that parents—especially fathers—are worried about a boy who is notably unaggressive, seeing it as a sign of his being a "sissy," the situation is different than in the case of the boy's putting on lipstick. In the latter case, there is a clear action on the part of the child that can serve as a signal for the parent's counteraction. In the case of a child's failure to fight, there is seldom a clear occasion calling for the parent's intervention, even though he may be worried about the total character pattern he sees his child developing. If parents want their sons to be tough in a fight, we might expect, at the least, that they would punish them less severely for fighting; we have not found this to be true, but the data are by no means adequate to provide a totally convincing picture. Studies often report the *frequency* with which a child is punished for fighting, without reporting the frequency of fighting itself. It may be that boys are punished equally often, or more often, than girls for this behavior, but that there are also more boy fights that go unpunished. And, of course, parents may be transmitting a mixed message to their sons in the midst of their discipline, so that the boy really understands his parents to be saying, "You are not supposed to fight, but I'm glad you did." On the basis of existing information on parent-child interaction, all that can be said is that there is no evidence that parents are systematically reinforcing sons, more than daughters, for aggressive behavior.

The same picture of lack of differential socialization emerges with respect to other aspects of behavior that are thought to be relevant for the development of sex typing. For example, parental reactions to the child's displays of sexual behavior or sexual curiosity might be expected to be different for boys and girls, considering the different standards that exist in most cultures for adult male and female sexual conduct. Yet in the three available studies—all interview studies—no tendencies have been found for girls to be more reinforced for modesty or punished more for sexual exploration.

With respect to allowing the child autonomy—encouraging independent, exploratory behavior or, on the contrary, restricting such behavior—we again find very little difference in the treatment of boys and girls, although the tendency is for parents (or at least mothers) to restrict boys somewhat more. Parental treatment of young children's dependency is also not clearly differentiated by sex. In the relatively few studies that report parental re-actions to children's clinging, proximity seeking, separation resistance, and demands for attention, positive and negative parental reactions seem to be about evenly distributed to boys and girls.

Of course, "shaping" a child toward a particular form of behavior may take more than one form. In the usual meaning of the term, parental reac-tions would have to be contingent on particular actions by the child. That is, in the development of dependent behavior, for example, it is reinforce-ment of the child specifically for approaching the parent, or clinging to him, or crying when he attempts to leave, that ought to increase the be-havior. It is precisely these kinds of contingencies that do *not* appear to be different for the two sexes with respect to a wide range of behaviors that are normally thought to be relevant to sex typing. However, there might be differences in more global aspects of child rearing that would have similar effects, even if the contingencies are less explicit. If it were true that mothers held and caressed their daughters more than their sons, for example, or interacted with them more frequently, this might have the effect of increasing the child's orientation and proximity seeking toward the mother. Here again, the evidence does not point to differential sociali-zation. The total amount of interaction between mother and child is simi-lar for the two sexes, as is the amount of expressed affection and "warmth," so that neither the global reinforcement conditions nor the specifically con-tingent ones are such as to differentiate the dependency behavior of young boys and girls. The only global difference in child rearing that might affect the child's dependency is the more frequent physical punishment and other negative sanctions administered to boys. These might cause the boy to dis-tance himself from his caretaker, and thus to score lower on certain mea-sures of dependency. However, there is evidence that punishment some-times increases a child's anxiety, which in turn can lead directly to contact seeking and proximity seeking, so it is by no means clear that differential punishment would differentiate the sexes in the direction consistent with our concepts of masculinity and femininity. And in any case, a generally punitive home atmosphere could hardly be regarded as an instance of "shaping" behavior in the sense that is implied in hypothesis 1. We must summarize our analysis of this hypothesis with the conclusion that we have been able to find very little evidence to support it, in relation to behaviors other than sex typing as very narrowly defined (e.g. toy preference). The reinforcement contingencies for the two sexes appear to be remarkably similar.

Different Eliciting Qualities of Boys and Girls

The second hypothesis was that boys and girls begin life with different behavioral tendencies that are biologically based: that because of their different initial behaviors they stimulate their parents differently, and thus initiate a different sort of circular process that becomes established as a habitual mode of interaction between parent and child. An example of such a presumed situation may be found in Moss (1967). Moss noted that at age 3 weeks, the more an infant cried, the more a mother interacted with it, and his inference was, reasonably enough, that the infant was controlling the mother—that its cry was a signal to the mother and the rate of her response was closely related to the frequency of her receiving this signal. At age 3 months, however, Moss found that the infant's irritability continued to be positively related to the amount of mother-infant interaction for girls only ($r = .54$ for girls), but *negatively* for boys ($r = -.47$, $p < .10$ for this sample size). His hypothesis is that female infants may be more readily quieted than male infants, so that when a female infant cries and the mother goes to it and picks it up, the mother's nurturant behavior is reinforced by the cessation of the infant's crying; if boys, on the other hand, continue to cry while the mother attempts to minister to them, her nurturant behavior is *not* reinforced and she may become more and more reluctant to pick up her crying child. As we have seen in Chapter 2, it is doubtful that girls are more easily quieted than boys. The Moss hypothesis, however, serves as an example of a kind of differential parent behavior that *could* occur in response to preexisting behavioral sex differences. Are there any instances among the studies summarized above where a similar interpretation would be reasonable?

As noted above, there is some evidence that boys are more "resistive" than girls. In the Minton et al. study with 2-year-olds (1971) and the Serbin et al. (1973) study with 3–4-year-olds, boys did not comply as readily as girls to directions from the mother or a teacher. The Minton study showed that it was following noncompliance on the part of the child that mothers tended to move to somewhat more coercive methods to obtain compliance. In the Serbin study, controlling and sanctioning behavior of all sorts by the teacher was more frequent toward boys, but it is difficult to say whether this was a consequence or a cause of the boys' greater tendency to ignore the teacher's directions, since detailed sequential analysis was not reported.

In any case, the boy's greater resistiveness to directions, and his lesser susceptibility to milder forms of pressure, may be part of the explanation of the fact that parents use more punishment with boys. The finding of greater punishment administered to sons is, then, compatible with hypothesis 2—more compatible, we think, than it is with hypothesis 1. But there may be other explanations, as we shall see below.

Our major finding, however—that parents treat boys and girls much alike—would suggest that there are probably not very many initial biologically based behavioral differences, at least not many that are strong enough to elicit clear differential reactions from caretakers.

Parents' Conceptions of What the Two Sexes Are Like

Parents and teachers, of course, operate on the basis of certain stereotypes about children's characters. Having labeled a child "shy" or "rambunctious," they then govern their own actions accordingly. Do they characteristically label the two sexes differently? And if so, what implications does this have for the way they socialize their children?

Few studies have asked parents directly how they believe the two sexes do in fact differ, apart from what behavior the parent would prefer to see in a boy or girl. Lambert et al. (1971) worked with French-Canadian and English-Canadian parents, using a modification of the "Perception" and "Expectation" scales originally used by Rothbart and Maccoby (1966)[R].[*] In the Perception scale, parents were given a series of 40 items such as "more helpful around the house," "more likely to be rough and boisterous at play," "more likely to act scared," and were asked to check whether they believed a boy or girl would be more likely to engage in the behavior described. A box was provided where the parent could check if he believed that neither sex was more likely than the other to show the behavior. In the Expectation scale, the parent was asked how important he thought it was for a child of each sex to have each behavioral characteristic. A five-point scale was provided, ranging from "very important *not* to" to "very important to," with the central point being "unimportant," and the parents rated each item separately for boys and girls.

The finding of greatest interest for our present purposes was that these groups of parents thought the typical behavior of boys and girls was different on many items, but their values concerning how the two sexes ought to behave were quite similar. Boys were described as being more likely to be rough at play, be noisy, defend themselves, defy punishment, be physically active, be competitive, do dangerous things, and enjoy mechanical things. Girls were described as being more likely to be helpful around the house, be neat and clean, be quiet and reserved, be sensitive to the

[*] The authors are grateful to W. Lambert and J. Hammers for making the data available for an item-by-item analysis.

feelings of others, be well mannered, be a tattletale, cry or get upset, and be easily frightened. But when asked which of these characteristics they thought it was important for boys and girls to have (or *not* to have) parents said they thought it was important for *both* boys and girls to be neat and clean, to be helpful around the house, to be able to take care of themselves, not to be easily angered, not to do dangerous things, not to cry, and to be thoughtful and considerate of others. Surprisingly, it was also thought important for both boys and girls to defend themselves from attack, and to be competitive. There were unexpectedly few differences in the values held for the behavior of sons and daughters. Similar results were obtained by W. Smith (1971)[R] working with 48 pairs of American black parents. On the whole, these studies indicate that parents are trying to socialize children of both sexes toward the same major goals, but that they believe they are starting from different points, with each sex having a different set of "natural" assets and liabilities.

A similar conclusion can be reached from the Levitin and Chananie (1972) study with first- and second-grade teachers, although this study focuses on a narrower range of behaviors. In this study, teachers were given a description of a hypothetical child who might be in their classroom: "Tom (Alice) is sometimes disobedient to the teacher and often aggressive with other children in his (her) class." The teachers were then asked whether they approved of the child's behavior, how much they thought they would like this child, and how typical they thought the behavior was of other boys (girls) of the same age. Aggressive behavior was more often thought to be typical of boys, but it was disapproved (and equally so) in both sexes. Dependent behavior was not thought to be especially typical in either sex, and although a dependent girl was somewhat better liked than a dependent boy, the difference was not significant. The aggression findings again point to an area of behavior where adults believe that a sex difference exists but they do not value it more (or depreciate it less) in the sex for which it it believed typical.

When parents consider a kind of behavior "natural" for a given sex, and the behavior is undesired, do they direct stronger socialization efforts toward the behavior, or do they assume that there is little they can do to change it and hence reconcile themselves to the behavior? Unfortunately we do not have a sufficiently detailed listing of parents' beliefs concerning behavioral sex typing, or sufficiently detailed descriptions of usual parental reactions to these same behaviors, to answer the question. For example, the Smith (1971)[R] and Lambert et al. (1971) studies indicate that parents believe girls cry more easily, and that they think it is important for children not to cry frequently. But we do not know how widely this finding applies to other samples of parents, or whether parents react more harshly or more sympathetically to this behavior in a girl. We can make a rough assessment with respect to two categories of behavior: dependency and aggression. We have seen earlier that these behaviors are treated quite similarly in boys and girls. If the findings of Lambert et al. and Smith replicate on other populations, this would mean that although aggression is seen as typical for boys, and is undesired, parents neither direct more intense socialization toward boys because aggression is seen as a greater "danger" in them, nor ignore the behavior more often because it is seen as "natural." The same situation applies to the treatment of dependency in girls.

Earlier, we mentioned another possible effect of a parent's believing that a particular behavior is more typical of one sex than the other: perhaps the probability of a child's behavior being *noticed* is a function of the probability level the parent unconsciously assigns to it. This was called the "perceptual adaptation level" hypothesis. Let us consider some of the implications of this hypothesis. Many (perhaps most) of the actions a child performs do not call for any parental response at all. Only when the child's action is defined by the parent as naughty, or dangerous, or especially nice, does it call for the parent to react with positive or negative sanctions. In the case of aggression, there are many ambiguous actions that a child performs concerning which the parent has some latitude. The parent could see a given action either as exuberant horseplay or as the beginning of a fight. The way he defines an action by a particular child will depend on his range of expectations for that child. If the parent is adapted to a rather high continuous level of exuberant horseplay, only the rare especially vigorous action, or the one that makes another child cry, will be seen as aggressive. If the parent expects this particular child to be normally quiet and gentle, however, any vigorous social action will be noticed, and any mild protest from another child may cause the action to be defined as aggressive. Because parents have different levels of expectation for the two sexes, the hypothesis says, parents will be more likely to define a given ambiguous action as aggressive if performed by a girl than if by a boy.

J. Meyer and Sobieszek (1972) made a study bearing on the issue. They showed video tapes of behavior sequences of young children at play to adult viewers of both sexes. The children on the film were dressed in play clothes that would be appropriate for either sex, and their appearance was not sex-typed. A given child was identified as a boy for some observers, and as a girl for others. After viewing a tape, the adult viewer was asked to rate the child on a series of sex-typed traits, saying how "independent," "aggressive," "confident," "cooperative," "shy," and "affectionate," among other traits, the child on the tape had seemed. One possible outcome of the study might have been, of course, that raters would tend to see children as conforming to the raters' stereotypes, so that boys would be seen as more aggressive and girls as more cooperative or shy. In fact, however, the reverse was true, at least for the subsample of subjects who had previous experience with children. If a child behaved in a vigorous, uninhibited way on the screen, the behavior was more likely to be labeled aggressive if the actor was thought to be a girl than if the same actor was thought to be a boy. In other words, behaviors were especially noticed if they ran counter to sex-role stereotypes.

A mechanism has been identified whereby parents will notice and punish sex-inappropriate behavior. But, unfortunately, the explanation cuts two ways, and does not help to explain why a parent should reward sex-appropriate behavior. As noted above, many parents see girls as naturally more cooperative, more tractable, more sociable than boys, and on the whole they see these as attractive traits; but they also see girls as more timid and more likely to cry, and many parents do not especially like these aspects of "feminine" personality. Similarly for boys: parents generally see boys as naturally stronger and more self-reliant than girls, and they may like this about boys; but at the same time they see them as more aggressive and less obedient. Particularly when aggression is directed by a boy toward his parents, it is not seen as praiseworthy; neither is his disobedience.

The principle of perceptual adaptation level predicts that when a girl behaves in a cooperative, helpful manner, this will either tend to go unnoticed or draw only moderate approval because that is the way a girl is expected to act. When a boy behaves in this manner, however, his mother will react with pleased surprise and reinforce him vigorously. As the principle works out, then, punishment from parents will tend to support existing sex stereotypes—each sex will be punished more for behavior seen as unusual, or wrong, for his sex. *Positive* reinforcement, however, will run counter to sex stereotypes. Each sex will be rewarded for desirable behavior when it is seen as relatively unusual for his sex. Hence, the perceptual-adaptation-level theory does not seem so promising as it might have seemed at first glance as a basis for explaining the role of parental socialization in children's sex differentiation.

Cross-Sex and Same-Sex Effects

At the beginning of this chapter, it was suggseted that a parent's reaction to a child might depend on whether the child was the same sex as the parent. This would mean that, in some respects, fathers would tend to react to daughters as mothers do to sons. We suggested that parents might show rivalry with a same-sex child, and flirtation, submissiveness, or dominance with an opposite-sex child, depending upon the parent's usual relationship with opposite-sex adults.

Most of the research summarized in the present chapter involves observations or interviews with mothers. Hence, cross-sex or same-sex effects can rarely be assessed. However, the studies that have obtained data concerning both maternal and paternal behavior have revealed some extremely interesting cross-sex effects, particularly in the area of aggressive behavior directed by a child toward an adult. Fathers appeared to be more tolerant of aggression from a daughter, mothers from a son. Why should this be so? In Chapter 6, we saw that there is some reason to believe that boys are more likely to be aggressive when interacting with other boys than they are with other persons. Young males appear to challenge one another, and to react with counterthreat when challenged by another male. Perhaps a father, at least on some occasions, is reacting to a son simply as another male—reacting as though a threat to his dominance were involved when his son is angry toward him, whereas he feels no such threat when challenged by a girl. Most women, on the other hand, are accustomed to moderating their reaction to male threat; frequently, they would have a good deal to lose, in terms of actual or potential status derived from men, if they reacted with open counterthreat, although of course the more subtle forms of resistance and retaliation have long been a woman's game. When a woman is challenged by another woman, however (and this does not happen as often as male–male threat), the challenge may be more safely resisted in an open way. If a woman's experience in this regard is transferred in any degree to the family arena, a mother would be more likely, then, to take direct countermeasures against a daughter's aggression than a son's.

With respect to dependency, one study (Rothbart and Maccoby 1966[R]) found cross-sex effects, with mothers being more supportive of dependency behavior in sons and fathers in daughters; this finding, however, was not replicated in the Lambert et al. (1971) study, where mothers and fathers both treated the two sexes similarly when asked for help, and gave girls more positive response when asked for comfort. Until further information is available that will help to identify the conditions under which cross-sex effects occur, it is fruitless to speculate about their meaning for intrafamily dynamics. It is worth noting, however, that when cross-sex effects *do* occur, they present a problem for simple reinforcement theory. If fathers react repressively to a boy's aggression and mothers do likewise toward girls while being permissive toward a son's aggression, the two parents are working against one another in terms of sex-typing pressure. One parent is differentiating between boys and girls in a sex-typed direction, the other in the opposite direction. When the two parents are behaving inconsistently with respect to reinforcing a particular kind of behavior in a child, the analogy to a Skinnerian "shaping" process becomes unclear. Is the situation analogous to an intermittent schedule of reinforcement—one that produces a strong habit that is resistant to extinction? If so, then a strong habit is being produced in both sexes. Although the identity of the parent who is punishing and the identity of the parent giving positive reinforcement differ for boys and girls, intermittent reinforcement is occurring for both sexes. Thus the situation does not produce an explanation of the fact that a given behavior develops more strongly in one sex than in the other.

Of course, in early childhood children of both sexes spend more time with the mother. And when they enter school, they are usually under the supervision of a female teacher. Thus, if cross-sex indulgence and same-sex severity are the rule, boys should have an easier time in both the home and school settings. We suspect, however, that the sheer amount of time spent in the presence of a particular socializing agent may not be the most important index of that agent's influence and that fathers may be very effective despite their fewer hours at home. Furthermore, any tendency for mothers and teachers to be more indulgent toward boys for any given bit of behavior is tempered by their belief that boys are more mischievous and more difficult to socialize. We cannot conclude that either sex is dealt with more leniently, on the whole.

Overview

Our survey of data has revealed a remarkable degree of uniformity in the socialization of the two sexes. In many instances, however, the evidence has been quite limited and the data have not been adequate for testing our initial hypotheses. Particularly handicapping has been the lack of information about fathers; it may be that fathers differentiate between the sexes to a much greater degree than do mothers, from whom most of our information comes. It is also possible that we would have obtained a more differentiated picture if more research on working-class families had been available. In any case, existing evidence has not revealed any consistent process of "shaping" boys and girls toward a number of behaviors that are normally part of our sex stereotypes.

Some unanticipated themes have emerged, however. Boys seem to have more intense socialization experiences than girls. They receive more pressure against engaging in sex-inappropriate behavior, whereas the activities that girls are not supposed to engage in are much less clearly defined and less firmly enforced. Boys receive more punishment, but probably also more praise and encouragement. Adults respond as if they find boys more interesting, and more attention-provoking, than girls. The simplest hypothesis to explain this fact would be that boys are more active, thus providing more stimulation to observers. But we have seen in Chapter 5 that there is not a reliable sex difference in total activity level, so that the issue becomes one of whether boys' actions are qualitatively, rather than quantitatively, more attention-getting. Other possible explanations come to mind: perhaps boys are valued more; or perhaps their greater strength and aggressiveness make it more important that they be adequately socialized. Whatever the explanation, the different amounts of socialization pressure that boys and girls receive surely have consequences for the development of their personalities.

CHAPTER TEN

Summary and Commentary

In Chapters 2–7 we set out to discover which of the widely held beliefs about sex differences are myth, which are supported by evidence, and which are still untested. We shall now summarize some of the answers that have emerged, and shall then return to the question, raised in Chapters 8 and 9, of how the patterns of similarity and difference are to be explained. Finally, we shall consider the social implications of what has been learned.

SUMMARY OF OUR FINDINGS

Unfounded Beliefs About Sex Differences

1. *That girls are more "social" than boys.* The findings: First, the two sexes are equally interested in social (as compared with nonsocial) stimuli, and are equally proficient at learning through imitation of models. Second, in childhood, girls are no more dependent than boys on their caretakers, and boys are no more willing to remain alone. Furthermore, girls are not more motivated to achieve for social rewards. The two sexes are equally responsive to social reinforcement, and neither sex consistently learns better for this form of reward than for other forms. Third, girls do not spend more time interacting with playmates; in fact, the opposite is true, at least at certain ages. Fourth, the two sexes appear to be equally "empathic," in the sense of understanding the emotional reactions of others; however, the measures of this ability have so far been narrow.

Any differences that exist in the "sociability" of the two sexes are more of kind than of degree. Boys are highly oriented toward a peer group and congregate in larger groups; girls associate in pairs or small groups of age-mates, and may be somewhat more oriented toward adults, although the evidence for this is weak.

2. *That girls are more "suggestible" than boys.* The findings: First, boys and girls are equally likely to imitate others spontaneously. Second, the two sexes are equally susceptible to persuasive communications, and in face-to-face social-influence situations (Asch-type experiments), sex dif-

ferences are usually not found. When they are, girls are somewhat more likely to adapt their own judgments to those of the group, although there are studies with reverse findings. Boys, on the other hand, appear to be more likely to accept peer-group values when these conflict with their own.

3. *That girls have lower self-esteem.* The findings: The sexes are highly similar in their overall self-satisfaction and self-confidence throughout childhood and adolescence; there is little information about adulthood, but what exists does not show a sex difference. However, there are some qualitative differences in the areas of functioning where the two sexes have greatest self-confidence: girls rate themselves higher in the area of social competence; boys more often see themselves as strong, powerful, dominant, "potent."

Through most of the school years, the two sexes are equally likely to believe they can influence their own fates, rather than being the victims of chance or fate. During the college years (but not earlier or later), men have a greater sense of control over their own fate, and greater confidence in their probable performance on a variety of school-related tasks that they undertake. However, this does not imply a generally lower level of self-esteem among women of this age.

4. *That girls are better at rote learning and simple repetitive tasks, boys at tasks that require higher-level cognitive processing and the inhibition of previously learned responses.* The findings: Neither sex is more susceptible to simple conditioning, or excels in simple paired-associates or other forms of "rote" learning. Boys and girls are equally proficient at discrimination learning, reversal shifts, and probability learning, all of which have been interpreted as calling for some inhibition of "available" responses. Boys are somewhat more impulsive (that is, lacking in inhibition) during the preschool years, but the sexes do not differ thereafter in the ability to wait for a delayed reward, to inhibit early (wrong) responses on the Matching Familiar Figures test (MFF) or on other measures of impulsivity.

5. *That boys are more "analytic."* The findings: The sexes do not differ on tests of analytic cognitive style. Boys do not excel at tasks that call for "decontextualization," or disembedding, except when the task is visual-spatial; boys' superiority on the latter tasks seems to be accounted for by spatial ability (see below), and no sex differences in analytic ability are implied. Boys and girls are equally likely to respond to task-irrelevant aspects of a situation, so that neither sex excels in analyzing and selecting only those elements needed for the task.

6. *That girls are more affected by heredity, boys by environment.* The findings: Male identical twins are more alike than female identical twins, but the two sexes show equivalent amount of resemblance to their parents.

Boys are more susceptible to damage by a variety of noxious environmental agents, both prenatally and postnatally, but this does not imply that they are generally more influenced by environmental factors. The correlations between parental socialization techniques and child behavior are higher for boys in some studies, higher for girls in others. Furthermore, the two sexes learn with equal facility in a wide variety of learning situations; if learning is the primary means whereby environmental effects come about, sex equivalence is indicated.

7. *That girls lack achievement motivation.* The findings: In the pioneering studies of achievement motivation, girls scored higher than boys in achievement imagery under "neutral" conditions. Boys need to be challenged by appeals to ego or competitive motivation to bring their achievement imagery up to the level of girls'. Boys' achievement motivation does appear to be more responsive to competitive arousal than girls', but this does not imply a generally higher level. In fact, observational studies of achievement strivings either have found no sex difference or have found girls to be superior.

8. *That girls are auditory, boys visual.* The findings: The majority of studies report no differences in response to sounds by infants of the two sexes. At most ages boys and girls are equally adept at discriminating speech sounds. No sex difference is found in memory for sounds previously heard.

Among newborn infants, no study shows a sex difference in fixation to visual stimuli. During the first year of life, results are variable, but neither sex emerges as more responsive to visual stimuli. From infancy to adulthood, the sexes are highly similar in interest in visual stimuli, ability to discriminate among them, identification of shapes, distance perception, and a variety of other measures of visual perception.

Sex Differences That Are Fairly Well Established

1. *That girls have greater verbal ability than boys.* It is probably true that girls' verbal abilities mature somewhat more rapidly in early life, although there are a number of recent studies in which no sex difference has been found. During the period from preschool to early adolescence, the sexes are very similar in their verbal abilities. At about age 11, the sexes begin to diverge, with female superiority increasing through high school and possibly beyond. Girls score higher on tasks involving both receptive and productive language, and on "high-level" verbal tasks (analogies, comprehension of difficult written material, creative writing) as well as upon the "lower-level" measures (fluency). The magnitude of the female advantage varies, being most commonly about one-quarter of a standard deviation.

2. *That boys excel in visual-spatial ability.* Male superiority on visual-spatial tasks is fairly consistently found in adolescence and adulthood, but not in childhood. The male advantage on spatial tests increases through

the high school years up to a level of about .40 of a standard deviation. The sex difference is approximately equal on analytic and nonanalytic spatial measures.

3. *That boys excel in mathematical ability.* The two sexes are similar in their early acquisition of quantitative concepts, and their mastery of arithmetic during the grade-school years. Beginning at about age 12–13, boys' mathematical skills increase faster than girls'. The greater rate of improvement appears to be not entirely a function of the number of math courses taken, although the question has not been extensively studied. The magnitude of the sex differences varies greatly from one population to another, and is probably not so great as the difference in spatial ability. Both visual-spatial and verbal processes are sometimes involved in the solution of mathematical problems; some math problems can probably be solved in either way, while others cannot, a fact that may help to explain the variation in degree of sex difference from one measure to another.

4. *That males are more aggressive.* The sex difference in aggression has been observed in all cultures in which the relevant behavior has been observed. Boys are more aggressive both physically and verbally. They show the attenuated forms of aggression (mock-fighting, aggressive fantasies) as well as the direct forms more frequently than girls. The sex difference is found as early as social play begins—at age 2 or 2½. Although the aggressiveness of both sexes declines with age, boys and men remain more aggressive through the college years. Little information is available for older adults. The primary victims of male aggression are other males—from early ages, girls are chosen less often as victims.

Open Questions: Too Little Evidence, or Findings Ambiguous

1. *Tactile sensitivity.* Most studies of tactile sensitivity in infancy, and of the ability to perceive by touch at later ages, do not find sex differences. When differences are found, girls are more sensitive, but such findings are rare enough that we cannot have confidence that the difference is a meaningful one. Additional work is needed with some of the standard psychophysical measurements of tactile sensitivity, over a range of ages. Most of the existing studies in which the data are analyzed by sex have been done with newborns.

2. *Fear, timidity, and anxiety.* Observational studies of fearful behavior usually do not find sex differences. Teacher ratings and self-reports, however, usually find girls to be more timid or more anxious. In the case of self-reports, the problem is to know whether the results reflect "real" differences or only differences in the willingness to report anxious feelings. Of course, the very willingness to assert that one is afraid may lead to fearful behavior, so the distinction may not turn out to be important. However, it would be desirable to have measures other than self-report (which make up the great bulk of the data from early school age on) as a way of

clarifying the meaning of the girls' greater self-attribution of fears and anxiety.

3. *Activity level.* Sex differences in activity level do not appear in infancy. They begin to be seen when children reach the age of social play. During the preschool years, when sex differences are found they are in the direction of boys' being more active. However, there are many instances in which sex differences have not been found. Some, but not all, of the variance among studies can be accounted for by whether the measurement situation was social. That is, boys appear to be especially stimulated to bursts of high activity by the presence of other boys. But the exact nature of the situational control over activity level remains to be established. Activity level is responsive to a number of motivational states—fear, anger, curiosity—and is therefore not a promising variable for identifying stable individual or group differences. More detailed observations are needed on the vigor and qualitative nature of play.

4. *Competitiveness.* When sex differences are found, they usually show boys to be more competitive, but there are many studies finding sex similarity. Madsen and his colleagues find sex differences to be considerably weaker than differences between cultures and, in a number of studies, entirely absent. Almost all the research on competition has involved situations in which competition is maladaptive. In the Prisoner's Dilemma game, for example, the sexes are equally cooperative, but this is in a situation in which cooperation is to the long-run advantage of both players and the issue is one of developing mutual trust. It appears probable that in situations in which competitiveness produces increased individual rewards, males would be more competitive, but this is a guess based on commonsense considerations, such as the male interest in competitive sports, not upon research in controlled settings. The age of the subject and the identity of the opponent no doubt make a difference—there is evidence that young women hesitate to compete against their boyfriends.

5. *Dominance.* Dominance appears to be more of an issue within boys' groups than girls' groups. Boys make more dominance attempts (both successful and unsuccessful) toward one another than do girls. They also more often attempt to dominate adults. The dominance relations between the sexes are complex: in childhood, the sex segregation of play groups means that neither sex frequently attempts to dominate the other. In experimental situations in which the sexes are combined, the evidence is ambiguous on whether either sex is more successful in influencing the behavior of the other. Among adult mixed pairs or groups, formal leadership tends to go to males in the initial phases of interaction, but the direction of influence becomes more sex-equal the longer the relationship lasts, with "division of authority" occurring along lines of individual competencies and division of labor.

6. *Compliance.* In childhood, girls tend to be more compliant to the de-

mands and directions of adults. This compliance does not extend, however, to willingness to accept directions from, or be influenced by, age-mates. Boys are especially concerned with maintaining their status in the peer group, and are probably therefore more vulnerable to pressures and challenges from this group, although this has not been well established. As we have seen in the discussion of dominance, it is not clear that in mixed-sex interactions either sex is consistently more willing to comply with the wishes of the other.

7. *Nurturance and "maternal" behavior.* There is very little evidence concerning the tendencies of boys and girls to be nurturant or helpful toward younger children or animals. Cross-cultural work does indicate that girls between the ages of 6 and 10 are more often seen behaving nurturantly. Within our own society, the rare studies that report nurturant behavior are observational studies of free play among nursery school children; sex differences are not found in these studies, but the setting normally does not include children much younger than the subjects being observed, and it may be that the relevant elicitors are simply not present. Female hormones play a role in maternal behavior in lower animals, and the same may be true in human beings, but there is no direct evidence that this is the case. There is very little information on the responses of adult men to infants and children, so it is not possible to say whether adult women are more disposed to behave maternally than men are to behave paternally. If there is a sex difference in the tendency to behave nurturantly, it does not generalize to a greater female tendency to behave altruistically over varying situations. The studies of people's willingness to help others in distress have sometimes shown men more helpful, sometimes women, depending on the identity of the person needing help and the kind of help that is needed. The overall finding on altruism is one of sex similarity.

In Chapters 5 and 6, we raised the question of whether the female is more passive than the male. The answer is complex, but mainly negative. The two sexes are highly similar in their willingness to explore a novel environment, when they are both given freedom to do so. Both are highly responsive to social situations of all kinds, and although some individuals tend to withdraw from social interaction and simply watch from the sidelines, such persons are no more likely to be female than male. Girls' greater compliance with adult demands is just as likely to take an active as a passive form; running errands and performing services for others are active processes. Young boys seem more likely than girls to put out energy in the form of bursts of strenuous physical activity, but the girls are not sitting idly by while the boys act; they are simply playing more quietly. And their play is fully as organized and planful (possibly more so), and has as much the quality of actively imposing their own design upon their surroundings as does boys' play. It is true that boys and men are more aggressive, but this does not mean that females are the passive victims of aggression—they do not yield or withdraw when aggressed against any more frequently than males do, at least during the phases of childhood for which observations are available. With respect to dominance, we have noted the curious fact that while males are more dominant, females are not especially submissive, at least not to the dominance attempts of boys and girls their own age. In sum, the term "passive" does not accurately describe the most common female personality attributes.

Returning to one of the major conclusions of our survey of sex differences, there are many popular beliefs about the psychological characteristics of the two sexes that have proved to have little or no basis in fact. How is it possible that people continue to believe, for example, that girls are more "social" than boys, when careful observation and measurement in a variety of situations show no sex difference? Of course it is possible that we have not studied those particular situations that contribute most to the popular beliefs. But if this is the problem, it means that the alleged sex difference exists only in a limited range of situations, and the sweeping generalizations embodied in popular beliefs are not warranted.

However, a more likely explanation for the perpetuation of "myths," we believe, is the fact that stereotypes are such powerful things. An ancient truth is worth restating here: if a generalization about a group of people is believed, whenever a member of that group behaves in the expected way the observer notes it and his belief is confirmed and strengthened; when a member of the group behaves in a way that is not consistent with the observer's expectations, the instance is likely to pass unnoticed, and the observer's generalized belief is protected from disconfirmation. We believe that this well-documented process occurs continually in relation to the expected and perceived behavior of males and females, and results in the perpetuation of myths that would otherwise die out under the impact of negative evidence. However, not all unconfirmed beliefs about the two sexes are of this sort. It is necessary to reconsider the nature of the evidence that permits us to conclude what is myth and what is (at least potentially) reality.

HOW MUCH CONFIDENCE CAN BE PLACED IN THESE CONCLUSIONS?

Having gone through the often tedious process of summarizing and analyzing existing research, we must ask ourselves about the adequacy of this method as a way of knowing the truth about sex differences. We have tallied studies—the number showing higher scores for boys, the number favoring girls, and the number showing no difference—knowing, of course, that the studies differ widely in the rigor of their design and procedures, the number of subjects used, the definition of variables, etc. It is not uncommon to find a "box score" in which the majority of studies find no difference, but where the studies that do find a difference favor one sex by a considerable margin (say, two or three to one). We have interpreted such an outcome as a weak trend in the direction indicated by the largest number of studies, but recognize that it is quite possible that the minority of studies might turn out to have more than a kernel of truth. With stereotypes and biases being as common as they are in the field of sex differences, it is quite possible that the majority of studies were all distorted in the same direction. We think it equally likely, however, that the appearance of a sex difference often depends upon detailed aspects of the situation in which behavior was studied—details that have so far gone unrecognized, but that interact with the more obvious aspects of a situation to change the way in which it is perceived.

We have repeatedly encountered the problem that so-called "objective" measures of behavior yield different results than ratings or self-reports. Ratings are notoriously subject to shifting anchor points. For example, if a parent is asked, "How often does your daughter cry?," the parent may answer "Not very often," meaning "Not very often *for a girl.*" The same frequency of behavior might have been rated "quite often" for a son, from whom the behavior was less expected. Ratings, then, if they are made against different subjective standards, should minimize sex differences where they exist. Where they do not exist, ratings might produce them, but in the opposite direction from stereotypical behavior. It is puzzling that ratings so frequently yield sex differences in the stereotypical direction. For example, in one study, teachers rated each child in their class on activity level; the boys received higher average ratings; but "actometer" recordings for the same group of children did not show the boys to be engaging in more body movement. Obviously, the possibility exists that teachers are noticing and remembering primarily the behavior that fits their stereotypes. There is another possibility, however: that teachers are analyzing clusters or patterns of behavior that a simple single-attribute measurement such as an actometer score does not capture. If this is so, however, and the teachers are reporting something real about sex differences, the cluster that they are attending to should not be named "activity level," for the label implies that the behavior is simpler than it is.

The problems of shifting anchor points for ratings, selective perceptions of raters, and unclear definitions of what is being rated are not the only problems that beset the student of sex differences. It matters how large a "chunk" of behavior is chosen for analysis. This point has been nicely illustrated in work by Raush (1965)[R], in which he compared the social interactions of a group of clinically diagnosed "hyperaggressive" boys with a group of normals. The sequences of aggressive behavior were monitored. The two groups of boys were similar in the frequency and kind of response the victim first made. They were also similar in the aggressor's response to the victim's response. It was only in the fourth and fifth actions in the sequence that the groups diverged—the "hyperactives" continued to respond intensely; the normals "let it go" without continuing the sequence. It may be that sex differences, too, emerge at only certain points in a sequence, and the results of a study will depend upon how detailed and continuous the measurements are. Often, of course, an experimental situation is arranged in such a way that only single responses are recorded, and then summed across trials. Such a procedure makes it nearly impossible to detect either sequences or other patterning of behavior.

We have found a number of instances in which sex differences are situation-specific. For example, although boys and girls do not differ in their attachment to their parents in early childhood (that is, their tendency to remain close to them, interact with them, and resist separation from them), or in the amount of positive interaction with nonfamily adults, boys do interact more with same-sex age-mates. Unfortunately, many studies tally social behavior without specifying the "target" of this behavior. Similarly, studies of "nurturance" behavior (rare in the first place) have usually not identified the beneficiary of the behavior. Clearly, if a child brings a glass of water to his mother, the behavior is subject to different interpretations than if he does the same helpful act for a younger sibling. Furthermore, it makes a difference who is watching. We suspect, for example, that a man may behave more dominantly toward his girl friend and she more submissively when other men are present than they would do in private. It is possible, too, that marriage partners are especially likely to become more equal in dominance with time if there are children—that it is the need to maintain a united front before the children and to support one another's disciplinary moves that is a primary factor producing a change in the dominance relations of a married pair. These situational subtleties have gone largely unnoticed in existing research; we have had no choice but to report the data that researchers have obtained, but we think findings will be much clearer when these distinctions begin to be introduced.

We have attempted to understand the relationship of sex differences to age; we have wanted to know at what age a particular difference first manifests itself, whether it is temporary, whether it increases or decreases with development. We have been able to make only a tantalizing beginning to a genuinely developmental analysis. It is reasonably clear that differences in "temperament" and in social behavior emerge much earlier than differences in specific intellectual abilities. Furthermore, there are a few instances in our review where a difference was evident only briefly, during a limited age period. This appears to be true, for example, on certain measures of "impulsivity," where boys are more impulsive only during the preschool years. On the whole, however, our efforts to understand developmental change have been frustrated by two things: (1) the fact that certain ages are overrepresented, others underrepresented, in research on a given topic; and (2) the fact that the methods of measuring a given attribute change so drastically with age that cross-age comparison becomes virtually impossible. Newborn infants in the first two or three days of life, nursery school children, and college students are the groups most frequently studied. In addition, extensive data are available for school-age children on attributes that are clearly relevant to school success (e.g. intellectual aptitudes and achievement scores), with much less information available on social behavior. Very little is known about age changes during adulthood with respect to either cognitive or social measures.

The problem of changing measures over ages is a ubiquitous one in developmental psychology. One can learn something about a young child's attachments and fears by tallying the frequency with which he literally hides behind his mother's skirts; to attempt to do so with an adult would be absurd. One may measure quantitative skill in a preschooler by finding how accurately he can count, and of a fifth- or sixth-grader by asking him to do percentages; but by college age, subjects must be asked to solve differential equations before stable individual differences can be identified. There are great shifts with age not only in *what* is measured but in *how* measurement is done. Behavioral observation is fairly frequent with young children. From the time children become literate through adulthood, however, observational studies in naturalistic settings are very rare, and scores are based either on questionnaires or other self-reports, or on experimental situations using a deliberately restricted set of eliciting conditions and behavioral measures.

It is to be expected that results of experiments may yield quite different results than "real life" observations. It is possible, for example, that if a girl is put into a foot race, she will be as competitive and active as a male. But she might be much less likely to enter such a race spontaneously, and naturalistic observation would show her to be less frequently engaged in competitive behavior, whereas the foot race "experiment" would not. The conclusions of both kinds of studies are correct, but they have rather different implications. The shift from naturalistic observation in early childhood to experimental studies at later ages may mean that sex differences in self-selection of activities have had a better chance of being detected in the early years, rather than that there has been any decline in the importance of motivation and interest with growth.

In a certain sense it is reasonable to make the shift from observational data to questionnaires or self-reports. If one is sampling behavior in a nursery school, it may be meaningful to record simply that a child moved across the room. If one looked out the window at a college student walking down the sidewalk just before the bell rang, however, what is meaningful to record about his behavior? The fact that he was walking? The fact that he was going to class? The fact that he was taking a course in psychology? The fact that his attendance at this class was part of his four-year program to obtain a bachelor's degree? Elements of an adult's behavior are usually part of a nested set of organized action sequences (i.e. "plans"). Judging by the data we collect about people at different ages, researchers implicitly assume that a young child's behavior is less so. This is probably correct, although there are probably many more nested sequences in children's behavior than have been detected with the usual techniques of time sampling and frequency tallies of individual behavior elements. If plans of varying duration and complexity do assume more and more control of behavior as the individual develops, it would be reasonable to ask about the plans, rather than to spend so much time enumerating specific responses, as is done for young children. However, the value of observational data surely does not decline to zero with increasing age. We can point out here only that, reasonable though the shift in methods may be, it makes the meaning of measured age changes quite ambiguous. We hope there will be an increase in observational work in naturalistic settings with subjects beyond nursery school age, so that a few more cross-age comparisons will be possible.

One interesting age trend emerged in our survey that is probably *not* a reflection of changes in methods of measurement: this is the tendency for young women of college age to lack confidence in their ability to do well on a new task, and their sense that they have less control over their own fates than men do. These trends are not seen among older or younger women. Age 18–22 is the period of their lives when many young adults are marrying or forming some other kind of relatively enduring sexual liaison. In the dating and mating game, women traditionally are expected to take less initiative than men. Perhaps it is at this period of their lives more than any other that individuals define themselves in terms of their "masculinity" and "femininity," and when greater sex differences may therefore appear than at earlier or later ages, with respect to any attribute considered central to this definition.

This brings us to a related point: that sex differences may be greater among certain subgroups of men and women than among others. In a recent paper, "On Predicting Some of the People Some of the Time," Bem and Allen (1974)[R] suggest that an individual's behavior is likely to be stable across situations and across time with respect to only those attributes that are central to his self-definition. If the individual thinks of himself as a "friendly" person, and considers it important to be as friendly as possible, then he should be consistently friendly in many situations, partly because he will continually monitor his own behavior to take note of how friendly he is being and will correct his own behavior if he is not behaving in ways that are consistent with his self-definition. For other individuals, however, friendliness is not a defining attribute; self-monitoring activity will not be directed toward maintaining consistency with respect to friendly behavior, and hence such behavior will vary greatly depending on the situation in which the person finds himself. In this vein, it is reasonable to believe that "masculinity" and "femininity" are essential self-defining attributes for some people but not for others. If the studies summarized in previous chapters of this book had been based on selected subsamples of subjects, including only those women who consider it important to be feminine and those men for whom masculinity is central to their self-concept, the chances are that greater sex differences would have been reported and the findings would have been much more consistent than we have found them to be. The variations in findings from one study to another probably reflect, in part, the relative concentration of people of this type in the subject population, as well as subtle variations in experimental situations that would signal to the subjects whether the tasks they were called on to perform had any relevance to masculinity or femininity.

ON THE ETIOLOGY OF PSYCHOLOGICAL SEX DIFFERENCES

In previous chapters we have discussed three kinds of factors that affect the development of sex differences: genetic factors, "shaping" of boylike and girl-like behavior by parents and other socializing agents, and the child's spontaneous learning of behavior appropriate for his sex through imitation. Anyone who would hope to explain acquisition of sex-typed behavior through one or two of these processes alone would be doomed to disappointment. Not only do the three kinds of processes exert their own direct influence, but they interact with one another.

Biological factors have been most clearly implicated in sex differences in aggression and visual-spatial ability. We have argued that the male's greater aggression has a biological component, citing in support the fact that (1) the sex difference manifests itself in similar ways in man and subhuman primates; (2) it is cross-culturally universal; and (3) levels of aggression are responsive to sex hormones. We have also found, surprisingly, that there is no good evidence that adults reinforce boys' aggression more than girls' aggression; in fact, the contrary may be true. Here, however, there are questions about the adequacy of our information. Direct observational studies of parental reactions to aggression have been carried out in settings in which only the responses to a child's aggression *toward the parents* (or sometimes toward siblings) could be observed. When it comes to permissiveness for fighting among unrelated children, we must rely on parent interviews. Parents *say* they encourage daughters to defend themselves as much as they do sons, and that they attempt to teach nonaggression to the same degree to both sexes. Serbin et al. (1973) found that in the case of aggressive or destructive behavior by one child toward another child in nursery school, teachers were more likely to intervene (and perhaps scold the guilty child) if the aggressor was a boy. It is possible that mothers react in an opposite way when they are supervising groups of children in neighborhoods and parks. We doubt it, but we do not know. Meanwhile, the available evidence is that adults do not generally accept or approve aggression in either sex. Either their reaction is equally negative for the two sexes, or they react somewhat more strongly to boys' aggression, on the grounds that boys are stronger and more given to fighting and therefore must be kept under closer control. Although strong negative reactions by parents and teachers may actually be "reinforcing" to some children, this is not usually what is meant when it is alleged that parents shape the aggressive behavior of the two sexes differently. What is usually meant is that they allow, accept, or encourage the behavior more in boys, and this we have not found to be true. The negative evidence on differential socialization has strengthened the case for biological origins of the sex differences in aggression. This does not mean that we believe aggressive behavior is unlearned. There is plentiful evidence that it *is* learned. We argue only that boys are more biologically prepared to learn it.

Does the male predisposition toward aggression extend to other behavior, such as dominance, competitiveness, and activity level? Probably yes, to some degree, but the case is not strong. Among subhuman primates, dominance is achieved largely through aggression, and an individual's position in the dominance hierarchy is related to levels of sex hormones. However, there is no direct evidence that dominance among adult human groups is linked either to sex hormones or to aggressiveness. The fact that "dominance" in most human groups is called "leadership" provides a clue to the fact that adult human beings influence one another by persuasion, charisma, mutual affection, and bargaining, as well as by force or threats thereof. To the extent that dominance is *not* exercised by coercion, the biological male aggressiveness is probably not implicated in it.

The case for biological control of visual-spatial ability rests primarily with genetic studies. There is evidence of a recessive sex-linked gene that contributes an element to high spatial ability. Present estimates are that approximately 50 percent of men and 25 percent of women show this element phenotypically, although of course more women than this are "carriers." This sex-linked element is not the only genetic element affecting spatial ability, and the others appear not to be sex-linked. There is so far little evidence for sex linkage of any of the genetic determiners of other specific abilities such as mathematical or verbal ability. The existence of a sex-linked genetic determiner of spatial ability does not imply that visual-spatial skills are unlearned. The specific skills involved in the manifestation of this ability improve with practice. Furthermore, cross-cultural work indicates that the sex difference can be either large or small, or may even disappear, depending upon cultural conditions affecting the rearing of the two sexes. Where women are subjugated, their visual-spatial skills are poor relative to those of men. Where both sexes are allowed independence early in life, both sexes have good visual-spatial skills.

Our review of the socialization pressures directed at the two sexes revealed a surprising degree of similarity in the rearing of boys and girls. The two sexes appear to be treated with equal affection, at least in the first five years of life (the period for which most information is available); they are equally allowed and encouraged to be independent, equally discouraged from dependent behavior; as noted above, there is even, surprisingly, no evidence of distinctive parental reaction to aggressive behavior in the two sexes. There *are* differences, however. Boys are handled and played with somewhat more roughly. They also receive more physical punishment. In several studies boys were found to receive both more praise and more criticism from their caretakers—socialization pressure, in other words, was somewhat more intense for boys—but the evidence on this point is inconsistent. The area of greatest differentiation is in very specifically sex-typed behavior. Parents show considerably more concern over a boy's being a "sissy" than over a girl's being a tomboy. This is especially true of fathers, who seem to take the lead in actively discouraging any interest a son might have in feminine toys, activities, or attire.

Is the direct socialization pressure from parents sufficient to account for known sex differences? For some behaviors, probably so. In some areas, clearly not. Aggression is a case of the second kind. Also, we see nothing in the socialization of the two sexes that would produce different patterns of intellectual abilities. In the area of sex typing as narrowly defined, there is clear parental pressure, particularly on boys; nevertheless, children seem to adopt sex-typed patterns of play and interests for which they have never been reinforced, and avoid sex-inappropriate activities for which they have never been punished. Observations of parental behavior may not have been detailed enough to pick up the more subtle pressures exerted, but it is our impression that parents are fairly permissive where many aspects of sex typing are concerned, and that direct "shaping" by parents does not, in most instances, account for the details of the behavior that is acquired. Parents seem to treat a child in accordance with their knowledge of his individual temperament, interests, and abilities, rather than in terms of sex-role stereotypes. We suspect that others who do not know the child well as an individual are more likely to react to him according to their stereotyped views of what a child of a given sex is likely to be like. Although this conclusion runs counter to common sense, it appears possible that relative strangers exert more stereotyping pressure on children than their own parents do. In any case, we believe that socialization pressures, whether by parents or others, do not by any means tell the whole story of the origins of sex differences.

How then does psychological sex differentiation come about? The psychoanalytic theory of identification would have it that the child identifies with the same-sex parent and learns the details of a sex role through imitation of this parent. Social-learning theory also emphasizes imitation, but argues that children are more often reinforced when they imitate a same-sex than an opposite-sex model, so that they acquire a generalized tendency to imitate not only the same-sex parent but other same-sex models as well. The distinction between acquisition and performance of a given item of behavior is stressed. A child may learn how to do something by watching an opposite-sex model, but may seldom do it because he learns (through observation or otherwise) that such action would probably be punished if performed by a person of his own sex.

We have found several reasons to be dissatisfied with these theories. The first is that children have not been shown to resemble closely the same-sex parent in their behavior. In fact, the rather meager evidence suggests that a boy resembles other children's fathers as much as he does his own, at least with respect to most of the behaviors and attributes measured so far. The same applies to girls' resemblance to their mothers. When people believe they see parent-child resemblance, we suspect they are often noticing physical resemblance rather than behavioral resemblance.

A second problem is that when offered an opportunity to imitate either a male or female model, children (at least those under age 6 or 7) do not characteristically select the model whose sex matches their own; their choices are fairly random in this regard. Yet their behavior is clearly sex-typed at a much earlier age than the age at which choice of same-sex models begins to occur. A final problem is that children's sex-typed behavior does not closely resemble that of adult models. Boys select an all-male play group, but they do not observe their fathers avoiding the company of females. Boys choose to play with trucks and cars, even though they may have seen their mothers driving the family car more frequently than their fathers; girls play hopscotch and jacks (highly sex-typed games), although these games are totally absent from their mother's observable behavior.

To recapitulate briefly: we have been discussing the biological factors and the learning processes that have been alleged to underlie the development of behavioral sex differences. It is tempting to try to classify the differential behaviors as being either innate or learned, but we have seen that this is a distinction that does not bear close scrutiny. We have noted that a genetically controlled characteristic may take the form of a greater *readiness to learn* a particular kind of behavior, and hence is not distinct from learned behavior. Furthermore, if one sex is more biologically predisposed than the other to perform certain actions, it would be reasonable to expect that this fact would be reflected in popular beliefs about the sexes, so that innate tendencies help to produce the cultural lore that the child learns. Thus he adapts himself, through learning, to a social stereotype that has a basis in biological reality. (Of course, not all social stereotypes about the sexes have such a basis.) It is reasonable, then, to talk about the process of acquisition of sex-typed behavior—the *learning* of sex-typed behavior— as a process built upon biological foundations that are sex-differentiated to some degree.

So far we have discussed two learning processes that have been presumed to account for the development of socially defined sex-appropriate behavior. The first emphasizes direct parental reinforcement. We have seen that, although differential reinforcement of boys and girls may account for some sex typing as narrowly defined (e.g. the fact that boys avoid wearing dresses and playing with dolls), there are large areas of sex-differentiated behavior where parental sanctions and encouragement seem to play only a very minor role. A second process widely believed to be crucial in differentiation is the child's identification with (and imitation of) the same-sex parent and, by generalization, other same-sex models. The weaknesses of this process in accounting for the evidence have been delineated above.

We turn now to a third kind of process—the one we entitled "self-socialization" in Chapter 1. This process has been most explicitly enunciated by Kohlberg (1966)[x]. Kohlberg stresses that sex-typed behavior is not made up of a set of independent elements acquired by imitating actions the child has seen same-sex people perform. It stems from organized rules the child has induced from what he has observed and what he has been told, and these rules are in many ways a distortion of reality. They are based upon a limited set of features that are salient and describable from a child's point of view (e.g. hair styles and dress); the child's sex-role conceptions are cartoon-like—oversimplified, exaggerated, and stereotyped. He fails to note the variations in the sex-role behavior of his real-life models. A compelling example of this is seen in the case of a 4-year-old girl who insisted that girls could become nurses but only boys could become doctors. She held to this belief tenaciously even though her own mother was a doctor. Hers was a concept clearly not based upon imitation of the most available model. It represented an induction from instances seen and heard (in fiction as well as fact), and like most childish rule inductions it did not easily take account of exceptions.

The child's problem in behaving in ways appropriate to his sex is twofold: he not only must have some conception of what boylike and girl-like behavior is, but also must have a clear conception of his own sex identity so that he knows which kind of behavior to adopt. Kohlberg notes that neither a child's conception of his own sexual identity nor his notions of what it means to be "masculine" or "feminine" are static. Both change with intellectual growth. Initially a child might know only what his or her own sex is without understanding that his own gender is unchangeable. When sex constancy has been achieved, the child then seeks to determine what behavior is appropriate for his own sex. Early in development, he may not know precisely which other people share a sex category with him; a boy of 4 may know, for example, which other children are also boys, but he may class all adults together as "grown-ups" and fail to make consistent distinctions between men and women or to realize that men and boys are similar in the sense of all being males. When sex groupings have been understood, the child is then in a position to identify what behavior is appropriate for his sex by observing what kinds of things males, as distinct from females, do and to match his own behavior to the conceptions he has constructed.

There is a problem with the Kohlberg view: sex typing of behavior occurs much earlier than gender constancy normally develops. We do not question that the achievement of gender constancy may accelerate the process of sex typing. Indeed, R. G. Slaby* has found that those kindergartners who have come to understand that gender is constant choose to observe same-sex models (as compared with opposite-sex models), whereas other children of the same age do not. But we would like to argue that gender constancy is not necessary in order for self-socialization into sex roles to begin. Children as young as 3, we suggest, have begun to develop a rudimentary understanding of their own sex identity, even though their ability to group others according to sex is imperfect and their notion about the permanence of their own sex identity incomplete. As soon as a boy knows that he is a boy in any sense, he is likely to begin to prefer to do what he conceives to be boylike things. Of course, he will not selectively imitate male models if he does not yet know which other people around him are in the same sex category as himself. But he will nevertheless try to match his own behavior to his limited concept of what attributes are sex-appropriate.

We believe that the processes of direct reinforcement and simple imitation are clearly involved in the acquisition of sex-typed behavior, but that they are not sufficient to account for the developmental changes that occur in sex typing. The third kind of psychological process—the one stressed by cognitive-developmental theorists such as Kohlberg—must also be involved. This third process is not easy to define, but in its simplest terms it means that a child gradually develops concepts of "masculinity" and "femininity," and when he has understood what his own sex is, he attempts to match his behavior to his conception. His ideas may be drawn only very

* R. G. Slaby, University of Washington, personal communication, 1974.

minimally from observing his own parents. The generalizations he constructs do not represent acts of imitation, but are organizations of information distilled from a wide variety of sources. A child's sex-role concepts are limited in the same way the rest of his concepts are, by the level of cognitive skills he has developed. Therefore the child undergoes reasonably orderly age-related changes in the subtlety of his thought about sex typing, just as he does with respect to other topics. Consequently, his *actions* in adopting sex-typed behavior, and in treating others according to sex-role stereotypes, also change in ways that parallel his conceptual growth.

IMPLICATIONS FOR SOCIAL ISSUES

Schooling

If boys and girls, on the average, have somewhat different areas of intellectual strength and weakness, does this imply that they should be taught in different ways? There have been a number of attempts to match instructional techniques to the specific aptitudes and learning styles of specific groups of students. The reader is referred to a review paper on this subject by Glaser (1972)[R]. Glaser shows that the results of these attempts have been disappointing. To date there is no evidence that an individual learns better if an instructional program is geared to his areas of strength. That is, it has not proved especially effective to instruct people with high visual-spatial abilities through visual-spatial (rather than verbal) means. Glaser believes that one reason for the failure to find such matches is that diagnosis of special abilities has been made with tests based upon psychometric, factor-analytic definitions of what these abilities are. He argues that instructional techniques must be adapted to the individual's repertoire of *learning processes*, not to "abilities" as psychometrically defined. Now it is just in the area of learning processes that sex differences have not been found. We have found the two sexes to be equally adept at paired-associates learning, discrimination learning, complex problem solving, adoption of useful strategies in memorizing, etc. Taking the Glaser position, then, there would be no grounds for separate instructional programs for the two sexes. It should be added that Glaser does not advocate working primarily with the skills that a child already has, and sidestepping the areas of weakness. He argues, rather, that the educator should focus directly upon teaching the strategies (processes) that are missing from a child's repertoire. This means that if a child seems to have a poor level of visual-spatial skills, one should *not* attempt to teach him exclusively by verbal means, but should attempt to improve his visual-spatial skills.

Schools are already coping with some of the educational handicaps wherein the sexes differ. There are special remedial classes for poor readers, and boys are considerably overrepresented in such classes. However, special remedial instruction in visual-spatial skills is not normally offered in the schools. If such skills do prove to be important in higher education or adult occupations, it might well be the case that many students, especially girls, would profit from such remedial instruction.

Sex differences in the social-emotional sphere have implications for the classroom, too, bearing not so much upon teaching strategies as upon the nature of the organization of classroom activities that may be optimal for the two sexes. We have seen that boys stimulate one another to increased activity and mock fighting. We also found, however (Chapter 4), that boys perform better on certain experimental tasks in the presence of other boys, so the possibility clearly exists that the competitive spirit among boys may feed into improved academic performance under certain circumstances. Little is known concerning the cross-sex effects of boys and girls upon each other's performance in the classroom. Do boys "show off" for girls or primarily for each other? Does the desire to impress the other sex take pro-academic or anti-academic forms? Does the presence of girls have a "gentling" effect on boys? Do boys stimulate girls to greater competitive striving? We cannot rely on our intuition for the answers to these questions, and, to our knowledge, data are not yet available. All we can say is that the sex mix in the classroom undoubtedly makes a difference in the motivation of students, and it would be worthwhile to consider how these motivations could be constructively utilized. Instructional techniques and classroom organization are not, of course, the only educational issues related to sex. There is the problem of admissions quotas. If girls are, on the average, less skilled in visual-spatial tasks, does this mean that fewer of them should be admitted to graduate schools in engineering, architecture, and art? Should fewer men be admitted to training in languages, linguistic science, and creative writing, on the grounds that girls, with their greater verbal skills, are more likely to profit from advanced training? Here we must emphasize once again the overlap in the sex distributions. There are many girls with high-level visual-spatial skills. It is by no means self-evident that visual-spatial skill is the intellectual ability that is most needed by engineers, but even if it were, and even if the elusive sex-linked recessive gene carried the major part of the variance in these skills (which it probably does not), current estimates are that at least 25 percent of women have it, as compared with approximately 50 percent of men. This is more than enough women to fill our engineering schools, if women's talents were developed through the requisite early training and interests. Women are now considerably underrepresented in engineering in terms of any criterion by which potential talent can be measured. We have no wish to push women toward careers that do not attract them. At the same time, we believe it would be a grievous injustice to establish formal or informal quotas

368   Summary and Commentary

that would exclude any women with the requisite talents and interests.
We are discussing quotas that exclude women because, historically, women
have been excluded from training for high-status careers more frequently
than men, but of course the argument applies in both directions. After a
certain amount of positive recruiting of qualified women to redress historical imbalances, the reasonable approach would appear to be to assess
an applicant on the basis of his or her measurable talents, not on the basis
of probabilities based on sex.

Dominance, Leadership, and Vocational Success

We have seen that the greater aggressiveness of the male is one of the
best established, and most pervasive, of all psychological sex differences.
We have also seen reason to believe there is a biological component underlying this difference. It has been alleged (see, for example, Goldberg
1973[R]) that aggression is the primary means whereby human beings dominate one another, so that in cross-sex encounters it will be true that (with
rare exceptions) men will dominate women, and will therefore come to
occupy the positions in society in which status and authority are vested.
In this view, the implications of male aggressiveness go very deep. In a
business setting, for example, it would be the man who would be (and
should be) the foreman, the supervisor, the chairman of the board. Leadership would also properly be assumed by men in politics, in the profes-
sions, and within the family.

We believe it is true that males have occupied the high-status positions
in the large majority of human social groupings through the history of man.
We do not think this is a historical accident. We doubt, however, that
dominance and leadership are inevitably linked to aggression.

Aggression may be the primary means by which apes and little boys
dominate one another (although even here the ability to maintain alliances
is important). However, aggression is certainly not the method most usually employed for leadership among mature human beings. Perhaps it
once was. But the day of the iron-fisted tycoon appears to be waning.
Business leadership is now exercised (especially at the highest levels in
the management of conglomerates) by negotiation and attempts to reach
agreement among managerial groups; leaders must be supportive toward
the people with whom they work, and more skilled in guiding a group toward consensus than in imposing their own wills. We must leave it to the
reader's judgment to estimate how often the "killer instinct" is involved in
achieving success in the business or political world. Clearly, it sometimes
is, and in these cases there will be a smaller number of women than men
who will have the temperament for it. We wish only to suggest that it is
entirely possible to achieve status by other means, and that the sexes have

a more equal chance at success by these alternative routes. We believe we see a shift toward more nonaggressive leadership styles in high-level management, but at the moment this is speculation.

In small face-to-face groups and within families, it may be that similar shifts have occurred. We do not know whether wife beating was ever the norm. Certainly in earlier times husbands had formal control over their wives' lives and fortunes to a degree that would be highly unusual now, and although physical force may not have been frequently used in maintaining this control, the possibility of its use as a last resort no doubt helped to support male authority. Nowadays, marriages are maintained to a much greater degree by mutual consent. Expanding the argument presented at the close of Chapter 7, we would like to suggest the following generalizations concerning the role of aggression in dominance and submission:

1. Aggression is a relatively primitive means of exerting influence over others. It entails risks and costs for the aggressor as well as the victim, and will normally be superseded by alternative forms of interaction as individuals acquire the skills needed for these more mature approaches.

2. Dominance of one individual over another can be maintained by aggression only to the degree that the dominee is not free to leave the relationship (i.e. to the degree that the individual needs the relationship and has no good alternatives). This, indeed, is one of the reasons why aggression is of limited effectiveness (see point 1 above).

2a. Young children have few alternatives to the same-sex play group. A boy cannot easily escape the aggression-maintained hierarchy of the male play group unless he is willing to be solitary or to play with girls.

2b. As children grow older, a variety of social groups become available, and hence aggression declines in importance as a means by which the leaders of these groups maintain their dominance.

2c. The amount of aggression displayed by adult men toward women in the maintenance of dominance depends, in part, on the degree to which the social system gives women a "way out" in marriage. In modern times, divorce is always an alternative, albeit not an attractive one in many cases. In some traditional societies, a woman can return to her parents' home to escape the brutality of a mate, or she may claim the protection of her brothers. All societies provide women and girls some protection against the aggression of men.

Social restraints on the expression of aggression by men toward women go a long way to create equality of bargaining power between them, but they do not necessarily equalize this power. Other aspects of the social system determine whether "institutionalized" dominance relations exist. The evidence is that the formal role structure of a society may determine the initial dominance-submission relations of men and women toward one another when they first become acquainted. But dominance within long-standing relationships has surprisingly little relationship to formal role structure. It is doubtful whether most long-standing relationships between individual human beings can be described in terms of a single "dominance-submission" dimension. One member of a pair will usually be more influential with respect to certain kinds of decisions, the other member with respect to others. The dominance relationship within a pair or social group fluctuates, depending on changes in coalitions and patterns of interpersonal loyalty or antagonism. What matters is the individual competencies, motivations, and commitments of the parties to a relationship, and their mutual affection.

These considerations imply that there is nothing inevitable about male achievement of all available leadership positions. As women acquire the relevant competencies, and as these competencies become known to themselves and others, groups will less and less be formed on the initial assumption that the male members will have more of the needed skills. Leadership roles should thus gradually become more equitably distributed. There will no doubt continue to be groups in which physical strength, or aggression-based dominance, will be the means of seizing leadership, or in which these traits are needed in a leader if the group is to achieve its goals. In such cases, we would expect leadership to gravitate to males. But in groups where leadership is achieved and held through skill in setting achievable goals, in planning, organizing, persuading, conciliating, and conveying enthusiasms, we see no reason for a sex bias.

Apart from leadership, we may ask whether the characteristics of men and women suit them particularly for certain occupations. We have already seen that intellectual aptitudes are similarly distributed by sex, at least enough so as to rule out reserving certain occupations for one sex or the other on the basis of ability patterns. Clearly, there are some occupations that call for great physical strength, and men can be expected to predominate in them. Some women, however, are strong enough to do any task, and if one looks at work assignments across the world, it is surprising how often women's work matches or exceeds men's work in strenuous physical exertion: thus we often find women carrying huge burdens on their heads, hoeing weeds for hours on end, and so on. In any case, physical exertion is not a prominent requirement of most jobs these days, and there are fewer and fewer jobs that must be assigned to men simply because men alone have the strength to perform them.

What about the male pattern of aggression and dominance attempts—are there occupations to which these contribute positively? Undoubtedly there are some, although it is difficult to know precisely what they are. It was once thought that a salesman needed to be "aggressive," but it is now known that a softer approach can be equally or sometimes more effective. A salesman does need to convey a sense of confidence in himself and his product, but the ability to do this is by no means a special province of the male.

Perhaps the traditional assignment of certain jobs to men and others to women has come about not so much because men are in jobs that call for aggressiveness as because women, being slower to anger, are less likely to protest onerous assignments. We have seen that girls are more likely than boys to comply with demands that adults make upon them; although it has not been demonstrated, it appears likely that in adulthood as well they will "take orders" from authority figures with less coercion. To put the matter bluntly, they are easier to exploit.

Childbearing and Child Care

We saw in Chapter 5 that, among lower animals, the hormones associated with pregnancy and childbirth produce a state of "readiness" to care for the young. It is not known whether there are similar biochemical elements in human responsiveness to young infants.

Hormonal priming or not, it is obvious that when a woman is breast-feeding her infant, this increases the likelihood of her being the infant's primary caretaker. It probably also imposes some constraints on the nature of the outside occupational duties she can undertake, although this issue is complex. In traditional agricultural societies, women who were breast-feeding frequently took their infants with them to the fields, and their assignment to certain other kinds of "heavy" labor was scarcely impeded. On the other hand, it is possible that some occupations (e.g. coal mining) became largely male because a breast-feeding woman could not take her infant to the work site. If some of the traditional division of labor between the sexes was indeed initially based upon the biological fact of breast-feeding, it is well to remember that these occupational distinctions grew up in a time when a woman would bear and nurse a very large number of children, so that she would be involved in this especially demanding form of care-taking for a high proportion of her adult life. During a time when families are small, breast-feeding briefer, and the woman's life span much longer, many of the traditional occupational constraints need no longer apply, even if they were at one time truly relevant. Furthermore, in societies where women's labor is needed, it has been found possible to organize nurseries near places of work, so that nursing mothers can be brought into occupations previously reserved for men.

Cross-cultural work has indicated that girls are more likely than boys to engage spontaneously in care-taking behavior toward younger children, but it is not known whether this stems entirely from their more intensive training as babysitters or whether they also have a greater readiness to acquire this behavior with appropriate training. Whether a boy can as easily learn to care for children depends in part upon whether his aggressive tendencies interfere.

We did see, in our review of the animal literature, that in rodents and some monkeys there is an initial tendency for males to attack the young, a tendency that must be weakened before "maternal" behavior develops in a male. That the same tendencies may exist in higher species is suggested by an incident recently observed in the course of a field study of free-living chimpanzees. David Hamburg* saw an adult male chimpanzee, in a fit of violent rage, seize an infant from the arms of its mother, swing it around by the feet, and dash its head against a rock; the mother attempted to retrieve it and was herself severely beaten. Of course, such incidents are very rare. In fact, this is the only incident of its kinds that has been witnessed over many years of observing this species; but the potentiality of its occurring must be one of the reasons why primate mothers keep their infants away from males as much as possible. To balance the picture, we should recall that there are subspecies of apes in which males play a considerable part in caring for infants. There are also instances (described in Chapter 5) in which male primates have "adopted" younger animals and cared for them effectively. Among humankind, is the danger of male aggression toward infants one of the reasons why child care has been assigned so exclusively to women? We do not know. Studies of battered children indicate that mothers are at least as likely as fathers to brutalize their children.

Of course, the vast majority of men and women are not notably aggressive toward children. Whether they are positively nurturant or merely indifferent seemingly depends in large measure on how much contact they have with children and how much responsibility they have for child care. C. E. Baldwin, using observations of children in six cultures (Whiting and Pope 1974), found that boys who had been involved in caring for younger siblings were less aggressive in their daily encounters with age-mates than boys who had not had such responsibilities. It would appear, then, that aggression is largely incompatible with child care, and that the process of caring for children moderates aggressive tendencies.

The role of dominance in child rearing is an important issue that has seldom been discussed. We have seen that boys are more likely than girls to try to dominate the adults with whom they deal. There is some reason to believe that women yield to these attempts from boys more readily than men do. Men, on the other hand, yield to the blandishments of small girls. Both men and women take a tougher stance toward children of their own sex. Thoughtful people differ in whether they value strictness toward chil-

---

* Professor of biological sciences and psychiatry, Stanford University, personal communication, 1974.

dren, and in how important they believe it is for adults to maintain "control" over children's behavior. In any case, when boys need control, men can probably provide it more effectively than women; when boys need support for independent action, they are more likely to get it from women. The reverse situation probably applies for girls: closer control from their mothers, indulgence and/or encouragement in adultlike behavior from their fathers. The major implication of these considerations would appear to be that a healthy balance of forces is best maintained when adults of both sexes are involved in the care of children of both sexes.

Is Biology Destiny?

We have seen that the sexes are psychologically much alike in many respects. We have also seen that some of the ways in which they do differ probably have a biological basis, whereas others do not. It has been argued (Goldberg 1973[R]) that where a biological basis exists, it behooves societies to socialize children in such a way as to emphasize and exaggerate the difference. That is, since males are more aggressive, girls should be carefully trained in nonaggression throughout childhood; otherwise they will be doomed to failure and disappointment as adults in their encounters with men. By extension, if women's greater propensity for nurturance has a biological basis, it would follow that men should not be trained in nurturance, leaving all nurturant activity to the sex biologically better suited for it.

The curious fact is, however, that social pressures to shape individuals toward their "natural" sex roles sometimes boomerang. Traits that may be functional for one aspect of a sex role may be dysfunctional for other aspects. A man who adopts the "machismo" image may gain prestige with his peers, or enhance his short-term attractiveness to women, at the expense of his effectiveness as a husband and father. A similar problem exists for the highly "feminine" woman. Effective care-taking of the young, for example, involves a good deal of assertiveness; people are more likely to be helpful toward others when they have had ego-enhancing experiences that make them feel competent in coping with problem situations (Moore et al. 1973). Training a girl to be "feminine" in the traditional nonassertive, "helpless," and self-deprecatory sense may actually make her a worse mother. Consistent with this possibility is a recent finding of E. Cohen (1973)[R] that schoolteachers who wanted to be promoted to principal had a more child-centered view of education, and more maternally warm feelings toward their pupils, than teachers who lacked this ambition. Of course, we need more information on the possible side effects of attempting to change the definitions of "masculine" and "feminine" that are used as yardsticks in the rearing of boys and girls. But it is by no means obvious that attempts to foster sex-typed behavior (as traditionally defined) in boys and girls serve to make them better men and women. Indeed, in some spheres of adult life such attempts appear to be positively handicapping. We suggest that societies have the option of minimizing, rather than maximizing, sex differences through their socialization practices. A society could, for example, devote its energies more toward moderating male aggression than toward preparing women to submit to male aggression, or toward encouraging rather than discouraging male nurturance activities. In our view, social institutions and social practices are not merely reflections of the biologically inevitable. A variety of social institutions are viable within the framework set by biology. It is up to human beings to select those that foster the life styles they most value.

References Cited

References Cited

Works cited in the text (or in the summary tables) that bear the superscript letter R are listed here. Works not bearing the superscript are listed in the Annotated Bibliography (Volume II). The distinction is explained in the Introduction, p. 8. Works designated by an asterisk in the following list appear in Roberta M. Oetzel's Annotated Bibliography in Eleanor E. Maccoby, ed., *The Development of Sex Differences* (Stanford, 1966), pp. 224–321, where they are annotated much in the manner of the present Annotated Bibliography.

Ainsworth, M. D. S., Bell, S. M. V., and Stayton, D. J. Individual differences in strange-situation behavior of one-year-olds. In H. R. Schaffer, ed., *Origin of human social relations*. London: Academic Press. 1971.

Alper, T. G. Role orientation in women. *J. Personality*, 1973, *41*, 9–31.

Anastasi, A. *Differential psychology*. 3d ed. New York: Macmillan, 1958.

Andrew, R. J. Changes in search behavior in male and female chicks, following different doses of testosterone. *Animal Behaviour*, 1972, *20*, 741–50.

*Bandura, A. Influence of models' reinforcement contingencies on the acquisition of imitative responses. *J. Personality & Social Psychology*, 1965, *1*, 589–95.

Bandura, A. Aggression: a social learning analysis. Englewood Cliffs, N.J.: Prentice-Hall, 1973.

Bandura, A., and Barab, P. G. Conditions governing nonreinforced imitation. *Developmental Psychology*, 1971, *5*, 244–55.

Bandura, A., and Barab, P. G. Processes governing disinhibitory effects through symbolic modeling. *J. Abnormal Psychology*, 1973, *82*, 1–9.

Bandura, A., and Walters, R. *Social learning and personality development*. New York: Holt, Rinehart & Winston, 1963.

*Bandura, A., Ross, D., and Ross, S. A. Transmission of aggression through imitation of aggresive models. *J. Abnormal & Social Psychology*, 1961. *63*, 575–82.

*Bandura, A., Ross, D., and Ross, S. A. Imitation of film-mediated aggressive models. *J. Abnormal & Social Psychology*, 1963a, *66*, 3–11.

Bandura, A., Ross, D., and Ross, S. A. A comparative test of the status envy, social power, and secondary reinforcement theories of identificatory learning. *J. Abnormal & Social Psychology*, 1963b, *67*, 527–34.

Bandura, A., Blanchard, E. B., and Ritter, B. Relative efficacy of desensitization and modeling approaches for inducing behavioral, affective and attitudinal changes. *J. Personality & Social Psychology*, 1969, *13*(3), 173–99.

Bandura, A., Jeffery, R. W., and Wright, C. L. Efficacy of participant modeling as a function of response induction aids. *J. Abnormal Psychology*, 1974, *83*, 56–64.

Bardwick, J. M. *Psychology of Women*. New York: Harper & Row, 1971.

Barrett, R. J., and Ray, O. S. Behavior in the open field, Lashley III maze, shuttle-box, and Sidman avoidance as a function of strain, sex, and age. *Developmental Psychology*, 1970, *3*, 73–77.

Barry, H., Child, I. L., and Bacon, M. K. Relation of child training to subsistence economy. *American Anthropologist*, 1959, *61*, 51–63.

Bayley, N. The development of motor abilities during the first three years. *Monographs of the Society for Research in Child Development*, 1936, *1*, 1–26.

Bayley, N. Individual patterns of development. *Child Development*, 1956, *27*, 45–74.

*Bayley, N., and Schaefer, E. S. Correlations of maternal and child behaviors with the development of mental abilities: data from the Berkeley Growth Study. *Monographs of the Society for Research in Child Development*, 1964, *29*, serial no. 97.

Bell, R. Q. Relations between behavior manifestations in the human neonate. *Child Development*, 1960, *31*, 463–77.

*Beller, E. K., and Turner, J. L. A study of dependency and aggression in early childhood. From progress report on NIMH project M-849, National Institute of Mental Health, Washington, D.C., 1962.

Bem, D. J., and Allen, A. On predicting some of the people some of the time: the search for cross-situational consistencies in behavior. *Psychological Review*, 1974, in press.

Bentzen, F. Sex ratios in learning and behavior disorders. *J. Orthopsychiatry*, 1963, *23*, 92–98.

Berger, E. M. Relationships among acceptance of self, acceptance of others and MMPI scores. *J. Counseling Psychology*, 1955, *2*, 279–84.

Bhavnani, R., and Hutt, C. Sexual differentiation in human development. In C. Ounsted and D. C. Taylor, eds., *Gender differences: their ontogeny and significance*. Baltimore: Williams & Wilkins, 1972.

*Bing, E. Effects of childrearing practices on development of differential cognitive abilities. *Child Development*, 1963, *34*, 631–48.

Blade, M. F., and Watson, W. S. Increase in spatial visualization test scores during engineering study. *Psychological Monographs*, 1955, *69* (12, whole no. 397).

Block, J. (Discussant). Longitudinal relations between newborn tactile threshold, preschool barrier behavior, and early school age imagination and verbal development. Symposium presented at the meeting of the Society for Research in Child Development, Minneapolis, 1971.

Bock, D. R., and Kolakowski, D. Further evidence of sex-linked major-gene influence on human spatial visualizing ability. *American J. Human Genetics*, 1973, *25*, 1–14.

Bowlby, J. *Attachment*. New York: Basic Books, 1969.

Brackett, C. W. Laughing and crying of preschool children. *Child Development Monographs*, 1934, *14*, 1–90.

Brinkmann, E. H. Programmed instruction as a technique for improving spatial visualization. *J. Applied Psychology*, 1966, *50*, 179–84.

Brody, E. G. Genetic basis of spontaneous activity in the albino rat. *Comparative Psychology Monographs*, 1942, *17*, serial no. 89.

*Bronfenbrenner, U. Some familial antecedents of responsibility and leadership in adolescents. In L. Petrullo and B. M. Bass, eds., *Studies in leadership*. New York: Holt, 1960.

Bronson, F. H., and Desjardins, C. Aggression in adult mice: modification by neonatal injections of gonadal hormones. *Science*, 1968, *161*, 705–6.

Broverman, D. M., Klaiber, E. L., Kobayashi, Y., and Vogel, W. Roles of activation and inhibition in sex differences in cognitive abilities. *Psychological Review*, 1968, 75, 23–50.

Broverman, I. K., Broverman, D. M., Clarkson, F. E., Rosenkrantz, P. S., and Vogel, S. R. Sex-role stereotypes and clinical judgments of mental health. *J. Consulting & Clinical Psychology*, 1970, 34, 1–7.

Brown, D. G. Sex-role preference in young children. *Psychological Monographs*, 1956, 70, no. 14.

Brown, D. G. Sex-role preference in children: methodological problems. *Psychological Reports*, 1962, 11, 477–78.

Bruner, J. S., Olver, R. R., and Greenfield, P. M. *Studies in Cognitive Growth*. New York: Wiley, 1966.

Buffery, A. W. H. Sex differences in the development of hemispheric asymmetry of function in the human brain. *Brain Research*, 1971, 31, 364–65.

Buffery, A. W. H., and Gray, J. A. Sex differences in the development of spatial and linguistic skills. In C. Ounsted and D. C. Taylor, eds., *Gender differences: their ontogeny and significance*. Baltimore: Williams & Wilkins, 1972.

Burke, P. J. Leadership role differentiation. In C. G. McClintock, ed., *Experimental social psychology*. New York: Holt, Rinehart & Winston, 1972.

Buss, A. H., and Buss, E. H. Stimulus generalization with words connoting anxiety. *J. Personality & Social Psychology*, 1966, 4, 707–10.

Cairns, R. B. Fighting and punishment from a developmental perspective. In J. K. Cole and D. D. Jensen, eds., *Nebraska Symposium on Motivation*. Lincoln: University of Nebraska Press, 1972.

Chamove, A., Harlow, H. F., and Mitchell, G. D. Sex differences in the infant-directed behavior of preadolescent rhesus monkeys. *Child Development*, 1967, 38, 329–35.

Clifford, M. M., and Cleary, T. A. The relationship between children's academic performance and achievement accountability. *Child Development*, 1972, 43, 647–55.

Cohen, E. G. Open-space schools: the opportunity to become ambitious. *Sociology of Education*, 1973, 46, 143–61.

Cohen, E. G., and Roper, S. Modification of interracial interaction disability. *American Sociological Review*, 1973, 37, 643–47.

*Coleman, J. S. *The adolescent society*. New York: Free Press of Glencoe, 1961.

Collins, B. E., and Raven, B. E. Group structure: attraction, coalitions, communication, and power. In G. Lindzey and E. Aronson, eds., *Handbook of social psychology*, vol. 4. Reading, Mass.: Addison-Wesley, 1968.

Conel, J. L. *The cortex of the newborn*. Cambridge: Harvard University Press, 1939.

Conel, J. L. *The cortex of the one-month infant*. Cambridge: Harvard University Press, 1941.

Conel, J. L. *The cortex of the three-month infant*. Cambridge: Harvard University Press, 1947.

Conel, J. L. *The cortex of the six-month infant*. Cambridge: Harvard University Press, 1951.

Conel, J. L. *The cortex of the fifteen-month infant*. Cambridge: Harvard University Press, 1955.

Conel, J. L. *The cortex of the twenty-four-month infant*. Cambridge: Harvard University Press, 1959.

Conel, J. L. *The cortex of the four-year child.* Cambridge: Harvard University Press, 1963.

Connolly, K. Locomotor activity in Drosophila. II. Selection for activity and inactive strains. *Animal Behavior,* 1966, *14,* 444–49.

Conrad, H. S., and Jones, H. E. A second study of familial resemblance in intelligence: environmental and genetic implications of parent-child and sibling correlations in the total sample. In G. M. Whipple, ed., *The thirty-ninth yearbook of the National Society for the Study of Education.* Bloomington, Ill.: Public School Publishing Co., 1940.

Craig, J. W., and Baruth, R. A. Inbreeding and social dominance. *Animal Behavior,* 1965, *13,* 109–13.

*Cunningham, J. D. Einstellung rigidity in children. *J. Experimental Child Psychology,* 1965, *2,* 237–47.

Dalton, K. Ante-natal progesterone and intelligence. *British J. Psychiatry,* 1968, *114,* 1377–82.

*Dawe, H. C. An analysis of two hundred quarrels of preschool children. *Child Development,* 1934, *5,* 139–57.

Dawson, J. L. M. Cultural and physiological influences upon spatial-perceptual processes in West Africa. *International J. Psychology,* 1967, *2,* 115–28, 171–85.

DeFries, J. C., Hegmann, J. P., and Weir, M. W. Open-field behavior in mice: evidence for a major gene effect mediated by the visual system. *Science,* 1966, *154,* 1577–79.

*De Jung, J. E., and Meyer, W. J. Expected reciprocity, grade trends, and correlates. *Child Development,* 1963, *34,* 127–39.

*DeLucia, L. A. The toy preference test: a measure of sex-role identification. *Child Development,* 1963, *34,* 107–17.

Deutsch, H. *The psychology of women.* New York: Grune & Stratton, 1944.

DeVore, I. Mother-infant relations in free-ranging baboons. In H. L. Rheingold, ed., *Maternal behavior in mammals.* New York: Wiley, 1963.

DeVore, I., ed. *Primate behavior: field studies of monkeys and apes.* New York: Holt, Rinehart & Winston, 1965.

Douvan, E., and Adelson, J. *The adolescent experience.* New York: Wiley, 1966.

*Droppleman, L. F., and Schaefer, E. S. Boys' and girls' reports of maternal and paternal behavior. *J. Abnormal & Social Psychology,* 1963, *67,* 648–54.

Duffy, E. *Activation and behavior.* (See esp. sex differences in measures of activation, pp. 224–28.) New York: Wiley, 1962.

Edwards, D. A. Early androgen stimulation and aggressive behavior in male and female mice. *Physiology & Behavior,* 1969, *4,* 333–38.

Ehrhardt, A. A., and Baker, S. W. Hormonal aberrations and their implications for the understanding of normal sex differentiation. Paper presented at the meetings of the Society for Research in Child Development, Philadelphia, 1973.

Ehrhardt, A. A., and Money, J. Progestin-induced hermaphroditism: IQ and psychosexual identity in a study of ten girls. *J. Sex Research,* 1967, *3*(1), 83–100.

Elliott, R., and McMichael, R. E. Effects of specific training on frame dependence. *Perceptual & Motor Skills,* 1963, *17,* 363–67.

Entwisle, D. R. To dispel fantasies about fantasy-based measures of achievement motivation. *Psychological Bulletin,* 1972, *77,* 377–91.

Eriksson, J. Genetic selection for voluntary alcoholic consumption in the albino rat. *Science*, 1968, *159*, 739–41.

Escalona, A., and Heider, G. M. *Prediction and outcome: a study in child development*. New York: Basic Books, 1959.

Feldman, S. S. Some possible antecedents of attachment behavior in two-year-old children. Unpublished manuscript, Stanford University, 1974.

Feshbach, S. Aggression. In P. H. Mussen, ed., *Carmichael's manual of child psychology*. New York: Wiley, 1970.

Fidell, L. S. Empirical verification of sex discrimination in hiring practices in psychology. *American Psychologist*, 1970, *25*, 1094–98.

Fidell, L. S. Put her down on drugs: prescribed drug usage in women. Paper presented at the meetings of the Western Psychological Association, Anaheim, California, 1973.

Fiedler, F. E. Assumed similarity measures as predictors of team effectiveness. *J. Abnormal & Social Psychology*, 1954, *49*, 381–88.

Flavell, J. H. Concept development. In P. H. Mussen, ed., *Carmichael's manual of child psychology*. New York: Wiley, 1970.

Flory, C. D. Osseous development in the hand as an index of skeletal development. *Monographs of the Society for Research in Child Development*, 1936, *1*, 96–97.

Fourr, J. S. Strength, timidity, and sleep cycles in the six-month-old infant: stability, sex differences, and relationships to newborn behaviors. Unpublished honors thesis, Stanford University, 1974.

Freedman, D. G. The development of social hierarchies. Paper presented at the World Health Organization conference, 1971. In Lennart Levi, ed., *Society, stress and disease in childhood and adolescence*, vol. 2. New York: Oxford University Press, in press.

Freud, A., and Dann, S. An experiment in group upbringing. *Psychoanalytic Studies of the Child*, 1951, *6*, 127–68. (See also in C. B. Stendler, ed., *Readings in child behavior and development*. New York: Harcourt, Brace & World, 1964.)

Furchgott, E., and Lazar, J. Maternal parity and offspring behavior in the domestic mouse. *Developmental Psychology*, 1969, *1*, 227–30.

Garai, J. E., and Scheinfeld, A. Sex differences in mental and behavioral traits. *Genetic Psychology Monographs*, 1968, 77, 169–299.

Garcia, J., and Koelling, R. Relation of cue to consequence in avoidance learning. *Psychonomic Science*, 1966, *4*, 123–24.

Glaser, Robert. Individuals and learning: the new aptitudes. *Educational Researcher*, 1972 *1*(6), 5–13.

Gold, M. Power in the classroom. *Sociometry*, 1958, *21*, 50–60.

Goldberg, S. *The inevitability of patriarchy*. New York: Morrow, 1973.

Goodall, J. Chimpanzees of the Gombe Stream Reserve. In I. DeVore, ed., *Primate behavior*. New York: Holt, Rinehart & Winston, 1965.

Goodenough, D. R., and Karp, S. A. Field dependence and intellectual functioning. *J. Abnormal & Social Psychology*, 1961, *63*, 241–46.

Goodenough, F. L. *Anger in young children*. Minneapolis: University of Minnesota Press, 1931.

*Gordon, J. E., and Smith, E. Children's aggression, parental attitudes, and the effects of an affiliation-arousing story. *J. Personality & Social Psychology*, 1965, *1*, 654–59.

Gordon, N. S., and Bell, R. Q. Activity in the human newborn. *Psychological Report*, 1961, 9, 103–16.

Gray, J. *The psychology of fear and stress*. London: Weidenfeld & Nicolson, 1971.

Gray, J. A., and Levine, S. Effect of induced oestrus on emotional behavior in selected strains of rats. *Nature*, 1964, *201*, 1198–2000.

Gray, J. A., Levine, S., and Broadhurst, P. S. Gonadal hormone injections in infancy and adult emotional behavior. *Animal Behavior*, 1965, *13*, 33–45.

*Guetzkow, H. An analysis of the operation of set in problem-solving behavior. *J. General Psychology*, 1951, *45*, 219–44.

Guhl, A. A., Craig, J. V., and Mueller, C.D. Selective breeding for aggressiveness in chickens. *Poultry Science*, 1960, *39*, 970–80.

Guilford, J. P. A revised structure of intellect. Rep. Psychol. Lab., no. 19, University of Southern California, Los Angeles, 1957.

Hagen, J. W. The effect of distraction on selective attention. *Child Development*, 1967, *38*, 685–94.

Hall, K. R. L., and DeVore, I. Baboon social behavior. In I. DeVore, ed., *Primate behavior*. New York: Holt, Rinehart & Winston, 1965.

Hamburg, D. A., and Van Lawick–Goodall, J. Factors facilitating development of aggressive behavior in chimpanzees and humans. Unpublished manuscript. Stanford University, 1973.

Hamers, J., and Lambert, W. Unpublished data, McGill University, 1973.

Harlow, H. F. The heterosexual affectional system in monkeys. *American Psychologist*, 1962, *17*, 1–9.

Hartlage, L. C. Sex-linked inheritance of spatial ability. *Perceptual & Motor Skills*, 1970, *31*, 610.

*Hartup, W. W., and Keller, E. D. Nurturance in preschool children and its relation to dependency. *Child Development*, 1960, *31*, 681–89.

*Hartup, W. W., Moore, S. G., and Sager, G. Avoidance of inappropriate sex-typing by young children. *J. Consulting Psychology*, 1963, *27*, 467–73.

*Hattwick, L. A. Sex differences in behavior of nursery school children. *Child Development*, 1937, *8*, 343–55.

*Heathers, G. Emotional dependence and independence in nursery school play. *J. Genetic Psychology*, 1955, *87*, 37–57.

*Hetherington, E. M. A developmental study of the effects of sex of the dominant parent on sex-role preference, identification, and imitation in children. *J. Personality & Social Psychology*, 1965, *2*, 188–94.

Hetherington, E. M. The effects of familial variables on sex typing, on parent-child similarity, and on imitation in children. In J. P. Hill, ed., *Minnesota Symposia on Child Psychology*, vol. 1. Minneapolis: University of Minnesota Press, 1967.

*Hicks, D. J. Imitation and retention of film-mediated aggressive peer and adult models. *J. Personality & Social Psychology*, 1965, *2*, 97–100.

Hoffman, L. W. Early childhood experiences and women's achievement motives. *J. Social Issues*, 1972, *28*, 129–55.

*Honzik, M. P. Sex differences in the occurrence of materials in the play constructions of preadolescents. *Child Development*, 1951, *22*, 15–35.

*Honzik, M. P. A sex difference in the age of onset of the parent-child resemblance in intelligence. *J. Educational Psychology*, 1963, *54*, 231–37.

Honzik, M. P. Environmental correlates of mental growth: prediction from the family setting at 21 months. *Child Development*, 1967, *38*, 337–64.

Horner, M. S. Sex differences in achievement motivation and performance in competitive and noncompetitive situations. Unpublished Ph.D. dissertation, University of Michigan, 1968.

*Hovland, C. I., and Janis, I. L., eds. *Personality and persuasibility*. New Haven: Yale University Press, 1959.

Hundleby, J. D., and Cattell, R. B. Personality structure in middle childhood and the prediction of school achievement and adjustment. *Monographs of the Society for Research in Child Development*, 1968, *33*, serial no. 121.

Hutt, C. *Males and females*. Middlesex, England: Penguin Books, 1972.

Jacklin, C. N., and Bonneville, L. The 9½-month-old infant: stability of behavior, sex differences, and longitudinal findings. Unpublished manuscript, Stanford University, 1974.

Jacklin, C. N., and Mischel, H. N. As the twig is bent—sex role stereotyping in early readers. *School Psychology Digest*, 1973, *2*, 30–37.

Jensen, G. D., Bobbitt, R. A., and Gordon, B. N. Sex differences in the development of independence of infant monkeys. *Behavior*, 1968, *30*, 1–14.

Johnson, D. D. Sex differences in reading across cultures. *Reading Research Quarterly*, 1973–74, *9*, 67–86.

Jones, S. E. A comparative proxemics analysis of dyadic interaction in selected subcultures of New York City. *J. Social Psychology*, 1971, *84*, 35–44.

Joslyn, W. D. Androgen-induced social dominance in infant female rhesus monkeys. *J. Child Psychology & Psychiatry*, 1973, *14*, 137–45.

*Kagan, J. The child's sex role classification of school objects. *Child Development*, 1964, *35*, 1051–56.

Kagan, J., and Kogan, N. Individuality and cognitive performance. In P. H. Mussen, ed., *Carmichael's manual of child psychology*. New York: Wiley, 1970.

*Kagan, J., and Lemkin, J. The child's differential perception of parental attributes. *J. Abnormal & Social Psychology*, 1960, *61*, 440–47.

Kagan, J., and Moss, H. A. Parental correlation of child's IQ and height: a cross-validation of the Berkeley Growth Study results. *Child Development*, 1959, *30*, 325–32.

*Kagan, J., and Moss, H. A. *Birth to maturity: a study in psychological development*. New York: Wiley, 1962.

Kaplan, A. R., and Fischer, R. Taste sensitivity for bitterness: some biological and clinical implications. In J. Wortis, ed., *Recent advances in biological psychiatry*, vol. 8. New York: Plenum Press, 1964.

Keating, D. P. The study of mathematically precocious youth. Paper presented at the meetings of the American Association for the Advancement of Science, Washington, D.C., 1972.

Kimura, D. Speech lateralization in young children as determined by an auditory test. *J. Comparative & Physiological Psychology*, 1963, *56*, 899–902.

Klaiber, E. L., Broverman, D. M., and Kobayashi, Y. The automatization cognitive style, androgens, and monoamine oxidase (MAO). *Psycholopharmacologia*, 1967, *11*, 320–36.

Klaiber, E. L., Broverman, D. M., Vogel, W., Abraham, G. E., and Cone, E. L. Effects of infused testosterone on mental performances and serum LH. *J. Clinical Endocrinology & Metabolism*, 1971, *32*, 341–49.

Kohlberg, L. Development of moral character and moral ideology. In M. L. Hoffman and L. W. Hoffman, eds., *Review of child development research*, vol. 1. New York: Russell Sage Foundation, 1964.

Kohlberg, L. A cognitive-developmental analysis of children's sex-role concepts and attitudes. In E. E. Maccoby, ed., *The development of sex differences*. Stanford, Calif.: Stanford University Press, 1966.

*Kohlberg, L., and Zigler, E. The impact of cognitive maturity on the development of sex-role attitudes in the years 4–8. *Genetic Psychology Monographs*, 1967, 75, 84–165.

*Kohn, A. R., and Fiedler, F. E. Age and sex differences in the perception of persons. *Sociometry*, 1961, 24, 157–64.

Konstadt, N., and Forman, E. Field dependence and external directedness. *J. Personality & Social Psychology*, 1965, 1, 490–93.

Kreuz, L. E., and Rose, R. M. Assessment of aggressive behavior and plasma testosterone in a young criminal population. *Psychosomatic Medicine*, 1972, 34, 321–32.

Kummer, H. Two variations in the social organization of baboons. In P. C. Jay, ed., *Primates—studies in adaptation and variability*. New York: Holt, Rinehart & Winston, 1968.

Kuo, Z. Y. *The dynamics of behavior development: an epigenetic view*. New York: Random House, 1967.

Lacey, J. I. Semantic response patterning and stress: some revisions of activation theory. In M. H. Appley and R. Turnbull, eds., *Psychological stress: some issues in research*. New York: Appleton-Century-Crofts, 1967.

Landreth, C. Factors associated with crying in young children in the nursery school and the home. *Child Development*, 1941, 12, 81–97.

Langlois, J. H., Gottfried, N. W., and Seay, B. The influence of sex of peer on the social behavior of preschool children. *Developmental Psychology*, 1973, 8, 93–98 (and personal communication).

*Lazowick, L. M. On the nature of identification. *J. Abnormal & Social Psychology*, 1955, 51, 175–83.

Leifer, A. D. The relationship between cognitive awareness in selected areas and differential imitation of a same-sex model. Unpublishd M.A. thesis, Stanford University, 1966.

Leifer, A. D. Effects of early, temporary mother-infant separation on later maternal behavior in humans. Unpublished Ph.D. dissertation, Stanford University, 1970.

Leifer, A. D., Leiderman, P. H., Barnett, C. R., and Williams, J. A. Effects of mother-infant separation on maternal attachment behavior. *Child Development*, 1972, 43, 1203–18.

Leik, R. K. Instrumentality and emotionality in family interaction. *Sociometry*, 1963, 26, 131–45.

Levine, S. Sex differences in the brain. *Scientific American*, 1966, 214, 84–90.

Levine, S. Sexual differentiation: the development of maleness and femaleness. *California Medicine*, 1971, 114, 12–17.

Levine, S., and Mullins, R. Estrogen administered neonatally affects adult sexual behavior in male and female rats. *Science*, 1964, 144, 185–87.

Levy-Agresti, J. Ipsilateral projection systems and minor hemisphere function in man after neocomissurotomy. *Anatomical Record*, 1968, 61, 1151.

Levi-Agresti, J., and Sperry, R. W. Differential perceptual capacities in major and minor hemispheres. Paper presented at fall meetings, National Academy of Sciences, California Institute of Technology, Pasadena. *Proceedings of the National Academy of Science*, 1968, 61.

*Lipsitt, L. P., and Levy, N. Electroactual threshold in the human neonate. *Child Development*, 1959, 30, 547–54.

Luchins, A. S. Mechanization in problem-solving—the effect of Einstellung. *Psychological Monographs*, 1942, *54*, no. 6.

Lunde, D. T. Sex hormones, mood and behavior. Paper presented at the Sixth Annual Symposium, Society of Medical Psychoanalysis, New York, 1973.

Lynn, D. B. *Parental and sex role identification: a theoretical formulation.* Berkeley, Calif.: McCutchan, 1969.

Lyon, M. F. Gene action in the X-chromosome of the mouse (*Mus musculus L.*) *Nature*, 1961, *190*, 372.

McCall, R. B., Appelbaum, M., and Hogarty, P. S. Developmental changes in mental performance. *Monographs of the Society for Research in Child Development*, 1973, *38*, serial no. 150.

McCarthy, D. Language development in children. In L. Carmichael, ed., *Manual of child psychology*, 2d ed. New York: Wiley, 1954.

°McClelland, D. C., Atkinson, J. W., Clark, R. A., and Lowell, E. L. *The achievement motive.* New York: Appleton-Century-Crofts, 1953.

McClintock, C. G. Game behavior and social motivation in interpersonal settings. In C. McClintock, ed., *Experimental social psychology.* New York: Holt, Rinehart & Winston, 1972.

McClintock, C. G., Messick, D. M., Kuhlman, D., and Campos, F. Assessing social motivation in a triple decomposed game. *J. Experimental Social Psychology*, 1973, in press.

Maccoby, E. E. Role-taking in childhood and its consequences for social learning. *Child Development*, 1959, *30*, 239–52.

Maccoby, E. E. Sex differences in intellectual functioning. In E. E. Maccoby, ed., *The development of sex differences.* Stanford, Calif.: Stanford University Press, 1966a.

Maccoby, E. E., ed. *The development of sex differences.* Stanford, Calif.: Stanford University Press, 1966b.

Maccoby, E. E. The development of stimulus selection. In J. P. Hill., ed., *Minnesota Symposium on Child Development*, 1969, *3*, 68–98.

Maccoby, E. E., and Jacklin, C. N. Sex differences and their implications for sex roles. Paper presented at the meetings of the American Psychological Association, Washington, D.C., 1971.

Maccoby, E. E., and Masters, J. C. Attachment and dependency. In P. H. Mussen, ed., *Carmichael's manual of child psychology*, vol. 2, 1970.

°Maccoby, E. E., and Wilson, W. C. Identification and observational learning from films. *J. Abnormal & Social Psychology*, 1957, *55*, 76–87.

°Maccoby, E. E., Wilson, W. C., and Burton, R. V. Differential movie-viewing behavior of male and female viewers. *J. Personality*, 1958, *26*, 259–67.

McDonnell, G. J., and Carpenter, J. A. Manifest anxiety and prestimulus conductance levels. *J. Abnormal & Social Psychology*, 1960, *60*, 437–38.

McKenzie, B. E. Visual discrimination in early infancy. Ph.D. dissertation, Monash University, Australia, 1972.

Marks, J. B. Interests and leadership among adolescents. *J. Genetic Psychology*, 1957, *91*, 163–72.

°Mellone, M. A. A factorial study of picture tests for young children. *British J. Psychology*, 1944, *35*, 9–16.

Messick, S., and Damarin, F. Cognitive styles and memory for faces. *J. Abnormal & Social Psychology*, 1964, *69*, 313–18.

Metzner, R., and Mischel, W. Achievement motivation, sex of subject, and delay behavior. Unpublished manuscript, Stanford University, 1962.

Miles, C. C. Gifted children. In L. Carmichael, ed., *Manual of child psychology*, 2d ed. New York: Wiley, 1954.

Minturn, L., and Hitchcock, J. T. The Pajputs of Khalapur, India. In B. B. Whiting, ed., *Six cultures*. New York: Wiley, 1963.

Mischel, H. Sex bias in the evaluation of professional achievements. *J. Educational Psychology*, 1974, 66, 157–66.

Mischel, W. Sex-typing and socialization. In P. H. Mussen, ed., *Carmichael's manual of child psychology*. New York: Wiley, 1970.

Mitchell, G. Attachment differences in male and female infant monkeys. *Child Development*, 1968, 39, 611–20.

Mitchell, G., and Brandt, E. M. Behavioral differences related to experience of mother and sex of infant in the rhesus monkey. *Developmental Psychology*, 1970, 3, 149.

Mitchell, G., and Brandt, E. M. Paternal behavior in primates. In F. E. Poirier, ed., *Primate socialization*. New York: Random House, 1972.

Moltz, H., Lubin, M., Leon, M., and Numan, M. Hormonal induction of maternal behavior in the ovariectomized rat. *Physiology & Behavior*, 1970, 5, 1373–77.

Money, J., and Ehrhardt, A. A. *Man and woman, boy and girl*. Baltimore: Johns Hopkins University Press, 1972.

Murray, H. A. Explorations in personality. New York: Oxford University Press, 1938.

Mussen, P. H. Early sex-role development. In D. A. Goslin, ed., *Handbook of socialization theory and research*. Chicago: Rand McNally, 1969.

*Mussen, P. H., and Rutherford, E. Parent-child relations and parental personality in relation to young children's sex-role preferences. *Child Development*, 1963, 34, 589–607.

*Nakamura, C. Y. Conformity and problem solving. *J. Abnormal & Social Psychology*, 1958, 56, 315–20.

Nerlove, S. B., Munroe, R. H., and Munroe, R. L. Effects of environmental experience on spatial ability: a replication. *J. Social Psychology*, 1971, 84, 3–10.

Notermans, S. L. H., and Tophoff, M. M. W. A. Sex differences in pain tolerance and pain apperception. *Psychiatria, Neurologia, Neurochirurgia*, 1967, 70, 23–29.

Osofsky, J. D., and Oldfield, S. Children's effects upon parental behavior: mothers' and fathers' responses to dependent and independent child behaviors (summary). *Proceedings of the 79th Annual Convention of the American Psychological Association*, Washington, D. C., 1971.

Parke, R., and O'Leary, S. Mother-father-infant interaction in the newborn period: some findings, some observations, and some unresolved issues. In K. Riegel and J. Meacham, Determinants of behavioral development, II, 1974 (in press).

Parlee, M. B. Comments on D. M. Broverman, E. L. Klaiber, Y. Kobayashi, and W. Vogel: Roles of activation and inhibition in sex differences in cognitive abilities. *Psychological Review*, 1972, 79, 180–84.

Parsons, T. The American family: its relations to personality and to the social structure. In T. Parsons and R. F. Bales, eds., *Family, socialization and interaction process*. New York: Free Press, 1955.

Patterson, G. R., Littman, R. A., and Bricker, W. Assertive behavior in children: a step toward a theory of aggression. *Monographs of the Society for Research in Child Development*, 1967, 32, serial no. 113.

Patterson, P., Bonvillian, J. D., Reynolds, P.C., and Maccoby, E. E. Mother and peer attachment under conditions of fear in rhesus monkeys. *Primates*, 1974, in press.

Peplau, A. Impact of sex-role attitudes and opposite-sex relationships on women's achievement: an experimental study of dating couples. Ph.D. dissertation, preliminary report, Harvard University, 1973.

Podell, J. E., and Phillips, L. A developmental analysis of cognition as observed in dimensions of Rorschach and objective test performance. *J. Personality*, 1959, *27*, 439–63.

Polansky, N., Lippitt, R., and Redl, F. An investigation of behavioral contagion in groups. *Human Relations*, 1950, *3*, 319–48.

Preston, D. G., Baker, R. P., and Seay, B. Mother-infant separation in the patus monkey. *Developmental Psychology*, 1970, *3*, 298–306.

*Rabban, M. Sex-role identification in young children in two diverse social groups. *Genetic Psychology Monographs*, 1950, *42*, 81–158.

Ramey, C. T., and Watson, J. S. Nonsocial reinforcement of infant's vocalizations. *Developmental Psychology*, 1972, *6*, 538 (extended version of brief report).

Raphelson, A. C. The relationships among imagination: direct, verbal, and physiological measures of anxiety in an achievement stimulus. *J. Abnormal & Social Psychology*, 1957, *54*, 13–18.

Raush, H. R. Interaction sequences. *J. Personality & Social Psychology*, 1965, *2*, 487–99.

Rescorla, R. A. Pavlovian conditioning and its proper control procedures. *Psychological Review*, 1967, *74*, 71–80.

Rescorla, R. A. Pavlovian conditioned inhibition. *Psychological Bulletin*, 1969, *72*, 77–94.

Reynolds, V., and Reynolds, F. Chimpanzees of the Budongo Forest. In I. Devore, ed., *Primate behavior*. New York: Holt, Rinehart & Winston, 1965.

Roff, M. Intra-family resemblances in personality characteristics. *J. Psychology*, 1950, *30*, 199–227.

Rose, R. M., Holaday, J. W., and Bernstein, I. S. Plasma testosterone, dominance rank, and aggressive behavior in male rhesus monkeys. *Nature*, 1971, *231*, 366–68.

Rose, R. M., Gordon, T. P., and Bernstein, I. S. Plasma testosterone levels in the male rhesus: influences of sexual and social stimuli. *Science*, 1972, *178*, 643–45.

Rosenberg, B. G., and Sutton-Smith, B. Family interaction effects on masculinity-femininity. *J. Personality & Social Psychology*, 1968, *8*, 117.

Rosenberg, K. M., Denenberg, V. H., Zarrow, M. X., and Bonnie, L. F. Effects of neonatal castration and testosterone on the rat's pup-killing behavior and activity. *Physiology & Behavior*, 1971, *7*, 363–68.

Rosenblatt, J. S. The development of maternal responsiveness in the rat. *American J. Orthopsychiatry*, 1969, *39* (1), 36–56.

*Rosenblith, J. F. Learning by imitation in kindergarten children. *Child Development*, 1959, *30*, 69–80.

*Rosenblith, J. F. Imitative color choices in kindergarten children. *Child Development*, 1961, *32*, 211–23.

Rosenkrantz, P. S., Vogel, S. R., Bee, H., Broverman, I., and Broverman, D. Sex-role stereotypes and self-concepts in college students. *J. Consulting & Clinical Psychology*, 1968, *32*, 287–95.

Rosenthal, M. K. The generalization of dependency behavior from mother to stranger. *J. Child Psychology & Psychiatry*, 1967, *8*, 117–33.

Rosner, J. A. The development and validation of an individualized perceptual skills curriculum. University of Pittsburgh, Learning Research and Development Center, 1973.

Rossi, A. M. An evaluation of the manifest anxiety scale by the use of electromyography. *J. Experimental Psychology*, 1959, *58*, 64–69.

*Rothaus, P., and Worchel, P. Ego-support, communication, catharsis, and hostility. *J. Personality*, 1964, *32*, 296–312.

*Rothbart, M. K., and Maccoby, E. E. Parents' differential reactions to sons and daughters. *J. Personality & Social Psychology*, 1966, *4*, 237–43.

Sackett, G. P. Isolation rearing in monkeys: diffuse and specific effects on later behavior. Unpublished manuscript, University of Washington, 1971.

Sander, L. W., and Cassel, T. Z. An empirical approach to the study of interactive regulation in the infant-caretaking system and its role in early development. Paper presented at the meetings of the Society for Research in Child Development, Philadelphia, 1973.

*Sarason, S. B., Lighthall, F. F., Davidson, K. S., Waite, R. R., and Ruebush, B. K. *Anxiety in elementary school children*. New York: Wiley, 1960.

Sarason, S. B., Hill, D. T., and Zimbardo, P. G. A longitudinal study of the relation of test anxiety to performance on intelligence and achievement tests. *Monographs of the Society for Research in Child Development*, 1964, *29*, serial no. 98.

Schachter, S. *Psychology of affiliation*. Stanford, Calif.: Stanford University Press, 1959.

*Schaefer, E. S., and Bayley, N. Maternal behavior, child behavior, and their intercorrelations from infancy through adolescence. *Monographs of the Society for Research in Child Development*, 1963, *28*, serial no. 87.

Schaller, J. Children's attitudes to newcomers. *Goteborg Psychological Reports*, 1973, *3*, 1–6.

Schneider, R. A., and Wolf, S. Olfactory perception thresholds for citral utilizing a new type olfactorium. *J. Applied Physiology*, 1955, *8*, 337–42.

Sears, P. S. The effect of classroom conditions on the strength of achievement motive and work output on elementary school children. Cooperative Research Project no. OE 873. Stanford University, 1963.

*Sears, R. R. Relation of early socialization experiences to aggression in middle childhood. *J. Abnormal & Social Psychology*, 1961, *63*, 466–92.

Sears, R. R. Development of gender role. In F. A. Beach, ed., *Sex and behavior*. New York: Wiley, 1965.

*Sears, R. R., Whiting, J., Nowlis, V., and Sears, P. S. Some child rearing antecedents of aggression and dependency in young children. *Genetic Psychology Monographs*, 1953, *47*, 135–234.

*Sears, R. R., Maccoby, E. E., and Levin, H. *Patterns of child rearing.* Evanston, Ill.: Row, Peterson, 1957.

*Sears, R. R., Rau, L., and Alpert, R. *Identification and child rearing*. Stanford, Calif.: Stanford University Press, 1965.

Seligman, M. E. P. On the generality of the laws of learning. *Psychological Review*, 1970, *77* (5), 406–18.

Sherman, J. A. Problem of sex differences in space perception and aspects of intellectual functioning. *Psychological Review*, 1967, *74*, 290–99.

Sherman, J. A. *On the psychology of women*. Springfield, Ill.: Charles C Thomas, 1971.

Shipman, V. C. Disadvantaged children and their first school experiences. Educational Testing Service, Head Start Longitudinal Study, 1972, Report PR-72-18, Princeton, N.J.

*Shirley, M., and Poyntz, L. The influence of separation from the mother on children's emotional responses. *J. Psychology*, 1941, *12*, 251–82.

Silverman, R. E. Manifest anxiety as a measure of drive. *J. Abnormal & Social Psychology*, 1957, *55*, 94–97.

*Simpson, M. Parent preferences of young children. *Contributions to Education* (Columbia University Teachers College), no. 652, 1935.

Singer, J. E., Westphal, M., and Niswander, K. R. Sex differences in the incidence of neonatal abnormalities and abnormal performance in early childhood. *Child Development*, 1968, *39*, 103–12.

Smith, I. M. *Spatial ability*. San Diego, Calif.: Knapp, 1964.

Smith, W. D. Black parents' differential attitudes toward childhood behaviors and child-rearing practices. Unpublished first year project, Stanford University, 1971.

Spence, K. W., and Spence, J. T. Sex and anxiety differences in eyelid conditioning. *Psychological Bulletin*, 1966, *65*, 137–42.

Stanley, J. C., Fox, L. H., and Keating, D. P. *Annual report to the Spencer Foundation*, The Johns Hopkins University, October 1972.

Stanton, A. M. Hormones and behavior in newborns: biochemical factors in the development of behavioral sex differences. Unpublished manuscript, Stanford University, 1972.

*Steiner, I. D., and Rogers, E. D. Alternative responses to dissonance. *J. Abnormal & Social Psychology*, 1963, *66*, 128–36.

Sternglanz, S. B. An ethological approach to neonatal quieting. Unpublished Ph.D. dissertation, Stanford University, 1972.

Stevenson, H. W. Learning in children. In P. H. Mussen, ed., *Carmichael's manual of child psychology*. New York: Wiley, 1970.

Strodtbeck, F. L., and Mann, R. D. Sex role differentiation in jury deliberations. *Sociometry*, 1956, *19*, 3–11.

Stroop, J. R. Studies of interference in serial verbal reactions. *J. Experimental Psychology*, 1935, *6*, 643–62.

*Sweeney, E. J. Sex differences in problem solving. Unpublished Ph.D. dissertation, Stanford University, 1953.

*Tasch, R. J. The role of the father in the family. *J. Experimental Education*, 1952, *20*, 319–61.

*Templin, M. C. *Certain language skills in children—their development and interrelationships*. Institute of Child Welfare Monograph no. 26. Minneapolis: University of Minnesota Press, 1957.

*Terman, L. M., and Tyler, L. E. Psychological sex differences. In L. Carmichael, ed., *Manual of child psychology*, 2d ed. New York: Wiley, 1954.

*Terman, L. M., et al. *Genetic studies of genius. I: Mental and physical traits of a thousand gifted children*. Stanford, Calif.: Stanford University Press, 1925.

Thompson, W. R. The inheritance of behaviour: behavioural differences in 15 mouse strains. *Canadian J. Psychology*, 1953, 7 (4), 145–55.

Thurstone, L. L. *A factorial study of perception*. Chicago: University of Chicago Press, 1944.

Troll, L. E., Neugarten, B. L., and Kraines, R. J. Similarities in values and other personality characteristics in college students and their parents. *Merrill-Palmer Quarterly*, 1969, *15*, 323–36.

*Vance, T. F., and McCall, L. T. Children's preferences among play materials as determined by the method of paired comparisons of pictures. *Child Development*, 1934, 5, 267–77.

Vandenberg, S. G. Twin data in support of the Lyon hypothesis. *Nature*, 1962, *194*, 505–6.

Vandenberg, S. G. Primary mental abilities or general intelligence? Evidence from twin studies. In J. M. Thoday and A. S. Parkes, *Genetic and environmental influences on behavior*. New York: Plenum Press, 1968.

Van Lieshout, C. F. M. Reactions of young children to barriers placed by their mothers. Unpublished manuscript, Stanford University, 1974.

Veroff, J., Wilcox, S., and Atkinson, J. W. The achievement motive in high school and college age women. *J. Abnormal & Social Psychology*, 1953, 48, 108–19.

Waldrop, M. F., and Halverson, C. F., Jr. Intensive and extensive peer behavior: longitudinal and cross-sectional analyses. Unpublished manuscript, Child Research Branch, National Institute of Mental Health, Washington, D. C., 1973.

Wallach, M. A. Creativity. In P. H. Mussen, ed., *Carmichael's manual of child psychology*. New York: Wiley, 1970.

Wallach, M. A., and Kogan, N. *Modes of thinking in young children*. New York: Holt, Rinehart & Winston, 1965.

Ward, W. C. Development of self-regulatory behaviors. ETS Head Start Longitudinal Study, 1973, Report PR-73-18, Educational Testing Service, Princeton, N.J.

Werdelin, I. *The mathematical ability*. Lund, Sweden: CWK Gleerup, 1958.

Werdelin, I. *Geometrical ability and the space factors in boys and girls*. Lund Studies in Psychology and Education. Lund, Sweden: CWK Gleerup, 1961.

White, S. H. Evidence for hierarchical arrangement of learning processes. In L. P. Lipsitt and C. C. Spiker, eds., *Advances in child development and behavior*, vol. 2. New York: Academic Press, 1965.

*White House Conference on Child Health and Protection, Section III. *The young child in the home. A survey of 3,000 American families*. New York: Appleton-Century, 1936.

Whiting, B. B., ed. *Six cultures*. New York: Wiley, 1963.

Wild, J. M., and Hughes, R. N. Effects of postweaning handling on locomotor and exploratory behavior in young rats. *Developmental Psychology*, 1972, 7, 76–79.

Williams, K. Father-child interaction in cooperation and competition with preschool children. Honors thesis, Stanford University, 1973.

*Witkin, H. A., Dyk, R. B., Faterson, H. F., Goodenough, D. R., and Karp, S. A. *Psychological differentiation*. New York: Wiley, 1962.

*Witryol, S. L., and Kaess, W. A. Sex differences in social memory tasks. *J. Abnormal & Social Psychology*, 1957, 54, 343–46.

Wolfe, D. M. Power and authority in the family. In D. P. Cartwright, ed., *Studies in social power*. Ann Arbor: University of Michigan Press, 1959.

Wolff, P. H. Observations on newborn infants. *Psychosomatic Medicine*, 1959, *21*, 110–18.

Wood-Gush, D. G. M. A study of sex drive of two strains of cockerels through three generations. *Animal Behavior*, 1960, 8, 43–53.

Woodrow, R. M., Friedman, G. D., Siegelaub, A. B., and Collen, M. F. Pain tolerance: differences according to age, sex, and race. *Psychosomatic Medicine*, 1972, *34*, 548–56.

Woolf, V. *A room of one's own.* New York: Harcourt, Brace & World, 1929.

Work, M. S., and Rogers, H. Effect of estrogen on food-seeking dominance among male rats. *J. Comparative & Physiological Psychology,* 1972, 79, 414–18.

Young, W. C., Goy, R. W., and Phoenix, C. H. Hormones and sexual behavior. *Science,* 1964, *143,* 212–18.

Zucker, I. Hormonal determinants of sex differences in saccharin preference, food intake and body weight. *Physiology & Behavior,* 1969, *4,* 595–602.

Zuckerman, N., Baer, M., and Monachkin, I. Acceptance of self, parents, and people in patients and normals. *J. Clinical Psychology,* 1956, *12,* 327–32.

*Zunich, M. Children's reactions to failure. *J. Genetic Psychology,* 1964, *104,* 19–24.

Index

Index

Personal names are indexed only if we have directly quoted the people in question or their works, or cited a personal communication from them, or discussed one or more of their works at length. All published works cited or listed in the text appear in either the References Cited section (pp. 377–91 herein) or the Annotated Bibliography (Volume II).

Index